Interactional Humor

Language Play and Creativity

Edited by
Nancy Bell

Volume 10

Interactional Humor

Multimodal Design and Negotiation

Edited by
Béatrice Priego-Valverde

ISBN 978-3-11-221482-4
e-ISBN (PDF) 978-3-11-098312-8
e-ISBN (EPUB) 978-3-11-098328-9
ISSN 2363-7749

Library of Congress Control Number: 2023943014

Bibliographic information published by the Deutsche Nationalbibliothek
The Deutsche Nationalbibliothek lists this publication in the Deutsche Nationalbibliografie;
detailed bibliographic data are available on the internet at http://dnb.dnb.de.

© 2025 Walter de Gruyter GmbH, Berlin/Boston
This volume is text- and page-identical with the hardback published in 2024.
Cover image: Samuel Zeller Photography
Typesetting: Integra Software Services Pvt. Ltd.
Printing and binding: CPI books GmbH, Leck

www.degruyter.com

Contents

Béatrice Priego-Valverde
Introduction —— 1

Part 1: **Face-to-face interactions**

Aliyah Morgenstern, Christelle Dodane and Marie Leroy-Collombel
1   A multimodal approach to children's development of humor in family life —— 15

Clarissa de Vries, Bert Oben and Geert Brône
2   On target. On the role of eye-gaze during teases in face-to-face multiparty interaction —— 53

Elisa Gironzetti
3   Humorous Smiling: A Reverse Cross-Validation of the Smiling Intensity Scale for the Identification of Conversational Humor —— 87

Hilal Ergül, Shelby Miller, Salvatore Attardo and Kevin Kramer
4   Alternative conceptualizations of the Smiling Intensity Scale (SIS) and their applications to the identification of humor —— 109

Béatrice Priego-Valverde and Stéphane Rauzy
5   Facial gestures and laughter as a resource for negotiating humor in conversation —— 131

Thomas Kiderle, Hannes Ritschel, Silvan Mertes and Elisabeth André
6   Multimodal humor in human-robot interaction —— 169

Part 2: **Mediated interactions**

Sabina Tabacaru
7   Facial expressions as multimodal markers of humor: More evidence from scripted and non-scripted interactions —— 209

Jia Qiu, Xinren Chen and Michael Haugh
8 Emojis and jocular flattery in Chinese instant messaging interactions —— 231

Agnese Sampietro
9 More than laughter: Multimodal humour and the negotiation of in-group identities in mobile instant messaging interactions —— 263

Kerry Mullan
10 Humour and creativity in a family of strangers on Facebook —— 289

Villy Tsakona
11 "Loanword translation and corrective acts are incongruous": Debating metapragmatic stereotypes through humorous memes —— 319

Index —— 355

Béatrice Priego-Valverde
Introduction

1 General presentation

It is a given that interactions are multimodal. This fact has been established at least since Birdwhistell (1968), whether or not multimodality has been concretely taken into account in analyses: *"[. . .] language and gesture [are] an integrated system"* (McNeill 2013: 135). McNeill focuses on hand gestures, but this integrated system also includes all the other nonverbal modalities such as gaze, head movement, posture, smiles, and prosody, and can be defined as a *"complex gestalt"* (Mondada 2013: 223) *"accounting for different levels of organization"* (Mondada 2013: 223) of the interaction as a social activity. As such, multimodality will refer here to an integrated set of multimodal resources:

> [. . .] in a holistic way and [which] make sense together; moreover, they can be seen as not being a priori hierarchized, but as having their relevance empirically and situatedly defined within the context of the activity and its ecology. (Mondada 2014: 139).

As for "resource", this term will refer to:

> [. . .] substance-based linguistic (and other) forms or entities that can be described with respect to their structure and use. Resources include single forms of different sizes, including verbal forms such as phones and other sound objects, morphs, words, phrases, clauses, sentences, and recurrent larger units, and non-verbal forms such as prosodies, gaze, facial/bodily gestures, and bodily position and movement; [. . .] (Couper-Kuhlen and Selting 2018: 29).

The term "resource", presented as such, has the benefit not only of making it possible to analyze all the modalities present during humor without prioritizing one over the other, but also to analyze how these various resources are combined (Mondada 2014).

It has also been well established that humor appears frequently in interaction. Within the Conversation Analysis framework, focused more specifically on canned jokes, Sack's study (1974/1989) is considered the foundation of humor studies: *"There is no question that the seminal and most influential analyses of jokes in conversational settings are due to Sacks"* (Attardo 2015: 169). Since then, in the broad fields of discourse analysis and interactional sociolinguistics, other landmark studies on humor in conversations have been published, covering various aspects of humor: humor as a personal style (Tannen 1984) which performs various functions using various linguistic and discursive devices (Norrick 1993) as a co-constructed activity (Davies 1984). This is not to mention Hay's very complete volume on humor, including everything from successful to failed humor (Hay 1995). In recent years, an increasing number of studies have been conducted, multiplying the approaches, the theoretical frameworks, and the settings where humor appears.

The aim of this volume is thus not to fill a gap in the research, but on the contrary, to report on the recent flurry of research on the way interactional humor is multimodally performed. This volume focuses on the way various modalities of language work together to create and negotiate humor, whether they are linguistic or semiotic, and the methodological issues raised by such analyses. Throughout this volume, following the way these chapters have been brought together in order to highlight both their diversity and their complementarity, two threads will be constantly woven together: multimodality on the one hand, and interactional humor on the other.

2 Aim of the volume

Knowing that humor appears frequently in interaction does not necessarily mean that it is conceived as interactional, i.e., influenced by the interaction in which it appears. This latter approach is precisely that of this volume. All the chapters will consider humor to be *interactional* (Tsakona and Chovanec 2018), i.e., an interactionally achieved activity, whether the interaction in which it is embedded is face-to-face or computer mediated, between humans or with a robot, oral or written. The variety of settings where humor appears leads, by choice, to an enlarged conception of multimodality. It is as much about analyzing the participants' linguistic resources such as lexicon, syntax, gesture, prosody, gaze or smiles, as the semiotic resources (i.e., affordances) that social networks and instant messaging platforms offer them, such as memes, gifs, or emojis. It is for this reason that the two threads are woven together. Whatever the nature of the interaction or the resources used, the central question remains the same: *how is humor multimodally produced, perceived, responded to, and negotiated?*

3 Analysis of multimodal and interactional humor under various scopes

This shared question, approached through various angles, allows us to highlight not the heterogeneity of the meanings of "multimodality" or "interaction," but on the contrary, what these various meanings have *in common*. Any activity is multimodal if it mobilizes more than one resource, whether this resource is verbal, vocal, gestural, iconic, or written. In the same way, an exchange is interactional when it is addressed or negotiated, and therefore necessarily subject to the collaboration of the participants, whether this exchange takes place face-to-face or in public or online interactions, and whether the participants know each other or not. Consequently, humor appearing in such interactions, whether it is considered a practice, an action, an activity, or a sequence (see Couper-Kuhlen and Selting 2018 for the definitions of these interactional units) will always be analyzed in this volume, not through the sole description of its devices, markers, or features, but through the way these characteristics allow participants to address it.

Needless to say, interactional humor is multipurpose and multifaceted (Priego-Valverde 2003). As such, humor is, per se, a deeply interdisciplinary phenomenon. Remaining within the field of linguistics, this volume aims at bringing together studies that are certainly very diverse, but all complementary.

3.1 Strengths of the corpora analyzed

Three chapters are entirely based on **face-to-face interactions** (Chapters 1, 2, and 5). Chapter 1 focuses on multimodal humor in interactions between *children and adults*. In this respect, this chapter differs from the other two which focus on adults. Following the same children at different ages, this chapter aims at observing the children's multimodal development of humor. As such, one of the strengths of such a corpus – contrary to corpora of face-to-face interactions between adults – is that it offers a *longitudinal* analysis of humor, which, to date, remains an underexplored topic in research on face-to-face interactions between adults.

Furthermore, while these three chapters are based on face-to-face interactions, they also explore a variety of practices and settings. While Chapters 1 and 5 focus on dyadic interactions, Chapter 2 analyses triadic interactions; the participants recorded in Chapter 1 are members of the same family, while they are friends in Chapters 2 and 5.

Chapter 3 proposes another kind of corpus constituted of dyadic video conversations, i.e., **computer mediated interactions**.

These four chapters are also based on corpora built in different methodological ways. The analyses provided in Chapter 1 are based on an *ecological corpus*, i.e., on interactions recorded in a natural setting, at the participants' home. Chapters 2, 3, and 5 provide analyses based on *semi-controlled corpora*. While the first type of setting is expected when analyzing humor in interaction, the second could seem more unusual. However, in this volume, we argue that both are not only legitimate but also necessary. In both conditions, the participants were free to talk about any subject of their choice; they were not given a script to follow. As such, all of the interactions are true interactions. But following semi-controlled protocols allowed us to use new technologies, including microphones to record each participant in order to analyze overlapping speech, video cameras filming participants to analyze their facial gestures, or eye-tracking systems to focus on their gazing behavior. In other words, multimodality in interaction, and especially in interactional humor – which not only appears often fleetingly but also through the combination of multiple modalities – can benefit from new technologies and new kinds of data:

> Progress toward a truly multimodal investigation of human interaction can only be made if the limitations of traditional video-recording as it is still exclusively used in orthodox conversation analysis are overcome (Auer 2021: 137).

Multimodal conversational corpora are increasingly used in research both on multimodality and interaction (see the "Cid" – Corpus of Interactional Data", Bertrand et al. 2008; "DCDS" – Dyadic Conversation Data Set, Pickering et al. 2009; "InSight Interaction Corpus", Brône and Oben 2015; "Cheese!", Priego-Valverde, Bigi, and Amoyal 2020; "Paco", Amoyal, Priego-Valverde, and Rauzy 2020), and various studies on humor have greatly benefitted from them (Gironzetti, Attardo, and Pickering 2016; Gironzetti 2022; Brône 2021; de Vries, Oben, and Brône 2021; Priego-Valverde, Bigi, Attardo, Pickering, and Gironzetti 2018). As will be shown in Chapter 6, these corpora and technonologies have also paved the way to more in-depth analyses of humor that can be applied to research involving humor generation and implemenation in robots.

Between multimodal corpora and online interactions as presented below, one chapter (Chapter 7) focuses on **public interactions** such as TV interviews. This chapter also analyzes occurrences of unscripted humor, demonstrating that both scripted and unscripted humor can share the same nonverbal cue – eyebrow movements – to frame an utterance as humorous.

Finally, four chapters of this volume analyze **online interactions** on various platforms: Instant Messaging interactions (Chapters 8 and 9) and Facebook (Chapters 10 and 11). The interests of such data are manifold. First of all, these kinds of studies enlarge the notion of multimodality, showing that memes, emojis, and GIFs, for instance, are not only humorous devices, but are also and above all resources used by participants to produce and negotiate humor in online interactions. Secondly, these corpora allow us to collect larger datasets than face-to-face interactions and as such, can facilitate the generalization of the results. Thirdly, these large corpora also include a larger variety of participants. Face-to face interactions are often recorded between acquaintances, who are often acquaintances of the analyst him/herself. This fact raises the issue of the representativity of the data, since participants are often students and within the same age group. Online interactions may allow us to avoid this issue. And although the researcher is often one of the participants analyzed (often to have access to the exchanges), s/he only one among many others. Finally, online interactions, as shown by the chapters presented here, provide the basis for a *longitudinal analysis of humor*. Following humorous exchanges between the same participants over the course of days and weeks can help reveal the way humor appears, but also the way it evolves and eventually transforms, until it becomes a "running gag." To date, and to the best of our knowledge, longitudinal studies constitute a gap in humor studies (at least between adults); these studies are needed to provide a better understanding of the way in which humor evolves between participants and, conversely, the way this evolution allows participants to bond even when they have never met in person (Chapter 10).

3.2 Diversity of the modalities

The modalities analyzed in this volume are diverse and numerous in terms of the variety of settings and types of interactions investigated. In addition to the verbal modality, the various chapters also analyze semiotic resources (such as memes, GIFs, or emojis in Chapters 8 to 11) and linguistics resources such as hand gestures, prosody (Chapter 1), laughter (Chapter 5), and various facial expressions such as smiling, gaze, and eyebrow movements (Chapters 2 to 6).

3.3 A rigorous look at methodology

Certain chapters in this volume are more empirical, while others focus more on methodological issues. However, all of them highlight the fact that analyzing the multimodal dimension of interactional humor raises a challenge: the technical quality of the data, and the care taken to collect and annotate them. For this reason, the methodological considerations surrounding the data are intrinsically linked to theoretical considerations; for instance, the status of observant participant is sometimes emphasized (see Chapters 8, 9, and 10) as a useful status both to gain access to humorous occurrences and to be able to analyze them.

In other respects, while most of the chapters provide an empirical analysis of multimodal humor, three chapters (Chapters 3, 4, and 6), reverse the perspective and prioritize methodological issues, each in their own way. Chapter 4 presents a new version of the Smiling Intensity Scale ("SIS", Gironzetti, Attardo, and Pickering 2016), which analyzes participant's smiling behavior in order to simplify it as a tool (the SIS is also used in Chapters 3 and 5). Chapter 3, using the original version of the SIS, shows how this tool, originally used to annotate smiles, can be used to predict humor. Chapter 6 investigates the methodological issues with implementing humor in robots.

In addition to these three chapters, we could add Chapter 5. Although this chapter does not address methodology per se, it combines both an empirical analysis of interactional humor and a methodological discussion about the SIS as a tool.

Finally, all the chapters presented here focus particular attention on the type of annotations needed to study the resources and reveal a large variety of practices, including discussions about software, tools, and types of orthographic transcriptions and how to combine them with multimodal information. These chapters also show that working on multimodality is not straightforward but is a constant back-and-forth process between the phases of annotation and analysis. The authors question the type(s) of annotation needed to analyze multimodal interactional humor and show how, sometimes, the analysis phase allows us to enrich the initial annotations.

3.4 A complementary diversity

As previously mentioned, this volume aims at bringing together diversified studies on multimodal interactional humor within various types of interactions: online, public, face-to-face, or computer-mediated interactions. A variety of different languages are also presented: American English, Australian English, Greek, French, (Mandarin) Chinese, and Spanish. Although a cross-cultural comparison of humor is beyond the scope of this volume, certain results presented here show that some kinds of universals appear to exist: for example, the way in which a humorous sequence is organized, i.e., who initiated and ended it, regardless of the language and type of interaction (Chapters 2, 5, 8, 9); or the function of a smile, whether it is displayed through a facial expression or an emoji (Chapters 3, 4, 5, 8, 9).

In other respects, while most of the chapters provide a qualitative analysis of humorous sequences and as such, provide data-driven analyses, Chapters 2 and 5 employ a mixed statistical and sequential approach, which highlights their useful complementarity. Chapter 3 presents a quantitative analysis of smiles and humor. Finally, Chapter 6 demonstrates how Artificial Intelligence can be applied to empirical studies on multimodal and interactional humor.

In sum, all the chapters presented here, while diverse, are also complementary, as each of them, in their own way and using their own approach, aim at investigating the same questions: what are the various *multimodal resources involved in interactional humor and how are they deployed?*

4 Presentation of the chapters

This volume contains 11 chapters divided into two sections. The first section of the volume focuses on the multimodal analysis of humor in *face-to-face interactions*. Six chapters will be presented in this section. The corpora analyzed in Chapters 1, 2, 3, and 5 are constituted of both naturally-occurring interactions and semi-controlled interactions. They all aim to analyze, moment-by-moment, the way humor appears and the way it is negotiated in interactions, using both verbal and nonverbal resources. Chapter 4, which are more methodological, explores the way these types of corpora can be more easily used and annotated.

Given the diversity of the participants recorded (children, both well-acquainted and unacquainted adults), the question of which multimodal resources are used in humorous interactions and how they are deployed will be addressed through various angles. In **Chapter 1, Aliyah Morgenstern, Christelle Dodane, and Marie Leroy-Collombel** analyze children's multimodal development of humor. For this purpose, they use a longitudinal dataset of children between the ages of 1 and 7 recorded at home while performing daily activities (Morgenstern and Parisse 2017). The authors use a "multi-linguistic level" and multimodal approach involving phonology, pragmatics, discourse, gesture, facial expressions, gaze, and posture, and take into account children's linguistic, cognitive, and social development. The authors analyze the way children begin to perceive humor and progressively produce it until they become co-operative actors of the ongoing interaction with an adult. Based on triadic interactions from the *Insight Interaction corpus* (Brône and Oben 2015), in **Chapter 2, Clarissa De Vries, Bert Oben, and Geert Brône** analyze eye-gaze in teasing sequences, hypothesizing that gaze patterns differ depending on whether the target is present ("internal tease") or absent ("external tease"). This chapter also focuses on the influence of the participation framework.

The three next chapters mainly focus on facial gestures and smiling, all using the *Smiling Intensity Scale* (SIS; Gironzetti, Attardo, and Pickering, 2016) which was developed to code the intensity of smiles quickly and simply. In **Chapter 3, Elisa Gironzetti** presents a study which aims at validating the SIS as an instrument identify humor in a multimodal corpus. To this end, a new set of conversations is analyzed by applying the SIS to identify moments in which speakers show evidence of humor-related smiling behavior. In **Chapter 4, Hilal Ergül, Shelby Miller, Kevin Kramer, and Salvatore Attardo** introduce a new training method using the SIS and their initial encouraging results, exposing the methodological issues raised by the analysis of smiling in humor and the way these issues could be resolved. Finally, based on this presentation of the SIS, in **Chapter 5, Béatrice Priego-Valverde and Stéphane Rauzy** present a mixed analysis of facial gestures, smiles, and laughter in humorous sequences. Analyzing a dyadic conversational corpus – *"Cheese!"* – (Priego-Valverde, Bigi and Amoyal 2020), and drawing on previous research, their chapter's aim is twofold: (1) Through a statistical analysis of the data, the chapter explores general trends about the way neutral face, smiles, and laughter are displayed in interactional humor; (2) A sequential analysis provides a deeper understanding of the multimodal achievement of interactional humor. Finally, as a transition between the two parts of the volume, **Chapter 6,** proposed by **Thomas Kiderle, Hannes Ritschel, Silvan Mertes, and Elisabeth André,** investigates the way humor could be implemented in robots in order to facilitate and enable more "natural" human-robot interactions. As such, it presents the methodological issues encountered in implementing humor and nonverbal human behaviors in robots. This chapter not only lays out the stakes and applications research on human-human interactions can have, but it also proposes an implementation guideline to applying the insights from humor research for the generation and implementation of humor in robots.

The second section of the volume focuses on the multimodal analysis of humor in *mediated interactions*, whether they take place in public or online. The five chapters of this section bring together different kinds of corpora and settings and are both methodological and empirical. **Chapter 7,** by **Sabina Tabacaru,** addresses the question of the existence of *markers* of humor or related phenomena such as sarcasm. This chapter focuses on facial expressions used by the speaker(s) in different contexts (TV shows, political debates, TV series, etc.), and more specifically on eyebrow movements, in order to analyze the frequency and the use of such facial expressions for humorous purposes.

Using and associating various frameworks such as sociolinguistics, discourse analysis, and interactional pragmatics, the last four chapters of this section deal with multimodal humor used in various social media platforms such as Facebook and Mobile Instant Messaging (MIM) applications. **Chapter 8,** by **Jia Qiu, Xinren Chen, and Michael Haugh,** presents an interactional analysis of conversational humor in multi-party instant messaging interactions in (Mandarin) Chinese. Focusing on the functions of emojis, this chapter demonstrates that in multi-party interactions emojis convey multiple meanings which systematically vary according to the footing of the participant(s) in relation to the conversational humor sequence in question. Secondly, the authors investigate the ways in which particular emojis have more generalized functions while others play more specific roles in sequences of conversational humor.

The other three chapters analyze more specifically the way creativity in humor (due to its multimodal dimension) allows participants of online exchanges to build a community, in order to negotiate ideological positions and in-group identity. In **Chapter 9, Agnese Sampietro** analyzes humor in Mobile Instant Messaging (MIM), and more precisely, in Spanish exchanges on WhatsApp. With a method combining computer-mediated discourse analysis (Herring and Androutsopoulos 2015) and digital conversation analysis (Giles et al. 2015), the chapter describes the various multimodal resources of humor in these exchanges (photos, screenshots, memes, videos, stickers, and GIFs) and their specific functions. It also analyzes the way these resources are used by the participants to negotiate in-group identity and reaffirm participants' masculinity. In **Chapter 10**, **Kerry Mullan** examines the exchanges within a local community Facebook group in which members of an inner suburb of an Australian city can request and offer help with recommendations for local services. While the members of this group did not necessarily know each other, they shared similar interests and values. In this respect, this chapter focuses on the way the creativity of multimodal humor in online exchanges is employed to foster a sense of belonging in this group of strangers. Finally, in **Chapter 11**, **Villy Tsakona** focuses on how speakers participate in debates about language which take place on social media platforms, and more specifically, the way they reject loanword translations and respective corrective acts. Using a framework based on metapragmatics (Verschueren 2000) and citizen sociolinguistics (Rymes and Leone 2014), the author analyzes the humorous examples in terms of the Discourse Theory of Humor (Tsakona 2020) to highlight the way the speakers use humorous memes as multimodal contributions to ongoing debates over how language should (not) be used.

A variety of theoretical frameworks are used in these chapters to analyze multimodal and interactional humor (discourse studies, Conversation Analysis, interactional linguistics, interactional sociolinguistics, cognitive linguistics, computer mediated analysis, metapragmatics). Different methodologies are also employed (data-driven, qualitative, quantitative analyses, based on ecological or semi-controlled corpora). Some chapters focus more on empirical analysis while other concentrate more on methodological issues. But despite their diversity, all of the chapters investigate the same question: *how is interactional humor multimodally produced, perceived, responded to, and negotiated?*

In short, this volume proposes a panorama of linguistic research on multimodal and interactional humor, based on various theoretical frameworks, corpora, and methodologies. The approaches presented are thus very diverse, but they do not reflect a fragmented field of research. On the contrary, by highlighting all the complexities of humor, these approaches show to what extent they are necessarily complementary and as such, must be jointly considered.

References

Amoyal, Mary, Béatrice Priego-Valverde & Stéphane Rauzy. 2020. PACO: A corpus to analyze the impact of common ground in spontaneous face-to-face interaction. In *Proceedings of the Twelfth Language Resources and Evaluation Conference, 628–633*. Marseille: European Language Resources Association.

Attardo, Salvatore. 2015. Humor and laughter. In Deborah Tannen, Heidi E. Hamilton & Deborah Schiffrin (eds.), *The Handbook of Discourse Analysis*, 168–188. Oxford: Wiley Blackwell.

Auer, Peter. 2021. Turn-allocation and gaze: A multimodal revision of the "current-speaker- selects-next" rule of the turn-taking system of conversation analysis. *Discourse Studies* 23(2). 117–140.

Bertrand, Roxane, Philippe Blache, Robert Espesser, Gaëlle Ferré, Christine Meunier, Béatrice Priego-Valverde & Stephane Rauzy. 2008. 'Le CID – Corpus of Interactional Data–Annotation et Exploitation Multimodale de Parole Conversationnelle. *Traitement Automatique des Langues* 49. 105–134.

Birdwhistell, Ray L. 1968. Kinesics: Inter- and intra-channel communication research. *Social Science Information* 7(6). 9–26.

Brône, Geert. 2021. The multimodal negotiation of irony and humor in interaction: On the role of eye gaze in joint pretense In Augusto Soares da Silva (ed.), *Figurative Language – Intersubjectivigy and Usage, 109–136*. Amsterdam: John Benjamins Publishing Company. https://doi.org/10.1075/ftl.11.04bro

Brône, Geert & Brian Oben. 2015. InSight Interaction: A multimodal and multifocal dialogue corpus. *Language Resources and Evaluation*, *49*(1). 195–214. https://doi.org/10.1007/s10579-014-9283-2.

Couper-Kuhlen, Elisabeth & Margret Selting. 2018. *Interactional Linguistics*. Cambridge: Cambridge University Press.

Davis, Catherine. E. 1984. 'Joint Joking: Improvisational Humorous Episodes in Conversation'. *Proceedings of the Tenth Annual Meeting of the Berkeley Linguistics Society*, 360–371. Berkeley: Berkeley Linguistics Society.

de Vries, Clarissa, Bert Oben & Geert Brône. 2021. Exploring the role of the body in communicating ironic stance. *Languages and Modalities* 1(1). 65–80. https://doi.org/10.3897/lamo.1.68876

Giles, David, Wyke Stommel, Trena Paulus, Jessica Lester & Darren Reed. 2015. Microanalysis of online data: The methodological development of "digital CA". *Discourse, Context & Media* 7. 45–51. https://doi.org/10.1016/j.dcm.2014.12.002

Gironzetti, Elisa, Salvatore Attardo & Lucy Pickering. 2016. Smiling, gaze, and humor in conversation. In Leonor Ruiz-Gurillo (ed.), *Metapragmatics of Humor: Current research trends*, 235–254. Amsterdam/Philadelphia: John Benjamins Publishing.

Gironzetti, Elisa. 2022. *The Multimodal Performance of Conversational Humor*. Amsterdam/Philadelphia: John Benjamins Publishing

Hay, Jennifer. 1995. *Gender and Humour: Beyond a Joke*. Master Thesis. Victoria University of Wellington.

Herring, Susan C. & Jannis Androutsopoulos. 2015. Computer-mediated discourse 2.0. In Deborah Tannen, Heidi E. Hamilton & Deborah Schiffrin (eds.), *The Handbook of Discourse Analysis, Vol. I*, 127–151. Chilchester, UK: John Wiley & Sons.

McNeill, David. 2013. The growth point hypothesis of language and gesture as a dynamic and integrated system. In Cornelia Müller, Alan Cienki, Ellen Fricke, Silva H. Ladewig, David McNeill, Sedina Tebendorf (eds.), *Body – Language – Communication. An International Handbook on Multimodality in Human Interaction*, Volume 1. 135–155. Berlin/Boston: De Gruyter.

Mondada, Lorenza. 2013. Conversation Analysis: Talk and bodily resources for the organization of social interaction. In Cornelia Müller, Alan Cienki, Ellen Fricke, Silva H. Ladewig, David McNeill & Sedina Tebendorf (eds.), *Body – Language – Communication. An International Handbook on Multimodality in Human Interaction*, Volume 1. 218–227.

Mondada, Lorenza. 2014. The local constitution of multimodal resources for social interaction. *Journal of Pragmatics* 65. 137–156.

Morgenstern, Aliyah & Christophe Parisse (eds.). 2017. *Le langage de l'enfant de l'éclosion à l'explosion*. Paris: Presses de la Sorbonne Nouvelle.

Norrick, Neal R. 1993. *Conversational Joking*. Bloomington: Indiana University Press.

Pickering, Lucy, Marcella Corduas, Jodi Eisterhold, Brenna Seifried, Alyson Eggleston & Salvatore Attardo. 2009. Prosodic Markers of Saliency in Humorous Narratives. *Discourse processes* 46. 517–540.

Priego-Valverde, Béatrice, Brigitte Bigi, Salvatore Attardo, Lucy Pickering & Elisa Gironzetti. 2018. Is smiling during humor so obvious? A cross-cultural comparison of smiling behavior in humorous sequences in American English and French interactions. *Intercultural Pragmatics* 15(4). 563–591.

Priego-Valverde, Béatrice, Brigitte Bigi & Mary Amoyal. 2020. Cheese!: A corpus of face-to-face French interactions. A case study for analyzing smiling and conversational humor. *Language Resources and Evaluation Conference*. 460–468. LREC2020, May 2020, Marseille, France.

Priego-Valverde, Béatrice. 2003. *L'humour dans la conversation familière: description et analyse linguistiques*. Paris: L'Harmattan.

Rymes, Betsy & Andrea R. Leone. 2014. Citizen sociolinguistics: A new media methodology for understanding language and social life. *Working Papers in Educational Linguistics* 29(2). 25–43.

Sacks, Harvey. 1989. [1974]. An analysis of the course of a joke's telling in conversation. In Richard Bauman & Joel Sherzer (eds.). *Explorations in the Ethnography of Speaking*, 2nd ed. 2nd ed., 337–353. Cambridge: Cambridge University Press.

Tannen, Deborah. 1984. *Conversation styles*. Oxford: Oxford University Press.

Tsakona, Villy & Jan Chovanec (eds.) 2018. *The Dynamics of Interactional Humour*. Amsterdam: John Benjamins.

Tsakona, Villy. 2020. *Recontextualizing humor: Rethinking the analysis and teaching of humor* (Language and Creativity 4). Boston: De Gruyter Mouton.

Verschueren, Jef. 2000. Notes on the role of metapragmatic awareness in language use. *Pragmatics* 10(4). 439–456.

Part 1: **Face-to-face interactions**

Aliyah Morgenstern, Christelle Dodane and Marie Leroy-Collombel
1 A multimodal approach to children's development of humor in family life

Abstract: The development and production of humor (McGhee 1979) involves all semiotic resources at the child's disposal. It is embedded in social-cultural contexts and requires specific cognitive, interactional and linguistic skills (Thalander and Aronsson 2003). Patterns of humor development depend on children's construction of these skills and on parental modeling or support for the child's efforts at humor. Adults transmit their socializing practices in their daily spontaneous exchanges with their children (Ochs and Schieffelin 1984). It is thus essential to study humor in its natural habitat: daily interactions.

In this chapter, we analyze the development of humor in two longitudinal follow-ups of children between 1 and 7 years old recorded at home in daily activities (Morgenstern and Parisse 2017). We use a multi-linguistic level and multimodal approach involving detailed analyses of phonology, pragmatics, discourse, gesture, facial expressions, gaze, posture, and taking into account children's linguistic, cognitive and social development. We study how children exploit the resources available to them within the discourse context and enter a collaboration in which the adults, as experts, provide important scaffolding. We analyze the reception and production of marked expression of amusement and humor with their specific acoustic, facial and gestural components.

The results of our analyses help us describe the paths the children take to go from first instances of shared amusement initiated by the adults, in which they produce mainly reactive multimodal behavior such as smiling and laughing, to their own production of successful humor. The children in our dataset are at first willing participants who express their amused reactions, but they are progressively socialized into becoming co-operative actors (based on Goodwin 2017) who initiate humor by combining their verbal, gestural and prosodic skills in interaction.

Keywords: multimodal humor, language acquisition, semiotic resource, child language, language socialization

---

Note: The video files can be accessed via the following link: https://www.degruyter.com/document/isbn/9783110983128/html

1 Introduction

Language development is a socializing as well as a linguistic process (Bruner 1981, Ochs et al. 1979; Slobin 1982). Collaborative discourse therefore has a very important role to play. We wish to analyze and highlight that role through the detailed study of the ontogenesis of humor which has a key function in social life. Humor is developed in spontaneous interactions and is linked to the appropriation of conversational skills such as turn construction and turn taking, of cognitive skills such as displacement and of advanced linguistic skills involving fictional narratives, perspective taking, intersubjective positioning and argumentation.

Despite the fact that there is a new wealth of literature on humor coming from linguistics (Raskin 1985; Attardo 2001; Attardo and Raskin 2017; Bröne 2017), with an interest in interaction and conversation (Norrick and Chiaro 2009; Chovanec and Tsakona 2018), research on children's development of humor with a linguistic approach is still scarce and multimodal approaches to interactive practices in ecological settings are underexplored. In this chapter, we combine those two scientific areas and analyze the multimodal development of humor in the longitudinal datasets of two children between 1 and 7 years old recorded at home in daily activities (Morgenstern and Parisse 2017). We use a multi-linguistic level and multimodal approach involving detailed analyses of phonology, pragmatics, discourse displayed in the visual-gestural and audio-vocal modalities. We take into account the children's linguistic, cognitive and social development, especially their capacity to express perspective taking and intersubjective positioning. We thus explore the multimodal resources involved in humor during spontaneous interactions in children's daily life.

We begin this chapter with our theoretical background grounded in an overview of the literature and define our approach to children's multimodal development of humor and of language in interaction. We then present our data and method. The focus of this study is on qualitative analyses of children's participation in shared amusement and humor in the family environment. We first illustrate how children are socialized to humor and resonate with their family by analyzing markers of amusement – facial expressions, laughter, *glee gestures* (gestures expressing children's glee, Aronsson and Morgenstern 2021), prosody. We then show how they develop the metalinguistic skills to initiate collective amusement and humor sequences.

2 Theoretical background

2.1 The development of shared amusement and humor

Humor is a constructive conduct in social interactions from infancy through adulthood. It plays a valuable role in children's socialization as it reflects the norms and values of the community in which it is grounded. It is tightly linked to social, linguistic and interactional practices transmitted by parents and internalized by children, as they grow older. In playful situations children experience "kinesic humor" (Bolens 2021) – that is humor elicited in the processing of gestures and actions in real-life situations – grounded in sensorimotor cognition and prompted in motor perception. As children develop their sensorimotor knowledge especially through touch and kinesthesia, and learn the laws of physics such as gravity, they can make predictive perceptions of movements thanks to their experience of motor patterns. If the adults around them socialize them to playing with those anticipations and create incongruities, children will develop their own creativity around such experiences. The same processes are elicited in verbal interactions through shared knowledge and deviations from routinized patterns. Children thus train their cognitive processing of dynamic shifts in anticipated actions, gestures, as well as verbal productions in interaction.

Humor production has been little studied and only anecdotally in everyday interactions (Horgan 1981; Johnson and Mervis 1997; Loizou 2007). There is more work on comprehension (Thommen and Rimbert 2005) but it is mainly focused on children over seven years old, with the exception of the work of Hoicka and Gattis (2008) and Hoicka, Jutsum and Gattis (2008). Most of the research seems to underestimate children's ability to produce and understand humor between the ages of one and seven years old, as well as the importance of the social context in which it may occur.

Norrick (2006) insists on the fact that humor is triggered by the awareness of some incongruity — a discrepancy between our representation of an event and reality. When we find something incongruous, it leads to a break in the unfurling of a script (Kintsch and van Dijk 1978), it creates a sudden semantic leap between two entirely different mental spaces (Coulson 2000) or some violation of conversational roles as defined for example by Levinson (1992) or Clark (1996). The discrepancy between the expectations of the interlocutors and the content expressed dialogically can provoke an emotional discharge shared through smiling and laughter (Del Ré, Dodane and Morgenstern 2013). As shown by Suls (1983:43), humor results from the identification and resolution of the incongruity, when an expectation is not met. The management of the incongruity in at least two different mental spaces and the way it might lead to humor vary according to the types of population. Cognitive deficits in the autistic spectrum for example may be based on the difficulty they have in integrating different contexts simultaneously (Frith 1989). According to Apte (1985), there are two types of infantile humor: physical and linguistic humor. Physical humor, (which is the basis for kinesic humor described in Bolens 2021) reflects children's curiosity towards their body. It enables them to discover their body and learn how to control its functions. Linguistic humor develops in parallel to language acquisition but also depends on the family environment (Del Ré et al. 2015).

Mac Ghee (1979) distinguished four stages in the development of children's humor. During Stage 1, they are fascinated by anything new that is viewed as incongruous, be it an object, an event or an experience. The perception of an incongruity can either provoke fear, curiosity or amusement. Children enter Stage 2 with the acquisition of their first words. Between age one and two, they will start using incongruous labels for things or people with either phonological or semantic malformations. As their language develops, children can intentionally manipulate its phonology, its semantics, its syntax or its conversational impact in order to provoke shared amusement, which leads them to Stage 3 in their third year. They learn to play with situations and words as they enter symbolic play and are more and more able to appreciate the subtleties of their own language. The complexity of children's linguistic humor increases with age. Linguistic humor first provided in the input is beneficial to children's metalinguistic skills as it is the basis for children to understand the phonological, semantic and discursive subtleties of their language. Later on, around age seven, children reach Stage 4 during which they can manipulate causal relations, the logic of their discourse and access more complex polysemy.

Bariaud (1983) only studied children over seven in order to analyze their explanations of what they find funny in parallel with their productions and uncover their metalinguistic skills. However, Figueira (2000) has shown that children can produce intentional verbal humor as early as age two. Hoicka worked on early humor production and revealed some interesting differences between humorous and sincere communicative intentions (Hoicka and Gattis 2008; 2012). The research showed for instance that mothers used a higher mean F0 to communicate visual humor as compared to visual sincerity, as well as greater F0 mean, range, and standard deviation; greater intensity mean, range, and standard deviation; and a slower speech rate to communicate verbal humor as compared to verbal sweet-sincerity. Mothers used a rising linear contour to communicate verbal humor, but used no specific contour to express verbal sweet-sincerity. Mothers thus provide acoustic cues enabling children to distinguish between various positive communicative intentions. Del Ré et al. (2010) have mainly found intentional verbal humor in their longitudinal data as of age three, but do indicate that signs of comprehension of their adult interlocutor's humor can be traced much earlier and have not been analyzed in detail.

The production of humor is embedded in socio-cultural contexts and requires specific cognitive, interactional and linguistic skills (Thalander and Aronsson 2003). Patterns of humor development depend on children's construction of these advanced skills and on parental modeling or support for the child's efforts at humor. As our focus in this study is on children's multimodal engagement in humor sequences in spontaneous interaction, a multimodal approach to language development in interaction is necessary to analyze children's pathway into shared amusement and humor.

2.2 A multimodal approach to language development in interaction

Vygotsky's theory of learning as socially co-constructed between collaborating partners within a cultural context (1934) gives a fundamental role to interaction in children's cognitive and linguistic development. They learn to understand language and action together, each providing support for the other. To examine how children come to use language in general, one must examine the broader context in which the child experiences events and interaction. We use a functional-constructivist approach to language development (see Morgenstern and Parisse, 2017; Morgenstern et al. 2017). Following Tomasello (2003), we assume that through interaction, children initially learn concrete chunks of language, linguistic gestalts that can take different sizes and shapes (Bomstein and Bruner 1989). They then generalize across those various elements and develop abstract constructions (Goldberg 2006) in the process of creating new utterances. These linguistic constructions contain multiple cross-modal elements used together for coherent communicative functions (Morgenstern 2014). We argue that language can be analyzed within situated activities and that theories from different domains and different frameworks, both formal and functional, can feed each other.

Mondada (2019: 47) explains that "research in multimodality – that is, the diversity of resources that participants mobilize to produce and understand social interaction as publicly intelligible actions, including language, gesture, gaze, body postures, movements, and embodied manipulations of objects – can be further expanded by considering not only embodied resources for interacting but also embodied practices for sensing the world in an intersubjective way." Sensory experiences and situated activities are indeed particularly important for all children's language development as "meaning comes about through praxis – in the everyday interactions between the child and significant others" (Budwig 2003: 108). Joint parent-child action/interaction provides the scaffold for children's growing ability to grasp both what is happening around them, and what is being said in the situation. They learn to understand language and action together, each providing support for the other. Zlatev (1997) suggests that sensorimotor schemes provide the "grounding" of language in experience and will then lead to children's access to the symbolic function. It thus is important to us to apply Mondada's (2019) suggestions and capture children's developmental path by analyzing their daily sensory experiences and their use of all the semiotic resources at their disposal (Morgenstern et al. 2021).

In his combat against the cultural filters that lead many linguists to deny the role of the body and its dynamics, to illuminate how language is structured by our bodily activity in all its materiality, our colleague Dominique Boutet constructed a kinesiological approach to language and constantly sought to place the body at the center of all language activity (Boutet 2018; Boutet and Morgenstern 2021; Morgenstern et al. 2021). Boutet considered that a merely semiotic approach to language evacuates the signifier as a mode of expression. His kinesiological approach, on the other hand, is based on the signifier, the body and all the segments whose constraints but also whose "affordances"[1] (Gibson 1977) make it possible to produce the signified and reveal how it structures meaning, how it can limit but also strengthen our expressivity.

Following his steps, we view language as fundamentally embodied. The multimodal nature of language has led us to investigate how various semiotic systems such as speech, gesture, posture, facial expressions and gaze (Kendon 1988; Goodwin and Goodwin 1992) are simultaneously deployed, transmitted and used in situated activities. Our theoretical framework combines language socialization, cognitive grammar, interactive and multimodal approaches to *languaging*. We borrow the term *languaging* to refer to multimodal language use – "linguistic actions and activities in actual communication and thinking" (Linell 2009: 274) expanding the term to include speaking, signing, gesturing but it could also integrate touching, object manipulation and other forms when they are used to construct meaning. We study how children's socialization to a variety of modes of expression in their daily *experiencing* (Ochs 2012) shapes their language development. The framework of Cognitive Grammar provides a means of taking into account all semiotic resources as a consequence of the usage-based (Langacker 1988) nature of the theory. The theory allows for linguistic *signs* (in the Saussurian sense, 1916) to be multimodal to varying degrees, based on the extent of schematization and entrenchment. Thus far, humans cannot yet be imitated in their

---

[1] Affordances can be defined here as the potential offered by physiological constraints that shape the possible movements of each part of the human body.

skill to coordinate the semiotic resources at their disposal, varying the use of the *scope of relevant behaviors* as needed (Cienki 2012), adjusting to the context of interaction, the activity, the age and identity of the interlocutor, the time of day, etc. Each language provides a certain set of options for the grammatical encoding of characteristics of objects and events. If children are "guided in how they choose to talk about experience by the most available grammatical means provided by their native language" (Slobin 1987: 443) as they are "thinking for speaking", the same could apply to "thinking for gesturing" (Cienki and Irishkhanova 2018). *Languaging* might thus not be solely relative to languages and cultures, but also to the mode of expression as we embody mental construals. And as we constantly adjust and co-construct the form and function of our multimodal productions with our interlocutors, according to the situation, the discursive context, we refer to interactive practices as multimodal *inter-languaging*.

Humor plays an important role in children's socialization as it reflects the norms and values of the community in which it is grounded. It is tightly linked to social, linguistic and interactional practices transmitted by the parents and internalized by the children, as they grow older. Analyzing the development of humor represents an important theoretical multidisciplinary challenge because it forces us to consider a combination of social, cultural and cognitive skills as well as multimodal and multi-functional uses of language. Humor is an affective and cultural phenomenon, which involves the sharing of attention, affect, and convention as well as the progressive mastery of all semiotic resources. Children's production of humor is an excellent marker of the attainment of new socio-cognitive levels with the assistance of multimodal inter-languaging and of "good-enough" (Winnicott 1964) scaffolding (Wood, Bruner and Ross 1976) provided to children by more expert interlocutors. The analysis of humor can provide important landmarks of children's meta-pragmatic knowledge of language use as it indicates whether thanks to multimodal cues and their semantic content, they discriminate adequate and acceptable productions in context.

3 Method and data

We find it absolutely essential to study humor in its natural habitat: daily spontaneous interactions. Adults transmit their socializing practices in their everyday exchanges with their children. We therefore use a longitudinal follow-up of spontaneous interactions as the main source for our coding and analyses of humor and the semiotic resources employed to express shared amusement. Video-recording tools have notably advanced the detailed analysis of the organization of human action and interaction (Mondada 2019). These tools have shaped new avenues of research on language in interaction, as it is deployed in multiple ecologies, both in time – the moment-to-moment unfurling of an interaction – and over time – multiple recordings over several years of the same children in their family environment (Morgenstern and Goldin-Meadow 2021). The study of humor and its development requires richly contextualized high-quality video-recordings of adult-child interaction since we need to analyze how the amusing and humorous frames are constructed, and how the participants collaborate, and display their understanding of multimodal productions. We study how adults and children exploit the resources available to them within the discourse context and enter a collaboration in which the adult, as an expert, provides important scaffolding. We thus analyze the production of marked expression of amusement as well as their specific acoustic and visual components.

We are interested in how the content of hearing children's spoken productions, prosody and gesture are deployed and coordinated in humor sequences. In line with McNeill (2016), we consider that speech and gesture are partners (Morgenstern and Goldin-Meadow 2021) and that they are "co-expressive but semiotically non-redundant. Each has its own means of packaging [a] shared idea" (McNeill 2016: 22). Simulations of kinesthetic sensations are crucial in language processing and are marked in interaction through gestures which embody the dynamics of actions or events. Just as gestures often depict the "movement dynamics" in verbal metaphor (Müller 2008: 100), our detailed analyses will strive to illustrate how they embody the inherent dynamics of interactive humor.

This study was conducted on the longitudinal corpus of Anaé and of Théophile, two monolingual French children. The corpus is part of the *Paris Corpus* (longitudinal follow-ups of 10 children) collected in the *ANR CoLaJE* project (ANR-08-COM-021, Morgenstern and Parisse 2012, 2017). Each video was transcribed and aligned to its transcript using the CLAN software (MacWhinney 2000), which also allows for queries. All of the recordings and their transcriptions are available online (http://modyco.inist.fr/data/colaje/) on the Equipex Ortolang website funded by the *Agence Nationale de la Recherche*. Anaé and Théophile were filmed from 7 months to 7 years of age approximately once a month until they were 4 years old, then 2 to 3 times a year. Anaé has two older brothers. Her language development was quite fast when compared to that of the other children in the *Paris corpus* who were from equivalent upper middle-class socio-economic backgrounds. Théophile is the first born in his family, his little brother was born in the middle of our longitudinal study and his sister at the end of the study. His vocal language development was slower, his mean length of utterance if we only take into account the verbal content was about 7 months behind Anaé's until he was 4 years old (then he caught up with her), but his multimodal expressive skills were extremely rich. A fairly large body of work has focused on their linguistic development, which provides us with very precise landmarks for this study (Leroy-Collombel and Morgenstern 2012; Parisse and Morgenstern 2012; De Pontonx et al. 2018, among others).

We chose those two families because in our multiple analyses of the longitudinal data, we were struck by the role of humor and play in the two families' ecosystem. The children and their parents seemed to spend a lot of their family time in a *playful mode*. They were constantly cooperating in their play with objects, their bodies, their verbal productions and their thoughts. Morreall (2009: 65) stresses how the "activities that humans and other animals seem to find the most fun are those in which they exercise their abilities in unusual and extreme ways, but in a relatively safe setting", which characterizes sequences of shared amusement and humor in the home environment. This *playful mode* is not only propitious to humor but it involves developing the ability to view events and situations from multiple perspectives with at least two interpretations at the same time. Thus, sensorimotor playful experimentations trigger cognitive shifts and mental abilities that facilitate "theory of mind" (Baron-Cohen 1991) and meta-cognitive as well as meta–linguistic skills. For our project on children's humor, in line with Kant and Schopenhauer's incongruity theory (see Morreall 1987), combined with a Vygotskian approach to language development, and linguistic approaches to humor that target the capacity to shift perspectives (Attardo and Raskin 2017; Bröne 2017), we identified four components of the situations involving humor in our previous research (Del Re et al. 2020):
1) Intentionality of the speaker who produced humor.
2) Marks of amusement on the part of the interlocutor (laughing, smiling, verbal or gestural reaction).
3) Complicity between the conversational partners.
4) A favorable context in which the children become aware of some discrepancy or incongruity.

The analyses were conducted on 46 hours of longitudinal of video data aligned with the transcriptions. We selected all the sequences in which at least one of those components is present along with marks of amusement from at least one participant. As children can produce utterances that are unintentionally amusing for adults, we annotated all marks of amusement (smiling, laughing) in order to identify the sequences to be analyzed. All the sequences were then coded in EXCEL in order to capture a variety of categories in an integrated format. Qualitative prosodic analyses were conducted using PRAAT (Boersma and Weenink 1992–2022) which is the software that allowed us to analyze prosodic patterns and qualitative analyses of actions, gestures, postures and facial expressions, gaze, using ELAN (Sloetjes and Wittenburg 2008). We compared our gestural and vocal analyses in order to look for directional and temporal patterns in parent-child interactions. The results of the coding help us describe the paths the children take to get from first instances of shared amusement initiated by the adult and expressed mainly through reactive behavior such as smiling and laughing, to their own verbal production of successful humor in dialogue. Children are at first willing participants who express their amused reactions but are progressively socialized into becoming actors who initiate playful moments that punctuate their interactions. The children's use of humor is thus studied in connection to their cognitive, social and linguistic development. In the specific study presented in this chapter, we focus on qualitative examples in order to draw the children's general pathways into multimodal humor.[2]

4 The children's multimodal participation in shared amusement and humor

4.1 Multimodal expression of shared amusement and family resonance to humor

As already mentioned, both Anaé and Théophile were surrounded by a playful family in which shared amusement and humor were particularly present. The video-recordings are peppered with laughter around incongruous situations initiated by the parents and the children. The two children were particularly sensitive to the incongruity of adults behaving like children using postural, gestural, facial and vocal cues. To give a few examples, when Théophile was 9 months old, his father or mother would follow him on all fours which amused their son so much that he would laugh himself out of breath. Seeing his adult father and mother aligning with his own posture exhilarated him. When Théophile was 1 year and two months, he would push his (very thin and petite) mother onto the little truck he used to wheel himself around and simply cracked up with laughter when she obeyed so that he could roll her around the living-room. Those situations were of course not only embodied in the parents' actions but also worded out, which would constantly provide the child with the explicit verbalization of the actions in progress. Their amusing incongruity would be marked in the prosodic patterns

---

[2] Collombel and Morgenstern (under review) present the quantitative results on Anaé's data and other papers are in preparation with quantitative analyses.

used by the parents enriched with high pitch, intensity and vowel lengthening, accompanied by laughter, smiling and gleeful gestures.

In the following extract, we give a more specific example of the playful atmosphere in which Théophile's family thrives. The three members of the family use gestures in a spirited orchestration making up the rules of a game in order to create a sort of variation of *Simon says* during dinner.

(1) Théophile 1;3 – MOT, FAT and CHI: Playful game at the dinner table
   https://www.degruyter.com/document/isbn/9783110983128/html
   1 MOT: *feeds C with a spoon*
   2 CHI: *opens his mouth and eats, but is not looking at Mama; he claps his hands, applauding, for no apparent reason* (figure 1)

Figure 1: illustration of line 2, child applauding.

   3 MOT: Tu as envie d'applaudir ce soir? (You want to applaud tonight?) *to Child*
   4 CHI: mhm *looks intently at FAT, leaning forward, pointing at him with his index finger* (figure 2)

Figure 2: illustration of line 4, child pointing at Father.

5 FAT: *raises both arms high up* (figure 3).

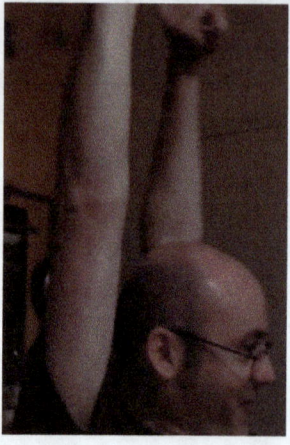

Figure 3: illustration of line 5: Father raising both arms.

6 MOT: Tu le ↑fais! (You do it!) *to CHI*
7 CHI: *raises both arms high up beaming with a proud smile* (figure 4).

Figure 4: illustration of line 7: CHI raising both arms and smiling.

8 MOT: ↑Ouais! (yeah)
9 FAT: ↑Ouais! Oh là oh là (<u>Yeah</u>! Oh là là !)
10 CHI: *points at FAT with his index finger.*
11 FAT: *lifts his arms high up above his head; waving both hands.*
12 CHI: *again points at FAT with his index finger.*
13 FAT: Oh pourquoi- pourquoi toujours moi? (Oh why- why always me?)

14 CHI: *points at MOT with his index finger*
15 MOT: à moi? (my turn?) *raising arms high and wide above her head* ah oui à toi! (yes now your turn) *points at CHI.*
16 CHI: *lifts his arms high and wide; smiling beamingly* (figure 5).

Figure 5: illustration of line 15–16: mother pointing at CHI and CHI raising both arms, smiling.

17 FAT: *applauds.*
18 MOT: bravo !(bravo!)
19 CHI: *claps his hands beamingly; shakes head in excitement and then as his mother brings a spoonful of food to his mouth slows down in time to open his mouth and eat.*

The mother's feeding (turn 1) is interrupted and gives way to a playful activity with its own rules. This activity is collectively constructed through the cooperation between the child and his parents in the middle of the family dinner in alternation with eating. This sequence shows how in line with other French middle–class families, both parents consider the dinner table not only as a place to eat and feed, but also as a commensal space and a time to communicate and share amusement (Morgenstern et al. 2021). The mother resonates with her child's applauds (turns 2–3) and verbalizes his gesture. Then when Theophile points at his father in a commanding gesture, the latter lifts both arms. This sequence of gestures composed of pointing, arm lifting and applauding is repeated several times throughout the sequence with each participant alternating roles and all of them having fun together. Both parents are constantly creating alignment and turn-taking with the child through words and gestures (turns 5 to 17). They follow Théophile's initiations joyfully and his outcries are upgraded by their own gleeful response cries (Goffman 1978). Théophile's enjoyment is marked by his beaming smiles, his energetic pointing, his lavish laughter and his vocalizations. In this shared game, Théophile designates who should raise his arms, alternately pointing to his father and mother, while gazing at the designated person. When initiating each sequence, he produces a very short nasal vocalization [m] with a rising intonation (from 244 to 346 Hz) and in synchrony with the pointing gesture. In turn 9, the father takes over this vocalization, thus integrating it into their shared game. Prosody, vocalization, gaze and gestures are thus combined here to convey Théophile's request to each of his parents to continue the game. His parents' participation in the game they have collectively created gives him the role of the maestro, the conductor of the activity and fills him with pride. This whole sequence involves a kind of role-reversal (as in the sequences we have described when he was a few months younger crawling and driving his truck) marking a deviation from their usual asymmetric positioning as adult and child, expert and novice. His parents and himself applaud his own performance both as the orchestra conductor and as the artist raising his arms in reciprocal imitation. Applauding is worded out as praise ("bravo") celebrating the child's accomplishments in a multimodal utterance or construction (Kendon 2009; Andren 2010; Goodwin 2018; Morgenstern 2014). The situation is thoroughly enjoyed by the whole family who is intensely participating in the collective activity as is marked by their gaze constantly shifting in unison towards the celebrated agent of the arm raising (see Aronsson and Morgenstern 2021 for a detailed analysis of this sequence and of children's self-praise). The same sense of accomplishment was celebrated in other situations in the two families under study for example when Théophile was able to blow bubbles in imitation of his mother at 1;5 or when Anaé proudly carried a glass from the dish-washer to the table and therefore gleefuly co-operated in setting up the family lunch table at 1;9.

The playful mood was constantly used as well to divert Théophile from the types of situations he did not particularly appreciate, such as putting on tight sleeves when he was 7 months or hair washing in his bath when he was one year old. Both mother and father would find ways to turn what was for him at first a stressful experience into a game. They would trap him into transforming screaming into laughter in fake combats around the actions of massaging the shampoo into his hair.

Not only did the children and the parents share collective playful episodes during their daily mundane activities, but even the children's own enjoyment of toys, books, videos were celebrated by the parents. Anaé's mother would participate affectionately when she saw her 18 months old daughter "read" a book on her own, and would echo her smiles and laughter. Théophile's mother would sit on the sofa next to her son and align with his own eager laughter when he watched episodes of *Wallace and Gromit* around the same age by laughing herself as well in resonance to his behavior. Both mothers simply relished in their children's fun and their own postures, gestures and facial expressions resonated with theirs.

This mutual echoing provided the children with an environment permeated with the promotion of amusement even in situations when they could not fully capture the actual source of adults' amusement and humor. In a sequence at 1;6, Théophile imitates his mother and produces the word "papa" (daddy), he then points at his father. In their effort to trigger verbal productions from their child, the mother then tries to have him say "caméra" (camera). His father repeats the word "caméra" (camera) and then says "c'est un paparazzi" (it's a paparazzi) playing on the situation and on words. The little boy does not know the meaning of paparazzi but the adults' laughter triggers a smile.

The same type of situation with the father playing on the verbalization of the situation occurs in the same session at the dinner table at a greater scale. Théophile is learning to use the fork the observer has brought back for him from Amsterdam. It is one of the first times he is actually eating by himself (with a little help from his mother).

(2) Théophile 1;6 (MOT, FAT, OBS, CHI): "C'est l'immigration choisie"
https://www.degruyter.com/document/isbn/9783110983128/html

1 OBS: je crois qu'il manifeste une certaine préférence... (I think he is showing a certain preference. . .)
2 MOT: pique . (prick.)
3 MOT: *helps CHI with his food. CHI is extremely concentrated on the pricking gesture and the food.*
4 OBS: *laughs.*
5 OBS: . . .pour les saucisses. (. . . for hot-dogs).
6 MOT : oh il aime bien les légumes normalement. (oh he usually likes vegetables.)
7 MOT: mais là c'est vrai qu'il l'air d'apprécier hein. (but he really seems to appreciate the hot-dogs this time I must say). *She laughs .*
8 MOT: voilà. (here you go). *She accompanies his gesture and helps him add a little bit of leek onto his piece of hot-dog.*
9 MOT: regarde, t'as vu ? (look, did you see ?) *she points at the fork.*
10 FAT: **c'est l' immigration choisie là**. (it's selected immigration.)
11 OBS: *laughs.*
12 CHI: *almost immediately lifts his head from his plate and laughs.*
13 MOT: *laughs (figure 6).*
14 CHI: *gazes at the adults, smiles and laughs.*
15 FAT: elle est bonne celle-là (that's a good one). *He laughs.*

Figure 6: illustration of line 12–13: Mother and child laugh.

16	OBS:	*laughs.*
17	FAT:	*laughs.*
18	CHI:	*laughs.*
19	MOT:	*laughs.*
20	MOT:	ça lui a plu. (he liked the joke)
21	FAT:	et ouais. (yeah).

During this sequence, the father who seizes every opportunity to make jokes and ironic comments, uses a metaphor in turn 10 to illustrate his son's preference to prick the pieces of hot–dog with his new fork rather than pieces of leeks that are also on his plate. "C'est l'immigration choisie" (it is selected immigration) refers to how some countries only allow the immigration of certain types of professionals to fill in the lack of specialists for certain jobs. This verbal representation of Théophile's dining behavior, which was commented on by the observer (turns 1 and 5) triggers laughter from all the adults present. Théophile, who was extremely concentrated on pricking his food and eating it (turn 3), immediately reacts to the observer's laughter (turns 11–12) as he lifts his head to gaze at her and laughs in direct response to her. There is not even a beat between the timing of his own laughter and hers. He then continues responding to all the participants' laughter and gleeful intonation (turns 15–19) and aligns with their amusement marking his participation with his own smiles and laughter. At 1;6, Théophile could not have understood the cultural reference and the semantics of his father's comment and is not reacting to the humorous content of the verbal metaphor. He simply and joyfully participates in the playful atmosphere that is extremely frequent in his household and probably proudly reacts as well to the adults' focus on his behavior. His alignment is therefore not "intellectual" but corporeal and fully embodied through the semiotic resources (facial expression and laughter) used to express amusement (turns 12 and 14). Interestingly enough, in this whole sequence, Théophile's visuo-gestural channel (gaze, posture, arm movements) was engaged in dining activities (pricking the food with the fork) but his audio-vocal channel was available (ears) and enabled him to react to his parents' vocal shared amusement. He then used both channels to find the source of the amusement (head lifting and gaze) and express his own amusement (smiling and laughing).

The father accompanies his child's laughter with a formulaic verbal expression used when someone makes a good joke and says "ah elle est bonne, elle est bonne celle-là" (oh that's a good one, that's a good one) which once again cannot be fully captured by the child. The father stages the child's reaction as if the child were taking an adult-like perspective and were marking an intentional stance. The father is using a transmodal recast as he reformulates the child's laughter and smile into a verbal production. Théophile probably reacts to the father's prosody as it makes him laugh even louder (turn 18). After the three members of the family continue to align their collective behavior through eating a mouthful at the same time (just after turn 19), both parents, fully aware that their son could not have understood the joke, comment on his sharing their "adult" amusement (turns 20 and 21). This humor sequence therefore plays out at two levels: 1) the intellectual level with the semantic content of the father's metaphor which could only be understood by adults sharing the same cultural background; 2) the collective amusement that propagates throughout the table and which Théophile shares. He therefore is able to take part in the adults' amusement at a global level, he can fully participate in the humorous collective bubble through his semiotic resources without producing or understanding the verbal content. Our data shows that Théophile's early socialization to both his parents' shared amusement and his father's jokes probably facilitates his own playful attitude at an early age and his later frequent production of his own jokes.

Similarly to Théophile's, Anaé's environment is permeated with shared amusement and humor. Her mother verbalizes and clarifies all the quirkiness, oddities, during the activities she shares with her daughter. Every sequence of situational comedy in the behavior of the members of the family or the dog is dissected as well as all the authors' and illustrators' creative incongruities that could be found in the illustrations and the text of the books they read together. For example, at 1;09, during the reading of an illustrated book in which the caterpillar Nini, who has just turned into a butterfly, flies away, the following exchange takes place:

(3)   Anaé 1;9 (MOT, CHI, BRO1, BRO2, OBS) : the flying chicken.
      1   MOT: elle vole? (does it fly?)
      2   CHI: *she is bended over the picture book and attentively looking at the illustrations.*

3 CHI: *gazes at her mother.*
4 CHI: [ɛ] poule? ([ɛ] chicken?)
5 MOT: nan. c'est pas une poule regarde! (no. look, it's not a chicken.)
6 MOT, OBS, BRO1, BRO2 *laugh all at once*
7 MOT: et les poules ça ne vole pas en plus. (and besides, chicken don't fly.)
8 BRO1: *laughs.* elle avait dit que les pigeons c'étaient des poules qui volent ! (she said that the pigeons were chickens that could fly).
9 MOT: oui ben toi t'avais dit que la poule c'était un pigeon alors. *laughs.* (yes, well you said that the chicken was a pigeon).

Anaé has unintentionally produced an incongruous response by using the wrong name to refer to the butterfly (turn 4, she calls it a chicken), which makes all the other participants laugh (turn 6). The mother then explains the reasons for their reaction, pointing out Anaé's error and providing additional information about her knowledge of the world (it cannot be a chicken since chickens do not fly, turn 7), which will allow the child to understand her error and eventually correct it in a subsequent sequence. The older brother then reminds them of another mislabeling Anaé produced one day (turn 8) and his mother replies by showing that he was prone to similar errors as well (turn 9). Anaé's specific mislabeling is thus viewed as amusing but also as an item in a list of similar semantic generalizations children make which can be corrected (her older brother does not make that type of confusion any longer). It is transitory and it can be repaired, semantic domains can be mastered in time with enough exposure to the referents and to their adequate names.

According to Cunningham (2004), the pleasure we derive from humor lies in the cognitive realization that the situation is unreal and incongruous in reference to the "rules" of the world we know. A number of studies have shown that humor can arrive in situations where expectations are violated (see Attardo 2020 for an overview). As children begin to use their perceptions and past experiences to formulate expectations about situations and events, when they have been confronted repeatedly to examplars of shared amusement in their environment in similar situations, they can respond with laughter when these expectations are violated.

In this section, we have shown how the daily repetition of children's experiencing of shared amusement and humor socializes them progressively to collective amusement and humor marked by multimodal cues. In the next section, we present analyses that support the development of their own ability to produce amusing incongruities.

4.2 The children's multimodal entry into amusing incongruities

The two children we focus on in this paper start producing incongruities that amuse them as early as their second year of life which indicates that their productive pathway into humor begins quite earlier than mentioned in some of the literature (del Ré et al. 2013). Incongruities can be enacted through the accomplishment of actions which divert an object from its principal function, such as a package of pasta which becomes a musical instrument in example 4.

(4) Anaé 1;9.- OBS – CHI – the musical pasta
    1 CHI: *shakes a package of pasta.*
    2 OBS: t(u) aimes mieux les pâtes! (you like pasta better !)
    3 OBS: *laughs.* ça fait d(e) la musique? (it makes music ?)
    4 CHI: *smiles, gazes at OBS.*
    5 CHI [əlɔ] *She continues to shake the pasta.*
    6 OBS : *laughs.*
    7 CHI: *laughs* e@fs pâtes! (fs pasta!)

It is the adult who verbalizes what the child is doing with the object diverted from its main function, but her own action makes the child laugh. By shaking the package vigorously, she seems to be asserting the discrepancy between the object first labeled as pasta both by the observer (turn 2) and later by the child herself (turn 7). The child's repeated action aligns with the observer's comment on her music making. Her uptake of the single word "pâte" preceded by a filler syllable signaling the early stage of her syntactic, phonological and morphological development at 1;9 echoes the observer's utterance about her liking pasta (turn 2). She is thus using several resources by combining an action (that happens to make noise or rather "music") and speech to mark how she redirects pasta from their function as food -to be eaten and "liked better" as the observer proposes – into becoming a musical instrument to be played with. She is thus aware that the same object, a package of pasta, can have two different functions, which is a perfect grounding to develop humor.

In the next session, Anaé initiates an incongruous behavior that triggers the amusement of all the other participants by untying her father's shoelaces.

(5) Anaé 1;10 (FAT, MOT, BRO): the shoe laces.
    1 CHI: toi chaussure. (you shoe).
    2 CHI *unfastens her father's shoe laces.*
    3 CHI: [e] d'aut(re). (and the other) *she fidgets with the shoes.*

4	CHI:	et chaussure a d'aut(re). (and shoe and also the other). *She works on the shoe laces.*
5	CHI:	là. (here.)
6	CHI:	*catches her father's other shoe.*
7	CHI:	oui lacet toi. (you, lace you.)
8	CHI :	*unfastens her father's shoe laces.*
9	FAT:	hé non! (hey, no!) *father performs large gestures with his arms but does not stop CHI.*
10	CHI:	*smiles, laughs.*
11	FAT:	ah non! (oh no!)
12	CHI:	*laughs.*
13	FAT:	ah non! (oh no!)
14	CHI:	*laughs.*
15	FAT:	t'as détaché mes chaussures? (you have unfastened my shoes?)
16	CHI:	*falls down on her bottom as she laughs.*
17	CHI:	détaché mes chaussures. (unfastened my shoes.)
18	FAT:	tu me les rattaches? (can you fasten them again ?)

The father overperforms and loudly verbalizes his reaction (turns 9, 11, 13, 15). This triggers Anaé's smile, then laughter, which increases all the way to her falling on her bottom in laughter (turns 10, 12, 14, 16). The father's loud reaction is part of a scenario with two actors, the child and the father, who collaborate to play out the comic scene. At first the child acts on her own and combines her fidgeting with her father's shoe laces and produces quasi monologic verbalizations (turns 1, 3, 4, 5, 7). Then the father participates by performing his reaction with emphatic prosodic patterns. He protests by saying *no* to his daughter but in a very particular way: the nasal vowel [a~] is very elongated, he uses a rising intonation in turn 9, and then a rising–descending intonation in turns 11 and 13 which elicit Anaé's laughter each time. The pitch of his voice is also very high, up to 306 Hz in turn 13 (Figure 7), while the average pitch of his voice is usually 180 Hz in this excerpt when he addresses his daughter without amplifying his prosody.

The incongruous behavior comes from a double role reversal: usually adults are the ones who act on children's shoe laces and help them because they are difficult for a child to tie on their own. In this case Anaé has the power to act on her father's shoe laces but she does not help him tie them. On the contrary, she unties them and disrupts the ongoing conversation. Her transgressive behavior is not viewed as negative and instead, it is valued as amusing as indicated by the father's role play and by her own smile and laughter. Not only does her father mark his participation in the amusement by overperforming his verbal reactions, but he does not stop her and thus allows her to accomplish her joke on him. Just like Théophile, who when he was younger ordered his mother to sit on his own toy truck, Anaé has the ability to initiate incongruous behaviors and to amuse her interactional partner.

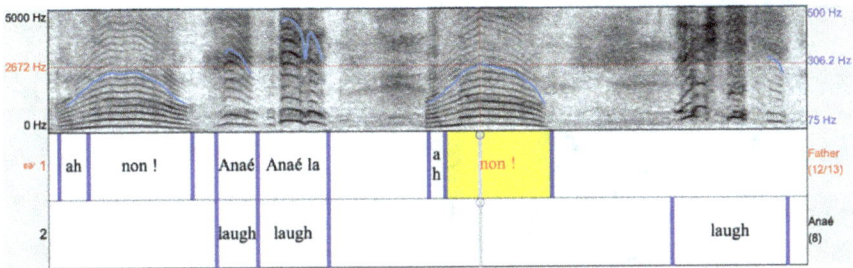

Figure 7: Representations of Anaé's laughter and her father's speech (turns 11–14). Narrow-Band spectrogram in black and white) and fundamental frequency visualization (in blue)

Another frequent illustration of incongruity and transgression is marked in what the literature calls "scatological humor". Both Anaé and Théophile gloat when they produce such words as "pipi" and "caca" ("pee" and "poo"). This type of amusement is not always shared with adults who do not fully enjoy the production of those words, especially in the presence of an observer and a camera. But children thrive when they can seize the opportunity to share their amusement with adults. Such an opportunity presents itself in the next example as the observer provides an opening to use the word "pipi" (pee).

(6) Anaé 2;0 (CHI, OBS): Fait pipi
https://www.degruyter.com/document/isbn/9783110983128/html
Anaé is playing with her new doll and a toy bathroom that has a shower and a toilet.
1 CHI: ɛ@fs fait pipi. (she is peeing.)
2 OBS: comment elle faisait avant pour faire pipi si elle avait pas de salle-de-bains ? (how did she manage before to pee if she did not have a bathroom?)
3 MOT: *laughs.*
4 CHI: ɛ@fs fait pipi. (she is peeing). *laughs.*
         After gazing at the observer, Anaé gazes down at her doll as she is peeing. She holds her doll on top of the toy shower.
5 CHI: *laughs* ɛ@fs fait pipi. (she is peeing). *Large smile at OBS.*
6 OBS: alors, qu' est-ce-que tu as eu d'autre montre-moi ! (so what else did you get, show me).

Figure 8: Illustration of line 5. Anaé shows how Dora is peeing and smiling at OBS.

7   CHI: ε@fs fait pipi ! (she is peeing !) *large smile at OBS.*
8   OBS: il est long son pipi dis-donc ! (Oh my, that's a very long pee!)
9   CHI: fait pipi xx . (peeing xx) *large smile at OBS.*
10 CHI: *lets her doll fall inside the shower.*

Anaé, who is two years old, is playing with her doll Dora, which her parents have just given her for her birthday. She places Dora over a plastic shower stall and says she is peeing. The observer asks her how Dora used to pee if she did not have a bathroom (turn 1). Anaé does not answer and continues to say "ε@fs is peeing" (turn 4), laughing, as she somewhat senses that her verbal production is part of the scatological register and starts embodying it as an accepted transgression (since it was initiated by the observer who used the word herself) to the polite verbal register. She gazes at the observer and then immediately turns down her head to watch the doll pee, and then lifts her head up again and repeats ε@fs is peeing" (turn 6) gazing at the observer with a large smile. The observer tries to distract her by asking her what else she got for her birthday (turn 5), but Anaé persists and repeats the same utterance again (turns 7, 9). In this situation, it is the word "pee" that makes her laugh (scatological amusement) and she prolongs her jubilation by repeating the same statement several times. She does not really interact with the adult, she does not answer her questions, but produces her verbal monologue, in front of others for the pleasure of speaking, and of repeating the words that make her laugh. She is enjoying her "egocentric speech" (Piaget, 1968: 20–21) but the pleasure is also derived from the fact that it is performed in front of adults – particularly the observer – as the repetition of the word "pipi" is often viewed as not quite proper and Anaé seems to gloat at the idea that she is repeating the word "pipi" in front of adults as her gaze, smiles and laughter indicate. Interestingly enough, the audio-vocal modality sounds like it is monologic, or egocentric. Even though the topic was in fact pursued by the observer (turn 2) and taken up again by the child who thus got some kind of license to use the word "pipi", the adults do not continue to align with her verbal productions. The observer tries to change the topic, the mother does not continue the exchange either. But the use of other semiotic resources shows the adults' joint attention and could indicate that they are in fact amused.[3] Both the adults' gaze are on the doll that Anaé has positioned to illustrate that she is peeing in her new bathroom. Anaé keeps looking at the observer when she uses the word "pipi" with a huge smile and her gleeful intonation marks her excitement over her own playful actions with the doll and her verbal productions. The two channels are thus used with different functions: the observer and the child express a different project at the verbal level (Anaé wants to repeat the word "pipi", the observer tries to change the topic), but they are sharing some form of amusement which is marked through the visual channel.

As far as the use of prosody is concerned, there are nuances in the production of the statement "ε@fs is peeing" produced on five occasions (turns 1, 4, 5, 7, 8). In turn 1, Anaé simply formulates the observation that Dora is peeing (with the primary French accent realized on the final syllable accompanied by a very slight intonational rise, from 328 to 340 Hz, Figure 9). In turn 4 which triggers her laughter, she produces a slight contrastive stress on the 1st syllable of "pipi" (marked by a higher pitch 302 Hz which contrast with the previous and following syllables, respectively produced at 278 Hz and 234 Hz, a longer duration and a stronger intensity, Figure 10), which she did not produce in the previous utterance. She therefore emphasizes the word "pipi". In turn 7, she repeats the same utterance with a more exaggerated prosody (maybe because the adult is trying to divert her attention) with a very marked final intonational rise (she solicits the adult without looking at her). There is still an initial accent on the 1st syllable of [pi] (it is so marked that she produces an occlusion with a long release phase and a longer syllable than the final syllable). The placement of this accent on the 1st syllable of the word "pipi" twice allows her to nuance the meaning of what she says and to introduce her own touch of subjectivity in an utterance that never varies at the segmental level. In this extract, the subtleties of the participants' amusement are

---

[3] As the adults are also two of the co-authors of this paper, we have insider information about their emotions.

thus marked thanks to their mutual use of gaze, the addition of contrasting accents and the use of different intonation contours.

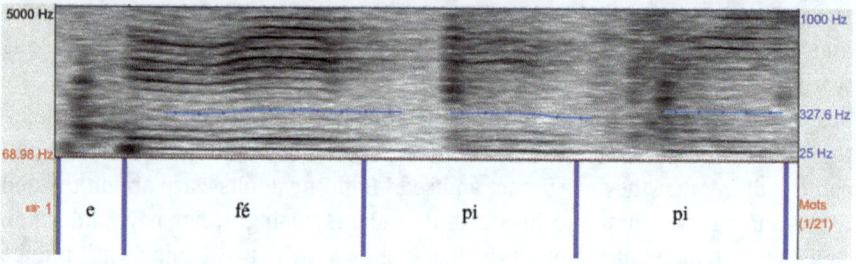

Figure 9: Representations of Anaé's speech (turn 1).
Narrow-Band spectrogram in black and white) and fundamental frequency visualization (in blue).

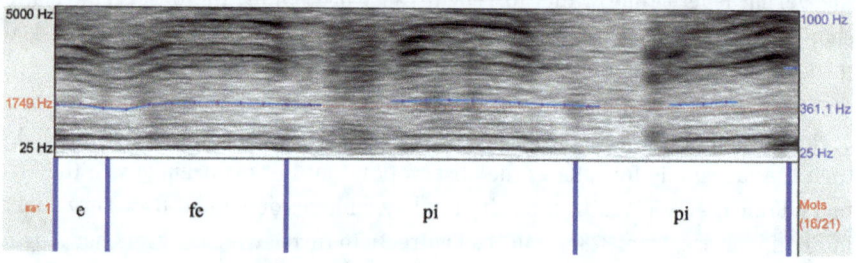

Figure 10: Representations of Anaé's speech (turn 4).
Narrow-Band spectrogram in black and white) and fundamental frequency visualization (in blue).

Those examples have shown that the children's transgressive and incongruous actions can generate amusement which is perceivable in their interlocutors' gestures, speech, prosodic patterns and laughter. The combination of the family's acceptance of those actions and the models the parents provide of verbal humor and collective amusement during their daily shared activities illustrated in 3.1. facilitate the two children's entry into the production of verbal humor complemented by other semiotic resources.

The following example is particularly interesting as Anaé does not share the same perspective as her older brother and the observer on her own behavior. Even though all the participants mark their amusement through multimodal cues, there is an asymmetry in their apprehension of the target event which comes from the difference in their metalinguistic knowledge of the word "langue" (it refers both to the "tongue" and to "language" in French).

(7) ANAE 2;11.22 (CHI, OBS, BRO2): « tu chantes en quelle langue? »

1 CHI: xxx *singing in a microphone.*
2 OBS: hé dis-moi ANAE **tu chantes en quelle langue** ? (well tell me Anaé, what language are you singing in ?)
3 CHI: **a celle-là>** (fs[4] this one)
4 CHI: ***sticks her tongue out** and smiles*

Figure 11: Illustration of line 4: child sticks out her tongue and smiles.

5 OBS: avec celle-là ? (with this one ?) *with an amused tone of voice.*
6 BRO2 *Brother smiles and looks at OBS.*
7 CHI: *resumes singing xxx*

In this video, Anaé is only answering the questions that are asked of her, she does not seem to be trying to trigger the others' laughter. However, her behavior could be viewed as transgressive since sticking one's tongue out is a way to provoke one's interlocutors in her cultural community. She seems to be aware of her transgression of some kind of politeness rule and of the fact that the situation allows it, as she smiles. That action does have the effect of provoking her brother's and the observer's laughter. We cannot call this humor, because Anaé, her older brother and the adult do not have the same perspective on the situation. She in-

---

[4] fs is a code to refer to a filler syllable, which is typical of child speech: the transcribers could not interpret the meaning and the grammatical category of the phoneme produced but it corresponds to the beginning of the preposition "avec" which means "with".

terprets the question literally, without thinking about the other meaning of the word "langue". She does not know at that age that it refers in French not only to the organ that allows her to speak or sing (the tongue), but also to different languages. Her two interlocutors are aware of Anaé's incongruous behavior at two different levels: 1) she has mistaken the two meanings of the word langue; 2) she has stuck out her tongue, not "at them" and not as a provocation, but "for them" to show them "which tongue" she is using. If Anaé had had the metalinguistic awareness of a 7 year old such as her older brother, her behavior could have been interpreted as humorous and slightly provocative. The awareness of the discrepancy between the child's perspective and their own triggers the observer and brother's amusement and complicity (turns 5 and 6) marked through their smile, tone of voice and gaze exchange.

We have analyzed extracts in which the child's production of incongruities initiates amusement. In the next section we focus on the children's multimodal production of humor and metalinguistic awareness.

4.3 Children's multimodal production of humor and metalinguistic awareness

Once the children have acquired all the linguistic means to "language" humor, they are eager to express their own creativity and receive the adults' amused multimodal feedback. Humor becomes an interactive and intersubjective strategy.

In the following extract, Anaé is one year older and she produces one of the first "jokes" in our longitudinal data when the observer questions her about her birthday and what she likes to eat.

(8) Anaé 2;11,22 (CHI, OBS): le piment
 https://www.degruyter.com/document/isbn/9783110983128/html
 1 OBS: Alors dis-moi, tu vas aller manger où pour ton anniversaire ? Tu sais ? Tu vas aller au restaurant ? (So tell me, where are you going to eat for your birthday? Do you know? You're going to the restaurant?)
 2 CHI: oui. (yes.)
 3 OBS: Qu'est-ce que tu aimes manger ? (what do you like to eat?)
 4 CHI: ehm. . .*she looks down, fidgets with her fingers, then gazes through the corner of her eyes at OBS and smiles. Du: . . .she gazes straight at OBS* piment ! (Hot pepper!). *She brings back her hands to a rest position under the table.*

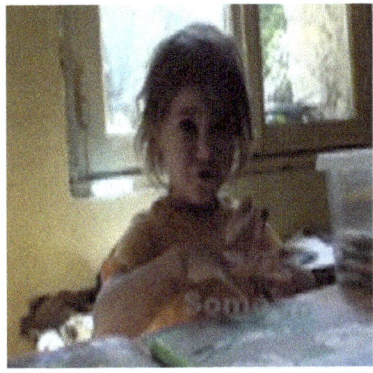

Figure 12: illustration of line 4-Anaé gazes through the corner of her eye before producing the target word an gestures with her two hands.

Figure 13: illustration of line 4-Anaé produces the word piment and gazes straight at OBS bringing back her hands on her lap.

```
5  OBS:  du piment ? (hot pepper?)
6  CHI:  non ! non ! She makes a large smile and laughs (no! no!)
7  OBS:  oh ! ça pique ! (oh! it's hot!) she laughs
8  CHI:  oui ! (yes). she laughs.
```

Just before turning three years old, Anaé is quite capable of injecting unexpected verbal elements into the dialogue with the intention of surprising her interlocutor to amuse herself and the observer. All the necessary elements for discursive humor are combined: the amusement shown by both the participants' laughter, the complicity between the interlocutors, Anaé's intentionality, and the incongruous food, hot pepper, in the context of a birthday meal. Anaé does not give the answer expected by the adult who knows that she does not like hot pepper. In this example humor flourishes in a pleasant context, conducive to playfulness (setting) with people capable of receiving it and a history of interactions, a habituation to playful formats. In this type of context, the child can produce an incongruity that provokes her own amusement indicated by her smile, the disfluencies in her vocal flow, her prosody and her gestures, turn 4) and that of the adult (marked through her prosody, turn 5).

The child's response establishes a discontinuity in the dialogue and this discontinuity is quite intentional on her part. It triggers surprise and laughter. But when the adult asks for confirmation of the child's answer ("du piment?" [hot pepper?] turn 5, Figure 14), Anaé quickly answers negatively with a playful intonation, certainly implying that of course she does not like hot pepper, and that her answer was a joke.

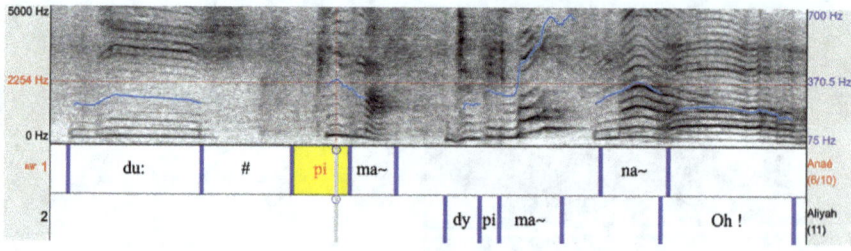

Figure 14: Representations of Anaé and Observer's speech (turns 5–6). Narrow-Band spectrogram in black and white) and fundamental frequency visualization (in blue)

Interestingly enough, even though we can capture the humor in both participants' speech, other semiotic resources are still at play. After OBS has asked her question "What do you like to eat? ", she produces a hesitation "ehm" then looks at her hands while pressing the fingers of her two hands together, looks again at OBS while saying "du" with a very pronounced lengthening (885 ms), followed by a 592 ms pause (she spares her effect at the temporal level by delaying the following production), then lowers her hands when producing "piment" with a focus on the first syllable (370 Hz) of "piment" (Figure 14). She then smiles. Her speech involves a clear focalization on the first syllable of "piment" with an extended intonation pattern (rise–fall intonation contour: 272–363–317). During the whole sequence, she does not take her eyes off of OBS so as not to lose a bit of her reaction. Just before the child answers the adult's question, in turn 4, her gaze alternates between her hands and the observer, she then gazes straight at the observer as she produces her challenging answer. These multimodal cues confirm her mastery of all the resources necessary to subtly express humor and her skill to coordinate speech, gaze, facial expressions and prosody.

The child and the adult both laugh, which indicates that the amusement is shared. Anaé is the source of the incongruity, which she seems to produce intentionally within the dialogue. The incongruity is identified and marked through the adult's reaction and her repetition of the incongruous element ("du piment" turn 5) with a rising and very large intonation contour (263–650 Hz > 19 semi-tones or 1 octave and a half), expressing her astonishment. Anaé's negative response to the observer's request for confirmation, accompanied by a large smile, and all the multimodal preparation described above allow us to assume that she is aware of the incongruity of her response – even if she may also have produced this response to escape the question-and-answer game, which is not her favorite activity. She thus perhaps marks a certain opposition to this "interview" conducted by the observer, which is transformed into a shared game thanks to humor. The child creates incongruity by selecting an inappropriate answer in the category of children's favorite foods, and there is thus a true discrepancy with the observer's expectations. Thanks to their complicity, this discrepancy is transformed into shared amusement.

This sequence was marked by a certain degree of provocation on the part of the child, but what could have been aggressive is turned into humor and amusement. A similar situation can be found in Théophile's data when he is 4;0 and is also discussing his birthday party.

(9) Théophile, 4 ;0 (CHI, MOT, OBS) : anniversaire
MOT is putting a shirt on Théophile who is quite excited and animated.
1   MOT: qu'est-ce-qu' a fait à ton anniversaire Théophile ? (what did we do for your birthday Théophile ?)
2   OBS: qu'est-ce que vous avez fait à ton anniversaire Théophile, vous avez fait avec tout le monde ? (what did you do for your birthday Théophile, you did it with everyone?)
3   CHI: *Just before his mother puts his shirt on his head, he gazes at the observer with a large smile.*
    Non on a fait **rien** . (no, we did **nothing**)
4   OBS: bah. *She laughs.*
5   MOT: bah.
6   MOT: on a rien fait ? (we did nothing ?)
7   CHI: nan ! (no !) *with a high-pitch voice.*
8   MOT: on a rien fait dimanche dernier ? (we did nothing last Sunday?)
9   CHI: y'a **pas** eu de cadeaux **rien** ! (there were **no** presents, **nothing**!)
10 MOT: *laughs. Throughout this sequence she is trying to pull the shirt down his head. Théophile does not seem to mind the inconvenience, he is busy answering her questions.*

11 OBS: oh!
12 CHI: rien! (nothing).
13 MOT: y avait pas d' cadeaux y avait pas d' gâteaux y avait pas d' copains ? (there were no presents, no cakes and no friends?)
14 CHI: c'était **pas** mon (an)niversaire . (it was **not** my birthday) *smiles*.
15 MOT: c'était quoi alors ? (what was it then ?)
16 CHI: c'était, c'était un **spec**tacle. (it was, it was a **show**.)
17 MOT: ah c'était un spectacle ? (oh it was a show ?)
18 CHI: oui. (yes.)
19 MOT: qu'est-ce-qu' y avait au spectacle ? (what was there in that show ?)
20 CHI: y avait des cacas y avait des kakabs[5] y avait des kakabs. Y avait des Spiderman y avait des kakabs. (there were poops, there were poopoos, there were poopoos. There were spidermen, there were poopoos).
21 MOT: *laughs*.
22 MOT: des kakabs c'est quoi les kakabs ? (poopoos ? what are poopoos ?)
23 CHI: c'est des des jouets c'est une voiture caca. (there are to toys, it's a poopoo car).

Probably because of the observer's presence, Théophile's mother initiates the process of narrative co-construction through questions. She is trying to get Théophile to narrate his birthday party that took place on the previous Sunday. The little boy is not in a compliant mood but instead of simply not answering, he chooses to annihilate the event the adults are referring to through a double negation "non on a fait rien" (no we did nothing, turn 3, Figure 15). Théophile produced a focalization accent on "rien" in turn 3 (with a stronger intensity on the last syllable and a falling intonation contour). The second negation produced on turn 7 with a rising intonation contour (as shown in Figure 15) is very high–pitched (274–378 Hz), giving the feeling that he is playing with his voice – a little baby's voice – and with the situation. His mother puts his assertions into question with a very high pitch (turns 6: 387–704 Hz, + 11 semi-tones, almost one octave, mean fundamental frequency is of 451 Hz) and turn 8 (+ 19 semi-tones, one and a half octave, with an even more high–pitched voice, mean fundamental frequency is of 534 Hz).

Théophile's negations are pursued (turns 7 and 9) and the characteristics of the event, especially receiving presents, denied with strong accentuations as well: "y'a pas eu de cadeaux rien!" (there were no presents, nothing, turn 9, Figure 16). The denial culminates in the turn 14: "c'était **pas** mon (an)niversaire" (it was not

---

5 Théophile invents the word « kakab » which is very close to "caca" (poop).

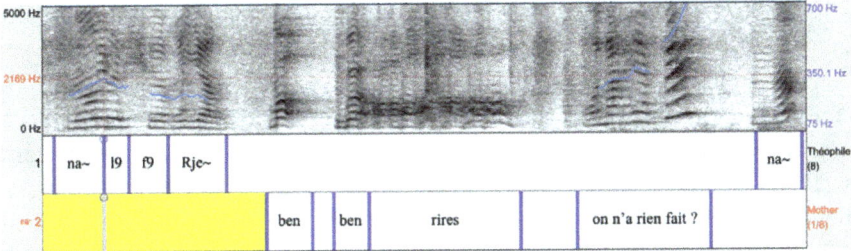

Figure 15: Representations of Théophile and his mother's speech (turns 3–7). Narrow-Band spectrogram in black and white) and fundamental frequency visualization (in blue).

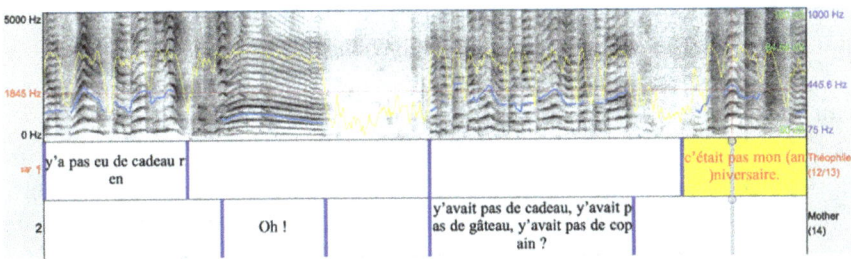

Figure 16: Representations of Théophile and his mother's speech (turns 9–14). Narrow-Band spectrogram in black and white) and fundamental frequency visualization (in blue)

my birthday) with an accent of focalization on the negative adverb "pas" (in yellow, Figure 16), which is produced on the higher point of the utterance of the rise–fall intonation contour (256-444-364 Hz, with 9 semi-tones higher pitch). The annihilation of the birthday goes even further: as an answer to his mother's question (turn 15), Théophile redefines the event as a show (turn 16). In answer to his mother's question (turns 19 and 22), Théophile's provocation and excitement, first expressed through negation and then the redefinition of the event, culminates through scatological speech, which particularly amuses him like most children his age. He starts with the word "caca" and then produces word play by inventing a variation: "kakab" which he uses repeatedly.

Théophile thus has the skills to express his provocative feelings towards the adults through different framings of the event and of its characteristics (as a "non-birthday", with no presents, as a show and transgressive language (caca, kakab) and transforms his aggressive mode into humor. Just as in example 8, humor has thus played its role as a contributor to harmonious social exchanges (Priego-Valverde 2003: 233) by enabling Théophile to express and transform his aggressivity into shared amusement.

At four years old, both Anaé and Théophile are capable of producing verbal humor subtly complemented by other multimodal cues. As soon as they can verbalize incongruities with the intent to amuse the other, the sequences form a script which includes multimodal markers. All the elements of this script have been progressively developed in the daily family interactions and the constant scaffolding of Anaé and Théophile's family members. It will continue in other settings, and in particular at school with other conversational partners who will broaden the framework for humor.

When she is a little older, Anaé has developed her metalinguistic skills even more and is becoming capable of explaining what a joke is. The sequence in example 10 happens very soon after April Fool's day, the day for jokes. Anaé explains how she has made drawings of fish in school and taped them on her teacher's back. The mother and the little girl then have a discussion about jokes.

(10) Anaé 4;08 (CHI, OBS, MOT): defining jokes
https://www.degruyter.com/document/isbn/9783110983128/html

1 MOT: vous lui avez pas fait d(e) blague ? vous lui avez pas dit qu' y avait un éléphant dans la cour ? (didn't you make a joke ? didn't you tell her that there was an elephant in the courtyard ?)
2 CHI: non. (no). *gazes at her mother.*
3 MOT: qu'est-ce-que c'est une blague ? (what's a joke ?)
4 OBS: ce serait bien. (it would be good)
5 CHI: c'est de dire *shrug* quelque chose que n'est pas *with each syllable clearly separated.* (it's to say something that isn't). *She is folding a piece of paper as she talks.*
6 CHI: *looks at MOT her hands still busy with her piece of paper. she rotates her head as if she were representing her search for words complemented with a facial expression.*
7 CHI: dedans. (inside) *laughs*
8 MOT: qui n'est pas quoi ? (that is not what ?)
9 CHI: DE DANS . (IN SIDE) *Produced with two distinct syllables.*
10 CHI: où i y'a. . . (where there is. . .)
11 MOT: est-ce-que tu connais des blagues ? (do you know any jokes?)
12 CHI: ben oui. (well yes.)
13 MOT: tu nous en dis une ? (could you tell us one ?)
14 CHI: *smiles.* euh maman t'as un éléphant derrière ton dos. (hum Mum, you have an elephant behind your back)
15 MOT: *forced laugh.*
16 MOT: c'est une blague ? (is that a joke ?)

17	OBS:	*laughs.*
18	CHI:	*laughs.* oui. (yes.)
19	OBS:	*laughs.*
20	CHI:	*to OBS* euh, t'as, t'as euh un ours derrière toi. *she points at OBS.* (hum, you have, you have, hum a bear behind you). *She makes an impressive facial expression as if she were seeing something quite extraordinary.*
21	OBS:	oh!
22	MOT:	*laughs.*

Even though she is still hesitant, and is still searching for the right formulation, Anaé does indicate that she understands what a joke is and defines it as "saying something that isn't" meaning "that is not true" or "not real". Interestingly enough, her posture indicates that she is actively searching for her formulation: her verbal production is complemented with a shrug, she articulates her words syllable after syllable (turn 5, Figure 17).

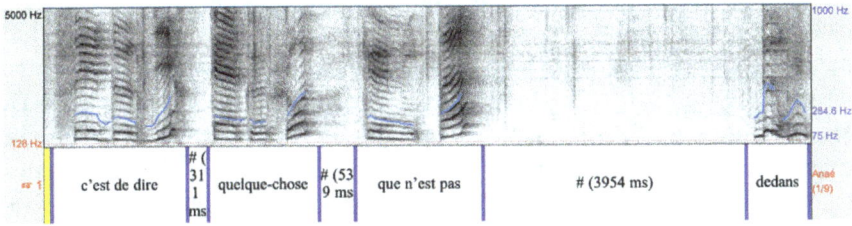

Figure 17: Representations of Anaé's speech (turn 5).
Narrow-Band spectrogram in black and white) and fundamental frequency visualization (in blue).

She then gazes at her mother (turn 6), her hands still busy with her piece of paper. Her prosody seems to match her hand movements as she manipulates the little piece of paper. There is thus a clear synchronization of her movements with the different accents located on "c'est de **dire** # quelque chose # que n'est **pas** ### **de**dans" with a rising intonation (Figure 17) and a beat gesture on each of the accents (before each pause). She rotates her head as if she were representing her search for words complemented with a facial expression. Anaé then takes up her mother's example (turn 1, an elephant in the courtyard) as an illustration of a joke (turn 14) which triggers her mother's forced or pretend laugh as it is not quite innovative. But Anaé is capable of slightly changing the joke when she addresses the observer (turn 20: you have, you have, hum, a bear behind you). The disfluency indicates her cognitive effort to change the target element of the joke.

Her facial expression embodies her pretend reaction to the bear that she is referring to and pointing at with her index.

Anaé has the metalinguistic skills not only to produce humor but to reflect on it. Her linguistic, metalinguistic, cognitive and expressive development are fully embodied through all the semiotic resources at play in her *languaging* of both the joke and the definition of the joke.

As early as four years old both children have the ability not only to participate in shared amusement, to initiate incongruities, but also to produce and embody humor with all the semiotic means at their disposal. They can subtly complement their verbal productions with the use of gaze, facial expressions, gestures and specific prosodic patterns.

5 Conclusion

In order to analyze humor, its reception and use by children under five years old, we focused on spontaneous interactions in a secure and playful environment. Family activities and interactions are a privileged locus for the development of humor. In this chapter, we analyzed the data of two children recorded at home during their daily activities (Morgenstern & Parisse 2017). We used a multimodal approach involving detailed analyses and taking into account children's linguistic, cognitive and social development, especially their capacity to express perspective taking and intersubjective positioning. We illustrated how children exploit the resources available to them within the discourse context and enter a collaboration in which the adults, as experts, provide important scaffolding. We analyzed the reception and production of marked expression of amusement and humor with their specific acoustic, facial and gestural components.

Humor is a complex phenomenon which involves multiple dimensions and is expressed and shared through multiple semiotic resources (Priego-Valverde 2003). Our detailed analyses of adult-child interactions illustrate how children internalize language through their senses in situated interactions grounded in the mundane activities of their everyday lives. Thanks to their sensory perceptions, and the languaging that surrounds them and is addressed to them, they are socialized to meaning making out of their experience. Children are wholistic multimodal languagers when they begin expressing themselves. The use of semiotic resources then progressively diversifies and varies according to the stage they are in, and to their cognitive, motor, and linguistic development.

The sequences we have analyzed in detail can help describe the paths children take to go from first instances of shared amusement initiated by the adults, in which they produce mainly reactive multimodal behavior such as smiling and laughing, to their own production of successful humor. The children in our dataset are at first willing participants who express their amused reactions, but then become co-operative actors (based on Goodwin 2017) who initiate humor by combining their verbal, gestural and prosodic skills in inter-action. Children are thus progressively socialized to co-operate with their conversation partner in the co-construction of multimodal interactional humor.

References

Andrén, Mats. 2010. *Children's Gestures from 18 to 30 months*, PHD dissertation, Centre for Languages and Literature, Centre for Cognitive Semiotics, Lund University.
Apte, Mahadev L. 1985. *Humor and Laughter: An Anthropological Approach*. Ithaca, NY: Cornell University Press.
Aronsson, Karin & Aliyah Morgenstern. 2021. "Bravo!": Co-constructing praise in French family life. *Journal of Pragmatics* 173. 1–14.
Attardo, Salvatore, and Victore Raskin. 2017. Linguistics and humor theory. In Salvatore Attardo, *The Routledge Handbook of Language and Humor*, 49–63. New York: Routledge.
Attardo, Salvatore. 2001. *Humorous Texts: A Semantic and pragmatic Analysis*. Berlin/New York: Mouton de Gruyter.
Attardo, Salvatore. 2020. *The Linguistics of Humor*. Oxford: Oxford University Press.
Bariaud, Françoise. 1983. *La genèse de l'humour chez l'enfant*, Paris: PUF.
Baron-Cohen, Simon. 1991. Precursors to a theory of mind: Understanding attention in others. In Andrew Whiten (ed.), *Natural theories of mind: Evolution, development and simulation of everyday mindreading*, 233–251. Oxford: Basil Blackwell.
Boersma, Paul & Weenik David. (1992–2022). Praat: doing phonetics by computer [Computer program]. Version 6.2.06, retrieved 23 January 2022 from https://www.praat.org.
Bolens, Guillemette. 2021. *Kinesic Humor*. Oxford: Oxford University Press.
Bornstein, Marc H. & Jerome S. Bruner (eds.). 1989. *Interaction in human development*. Hillsdale, NJ: Lawrence Erlbaum Associates.
Boutet, Dominique. 2018. *Pour une approche kinésiologique de la gestualité* [Habilitation á diriger des recherches, Université de Rouen-Normandie].
Boutet, Dominique & Aliyah Morgenstern. 2020. Prélude et Ode à une approche kinésiologique du geste. *Travaux Interdisciplinaires du Laboratoire Parole et Langage d'Aix-en-Provence* (TIPA), Laboratoire Parole et Langage. ID: 10.4000/tipa.3892
Bruner, Jerome S. 1981. The social context of language acquisition. *Language and Communication* 1(2–3). 155–178.
Brône, Geert. 2017. Cognitive linguistics and humor research. In *The Routledge handbook of language and humor*, 250–266. Abingdon, Oxon: Routledge.
Budwig, Nancy. 2003. Context and the dynamic construal of meaning in early childhood, In Catherine Raeff & Janette B. Benson (eds.), *Social and Cognitive Development in the Context of Individual, Social, and Cultural Processes*, 103–132. London, New York: Routledge.

Chovanec, Jan & Villy Tsakona. 2018. Investigating the dynamics of Humor: Towards a theory of interactional Humor. In Villy Tsakona & Jan Chovanec (eds.), *The Dynamics of Interactional Humor: Creating and Negotiating Humor in Everyday Encounters*, 1–26. Amsterdam/Philadelphia: John Benjamins Publishing Company.

Cienki, Alan. 2012. Usage events of spoken language and the symbolic units we (may) abstract from them. In Janusz Badio & Krzysztof Kosecki (eds.), *Cognitive processes in language*, 149–158. Bern: Peter Lang.

Cienki, Alan & Olga Iriskhanova. 2018. *Aspectuality across languages. Event construal in speech and gesture*. Amsterdam/Philadelphia: John Benjamins.

Cienki, Alan & Olga K. Iriskhanova (eds.). 2018. *Aspectuality across Languages: Event construal in speech and gesture*. Amsterdam: John Benjamins.

Clark, Herb H. 1996. *Using Language*. Cambridge: Cambridge University Press.

Coulson, Seana. 2000. *Semantic Leaps. Frame-Shifting and Conceptual Blending in Meaning Construction*. Cambridge: Cambridge University Press.

Cunningham, Jennifer. 2004. Children's humor. In W. George Scarlett, Sophie Naudeau, Dorothy Salanius-Pasternak & Iris Ponte (eds.), *Scarlett*, 93–109. Thousand Oaks/London/New Delhi: Sage Publications.

De Pontonx, Sophie, Marie Leroy-Collombel & Aliyah Morgenstern. 2018. How mother and child co-(re)construct non-conventional productions in spontaneous interaction. *First Language* 39(2). 1–23.

Del Ré, Alessandra, Aliyah Morgenstern, Christelle Dodane & Heitor Quimello. 2013. Diversão partilhada, humor e ironia: um estudo sobre a produção de enunciados por uma criança brasileira. In Alessandra Del Ré, Luciani de Paula & Marina Mendonça (eds.), *Explorando o discurso da criança*, 35–53. São Paulo: Contexto.

Del Ré, Alessandra, Christelle Dodane & Aliyah Morgenstern. 2015. De l'amusement partagé à la production de l'humour chez l'enfant. in M. Farhat & F. Lacoste (eds.), *L'Humour dans le Bassin Méditerranéen. Contacts linguistiques et Culturels*. 115–139. Gafsa: Nouha Editions.

Del Ré Alessandra, Christelle Dodane, Aliyah Morgenstern & Alessandra J. Vieira. 2020. Children's development of humour in everyday interactions: two case-studies in French and Brazilian Portuguese. *European Journal of Humour Research* 8(4). 112–131.

Figueira, Rosa Attié. 2001. Dados Anedóticos: Quando a Fala da Criança Provoca o Riso . . . Humor e Aquisição da Linguagem. *Língua e Instrumentos Linguísticos* 6. 27–61.

Frith, Uta. 1989. Autism and "Theory of Mind". In Christopher Gillberg (ed.), *Diagnosis and Treatment of Autism*, 33–52. New York: Plenum Press.

Gibson, James, J. 1977. The theory of affordances. In Robert E. Shaw & John Bransford (eds.), *Perceiving, acting, and knowing: Toward an eco- logical psychology*. 67–82. Hillsdale, N.J.: Lawrence Erlbaum Associates.

Goffman, Erving. 1978. Response cries. *Language* 54(4). 1787–1815.

Goldberg, Adèle E. 2006. *Constructions at Work: The Nature of Generalization in Language*. Oxford: Oxford University Press.

Goodwin, Charles. 2018. "Why Multimodality? Why Co-Operative Action?". In *Social Interaction. Video-Based Studies of Human Sociality* 2(1). 85–98.

Goodwin, Charles & Goodwin, Marjory H. 1992. Context, Activity and Participation, In Aldo Di Luzio & Peter Auer (eds.), *The Contextualization of Language*. 77–99. Amsterdam: John Benjamins.

Goodwin, Charles. 2017. *Co-Operative Action*. New York, NY: Cambridge University Press.

Hoicka, Elena & Meredith Gattis. 2008. Do the wrong thing. How toddlers tell a joke from a mistake. *Cognitive Development* 23(1). 180–190.

Hoicka, Elena & Meredith Gattis. 2012. Acoustic differences between humorous and sincere communicative intentions. *British Journal of Developmental Psychology* 30(4). 531–549.

Horgan, Dianne. 1981. Learning to tell jokes: A case study of metalinguistic abilities. *Journal of Child Language* 8(1). 217–224.

Johnson, Kathy E. & Carolyn B. Mervis. 1997. First steps in the emergence of verbal humor: A case study. *Infant Behavior & Development* 20(2). 187–196.

Kendon, Adam. 1988. "How gestures can become like words". In Fernando Poyatos, *Cross-cultural perspectives in non-verbal communication*, 131–141. Toronto: Hogrefe.

Kendon, Adam. 2009. Manual actions, speech and the nature of language. In Daniele Gambarara & Alfredo Giviigliano (eds.), *Origine e sviluppo del linguaggio, fra teoria e storia*, 19–33. Rome, Italy: Aracne Editrice.

Kintsch, Walter & Teun A. Van Dijk. 1978. Towards a Model of Text Comprehension and Production. *Psychological Review* 85. 363–394.

Langacker, Ronarld. 1988. A view of linguistic semantics. In Brygida Rudzka-Ostyn (ed.), *Topics in cognitive linguistics* 49–91. Amsterdam: Benjamins.

Leroy-Collombel, Marie & Morgenstern, Aliyah. 2012. Rising grammatical awareness in a French-speaking child from 18 months to 36 months: uses and misuses of possession markers. *French Language Studies* 22. 57–75.

Levinson, Stephen, C. 1992. Activity types and language. In Paul Drew and John Heritage (eds.), *In Talk at Work: Interaction in Institutional Settings*, 66–100. Cambridge: Cambridge University Press.

Linell, Per. 2009. *Rethinking Language, Mind and World dialogically*: Interactional and Contextual Theories of Human Sense-Making. Charlotte, NC: Information Age Publishing.

Loizou Eleni. 2007. Humor as a means of regulating one's social self: Two infants with unique humorous personas. *Early Child Development and Care* 177(2). 195–205.

MacWhinney, Brian. 2000. *The CHILDES Project: Tools for analyzing talk*, 3rd Edition. Vol. 2: The Database, Mahwah, NJ., Lawrence Erlbaum Associates.

McGhee, Paul E. 1979. *Humor, its Origin and Development*. San Francisco: W.H. Freeman.

McNeill, David. 2016. *Why we gesture: the surprising role of the hands in communication*. Cambridge: Cambridge University Press.

Mondada, Lorenza. 2019. Contemporary issues in conversation analysis: Embodiment and materiality, multimodality and multisensoriality in social interaction. *Journal of pragmatics* 145. 47–62.

Morgenstern, Aliyah. 2014. Children's multimodal language development. In Christiane Fäcke (ed.). *Manual of language acquisition*, 123–142. Berlin/Boston: De Gruyter.

Morgenstern, Aliyah, Léa Chevrefils, Marion Blondel, Coralie Vincent, Chloé Thomas, Jean-François Jego & Boutet, Dominique. 2021. "Of thee I sing": an opening to Dominique Boutet's kinesiological approach to gesture. *Languages and Modalities*. 1–14.

Morgenstern, Aliyah & Christophe Parisse. 2012. The Paris Corpus. *French Language Studies* 22(1). 7–12.

Morgenstern, Aliyah & Christophe Parisse (eds.). 2017. *Le langage de l'enfant de l'éclosion à l'explosion*. Paris: Presses de la Sorbonne Nouvelle.

Morgenstern, Aliyah, Marion Blondel, Pauline Beaupoil-Hourdel, Sandra Benazzo, Dominique Boutet, Angelika Kochan & Fanny Limousin. 2017. The blossoming of negation in gesture, sign and oral production. In Maya Hickmann, Edy Veneziano & Harriet Jisa (eds.), *Sources of variation in first language acquisition: Languages, contexts, and learners*, 339–363. Amsterdam: John Benjamins.

Morgenstern, Aliyah & Susan Goldin-Meadow. 2021. Foreword – Gesture as part of Language or partner to Language. In Aliyah Morgenstern & Susan Goldin-Meadow (eds.), *Gesture in language: Development across the lifespan*, 365–370. Amsterdam: De Gruyter Mouton.

Morgenstern, Aliyah, Stéphanie Caët, Camille Debras, Pauline Beaupoil & Marine Le Mené. 2021. Socialization to multi-party interactive practices in French family dinners: Who talks to whom about what, in Letizia Caronia (ed.), *Cultures in dialogue: learning through interaction at home and in school*, 45–86. Amsterdam: John Benjamins.

Morreall, John. 1987. *The Philosophy of laughter and Humor*. Albany: State University of New York Press.

Morreall, John. 2009. *Comic Relief: A Comprehensive Philosophy of Humor*. Oxford: Wiley-Blackwell.

Müller, Cornelia. 2008. What gestures reveal about the nature of metaphor. In Alan Cienki & Cornelia Müller (eds.). *Metaphor and Gesture*, 2019–245. Amsterdam: John Benjamins.

Norrick, Neal R. 2006. Humor in language. In Keith Brown (ed.), *Encyclopaedia of Language and Linguistics*, 425–426. Amsterdam: Elsevier.

Norrick, Neal, R. & Delia Chiaro. 2009. *Humor in Interaction*. Amsterdam/Philadelphia: John Benjamins.

Ochs, E., B. Schieffelin & M. Platt. 1979. Propositions across Utterances and Speakers. In *Developmental Pragmatics*, E. Ochs & B. Schieffelin (eds.), 251–68. New York: Academic Press.

Ochs, Elinor & Bambi Schieffelin. 1984. Language acquisition and socialization: Three developmental stories. in R. Shweder & R. LeVine (eds.), *Culture theory: Mind, self and emotion*. Cambridge: Cambridge University Press.

Ochs, Elinor. 2012. Experiencing Language. *Anthropological Theory* 12(2). 142–160.

Parisse, Christophe & Aliyah Morgenstern. 2012. The unfolding of the verbal temporal system in French children's speech between 18 and 36 months. *Journal of French Language Studies* 22. 95–114.

Piaget, Jean. 1968. Introduction, in M. Laurendeau & A. Pinard, *Les premières notions spatiales de l'enfant*. Neuchâtel: Delachaux & Niestlé.

Priego-Valverde, Béatrice. 2003. *L'humour dans la conversation familière : description et analyse linguistiques*. Paris: L'Harmattan.

Raskin, Victor. 1985. *Semantic Mechanisms of Humor*. Dordrecht: D. Reidel.

Slobin, Dan, 1982. Universal and particular in the acquisition of language. In Wanner, Eric, Gleitman, Lila R. (eds.), *Language Acquisition: The State of the Art*. 128–170. Cambridge: Cambridge University Press.

Slobin, Dan. 1987. Thinking for speaking. *Proceedings of the Thirteenth Annual Meeting of the Berkeley Linguistics Society*. 435–445.

Sloetjes, Han & Peter Wittenburg. 2008. Annotation by category – ELAN and ISO DCR. In: Proceedings of the 6th International Conference on Language Resources and Evaluation (LREC 2008).

Suls, Jerry M. 1983. Cognitive processes in humor appreciation. In Paul E McGhee & Jeffrey H. Goldstein (eds.), *Handbook of Humor Research*, Vol. 1: Basic Issues, 39–57. New York: Springer-Verlag.

Tholander, Michael & Karin Aronsson. 2003. Doing subteaching in school groupwork. Positioning, resistance, and participation frameworks. *Language and Education* 17(3). 208–234.

Thommen, Evelyne & Guillaume Rimbert. 2005. *L'enfant et les connaissances sur autrui*. Paris: Belin.

Tomasello, Michael. 2003. *Constructing a Language: A Usage-Based Theory of Language Acquisition*. Cambridge: Harvard University Press.

Vygotsky, Lev S. 1934–1985. *Thought and Language*, Cambridge, MA: The M.I.T. Press.

Winnicott, Donald, W. 1964. *The Child, the Family and the Outside World*. London: Pelican books.

Wood, David, Jerome Bruner & Gail Ross. 1976. The role of tutoring in problem solving, *Journal of Child Psychology and Psychiatry* 17(2). 89–100.

Zlatev, Jordan. 1997. *Situated Embodiment, Studies in the Emergence of Spatial Meaning*, Stockholm: Gotab Press.

Clarissa de Vries, Bert Oben and Geert Brône

2 On target. On the role of eye-gaze during teases in face-to-face multiparty interaction

Abstract: As this volume demonstrates, the multimodal construction of humor, and of teasing in particular, is increasingly at the center of attention in various fields of research. One multimodal marker in face-to-face interaction, the use of eye-gaze, serves a range of functions that are relevant for teasing, such as monitoring and eliciting response, displaying stance, and managing the participation framework. Surprisingly, there is little work available on the use of eye-gaze in teasing. The current study therefore investigates the use of eye-gaze in teases with a co-present target and teases in which the target is not present. Using a corpus of spontaneous triadic interactions in which participants wear head-mounted eye-trackers, we analyze the distribution of speaker gaze over both addressees, as well as the distribution of addressee gaze, in these two types of teases. Using both quantitative distributional analyses and qualitative micro-analyses of teasing sequences, we show that different gaze patterns emerge for internal versus external teases. During internal teases, speakers overwhelmingly look at the target of their tease, thereby not only verbally but visually targeting them. Furthermore, during internal teases, targets often avert their gaze, and the third participants alternate their gaze between the target of the tease, and the speaker. During external teases, the speaker's gaze is slightly more equally distributed over the addressees and all participants adhere to a more 'default' gaze pattern. Our findings highlight the multifunctionality of eye-gaze in interaction, and the influence of the specific participation framework and teasing constellation on gaze distribution over all participants in teases in conversation.

Keywords: teasing, irony, eye-gaze, eye-tracking, participation framework

1 Introduction

Teasing, the playful mocking of another person, is a ubiquitous social phenomenon that has been studied in many different languages and cultures (Chang & Haugh 2021; Haugh 2014; Lehtimaja & Tainio 2015; Priego-Valverde 2016). Moreover, other primate species have also been found to exhibit playful fighting behavior, which has evident evolutionary advantages (Eckert et al., 2020). In human interaction, teasing can occur in a wide range of settings and forms, such as physical mock aggression (Afshari Saleh 2020), or verbal re-enactments, self-mockery or other-directed teases. Depending on the interactional context, teases can fulfill a range of interactional functions such as sanctioning transgressions (Drew 1987), building or fostering solidarity (Dynel 2008; Yu 2013), identity construction (Boxer & Cortés-Conde 1997) and bringing shared amusement (Yu 2013). For an extensive review of previous work, we refer the reader to Haugh (2017).

More recently, there has been a growing interest in the multimodal marking of teases in face-to-face interaction. One such multimodal marker, the use of eye-gaze, has been recognized to serve a range of functions that appear relevant to the phenomenon of teasing. However, to the best of our knowledge there is very little work available on the use of gaze behavior in teasing in interaction. In the present contribution, we therefore aim to fill this gap in the literature. We present the results of a study investigating gaze behavior in two types of teasing: teases with a target that is physically present in the conversation and teases with a target that is not present. The data for this study consist of triadic interactions between friends, with all participants wearing mobile eye-trackers. This specific set-up allows us to compare the two types of teasing within the same conversation, and to gain fine-grained insights into gaze behavior of all participants involved. In what follows, we will give a brief overview of the literature on teasing in interaction and the role of gaze behavior in different social actions, before we present the aims and research questions of the current study.

2 Theoretical background

2.1 Teasing as pretense

In their extensive review of the literature concerning teasing, Keltner et al. (2001) argue that "the core elements of a tease are an intentional provocation and playful off-record markers, which together comment on something relevant to the target" (Keltner et al. 2001: 235). Other definitions also highlight the ambivalent nature of teasing, relating it to "bonding and biting" (Boxer & Cortés-Conde 1997: 275), or to diminishment "within a non-serious or playful frame" (Haugh 2014: 78). In this sense, verbal teasing can be regarded as a form of ironic pretense (Clark & Gerrig 1984). In the pretense theory of irony, a speaker S of an ironic utterance is argued to address an addressee A, while at the same time pretending to be another speaker S', addressing another addressee A' (1984: 122). Crucial to pretense-based theories of irony is that both speaker and addressee, or both writer and reader, manage to see through the pretense, and gain access to all the viewpoints at stake, as well as the contrast between those viewpoints. Consider for instance the example in *Extract 1*, taken from our dataset. Immediately preceding the excerpt, the participants (Paul, Gabriella and Mara) are talking about Mara's sister, who is a talented singer. In line 1 of the extract, Gabriella mumbles that she does not have any hidden talent, a self-directed tease that all three participants react to with laughter. In response, Paul proposes Gabriella's nose as a hidden talent, and Mara reacts by saying that "in your case, it just all radiates from you" (line 4).

Extract 1: ((Brainstorm7_PMG, 09:45.832–09:52.667, "verborgen talent"))

```
01.     Gabriella       <<mompelt> ik heb geen verborgen talent.>
                        <<mumbles> I have no hidden talent>
02.                     ((all three laugh))
03.     Paul            uw neuze.=
                        your nose
04.     Mara            =bij u straalt het er gewoon allemaal [af].
                        in your case it just all radiates from you
05.     Gabriella                                              [((laughs))
06.                     ((all three laugh))
```

In their remarks, both Paul and Mara continue in the jocular frame that Gabriella initiated, by exploiting the playful ambiguity of her first utterance, "I have no hidden talent". Instead of reacting to the serious layer of Gabriella's statement (which would be that she has no talents at all), Paul and Mara orient to another interpretation (which would be that all of her talents are obvious), mentioning "her nose" and saying "in your case it just all radiates from you", and join in with Gabriella's pretense (see Clark, 1996; Clark & Gerrig, 1984). All participants involved manage access to the different viewpoints, as demonstrated by their laughter in reaction to both Gabriella's self-directed tease and the other participants' follow-up. For a detailed multimodal transcript and analysis of this example, see De Vries et al. (2021).

In order for a tease to be successful, the addressee must recognize it as such. As Priego-Valverde (2016) puts it, "on the one hand, the target(s) has/have to *accept to switch into the play frame* the tease initiates, and, on the other hand, the target(s) has/have to *accept the biting illocutionary force*"(2016: 217). In the sequence above, this happens in Paul and Mara's teases, which build on the ironic play frame initiated by Gabriella, as well as in the laughter that follows.

2.1.1 The design of teases in interaction

In face-to-face interaction, the communication and negotiation of teases is accomplished by a combination of different semiotic resources, ranging from lexico-grammatical and acoustic, to visible embodied actions (see Haugh, 2014, for an elaborate overview). For instance, turn-final laughter can function as an invitation to join in laughter (Glenn 2003), and smiling of the speaker during a tease can mark the utterance as a "laughable", whereas smiling or laughter on the part of the addressee can function as a backchanneling device, or signal appreciation of the humor (Attardo et al. 2013; Drew 1987). Similarly, visible body movements such as hand gestures (Yu 2012) or head movements (De Vries, Oben & Brône 2021) can signal playfulness in interaction. These findings are in line with theories of irony as a form of pretense, as they involve the visible construction of a "staged communicative act" in interaction (Clark 1996).

As in *Extract 1*, the type of tease can vary and can shift rapidly in the course of an interaction. Typically, a distinction is made between teases that are self-directed, teases that are directed at a target that is physically present in the conversation, and teases with a target that is not physically present in the conversation. To our knowledge, little work has explicitly investigated differences in the ways in which the above-mentioned types of teases are designed and marked. The presence or absence of a target within the interaction, for instance, can be hypothesized to impact the design of a tease, with respect to both linguistic and nonlinguistic resources that are employed. In the current study, we therefore zoom in on two types of teases: those with an internal target (i.e. another participant that is present in the conversation) and those with an external target (someone who is not present in the conversation). In our analysis, we scrutinize the role of gaze behavior, which is assumed to play a significant role in achieving mutual understanding and has been shown to be relevant in the communication of irony (Gironzetti 2022) but has received little attention in research on teasing so far. Before we continue with the aims and research questions of the current study, we review existing literature on gaze behavior in interaction, and more specifically during playful language use.

2.2 Gaze behavior in interaction

Research in a variety of disciplines, including linguistics, sociology, psychology and human-computer interaction, has shown that eye-gaze plays a constitutive role in human face-to-face interaction and serves a multitude of –partly overlapping– functions. The vital importance of eye-gaze is especially relevant given that communication is essentially a joint action that involves negotiation and alignment between participants (Clark 1996; Linell 2009; Pickering & Garrod 2021). Throughout all stages of this interactive process eye-gaze is employed as a key semiotic resource, among others in the establishment of joint attention, the sequential organization of the interaction, feedback (elicitation), the signaling of engagement, (dis)interest and stance, etc.

With the introduction of video-recordings as a method for data collection in interactional studies, early work provided empirical evidence for several of these functions (Argyle & Cook 1976; Goodwin 1980; Kendon 1967). In a review of these pioneering studies and more recent work, Rossano (2012) distinguishes between three clusters of functions of eye-gaze in interaction:

1. *The distribution of participation roles*: One of the key findings of the above-mentioned early work is that speakers' and addressees' gaze patterns in turn-by-turn conversation seem to differ significantly (Argyle & Cook 1976; Brône et al. 2017; Goodwin 1981; Hirvenkari et al. 2013; Kendon 1967; Vertegaal 1999). The basic observation is that speakers tend to shift their gaze repeatedly during the production of turns-at-talk (reflecting cognitive planning and/or turn management, infra), and addressees typically display longer sequences of sustained gaze towards the speaker. Although this basic pattern may vary across different activity types (as shown, among others, in the work by Rossano, 2010), it illustrates the correlation between eye-gaze and participation in interaction. In the case of triadic interaction, which is the focus of the current study, special attention has been paid to asymmetry in the participation framework. For instance, Stivers (2021) argues that in multiparty interactions, there is a tendency towards serially dyadic participation, with one focal dyadic participation framework shifting to another over the course of an interaction. Here, sustained gaze of the speaker at one addressee as well as moments of mutual gaze between the speaker and addressee indicate the focal participation framework. However, gaze can also be used to momentarily extend the participation framework and involve all participants. For example, Rühlemann, Gee & Ptak (2019) and Stivers (2021) found that storytellers typically gaze at one addressee for longer stretches of time and alternate their gaze to others briefly to involve all participants in the conversation.

2. *The turn-taking machinery*: A key feature of turn-by-turn interaction is the smooth transition between speakers engaged in the joint activity. In order to achieve the orderly distribution of opportunities to participate in interaction (Sacks, Schegloff & Jefferson 1974; Schegloff 2000), a system of (multimodal) resources is employed, including gesture, body posture and eye-gaze (see e.g. Mondada, 2007 for an overview). Eye-gaze, in fact, may serve a variety of functions, ranging from turn-holding (by looking away) to turn-yielding (selecting the next

speaker through eye contact) (see e.g. Auer, 2018; Duncan, 1975). Also relevant in the context of the present contribution is the potential function of eye-gaze in eliciting or monitoring a response by co-participants, as illustrated in the work of Bavelas et al. (2002), Goodwin & Goodwin (1986), Thompson & Suzuki (2014), and Zima (2020).

3. *Action formation*: One line of research that is of particular importance to the study of teasing and irony, has pointed at the social-interactional meanings that eye-gaze patterns may acquire. These include actions such as warning or reprimanding (Kidwell 2005; Kidwell 2009), displaying a negative or positive stance (Haddington 2006), but also marking the shift between viewpoints or layers of action (Goodwin 2013; Parrill 2012; Rühlemann, Gee & Ptak 2019; Sidnell 2006; Sweetser & Stec 2016). For the latter function, it has been shown that in storytelling-in-interaction, speakers tend to use eye-gaze, in combination with head movements and gestures, to parse the telling in interactionally relevant units (Thompson & Suzuki 2014), e.g. by averting the gaze from the addressee(s) when shifting from the narrator to a character role in the story.

2.2.1 Gaze behavior in irony and teasing

Now that a variety of functions of eye-gaze in interaction have been highlighted, let us look more specifically at the role of gaze during humor in interaction. Somewhat surprisingly, to date only few studies have zoomed in on the particular case of speaker and/or addressee gaze in interactional humor. These studies report observations in experimental and corpus-based studies that may be of relevance to the present contribution. Speakers appear to avert their gaze more when producing sarcastic statements (Williams, Burns & Harmon 2009), and during ironic and humoristic utterances in general (Gironzetti 2022). In spontaneous interactions, speakers also tend to shift their gaze more during ironic utterances in comparison to non-ironic utterances in the same interaction (González-Fuente, Escandell-Vidal & Prieto 2015), which may support the view of irony and teasing as a staged communicative act (Clark 1996), involving shifts in the layer of action that can be marked verbally and nonverbally. Brône & Oben (2021) and Brône (2021) report similar findings using a corpus of three-party interactions enriched with mobile eye-tracking data. Apart from the speakers' increased number of gaze shifts in ironic compared to non-ironic utterances, Brône and Oben (2021) also observed that addressees displayed more mutual gaze (both in terms of quantity and duration) during ironic utterances, which can be considered as a form of visual monitoring of understanding or the establishment of a shared sense of complicity. De Vries et al. (2021) provide a more fine-grained account, showing that the difference in the amount of speakers' gaze shifts in ironic utterances is to be situated mainly in the final part of the ironic segment (i.e. in the final 1000ms), reflecting the visual monitoring of understanding with the addressees (or an invitation to join the pretense). In terms of the interaction between eye-gaze and other bodily resources, De Vries et al. observed a correlation between speaker laughter and marked gaze behavior (more gaze shifts, moments of mutual gaze and gaze aversion).

During teases specifically, gaze aversions may relate to the notion of face (Goffman 1967). Although there is little work on the use of gaze behavior during teases (but see Yu, 2013), studies outside of a teasing context show that gaze aversion tends to co-occur with a noncompliance (Kidwell 2006), a divergent stance (Haddington 2006) or dispreferred responses (Kendrick & Holler 2017). For the particular case of teasing and (self-)mockery, Yu (2013: 9) describes instances of self-mockery that are used to save the face of (one of) the interlocutors. Prior to these self-directed teases, the other interlocutors display a moment of embarrassment, which is made visible by gaze aversions and head lowering. During the teases then, the speaker re-establishes eye contact with the other interlocutor, involving a form of "invitational gaze" on their part. The re-establishment of eye contact with their addressees thus is part of a face-saving strategy, showing how teasing can accomplish complex face-work.

2.3 Current study

As is clear from the overview in Section 2.2, there is still much to learn about the role of gaze behavior in teasing in interaction. This not only relates to the notion of face-work, but also to the distribution of participation roles, as well as action formation. With the current study, we aim to help fill the gap in the literature and investigate gaze behavior during teases in interaction between friends. Specifically, we focus on triadic conversations, and analyze teases with a target that is physically present in the conversation (henceforth internal teases) and teases with a target that is not physically present in the conversation (henceforth external teases). A comparison of these constellations allows us to explore the role of both the participation framework and the activity type in gaze behavior in interaction.

We hypothesize that differences in participation framework between internal teases and external teases are reflected in the gaze behavior of the participants. During internal teases we expect speaker gaze to be relatively asymmetrically distributed across participants. The direction of this asymmetry can go two ways: either the speaker gazes primarily at the target (to index a participant as the primary addressee as well as the target of the tease) or the speaker gazes primarily away from the target (as part of a face-saving strategy or to achieve more indirectness).

During external teases the target of the tease is not present, which may lead to a different distribution of gaze behavior. Again, there are two contrasting hypotheses. Either speaker gaze is more symmetrically distributed, as both addressees have equal rights and opportunities to contribute to a tease. Alternatively, speaker gaze behavior could be asymmetric, which would confirm previous findings on multiparty interaction (Rühlemann, Gee & Ptak 2019; Stivers 2021).

As for addressee gaze, we explore whether they follow the 'default' listener gaze pattern of longer stretches of sustained gaze to the speaker, or whether the presence or absence of a target also influences the distribution of addressee gaze. One possibility is that during internal teases, the third participant (i.e. not the target) will alternate their gaze between the speaker and the target of the tease.

3 Data and method

3.1 Data collection

For this study, we used data from the Insight Interaction corpus (Brône & Oben 2015). This corpus consists of dyadic and triadic conversations between friends, in which the participants were equipped with mobile head-mounted eye-trackers. For the purpose of the current study, we only used data from triadic interactions, consisting of 11 triads or 33 participants (5 males and 28 females). Participants were recruited from a Flemish university population and were all L1 speakers of Dutch. Importantly, all participants were well acquainted with one another. They were rewarded with movie tickets after participation. The recordings took place in a room at KU Leuven, where participants were seated in a triad, so as to enable them to gaze at both co-participants with equal effort. All participants gave informed consent to participate in the study, and the study was approved by the local ethics committee with case number G-2021–3303.

The interactions consisted of two parts. For the first part, participants did not receive specific instructions and were allowed to speak about whatever they wanted. This *spontaneous conversation* lasted about 20 minutes on average. For 8 out of 11 triads there was also a second part of the task: here, participants received instructions to brainstorm about their ideal student house and their ideal student bar. In practice, this often resulted in spontaneous conversations about bars they went to, or student houses participants lived in. Given that the conversations during brainstorm sessions were very similar to the spontaneous conversations, we included both interaction types in our corpus. The *brainstorm* sessions lasted about 18 minutes on average. In total, this amounts to 308 minutes of data.

3.1.1 Recording equipment

The interactions were video-recorded with one external camera (Sony HDR-FX1000E, 25 frames per second, 720 × 576 pixels). All participants were also wearing eye-tracking glasses. Three triads were equipped with Pupil Pro Eye-Tracking Glasses (sample rate 30 Hz), and eight triads wore Tobii Pro Glasses 2 (sample rate 50 Hz). The eye-tracking glasses have an integrated scene camera and infrared cameras, which were used to capture participants' gaze fixations. To facilitate data analysis, all scene camera data, the audio and the external camera data were then edited together and synchronized into one video (see Figure 1). For a more detailed description concerning the eye-trackers and the set-up of the corpus, see Jehoul (2019).

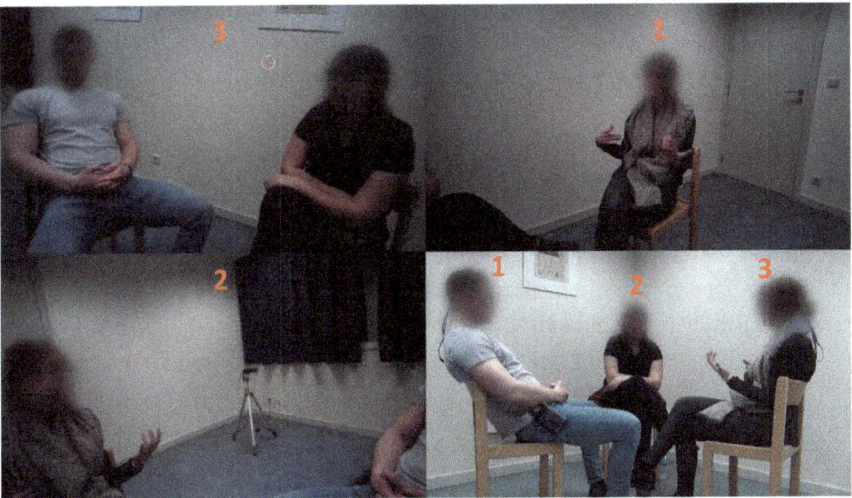

Figure 1: Screenshot of an overview video recording from the corpus. Numbers indicate the camera perspectives of the respective participants, as indicated on the bottom right image of the external camera perspective.

3.2 Data annotation

3.2.1 Speech and gaze annotation

The video data was annotated in ELAN (Wittenburg et al. 2006). All speech was transcribed using the GAT2 guidelines (Selting et al. 2011), at the level of the intonation unit. Intonation units have been characterized as segments that verbalize the focus of a speaker's idea of an event or state at a specific moment (Chafe 1994: 63), and are often used as a level of analysis in research in Interactional Linguistics and Cognitive Linguistics (e.g. Bressem, 2021). In the case of teases, one intonation unit typically corresponds with one teasing contribution. Analyzing our data at the level of the intonation unit thus allows us to see precisely what happens *during* each teasing contribution.

Gaze was annotated continuously (i.e. there were no boundaries between fixations: the gaze shift from one region of interest to another was included in the gaze annotation). In the annotation of gaze, a distinction was made between the following regions of interest:
1. Face: gaze at the face of one of the co-participants
2. Body: gaze at the body of one of the co-participants, or own body
3. Gestures: gaze at the gestures of one of the co-participants, or own gesture
4. Background: gaze at the background. A distinction was made between different parts of the background (floor, wall A, wall B, close to face of participant).

The resolution of the eye-tracking data did not allow us to distinguish between specific regions in the face, such as the eyes or the mouth. Furthermore, in our analysis we excluded fixations at the body or gestures of one of the co-participants, as previous research found that in general looking at the face is treated as the norm in western face-to-face interaction (Rossano 2012), and gestures are only rarely attended to (Gullberg & Holmqvist 2006).

See Figure 2 below, for a screenshot of gaze annotations in our dataset.

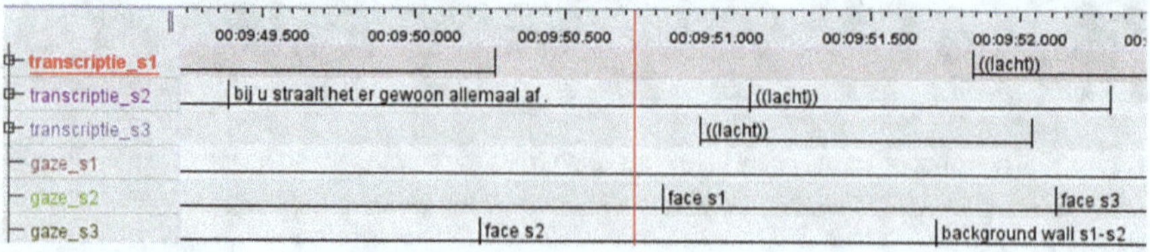

Figure 2: Screenshot of gaze annotation in ELAN.

For the quantitative analysis of gaze in different types of teases, we took into account speaker gaze durations at the face of addressees, as well as addressee gaze durations at the face of the speaker, the face of the target (for internal teases only) and the background. In our operationalization of gaze duration, we calculated the total duration of gaze at the region of interest. For instance, if during a teasing contribution a speaker first gazed at addressee 1 for 340 msec, then gazed at the background (wall) for 189 msec and then back at addressee 1 for 260 msec, there would be a total of 600 msec of gaze at addressee 1.

3.2.2 Annotation of ironic teases

We first identified all instances of verbal teases in the broad sense. We are fully aware that in some frameworks teases with an external target are in fact not categorized as forms of teasing. For this analysis, however, we followed Haugh (2014), who defines teasing as "social actions (as opposed to simply (non)verbal acts) whereby the speaker somehow diminishes something of relevance to self, other or a non–co-present third party, but does so within a non–serious or playful frame" (Haugh 2014: 78).[1] We annotated teases at the level of the intonation unit (see Section 3.2.1 supra). This means that for *Extract 1* for instance, only the gaze behavior during the utterance in lines 3–4 was included in the quantitative analysis. This resulted in a total of 197 cases. To be able to compare speaker gaze behavior in teases with an internal target versus teases with an external target, we then excluded all cases in which the eye-tracking data was unreliable, as well as all cases in which there was self-mockery or in which there was no clear target of the tease.[2] This resulted in the exclusion of 70 cases. For instance, in *Extract 1* in the introduction, the self-directed tease by Gabriella is excluded from the analysis, but the other-directed teases by Paul and Mara are included. All resulting cases of internal teases ($n = 70$) and external teases ($n = 57$) were checked by all three authors to ensure reliability of the annotations. For the qualitative analysis, our main focus was on the segments that were part of the quantitative analysis,

---

[1] To be precise, Haugh uses the term "jocular mockery". However, in the current contribution, we keep with the more broadly used term and colloquial term "teasing".
[2] Cases in which the eye-gaze data was unreliable included utterances during which there was a lot of laughter, causing participants to narrow their eyes or move their heads quickly, or cases in which there was no visible cursor for a large portion of the utterance. Cases in which there was no clear or relevant target of the tease included teases that were directed at the whole group and self-directed teases.

but here we also took into account the previous sequential environment, as well as the immediate reactions to the tease.

4 Results

The results section of this study is divided into two parts. First, we describe the quantitative analysis of speaker and addressee gaze. Next, we provide a more in-depth qualitative analysis of patterns of gaze behavior that were found in the quantitative analysis.

4.1 Quantitative analysis

4.1.1 Speaker gaze

Our first hypothesis was that there would be an asymmetric distribution of gaze during internal teases. That is, we expected the speaker to either look at the face of the target of the tease longer, or to show a preference for looking at the face of the other addressee.[3] To measure asymmetry, we calculated the relative difference in gaze at both participants. For instance, if a speaker looked at addressee A for 30 per cent of the utterance, and at addressee B for 20 percent of the utterance, the proportional difference of gaze at addressees is 0.10. Table 1 lists descriptive statistics of the teases for both internal and external teases. In the first column, it can be observed that there is no difference in total duration of the utterances between groups (W = 8550, p = 0.328). In the second column, it is shown that there is indeed a large asymmetry in gaze at the addressees in internal teases, with a median difference of almost 60 percent. As demonstrated in Figure 3 below, the direction of the asymmetry favors the target. That is, speakers look relatively longer at the targets during teases (Mdn = 0.586), and rarely look at the other addressees (Mdn = 0). At the same time, the proportion of speaker gaze that is directed at the target, as well as gaze asymmetry also shows a lot of variation (with an IQR of 0.885 for gaze asymmetry in internal teases). In Section 4.2 (infra) we elaborate on different reasons for speakers to avert their gaze from the target. Lastly, both during internal and external teases, speakers look at either one of their addressees for more than two thirds of the utterance. Interestingly, it seems

---

[3] For reasons of readability, we refer to gaze fixations at the face of the addressee as gaze fixations "at the addressee".

that speakers look at both of their addressees longer during internal compared to external teases. As we did not have specific hypotheses regarding this effect, we did not test this difference for significance.

Table 1: Median (Inter Quartile Range) of speaker gaze measures during internal and external teases.

	Utterance duration, in msec	Difference between proportional gaze at addressees	Total proportional gaze at addressees
Internal teases	1558 (1116)	0.599 (0.885)	0.834 (0.736)
External teases	1530 (1180)	0.341 (0.564)	0.681 (0.681)

For teases with an external target, we explored the question whether this type would yield a more symmetric distribution of speaker gaze over the addressees. In this group of utterances we still find an asymmetric distribution of gaze over the addressees, with a median proportional difference of 0.341. However, the difference seems to be smaller than for internal teases. A Wilcoxon Rank Sum test showed that there is a marginally significant difference between internal teases

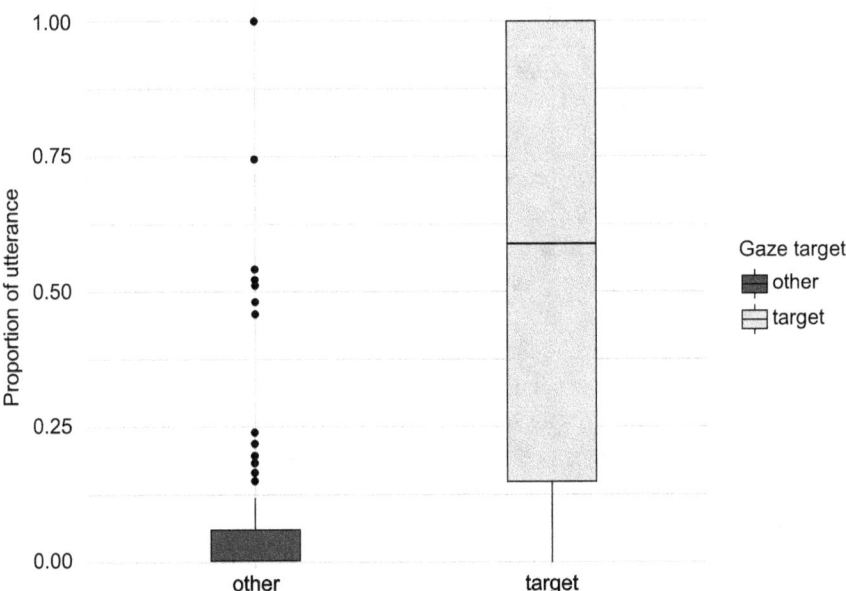

Figure 3: Proportion of speaker gaze at target and other addressee during internal teases.

and external teases in this regard (W = 6824, p = 0.0450), indicating that speakers may divide their gaze over the addressees slightly more in external teases. It also seems to be the case that speakers gaze at the addressees relatively more in internal teases compared to external teases.

4.1.2 Addressee gaze

As for addressee gaze, we explored possible differences in gaze durations at the speaker, the other addressee, and at the background. For this analysis, we excluded utterances with no reliable gaze data for either addressee (these cases were included in the analysis of speaker gaze). This left us with a total of 47 external teases and 49 internal teases. Table 2 below summarizes the gaze durations for the different areas of interest.

Table 2: Median (IQR) proportion of addressee gaze during external and internal teases.

		Face speaker	Face Addressee	Background
External teases	Addressee (average)	0.784	0	0
Internal teases	Addressee (average)	0.487	0	0.061
	Target	0.501	0	0.132
	Other	0.484	0.024	0

Note: Not all proportions add up to one, given (a) that the Median is listed, and (b) that participants could also look at other regions of interest such as the body of addressees or their own body.

There are several observations that we can gather from this table. First, during external teases, addressee gaze is mainly directed at the speaker, and very little at the other addressee or at the background. This pattern reflects the general distribution for addressee gaze behavior as described in the literature on eye-gaze in interaction (see Section 2.2 supra): addressees display sustained gaze towards the current speaker in face-to-face interaction.

For internal teases, a somewhat different pattern arises. Both addressees gaze relatively less at the speaker. Furthermore, the target of the tease gazes at the background relatively more, whereas the other addressee – the "accomplice" – looks relatively more at the target of the tease. These gaze patterns will be illustrated in Section 4.2 (infra).

4.2 Illustration of gaze patterns

In this section, we provide an illustration of the patterns that emerge from the distributional analyses presented above, in the form of qualitative micro-analyses of extracts from our dataset. We first focus on sequences with an internal target first, followed by an illustration of a pattern involving an external target. Both speaker and addressee gaze patterns will be considered, including the interdependency of both perspectives. Please note that for all extracts that follow, the video material has been made available in the supplementary materials.

4.2.1 Internal teases

As a first example, we take the sequence in *Extract 2*, which illustrates a basic pattern for speakers and their addressees in teasing utterances. Preceding this sequence, Joeri is talking about his part-time job at a supermarket and mentions that quite a few of his co–workers are of the same age. This leads to Amber and Lena asking questions about his age in a teasing way (lines 1–4) and to Lena producing a teasing utterance about Joeri's age in line 8.

The gaze data have been added to the transcriptions and should be read as a musical score: the dashed lines indicate that the gaze continues within the same region of interest, initials signal a gaze shift towards the participant with those initials, and BG indicates a gaze shift towards the background. The timing of the gaze shifts is placed in relation to the corresponding speech. If a gaze shift occurs during the pronunciation of the word "gij" (Flemish Dutch for "you") the gaze shift is located directly beneath the word "gij" in the transcription.

Extract 2: ((Conversatie1_ALJ, 15:46.973 – 15:54.772, "oude zak"))

```
-> 01.     A        beseft gij da ge naar de dertig aan het gaan zijt.
                    do you realize you're going on thirty
                    %(0.4)
           A        %leans forward, opens mouth, raises eyebrows,
                                                        and nods head->
           G_A      BG----J-------------------------------------
           G_L      J----A--------------------------------------
           G_J      L-A-----------------------------------------
    02.    J        *[nee.                         *
                    no
```

```
03.    L         *[hoe oud zijde gij% [nu?*
                 how old are you now
04.    A                            [ahha
       A         ------------------>%
       J         *shakes head------------>*
05.    J         ik word er zesentwintig [binnen] een $#(-) maand [en
                 half.=
                 I will be twenty-six in a month and a half
06.    L                                 [°h]
07.    A                                                      [u:
       hahahaha
       L                                               $covers mouth
                                                       with LH-->>
                 fig                                   #fig.4
```

```
-> 08. L         =zesentwintig, ou[de zak -
                 twenty-six, you old dog
   09. J                          [ja
                                  yeah
       G_A       L---------------------------
       G_L       J---------------------------
       G_J       L---------------------------
   10. A         [uhuhohoho °h
   11. J         [zeg gaat *da zo wa;*
                 hey, knock it off now
       J                  *raises eyebrows and tilts head down towards L*
```

In line 1, Amber teasingly asks Joeri whether he realizes that he is going on thirty. Immediately following her question, Amber leans forward, opens her mouth, raises her eyebrows and nods her head. This multimodal package is used to frame the question as playful, and emphasizing that Joeri is the target of a tease. Turning to the gaze scores, the speaker, Amber, displays sustained gaze at the target, and both addressees gaze at her, which corresponds to the general patterns for addressee gaze that have been described in the literature (see Section 2.2 supra). The talk about Joeri's age continues in lines 2–5. Leading up to the second tease then, Lena displays her shock with learning of Joeri's age by her audible inbreath (line 6) and by covering her mouth with her left hand (Figure 4), to which Amber reacts with laughter (line 7). Regarding the speaker and addressee gaze data during the production of the tease in line 8, they show that similar to the first tease in line 1, the teaser (Lena) displays sustained gaze directed at the target (Joeri) during the teasing utterance, while both the target and the third participant (Amber) keep looking at the teaser uninterruptedly. The speaker gaze pattern in these utterances illustrates the asymmetry as shown in Table 1 (supra): Lena not only verbally but also visually targets Joeri through her sustained gaze at him.

In the next example in *Extract 3*, taken from the same conversation, Amber is telling an anecdote about how she was threatened and robbed by a taxi driver on the first day of her holiday. When Amber's story is completed, Joeri reacts with a teasing comment on the stressful vacation (line 4).

Extract 3: ((Conversatie1_ALJ, 06:43.729 – 06:50.097, "wat hebt gij nog gedaan"))

```
      01.  A    zie dat die transactie goed verloopt en zo,
                make sure this transaction goes well and like
      02.  A    want %(-) ja dat was echt.%
                because (-) yeah that was really
           J          %raises eyebrows---%
      03.  A    [zo betaalt ge voor,
                that way you pay for
->    04.  J    [wat %hebt *gij nog gedaan voor de [rest* u:HE%heh
                what else did you do               u:HEheh
           J          %raises eyebrows---------------------%
           J                *shakes head rapidly--------*
      05.  A                                         [$hah$ hh°
                                                     $raises eyebrows and
                                                     tilts head slightly$
           G_A  J----BG-------------J-----------BG-----------
           G_L  A-----------------------------------------
           G_J  A-----------------------------------------
```

Joeri's tease in line 4 is shaped in a playful, casual way by his raised eyebrows and rapid head shake. He frames Amber's holiday as a series of calamities and casually asks what other things she did, which is immediately followed by laughter. Amber reacts by raising her eyebrows, tilting her head slightly, and producing one laughter particle, as if resisting Joeri's playful tease (Drew 1987), and breathes out. Note that the visible bodily behavior of Amber is similar to the target's behavior in *Extract 2*.

Contrary to the 'default' interactional gaze behavior in *Extract 2* (i.e. the speaker looks at the addressee(s) and they look back at the speaker), in this example the target avoids gaze twice during the tease by Joeri. Amber averts her gaze both during Joeri's statement, and when he finishes his tease and she reacts. Gaze aversion as an addressee, especially during gaze from the current speaker, is a marked case in the interactional gaze machinery (Haddington 2006; Kendrick & Holler 2017; Kidwell 2005; Yu 2013). The fact that Amber is suddenly catapulted into the position of the target of the tease might cause her to break eye contact with the current speaker.

A second way in which this example is a disruption of the 'default' interactional gaze behavior concerns the eye-gaze of the unaddressed third participant (Lena). As can be seen from the gaze score, during the entire teasing utterance by Joeri (line 4), Lena displays sustained gaze at the target of the tease (Amber), whereas a default gaze configuration would predict addressees to look at the current speaker (Joeri in this case). While we should be cautious with this interpretation, the joint focus of both the teaser (Joeri) and the third participant (Lena) on the target (Amber) might contribute to the gaze aversion of the target described in the previous paragraph.

Analogous to the previous example, *Extract 4* highlights the same pattern of the target avoiding eye-gaze, and the third participant not looking at the current speaker. Instead, the third participant alternates between looking at the target (Cara) and averting her gaze (while she is laughing). In this example, one of the participants (Cara) is talking about the recording set-up of the experiment, and more specifically the eye–tracking glasses. Cara is afraid that she might ruin the experiment, which is followed by a playful tease by Saskia in lines 5–6.

Extract 4: ((Conversatie3_CSS, 19:29.500 – 19:35.646, "opnieuw beginnen")

```
01.   C     maar ik *durf er niet aan# kom[en;
             but I don't dare to touch it
02.   Su                                  [nee.
                                           no
      C              *gestures palms together and away from her body->
      fig                                 #fig. 5
```

```
03. C     want ja* (.) als 't hier *₁[allemaal(-) ₂[verpest is door mij*
          because yeah (.) if it's all (-) ruined here because of me
-> 04. Sa          ₁[ik ook niet(.)seg sebiet moeten we opnieuw beginnen.
                   me neither(.)hey in a minute we will have to start again
   05. Su                                      ₂[ahh° a:h-
       C     ----->*                 *gestures RH  palm towards wall-->*
       G_C   BG----------------------------------------Sa-----------
       G_Su  C---------------------------------BG----------------
       G_Sa  C-----------------------------------------BG-----
-> 06. Sa   dat [zal zijn.
            yeah right.
   07. C        [mhm hehe °h
       G_C   Sa-------BG----
       G_Su  BG-----C-------
       G_Sa  BG-------------
```

In lines 1–3, Cara expresses that she is afraid to touch the eye-tracking glasses, because if she would, she might ruin the experiment. During her utterance, she produces a gesture with her hands away from her body, visually creating a distance between herself and the eye–tracking glasses that she doesn't want to touch (see Figure 5). Saskia interrupts her and playfully gets mad at Cara, when she produces the teasing utterance in lines 5–6. She imagines that they will have to start all over again with the experiment (line 5) and expresses that she does not want that (line 6).

As was the case in *Extract 3*, the teaser (Saskia) is not being looked at by the third participant (Susan). Instead, the third participant focuses on the target (Cara) continuously, only averting her gaze while she is laughing. In addition, Cara is not looking at Saskia during the utterance of the tease. Both observations are at odds with the 'default' gaze behavior of eye contact between speakers and addressees, and can serve to illustrate the results in Table 1 (asymmetry in gaze behavior by the speaker, caused by fixating the target) and Table 2 (target and third participant looking away from speaker).

In *Extract 5*, the role of speaker eye-gaze as an instrument in visually pinpointing one participant as the target of the tease seems to conflict with a different function of speaker gaze, as a resource for action formation, and more specifically for marking the shift from a narrator to a character viewpoint. Prior to the sequence, Saskia is talking about her experience with illegally downloading movies using the app Popcorn Time. Cara reacts by producing a teasing enactment in lines 4–5.

Extract 5: ((Brainstorm3_CSS, 14:42.140 – 14:51.475, "virussen"))

```
       01.   Sa    al *die virussen dat daarop* [komen, nie erg man, nie erg;
                   all those viruses that you get, no worries man, no worries
       02.   Su                                 [eheh (.) ja
                                                 eheh (.) yeah

             Sa         *gestures LH throw away-*
->     03.   C     ah ja inderdaad $en dan$- *oh (.) [mij*n computer is kapot;
                   ah yes indeed and then- oh (.) my computer is broken
       04.   Sa                              *      [dan* krijg de da,
                                                    then you get that
             C                        $shrugs shoulder$
             Sa                             *shrugs shoulders, tilts
                                             head, raises eyebrows*
             G_C    Sa---------------------------BG----------------------
             G_Su   BG-C------------------------------------Sa-----BG--
             G_Sa   BG--C---------------------------------------------
->     05.   C     ik &snap echt niet waar&hohom, ahah
                   I really don't understand why, ahah
             Su         &nods head---------&yawns-->>
             G_C    BG-----------------------Sa--------
             G_Su   BG-----------------------------C---
             G_Sa   C----------------------------------
```

In line 1, Saskia construes an ironic pretense utterance claiming that she does not mind that her computer gets infected by viruses due to illegal software, and produces a throw away hand gesture (Bressem & Müller 2014). visually dismissing worries about viruses on her laptop. This utterance, which can be considered as a form of self-deprecating humor, triggers a laughing response on the part of

Susan in line 2. In line 3, Cara picks up on the pretense initiated by Saskia, by first ratifying it verbally ("oh yes indeed and then") and gesturally by producing a shrug, which could be interpreted along the lines of dismissing worries or indifference (Debras 2017). This is followed by a viewpoint shift in which Cara enacts Saskia, in the pretense scenario of Saskia having downloaded illegal content and not understanding why her computer got infected (line 5). Note that during Cara's utterance in line 3, Saskia repeats her shrug and intensifies it by raising her eyebrows and tilting her head, potentially anticipating a tease by Cara and continuing the frame of dismissing worries about the viruses.

Looking at Cara's gaze behavior in lines 3–5, it is apparent that she first looks at Saskia (who is both the previous speaker and the target) when initiating the tease but then shifts her gaze towards the background at the start of the enacted sequence ("oh my computer is broken"). This pattern corresponds with findings reported in studies on storytelling in interaction, which observed that shifts from a narrator perspective to a character perspective (as well as more generally viewpoint shifts) co-occurred with a gaze shift to the background, marking a different layer of action (Sidnell 2006, Goodwin 2013, Thompson & Suzuki 2014, Parrill 2012, Sweetser & Stec 2016, Rühlemann et al. 2019). Interestingly, at the end of the teasing utterance, Cara shifts her gaze back to the target (Saskia) before bursting out into laughter herself. The gaze of the target is largely comparable to *Extract 2*: shortly after the onset of Cara's utterance in line 3, Saskia shifts her gaze to Cara and keeps her gaze focused on the speaker until the end of the utterance in line 5. The third participant (Susan), however, shifts her gaze between the teaser and the target, which may be interpreted as a form of response monitoring.

In the examples discussed so far, the teaser either displays sustained gaze towards the target of the tease, who serves as the primary addressee (*Extracts 2–4*) or shifts their gaze between the target and the background as part of an enactment (*Extract 5*). In *Extract 6*, the speaker shifts her gaze between the two addressees, which may be attributed to response elicitation or an invitation to join the tease. In this sequence, the participants (Paul, Mara and Gabriella) are talking about the regional Dutch dialects in Flanders, a beloved topic of stereotyping humor. In the target tease, Gabriella then teases Paul with his regional accent.

Extract 6: ((Conversatie7_PMG, 12:37.629 – 12:44.147, "uw taal"))

```
01.  G     maar ik vind dat het limburgs=
            but I think that the limburg dialect
02.  G     =nog vrij dicht *aanleunt* bij het AN,
            is relatively close to AN
     G                     *shrugs shoulder*
```

```
      03.  P     ja
                 yeah
->    04.  G     als ik dat *vergelijk me*t uw taal,
                 if I compare it to your language use
           G              *nods head toward P*
           G_P   G---------------------------------
           G_M   P----------------------------G---
           G_G   P-----------------------M-------
                 (0.5)
      05.  P     &pf&=
                 pf
           P     &tilts head back and towards M&
      06.  M     =u[h°:hAhaha
      07.  G     [uhuh ja& °h & ahahaha
                 uhuh yeah °h ahahaha
           P              &tilts head sideways and shakes head&
```

In the example, Gabriella starts by saying that the regional dialect of Limburg Dutch (situated in the East of the Flemish–speaking region) comes closest to what is generally considered to be standard Dutch (AN – Algemeen Nederlands) (lines 1–2). This is acknowledged by Paul in line 3, after which Gabriella continues with a tease towards target Paul and his regional dialect, (which is not from Limburg) in line 4, designating him as the referent and target by nodding her head towards him, gazing at him, and later by addressing him verbally ("als ik dat vergelijk met uw taal", if I compare that to your language use). Interestingly, Gabriella, although still predominantly focused on the target of the tease (Paul), shifts her gaze towards the third participant (Mara) while uttering the word "uw" (your). Shortly after Gabriella's gaze shift to Mara, Mara also shifts her gaze to Gabriella, establishing a moment of mutual gaze followed by laughter. In this sense, the gaze shift to Mara may be interpreted as an attempt to create a sense of complicity, the success of which is contingent upon Mara's (subsequent) behavior. The third participant (Mara) actively engages with the teaser (Gabriella) at the expense of the target (Paul). Paul reacts to the tease by a vocalization ("pf") indexing a change in orientation (Baldauf-Quilliatre 2016), as well as a backward head movement (as if being physically hit by the target), distancing himself from this tease.

4.2.2 External teases

The distributional analysis for gaze patterns in teasing sequences with an external target paints a fuzzier picture than was the case for internal targets. Generally, however, speaker gaze is still distributed asymmetrically across the addressees, even if this is slightly less pronounced. *Extract 7* may serve as an illustration of a relatively symmetric speaker gaze pattern. In this sequence, Seb is talking about a play he recently saw. He mentions that two critics differed substantially in their review and subsequently produces a teasing comment (line 9) about this.

Extract 7: ((Conversatie5_SAE, 06:08.317 – 06:19.494, "ander toneelstuk"))

```
   01. S      ne (-) echte aanrader
              a (-) real must-see
   02.        de morgen gaf wel maar twee sterren;
              'de morgen' only gave two stars though
   03.        ((sighs))*
       S              *smiles-->
   04. E      toch,
              still
   05. S      de standaard vier,
              'de standaard' four
   06. S      $en de knack ook vier,
              and 'knack' also four
       E      $retracts lips, tilts head and nods slowly-->
   07. S      %en de morgen dus $[twee;$
              and so 'de morgen' [two
   08. E                        [hh°
       S      %gestures, RH and LH moving back and forth
                                       as if comparing two items -->
       E      ----------------->$smiles$
-> 09. S      dan% toch precies een ander toneelstuk gezien he maar *ja;
              appears to have seen a different play then, but hey
       S      -->%
       S      ----------------------------------------------------->*
       G_S    A----BG--E----BG------A------------E----------------
       G_A    BG-S-------------------------------------------BG----
       G_E    S------BG------------S-------------------------------
```

In the extract, Seb displays with a sigh how surprised he was that a critic of one newspaper ('de morgen') only gave two stars out of five, whereas other newspapers were more favorable ('de standaard' in line 5 and 'knack' in line 6). This discrepancy, visualized by the conventionalized representational gesture, metaphorically 'weighing' the different reviews in an attempt to compare them, and Seb's continued smile, leads him to the ironic teasing conclusion that the negative critic must have seen a different play (line 9). The gaze score for this utterance visualizes the speaker's multiple gaze shifts between the two addressees as well as to the background, reflecting a more symmetric participation framework. The addressees on their part seem to be primarily oriented towards the speaker, even though they both avert their gaze during the teasing utterance.

The rather symmetrical distribution of gaze by the speaker across both addressees is not reflected in the overall picture we get from the quantitative analysis (see Table 1). In *Extract 8*, we exemplify the asymmetrical picture that arises for external targets (even though it is more distinct for internal targets). Here, the participants (Michelle, Lilian and Heleen) are discussing a drinking competition. During one specific night at the student bar, students can drink for their home province in Belgium: every beer that is sold, is assigned to the province of the person who drinks the beer; the province with the most beers wins the competition. For one of the friends of the speaker, Bill, this is a problem because Bill doesn't have a province to drink for (line 2). In the sequence that follows, Michelle ironically states that this is a terrible situation for Bill (line 5).

Extract 8: ((Conversatie6_MLH, 07:27.724 – 07:31.692, "geen provincie"))

```
01. H     en wat dan voor bill?
          and then what about bill
02.       bill die woont in brussel.
          bill lives in brussels
03.       *da is zelfs geen provincie.*
          that is not even a province
    H     *moves head forward and shakes head*
04.       (0.9)
->  05. M ja da's erg voor bill eh?
          yeah that's terrible for bill right
    G_M   H-----------------------
    G_L   H------M----------------
    G_H   M-----------------------
06  H     $h°ja ah ₁[ah ₂[a aha
          h°yeah ah aha
```

```
07.  L            ₁[hmh°
08.  M                ₂[h°
     M     $smiles -->>
```

In the sequence leading up to the tease, Heleen explains that Bill lives in Brussels, and given that Brussels is a city that does not belong to any of the Belgian provinces (it is a separate region), Bill has no province to drink for, highlighting this as problematic by shaking her head. After a long pause of 0.9 seconds, the teaser (Michelle) ironically states that this is a terrible situation for the external target (Bill) in line 5, which is responded to with laughter by Lilian and Michelle in lines 6–7.

Concerning the gaze behavior in this example, the asymmetry resides in the teaser only looking at one of the addressees (Heleen) and not at the other (Lilian). Lilian, receiving no visual attention in this extract, really is a by-stander in this part of the conversation. When zooming out from this example, Michelle and Heleen are having a subconversation about the drinking competition. In the 35 seconds leading up to this excerpt and the 20 seconds following it, Lilian does not utter any words, making her a bystander or secondary addressee. Precisely these types of subconversations among dyads within the triad contribute to the asymmetrical distribution of speakers' eye-gaze over the addressees, as has been described by Stivers (2021).

5 Discussion

Although teasing in interaction has received significant attention in literature from different backgrounds and is increasingly studied from a multimodal perspective, the use of eye-gaze in teases is an understudied phenomenon. Gaze behavior in social interaction plays an important role in different aspects that are relevant for teasing in interaction, such as signaling a positive or a negative stance (Haddington 2006), monitoring or eliciting a response (Bavelas, Coates & Johnson 2002), and announcing a shift between viewpoints (Sweetser & Stec 2016). Furthermore, the presence or absence of the target of a tease is expected to have a big influence on gaze behavior of all addressees involved. Following this, the current study aimed to describe gaze behavior in two types of teases: those with an internal target (internal teases) and those with an external target (external teases). In our analysis, we took a mixed-methods approach, combining a quantitative analysis of the distribution of participants' gaze, with a qualitative microanalysis of gaze patterns in teasing sequences.

5.1 Gaze patterns during internal teases

Our first research question related to the distribution of speaker gaze over addressees. We hypothesized that during internal teases, the speaker gaze would be relatively asymmetrically divided between participants. The direction of this asymmetry could go one of two ways: either the speaker could gaze primarily at the target, or the speaker could primarily gaze away from the target. Indeed, we found that speakers display a sustained gaze at the target of the tease during internal teases. With the target being the primary addressee of the speaker, this gaze pattern adheres to previous research demonstrating a sustained gaze of the speaker to their primary addressee (Auer 2018). The fact that gaze at the addressee is sustained provides evidence for the idea that gaze is not merely used to point to the addressee as the target of the tease or the referent of the utterance, but also to monitor uptake of the tease by the target.

Speakers also deviate from this pattern. In these cases, gaze was used either as a means for specific action formation, or as part of the turn-taking machinery (see Section 2.2, supra). In *Extract 5*, for instance, the speaker averted her gaze from the target as part of an enactment, when shifting from the narrator to the character role in a story (Thompson & Suzuki 2014). At the end of *Extract 6*, the speaker establishes mutual gaze with the other addressee, as a means to elicit a response from the other addressee, and to invite her to join the pretense (see Brône, 2021, for a detailed description of this phenomenon in humor in interaction).

Regarding the addressees' gaze behavior in internal teases, again, multiple patterns emerged. In the majority of cases, the target of the tease displayed a sustained gaze at the speaker (e.g. in *Extracts 2, 5* and *6*). This gaze pattern matches the 'default' pattern of addressee gaze in interaction (Kendon 1967). However, there were also cases in which the addressees averted their gaze from the speaker and looked at the background instead (such as in *Extracts 3* and *4*). This is in line with previous work locating gaze aversions preceding moments of a divergent stance (Haddington 2006) or dispreferred responses (Kendrick & Holler 2017), and research showing how gaze aversions relate to embarrassment prior to self-mockery (Yu 2013), and may signal something like embarrassment after having just been catapulted as the target of a tease. The other addressee (i.e. non-target) also deviated from the 'default' gaze pattern. In many cases, such as in *Extract 3, 4, 5* and *6*, they gazed not at the speaker but at the target of the tease, or shifted their gaze between the speaker and the target. This could indicate an awareness of other addressees of the delicacy of the tease, and suggests that the third participant visibly monitors the interactional dynamics between the speaker and the target, as well as the uptake of the tease by the target.

5.2 Gaze patterns during external teases

During external teases, the target of the tease is not present, which may lead to a different distribution of gaze behavior. Hypothetically, both addressees have equal rights and opportunities to contribute to a tease during this type of sequence. However, at the same time, there are indications for an asymmetric pattern of gaze behavior in multiparty interactions (see Section 2.2, supra, and Rühlemann et al., 2019; Stivers, 2021). We therefore explored the question whether this would yield a more symmetrical distribution of speaker gaze over both addressees. In our quantitative analysis, we found that the asymmetry of speaker gaze to addressees was relatively smaller in external compared to internal teases, meaning that speakers divide their attention more equally across the two addressees. *Extract 7* illustrated this pattern. However, our analysis also showed that although the asymmetry is more pronounced for internal teases, speakers still show a preference for gazing at one addressee rather than the other in external teases. A closer look at the data revealed that in many of these cases, there was a primary addressee, either because of epistemic primacy (the speaker uttered the external tease in response to a question by the current addressee) or other group dynamics, such as in *Extract 8* in which one of the participants did not utter any word for the last 35 seconds, making her a secondary addressee. This phenomenon has also been described by Rühlemann et al. (2019) and Stivers (2021) who investigated gaze behavior in storytelling sequences involving multiple participants. As for the addressees, during external teases, they followed a more default pattern of showing long sustained gaze to the speaker.

5.3 Gaze behavior during internal versus external teases

In sum, gaze behavior during internal versus external teases differed in a number of ways. During internal teases, speakers showed a preference for gazing at the target rather than at the other addressee, whereas speaker gaze during external teases was somewhat more equally divided (although there still was an asymmetry in the external teases). With regard to the addressees, during internal teases, in some cases the target would shift their gaze to the background, and the other addressee would shift their gaze towards the target. During external teases, however, they followed a more default pattern of longer stretches of gaze at the speaker. These findings show how the participation framework influences gaze behavior by all participants.

The longer stretches of gaze at the target from both the speaker and other addressee highlighted the delicacy of teases in interaction (Haugh 2016), and the need for constant visual monitoring of the ongoing response of the target. We also found frequent use of an "invitational gaze", as mentioned by Yu (2013) among others, which highlights the role of gaze in mobilizing a response (Bavelas, Coates & Johnson 2002; Brône 2021). The delicacy of teases in interaction was also reflected by gaze aversions by the targets of the tease, which can indicate embarrassment of having just been bombarded the target of a tease.

The current study also added to previous work on eye-gaze in irony. Whereas previous studies found more gaze aversions in sarcastic compared to neutral utterances (Williams, Burns & Harmon 2009) and ironic utterances more generally (Gironzetti 2022), we found an increase in gaze at the target participant during ironic teases. Here it must be noted that the study by Williams and colleagues used elicited stimuli, and Gironzetti studied dyadic interactions. Both differences in set-up could explain the contradictory results, highlighting the importance of taking into account the specific constellation and social action in investigating gaze behavior during irony in interaction.

5.4 Some notes on the multimodal design of teases

Although the main focus of our study was on gaze behavior, the qualitative analysis of teases allowed us to make some preliminary observations on the multimodal design of teases involving other resources as well. Corroborating findings of Yu (2013) and De Vries et al. (2021), ironic teases were often shaped in a playful way using body movements, such as head movements and eyebrow raises. Smiling and laughter similarly highlighted the playful nature of teasing, with both the teaser smiling to mark an utterance as a laughable (Glenn 2003), and addressees laughing to signal their appreciation of the humor (Attardo et al. 2013). Finally, in internal teases, the targets often playfully dismissed the tease by employing, among others, shoulder shrugs signaling disengagement (Debras 2017), head movements, and raised eyebrows etc. In some cases the visual dismissal was followed by a verbal one, but this was not always the case. Further investigating the precise timing of the employment of these different resources and their combinations into multimodal packages seems to be a promising avenue for future research. Mazzocconi et al. (2021), for instance, investigate the relation between the precise timing of gaze in relation to different functions of laughter, adding even more nuance to the study of gaze in interaction. In the context of internal versus external teases, we observed that the target of a tease can rapidly shift over the course of a short interaction, such as in *Extract 1*. This type of sequence would be very suitable for a follow-up study on the sequential development of teases, with a possible research question being: if the target of a tease shifts, do participants also adapt their gaze behavior? Furthermore, in future work, specific attention could be paid to the specific delineation of the tease. Perhaps it is possible to define a 'stroke' of the tease that corresponds to a heightened intensity. The timing of the 'stroke' could then be investigated parallel with the use of gaze at this specific moment.

Another avenue for future research could be to test if the current findings also hold in settings in which there are more visual distractions, or in which participants are involved in multiple actions that demand visual attention at the same time (such as playing a game together). Such studies would increase the ecological validity of the current study.

6 Conclusion

The multimodal nature of teasing, and more generally, of humor in face-to-face interaction, is increasingly well studied. However, the use of eye-gaze, an essential tool on many levels of social interaction, is less well documented. In the current study we investigated gaze behavior during teasing in spontaneous triadic interactions, using mobile eye-tracking. Specifically, we asked to what extent gaze behavior by all participants involved was affected by the presence or absence of a target of the tease in the interaction. Our results (both quantitative and qualitative) showed that speakers during external teases follow a more 'default' gaze distribution with regard to participant framework, with both addressees mainly looking at the speaker, and speakers dividing their gaze between the addressees. During internal teases a different pattern emerged: the target of the tease was not only targeted verbally, but also visually. Speakers gazed relatively longer at the target than at the third participant, and in some cases, the third participant also visibly monitored the interactional dynamics of the tease, by either gazing at the target, or shifting their gaze between the speaker and the target. These findings highlight the multifunctionality of eye-gaze in interaction, and the influence of the specific participation framework on gaze distribution over all participants in teases in conversation. We hope that future work will bring together this study with research with other semiotic resources that are all intricately connected in the construction of multimodal teasing in face-to-face interaction.

7 Author Contributions

CV, BO and GB conceptualized the study. CV annotated the data and carried out the quantitative analysis. CV, BO and GB contributed to the qualitative analysis. CV and GB wrote the introduction Section of the manuscript, CV wrote the methods Section, quantitative results Section, and discussion and conclusion Sections. CV, BO, and GB wrote the qualitative analysis Section and contributed to the revision of earlier versions of the manuscript.

8 Supplementary Materials

All videos of the extracts, as well as the replication data for the quantitative analysis, can be retrieved at https://doi.org/10.48804/MIOVLL

References

Afshari Saleh, Reihaneh. 2020. Mock Aggression: Navigating Affiliation and Disaffiliation in Interaction. *Research on Language and Social Interaction* 53(4). 481–499. https://doi.org/10.1080/08351813.2020.1833590.

Argyle, Michael & Mark Cook. 1976. *Gaze and mutual gaze*. Cambridge: Cambridge University Press.

Attardo, Salvatore, Lucy Pickering, Fofo Lomotey & Shigehito Menjo. 2013. Multimodality in Conversational Humor. *Review of Cognitive Linguistics* 11(2). 402–416. https://doi.org/10.1075/rcl.11.2.12att.

Auer, Peter. 2018. Gaze, addressee selection and turn-taking in three-party interaction. In Geert Brône & Bert Oben (eds.), *Eye-tracking in Interaction: Studies on the role of eye gaze in dialogue*, 197–232. Amsterdam: John Benjamins Publishing Company.

Baldauf-Quilliatre, Heike. 2016. "pf" indicating a change in orientation in French interactions. *Journal of Pragmatics* 104. 89–107. https://doi.org/10.1016/j.pragma.2016.07.006.

Bavelas, Janet Beavin, Linda Coates & Trudy Johnson. 2002. Listener Responses as a Collaborative Process: The Role of Gaze. *Journal of Communication* 52(3). 566–580. https://doi.org/10.1111/j.1460-2466.2002.tb02562.x.

Boxer, Diana & Florencia Cortés-Conde. 1997. From bonding to biting: Conversational joking and identity display. *Journal of Pragmatics* 27(3). 275–294. https://doi.org/10.1016/S0378-2166(96)00031-8.

Bressem, Jana & Cornelia Müller. 2014. The family of Away gestures: Negation, refusal, and negative assessment. In Cornelia Müller, Alan Cienki, Ellen Fricke, Silva Ladewig, David McNeill & Jana Bressem (eds.), *Body – Language – Communication (Handbooks of Linguistics and Communication Science), vol. 2*, 1592–1604. Berlin/Boston: De Gruyter. https://doi.org/10.1515/9783110302028.1592.

Bressem, Jana. 2021. *Repetitions in Gesture: A Cognitive-Linguistic and Usage-Based Perspective*. Berlin/Boston: De Gruyter.

Brône, Geert. 2021. The multimodal negotiation of irony and humor in interaction: On the role of eye gaze in joint pretense. In Augusto Soares da Silva (ed.), *Figurative Thought and Language*, 109–136. Amsterdam: John Benjamins Publishing Company. https://doi.org/10.1075/ftl.11.04bro.

Brône, Geert & Bert Oben. 2015. InSight Interaction: a multimodal and multifocal dialogue corpus. *Language Resources and Evaluation* 49(1). 195–214. https://doi.org/10.1007/s10579-014-9283-2.

Brône, Geert &Bert Oben. 2021. Monitoring the Pretence. Intersubjective grounding, gaze and irony. In Gitte Kristiansen, Karlien Franco, Stefano De Pascale, Laura Rosseel & Weiwei Zhang (eds.), *Cognitive Sociolinguistics Revisited*, 544–556. Berlin/Boston: De Gruyter. https://doi.org/10.1515/9783110733945-044.

Brône, Geert, Bert Oben, Annelies Jehoul, Jelena Vranjes & Kurt Feyaerts. 2017. Eye gaze and viewpoint in multimodal interaction management. *Cognitive Linguistics* 28(3). 449–483. https://doi.org/10.1515/cog-2016-0119.

Chafe, Wallace. 1994. *Discourse, Consciousness, and Time: The Flow and Displacement of Conscious Experience in Speaking and Writing*. Chicago: University of Chicago Press.

Chang, Wei-Lin Melody & Michael Haugh. 2021. Teasing and claims to non-serious intent in Chinese talk shows. *East Asian Pragmatics* 6(2). 135–159. https://doi.org/10.1558/eap.18158.

Clark, Herbert H. 1996. *Using Language*. Cambridge: Cambridge University Press.

Clark, Herbert H. & Richard J. Gerrig. 1984. On the pretense theory of irony. *Journal of Experimental Psychology: General* 113(1). 121–126. https://doi.org/10.1037/0096-3445.113.1.121.

Debras, Camille. 2017. The shrug: Forms and meanings of a compound enactment. *Gesture* 16(1). 1–34. https://doi.org/10.1075/gest.16.1.01deb.

Drew, Paul. 1987. Po-faced receipts of teases. *Linguistics* 25(1). 219–253. https://doi.org/10.1515/ling.1987.25.1.219.

Duncan, Starkey. 1975. Interaction units during speaking turns in dyadic face-to-face conversations. In Adam Kendon, Richard M. Harris & Mary R. Key (eds.), *Organization of behavior in face-to-face interaction*, 1999–213. Berlin/Boston: De Gruyter.

Dynel, Marta. 2008. No Aggression, Only Teasing: The Pragmatics of Teasing and Banter. *Lodz Papers in Pragmatics* 4(2). 241–261. https://doi.org/10.2478/v10016-008-0001-7.

Eckert, Johanna, Sasha L. Winkler & Erica A. Cartmill. 2020. Just kidding: the evolutionary roots of playful teasing. *Biology Letters* 16(9). 20200370. https://doi.org/10.1098/rsbl.2020.0370.

Gironzetti, Elisa. 2022. *The Multimodal Performance of Conversational Humor*. Amsterdam: John Benjamins. http://www.jbe.platform.com/content/books/9789027257857.

Glenn, Phillip. 2003. *Laughter in Interaction*. Cambridge: Cambridge University Press. https://www.cambridge.org/core/books/laughter-in-interaction/4629463A15293CFEBD21EE70AAC966F2.

Goffman, Erving. 1967. *Interaction ritual: Essays on face-to-face behavior*. Garden City: Anchor.

González-Fuente, Santiago, Victoria Escandell-Vidal & Pilar Prieto. 2015. Gestural codas pave the way to the understanding of verbal irony. *Journal of Pragmatics* 90. 26–47. https://doi.org/10.1016/j.pragma.2015.10.002.

Goodwin, Charles. 1980. Restarts, Pauses, and the Achievement of a State of Mutual Gaze at Turn-Beginning. *Sociological Inquiry* 50(3–4). 272–302. https://doi.org/10.1111/j.1475-682X.1980.tb00023.x.

Goodwin, Charles. 1981. *Conversational Organization: Interaction Between Speakers and Hearers*. Cambridge: Academic Press.

Goodwin, Charles. 2013. The co-operative, transformative organization of human action and knowledge. *Journal of Pragmatics* 46(1). 8–23. https://doi.org/10.1016/j.pragma.2012.09.003.

Goodwin, Marjorie Harness & Charles Goodwin. 1986. Gesture and coparticipation in the activity of searching for a word. *Semiotica* 62(1–2). 51–76. https://doi.org/10.1515/semi.1986.62.1-2.51.

Gullberg, Marianne & Kenneth Holmqvist. 2006. What speakers do and what addressees look at: Visual attention to gestures in human interaction live and on video. *Pragmatics & Cognition* 14(1). 53–82. https://doi.org/10.1075/pc.14.1.05gul.

Haddington, Pentti. 2006. The organization of gaze and assessments as resources for stance taking. *Text & Talk*. De Gruyter Mouton 26(3). 281–328. https://doi.org/10.1515/TEXT.2006.012.

Haugh, Michael. 2014. Jocular Mockery as Interactional Practice in Everyday Anglo-Australian Conversation. *Australian Journal of Linguistics* 34(1). 76–99. https://doi.org/10.1080/07268602.2014.875456.

Haugh, Michael. 2016. Jocular language play, social action and (dis)affiliation in conversational interaction. In Nancy Bell (ed.), *Multiple Perspectives on Language Play*. Berlin/Boston: De Gruyter. https://doi.org/10.1515/9781501503993-007.

Haugh, Michael. 2017. Teasing. In Salvatore Attardo (ed.), *The Routledge handbook of language and humor*, 204–218. New York: Routledge.

Hirvenkari, Lotta, Johanna Ruusuvuori, Veli-Matti Saarinen, Maari Kivioja, Anssi Peräkylä & Riitta Hari. 2013. Influence of Turn-Taking in a Two-Person Conversation on the Gaze of a Viewer. *PLOS ONE* 8(8). e71569. https://doi.org/10.1371/journal.pone.0071569.

Jehoul, Annelies. 2019. *Filled pauses from a multimodal perspective. On the interplay of speech and eye gaze*. Leuven, Belgium: KU Leuven Doctoral Dissertation. http://limo.libis.be/primo-explore/fulldisplay/LIRIAS2814932/Lirias.

Keltner, Dacher, Lisa Capps, Ann M. Kring, Randall C. Young & Erin A. Heerey. 2001. Just teasing: A conceptual analysis and empirical review. *Psychological Bulletin* 127(2). 229–248. https://doi.org/10.1037/0033-2909.127.2.229.

Kendon, Adam. 1967. Some functions of gaze-direction in social interaction. *Acta Psychologica* 26. 22–63. https://doi.org/10.1016/0001-6918(67)90005-4.

Kendrick, Kobin H. & Judith Holler. 2017. Gaze Direction Signals Response Preference in Conversation. *Research on Language and Social Interaction* 50(1). 12–32. https://doi.org/10.1080/08351813.2017.1262120.

Kidwell, Mardi. 2005. Gaze as Social Control: How Very Young Children Differentiate "The Look" From a "Mere Look" by Their Adult Caregivers. *Research on Language and Social Interaction* 38(4). 417–449. https://doi.org/10.1207/s15327973rlsi3804_2.

Kidwell, Mardi. 2006. 'Calm down!': the role of gaze in the interactional management of hysteria by the police. *Discourse Studies* 8(6). 745–770. https://doi.org/10.1177/1461445606069328.

Kidwell, Mardi. 2009. Gaze Shift as an Interactional Resource for Very Young Children. *Discourse Processes* 46(2–3). 145–160. https://doi.org/10.1080/01638530902728926.

Lehtimaja, Inkeri & Liisa Tainio. 2015. Encouraging participation or restraining teasing? Teacher responses to uninvited students' answers. *Journal of Applied Linguistics & Professional Practice* 12(1). 1–22. https://doi.org/10.1558/jalpp.36883.

Linell, Per. 2009. *Rethinking Language, Mind, and World Dialogically*. Charlotte: IAP.

Mazzocconi, Chiara, Vladislav Maraev, Vidya Somashekarappa & Christine Howes. 2021. Looking for Laughs: Gaze Interaction with Laughter Pragmatics and Coordination. In *Proceedings of the 2021 International Conference on Multimodal Interaction*, 636–644. Montréal QC Canada: ACM. https://doi.org/10.1145/3462244.3479947.

Mondada, Lorenza. 2007. Turn Taking in multimodalen und multiaktionalen Kontexten. In Heiko Hausendorf (ed.), *Gespräch als Prozess: Linguistische Aspekte der Zeitlichkeit verbaler Interaktion*, 247–276. Tübingen: Narr Francke Attempto Verlag.

Parrill, Fey. 2012. Interactions between discourse status and viewpoint in co-speech gesture. In Barbara Dancygier & Eve Sweetser (eds.), *Viewpoint in language: A multimodal perspective*, 97–112. Cambridge: Cambridge University Press.

Pickering, Martin J. & Simon Garrod. 2021. *Understanding Dialogue: Language Use and Social Interaction*. Cambridge: Cambridge University Press.

Priego-Valverde, Béatrice. 2016. Teasing in casual conversations: An opportunistic discursive strategy. In Leonor Ruiz-Gurillo (ed.), *Metapragmatics of Humor: Current research trends*, 215–233.

Amsterdam: John Benjamins Publishing Company. http://www.jbe-platform.com/content/books/9789027266378.

Rossano, Federico. 2010. Questioning and responding in Italian. *Journal of Pragmatics* 42(10). 2756–2771. https://doi.org/10.1016/j.pragma.2010.04.010.

Rossano, Federico. 2012. Gaze in Conversation. In Jack Sidnell & Tanya Stivers (eds.), *The Handbook of Conversation Analysis*, 308–329. Chichester, UK: John Wiley & Sons, Ltd. https://onlinelibrary.wiley.com/doi/10.1002/9781118325001.ch15.

Rühlemann, Christoph, Matt Gee & Alexander Ptak. 2019. Alternating gaze in multi-party storytelling. *Journal of Pragmatics* 149. 91–113. https://doi.org/10.1016/j.pragma.2019.06.001.

Sacks, Harvey, Emanuel A. Schegloff & Gail Jefferson. 1974. A Simplest Systematics for the Organization of Turn-Taking for Conversation. *Language* 50(4). 696–735. https://doi.org/10.2307/412243.

Schegloff, Emanuel A. 2000. Overlapping talk and the organization of turn-taking for conversation. *Language in Society* 29(1). 1–63. https://doi.org/10.1017/S0047404500001019.

Selting, Margret, Peter Auer, Dagmar Barth-Weingarten, Jörg Bergmann, Pia Bergmann, Karin Birkner, Elizabeth Couper-Kuhlen, et al. 2011. A system for transcribing talk-in-interaction: GAT 2 translated and adapted for English by Elizabeth Couper-Kuhlen and Dagmar Barth-Weingarten. *Gesprächsforschung* 12. 1–51.

Sidnell, Jack. 2006. Coordinating Gesture, Talk, and Gaze in Reenactments. *Research on Language and Social Interaction* 39(4). 377–409. https://doi.org/10.1207/s15327973rlsi3904_2.

Stivers, Tanya. 2021. Is Conversation Built for Two? The Partitioning of Social Interaction. *Research on Language and Social Interaction* 54(1). 1–19. https://doi.org/10.1080/08351813.2020.1864158.

Sweetser, Eve & Kashmiri Stec. 2016. Maintaining multiple viewpoints with gaze. In Barbara Dancygier, Wei-lun Lu & Arie Verhagen (eds.), *Viewpoint and the fabric of meaning: form and use of viewpoint tools across languages and modalities*, 237–257. Berlin/Boston: De Gruyter Mouton.

Thompson, Sandra A & Ryoko Suzuki. 2014. Reenactments in conversation: Gaze and recipiency. *Discourse Studies* 16(6). 816–846. https://doi.org/10.1177/1461445614546259.

Vertegaal, Roel. 1999. The GAZE groupware system: mediating joint attention in multiparty communication and collaboration. In *Proceedings of the SIGCHI conference on Human Factors in Computing Systems* (CHI '99), 294–301. New York: Association for Computing Machinery. https://doi.org/10.1145/302979.303065.

Vries, Clarissa de, Bert Oben & Geert Brône. 2021. Exploring the role of the body in communicating ironic stance. *Languages and Modalities* 1(1). 65–80. https://doi.org/10.3897/lamo.1.68876.

Williams, Jason A., Erin L. Burns & Elizabeth A. Harmon. 2009. Insincere Utterances and Gaze: Eye Contact during Sarcastic Statements. *Perceptual and Motor Skills* 108(2). 565–572. https://doi.org/10.2466/pms.108.2.565-572.

Wittenburg, Peter, Henie Brugman, Albert Russel, Alex Klassmann & Han Sloetjes. 2006. ELAN: a professional framework for multimodality research. In *Proceedings of the 5th International Conference on Language Resources and Evaluation (LREC 2006)*, 1556–1559.

Yu, Changrong. 2012. *Emotional display in argument, storytelling and teasing: a multimodal analysis*. Oulu, Finland: University of Oulu Doctoral Dissertation.

Yu, Changrong. 2013. Two interactional functions of self-mockery in everyday English conversations: A multimodal analysis. *Journal of Pragmatics* 50(1). 1–22. https://doi.org/10.1016/j.pragma.2013.01.006.

Zima, Elisabeth. 2020. Gaze and Recipient Feedback in Triadic Storytelling Activities. *Discourse Processes* 57(9). 725–748. https://doi.org/10.1080/0163853X.2020.1769428.

Elisa Gironzetti

3 Humorous Smiling: A Reverse Cross-Validation of the Smiling Intensity Scale for the Identification of Conversational Humor

Abstract: The Smiling Intensity Scale (SIS, Gironzetti, Pickering, Huang, Zhang, Menjo & Attardo, 2016) is a holistic FACS-based instrument developed for the study of smiling. The SIS comprises 5 different levels of smiling classified based on their visual properties (e.g., showing of teeth) and underlying muscle activation (e.g., the presence of AU 12; see Ekman & Friesen, 1978). The SIS has so far been employed to study the relationship between different levels of smiling and humor in computer-mediated and face-to-face conversations in English and Spanish (Gironzetti et al., 2016, 2019; Gironzetti, 2021), as well as in French (Priego-Valverde et al., 2018). Findings from these studies indicated that (a) people' smiling intensity is higher in the presence of humor as compared to each person's baseline, (b) interlocutors tend to display smiling patterns that frame the occurrence of humor, and (c) dyads show joint smiling behaviors at the same SIS level with humor. Based on these findings, the current study aims at reverse-validating the SIS as an instrument that could be applied to identify humor in a multimodal corpus. To this end, 2 dyadic, semi-naturalistic, computer-mediated conversations (approximately 26 minutes each, for a total of 52 minutes and 38 humor instances in total) were recorded. Each speaker was instructed to break the ice by telling a joke given by the researcher and then continue talking freely for about 20 minutes. Conversations were analyzed by applying the SIS to identify moments in which speakers show evidence of humor-related smiling behaviors (that is, increased smiling intensity and smiling intensity matching). This initial coding was done one speaker at a time and without having access to the audio of the conversations, therefore not knowing whether and when humor was present in each conversation and not seeing the facial expression of the other interlocutor, to eliminate the risk of rater bias. Then, the speech that co-occurs with these humor-related smiling behaviors is analyzed following the method outlined in Gironzetti et al. (2019) to verify whether any humor was in fact produced by any of the speakers. Findings from this study contribute to the growing body of research on the relationship between smiling and humor by assessing the degree of generalizability of SIS-based findings.

Keywords: smiling, conversational humor, smiling intensity scale, humor marker, synchronicity

1 Different types of smiling

Smiling is a ubiquitous behavior that people display virtually in any situation. Not all smiles are equal, though (Rychlowska et al., 2017). In fact, smiling differs based on the personality and the cultural and physical traits of the person, the situational context, the interlocutor or audience, and the underlying purpose or emotion (see, for example, Birdwhistell, 1970; Kaukomaa et al., 2013; Ekman et al., 1990). The study of smiling has attracted researcher's attentions for a long time and has led to a growing body of instruments (that is, physical instruments and methods) to measure and record different aspects of smiling; classifications that attend to quantitative and qualitative features, and theories that attempt to explain how and why people smile the way they do.

Among the first instruments employed to record and measure smiling is the "facial cinérecorder" (Lynn, 1940), an apparatus that comprised a sound movie projector to elicit the smiling expression through sound and movie, and a moving picture camera to record the smiling expression under standard conditions comparable across subjects. The researcher would then project the recordings of the smiling expression as a sequence of photographs and analyze the dynamic patterns of smiling by tracing them onto a translucent surface, and later translating these patterns into comparable numerical representations (what Lynn, 1940, calls a "mimetic smiledness quotient," p. 86).

The cinérecorder method focused on smiling by considering primarily changes in the corners of the mouth, which has remained the key region for the study of smiling in all subsequent research, and by attending to its physical (quantitative) characteristics. Lynn was not attempting, for example, at differentiating between genuine (Duchenne) and phony (non-Duchenne) smiling, which would require focusing on the qualitative aspects of smiling. Another such example is Blurton Jones' (1971), who developed precise descriptions of different facial expressions based on the analysis of 500 photographs of children and the anatomy of facial muscles. While his approach focused mostly on a quantitative description of the muscles and visual changes that can be recognized as contributing to a smiling expression (à la FACS), he also discussed the difficulty of arriving at a definition of an expression that looks like a smile (p. 387), because people do not agree on what parts of the face are involved (e.g., if only the mouth or also the eyes are involved) and how different types of smiles actually differ from one another.

However, already at the time of Blurton Jones' work, researchers had developed smiling taxonomies that encompassed both quantitative and qualitative differences in people's smiling expressions. One example is Grant's (1969), that considered quantitative and qualitative observations to classify different types of smiling. For example, according to his taxonomy (p. 528), a smile can be classified, among other options, as a "Simple smile. The lips are drawn slightly back and up and are closed", relying solely on quantitative elements, or as an "Upper smile. A smile showing the top teeth. This is the commonest social smile. It is used in greeting situations", described by combining quantitative (i.e., showing the top teeth) and qualitative (i.e., social smile used in greetings) elements.

Young and Décarie (1977) also proposed an early smiling taxonomy and differentiated between eight types of smiles (e.g., shy smile, ambivalent smile, semi-smile, etc.), all described as involving the mouth, eyes, and brows regions of the face, that is, attending to quantitative elements, but using qualitative labels. For example, they described a "coy smile" (p. 99) as one involving the mouth as in a slight open-mouth smile that "assumes a crescent appearance. The upper teeth are partly or greatly visible. The lips are fully retracted outward and upward . . ." (p. 100), and the brows that may be "drawn slightly down and in toward the center, creating a slight furrow between them" (p. 99). Interestingly enough, in their taxonomy laughter is described exclusively as an acoustic phenomenon (a vocalization, p. 104), although in the discussion, the authors briefly mention that it could co-occur with a play face or certain types of smiling, such as O-mouth smile and slight open-mouth smile.

Nowadays, the most widely employed instrument to study smiling is the Facial Action Coding System (FACS) developed by Ekman and Friesen (1978; Ekman et al., 2002). FACS relies on facial anatomy and muscle movements to identify 44 Action Units (AUs) that represent a finite set of anatomically separated and visually distinguishable changes that can occur on the appearance of someone's face and that can combine to configure different facial expressions. When it comes to smiling, FACS analyses have identified several types of smiling based on the AUs involved, which have also been associated with given underlying emotions or communicative intentions. For example, a genuine enjoyment smile (Duchenne smile) would be characterized by AU 6 (cheek raiser) and AU 12 (lip corner puller) and show visible changes in the mouth and eyes region of the face, while a contempt smile would involve changes in the mouth region only by means of AU 12 and AU 14 (dimpler). In addition to identifying the AUs responsible for a certain smiling expression, FACS also allows researchers to score the intensity of each AU on a scale from A to E, from slight to maximum intensity.

FACS has been widely applied to study static (i.e., photographs) and dynamic (i.e., videos) smiling expressions (e.g., Stewart, Bucy & Mehu, 2015, on political smiles; Kawulok, Nalepa, Kawulok & Smolka, 2021, on smiling perceived genuineness; Hertenstein, Hansel, Butts & Hile, 2009, on the relationship between smiling intensity in photographs and divorce) and has also been the basis for the development of additional instruments designed specifically for the study of smiling intensity: additive scoring systems and holistic ones. Additive scoring systems, such as Harker and Keltner's (2001), integrate the intensity of different AUs to arrive at an intensity score that is the sum of individual AUs' intensity. This is problematic because it does not consider or reflect the impact of each AU and its intensity on the facial expression as a whole. For example, a smiling expression of intensity 6 could be equally displayed with a strong AU 12 of intensity 5 and a weak AU 6 of intensity 1, and vice versa. With such a scoring system, it would be impossible to differentiate the two expressions, which would be visually different, or between the impact of each AU and their intensity on the resulting facial expression.

Holistic FACS-based scoring systems include a trichotomous scale that integrates AU 12 and AU 6 (Freese, Meland & Irwin, 2006; Abel & Kruger, 2010; Kaczmarek, Behnke, Kashdan, Kusiak, Marzec, Mistrzak & Włodarczyk, 2018) and the Smiling Intensity Scale (SIS, Gironzetti, Pickering, Huang, Zhang, Menjo & Attardo, 2016). The SIS is the instrument that is employed in the present study. It was developed explicitly for the study of smiling and conversational humor and to overcome some of the limitations of other similar instruments. Specifically, it was developed to be easily applied with lower-quality video recordings that would not allow a fine-grained FACS analysis of the intensity of each AU, and to integrate in a more meaningful way the different AUs that contribute to a smiling expression. Figure 1 represents the different behaviors of the SIS as produced by a speaker from the corpus analyzed in this study.

SIS 0   SIS 1   SIS 2   SIS 3   SIS 4

Figure 1: The five SIS behaviors (left to right) as displayed by participant N.

The SIS behaviors shown in Figure 1 are described as follows based on Gironzetti, Pickering, Huang, Zhang, Menjo, and Attardo (2016):

- Level 0: Neutral. No smile, no flexing of the zygomaticus (no AU12), may show squinting of the eyes (caused by AU6 or AU7), but no raised side of the mouth (no AU 12), the mouth may be closed or open (AU25 or AU26).
- Level 1: Closed mouth smile. Shows flexing of the zygomaticus (AU12), may show flexing of the orbicularis oculi (caused by AU6 or AU7).
- Level 2: Open-mouth smile. Showing upper teeth (AU25), flexing of the zygomaticus (AU12), may show flexing of the orbicularis oculi (caused by AU6 or AU7).
- Level 3: Wide open-mouth smile. Shows flexing of the zygomaticus (AU12), flexing of the orbicularis oculi (caused by AU6 or AU7). 3A: showing lower and upper teeth (AU25), or 3B: showing a gap between upper and lower teeth (AU25 and AU26).
- Level 4: Jaw-dropped smile. The jaw is dropped (AU26 or AU27), showing lower and upper teeth (AU25), flexing zygomaticus (AU12), flexing of the orbicularis oculi (AU6 or AU7).

So far, the SIS has been applied to study smiling as it co-occurs with humor in different languages (French, English, and Spanish) in computer-mediated (Gironzetti, Pickering, Huang, Zhang, Menjo & Attardo, 2016; Gironzetti, Attardo, & Pickering, 2019) and face-to-face conversational contexts (Amoyal & Priego-Valverde, 2019; Amoyal, Priego-Valverde & Rauzy, 2020; Gironzetti, 2022, 2021; Priego-Valverde, Bigi, Priego-Valverde, Bigi & Amoyal, 2020), and is the basis for the development of the SMAD script (https://github.com/srauzy/HMAD) for the automatic detection of facial movements (such as smiling) and head movements in video recordings (see Priego-Valverde & Rauzy, this volume).

2 Smiling behaviors and conversational humor

The relationship between smiling and conversational humor has begun to be explored in depth only recently as part of a research program that started at the Applied Linguistics Lab at Texas A&M University-Commerce. Attardo and Pickering (2011) noted that while humor is not clearly marked prosodically, it tends to co-occur with smiling and so it could potentially be marked visually. This hypothesis was further explored in Gironzetti et al. (2016, 2019), and Gironzetti (2021, 2022) with dyads of US English speakers or Mexican Spanish speakers interacting face-to-face in either a virtual or physical environment. Smiling was found to play a significant role in the performance of face-to-face conversational humor, regardless of whether the conversation would happen with both interlocutors present or via videoconference. More specifically, smiling intensity was found to increase in the presence of humor with respect to each speaker's baseline, although less so in the case of irony when compared with punchlines and jablines. Smiling was also found to be mobilized by speakers to frame a part of the conversation as humorous by displaying framing smiling patterns, that is, sustained increases of smiling intensity that would frame a humorous utterance. These patterns could be displayed only by one member of the dyad, which happened more frequently in the case of jablines and irony, or both members of the dyads, which characterized punchlines. Last, dyads also displayed an increased smiling dialogic synergy (Gironzetti, 2022, p. 45): they tended to synchronize their smiling and display the same smiling behavior at the same time in the presence of humor, but displaying more synchronic non-smiling in the absence of humor. Similar results were also obtained for French face-to-face conversations (Priego-Valverde et al., 2018). In comparison with US English speakers, however, French speakers displayed more non-synchronic smiling when humor was absent from the conversation, and more synchronic smiling when humor was present.

These findings are relevant for the study of conversational humor because they point to the fact that humor may be marked visually by means of smiling. The field has been searching for a reliable cue of humor to be used to identify the presence of humor in a conversation since its beginning, although most of the attention was placed on laughter and other prosodic means that could help speakers identify humor as such (see a discussion in Gironzetti, 2017; Attardo, 2019). However, it has been shown that laughter transcends humor as well as humor transcends laughter (Pickering, Corduas, Eisterhold, Seifried, Eggleston & Attardo, 2009), which means that laughter is a non-reliable cue for the presence of humor in conversation that would lead to false positives (laughter cueing humor when there is, in fact, no humor) and false negatives (no laughter cueing no humor when there is, in fact, humor). In the case of prosodic cues, it has been shown that there is not a specific cue or even set of cues that can serve this purpose, as speakers may or may not modify their pitch or speech rate, for example, to cue the listener towards a humorous interpretation of what was said (see Attardo & Pickering, 2011). Notably, this last strand of research focused on the *speaker*'s prosodic cues, excluding the interlocutor and their potential role in the negotiation of conversational humor. This speaker centered perspective assumes that humor cueing is done or initiated only or mostly by the speaker of the humorous utterance. In the present study, on the other hand, conversational humor is approached as a dialogical and negotiated activity, which means that both interlocutors in a dyadic conversation are considered to be equally capable and responsible for initiating or signaling, by means of a variety of cues, that a given utterance is being interpreted as humorous.

The search for a cue of conversational humor has some important methodological implications for researchers, because a reliable cue (in the sense of *indicator* as explained in Gironzetti, 2017, p. 405, that is, an element that is non-essential, but always co-occurring and intentionally cueing for humor) could facilitate and strengthen the identification of humor in a conversational corpus. Because no reliable cue of conversational humor has been found so far, a variety of methods have been employed to identify instances of humor in a corpus. The following are the two most common methods employed: (a) laughter, including laughter tracks employed in television shows, which has often been used as the sole default cue of humor with the limitations already described in the previous paragraphs, and (b) a full semantic and pragmatic analysis of the text to identify the humorous script opposition and resolution, which is very time consuming and adopt an etic or external perspective.

In the present study, I conduct a reverse, cross-validation of the SIS to explore the validity of different smiling behaviors as cues to identify, in a conversational corpus, the presence of humor. In the next paragraphs I discuss the methodology adopted to confirm whether the observed changes (increased smiling intensity, smiling synchronicity, and smiling intensity matching) in the smiling behavior of interlocutors can serve as an effective and reliable cue for conversational humor.

3 Methods

3.1 Procedures

The current study aims at validating the SIS as an instrument that could be applied to identify humor in a multimodal corpus. To this end, 2 semi-naturalistic, computer-mediated conversations (approximately 26 minutes each, for a total of 52 minutes) were recorded. The conversations occurred on videoconferencing software and were audio and video recorded. Before the recording, the researcher spent a few minutes with each participant separately to discuss the consent form and explain how the study was being conducted, without revealing the purpose of the study. At that stage, each speaker was given a joke (the donkey joke and the frog joke, reproduced in Attardo & Pickering, 2011). They were instructed to use the joke as an ice breaker to begin the conversation and then continue talking freely for about 20 minutes.

Each conversation recording included a video with both speakers visible, and an audio track. The researcher and author completed all the annotations. Each conversation was processed and analyzed as follows, ensuring that each step was completed in this order to avoid bias:

1. First, the video was edited to generate two separate videos, one per speaker. The two videos were uploaded and synchronized on ELAN, a software for multimodal annotations developed at the Max Planck Institute (Wittenburg, Brugman, Russel, Klassmann & Sloetjes, 2006).
2. Prior to the beginning of the smiling annotation in ELAN, the audio was muted and only one video was visible at a time, to avoid bias due to the audio (which could indicate when humor was present in the conversation) or the interlocutor's behavior.
3. Each video was continuously annotated by the researcher (a trained FACS rater) using the SIS to obtain individual smiling intensity measurements for each speaker. Two tiers were generated, i.e., Smile V and Smile G, one per speaker (G and V are the initials of participants' names in one of the conversations). Figure 2 shows the annotation window in ELAN where, to avoid bias, only one video is visible and there is no audio available to the annotator. The tier with the corresponding individual smiling intensity annotations is also visible in the bottom part of the image.
4. Dyadic humor-related smiling behaviors were then computed based on the SIS individual annotations to obtain measurements of smiling synchronicity behaviors, as shown in Figure 3 (i.e., Synch 1 is the tier for all smiling synchronicity at SIS level 1; Synch 2 shows annotations for smiling synchronicity at SIS level 2, and so on). This was done in ELAN using the function *create annotations from overlaps* and selecting specific criteria. One tier was created for overlaps in the smiling behaviors of the two participants with the same SIS value (e. g., both participants smiling at SIS level 2) to represent all cases of smiling intensity matching (that is, when both speakers are smiling at the same time at the same SIS level). Another tier was created for all cases of synchronic non-smiling behavior (that is, when the two participants are displaying a SIS level 0 behavior—not smiling—at the same time). One additional tier was created for smiling synchronicity without intensity matching (when both participants are smiling at the same time but at different SIS levels), and asynchronous smiling (when one speaker is smiling at any SIS level other than 0, while the other is at SIS level 0). This resulted in 7 new tiers (Synch and Asynch ones illustrated in Figure 3), each with annotations representing the duration, in milliseconds, of the observed behavior.
5. After the smiling annotations were completed for each conversation, the videos and the tiers were hidden, and the audio track was unmuted to proceed with the marking of humor. Humor was marked in a dedicated tier, *Humor (Observed)*, following the procedure outlined in Gironzetti et al. (2019), that is, relying on a semantic and pragmatic analysis and the presence of explicit metalinguistic comments such as "this is / is not funny," which indicated that

3 Humorous Smiling — 95

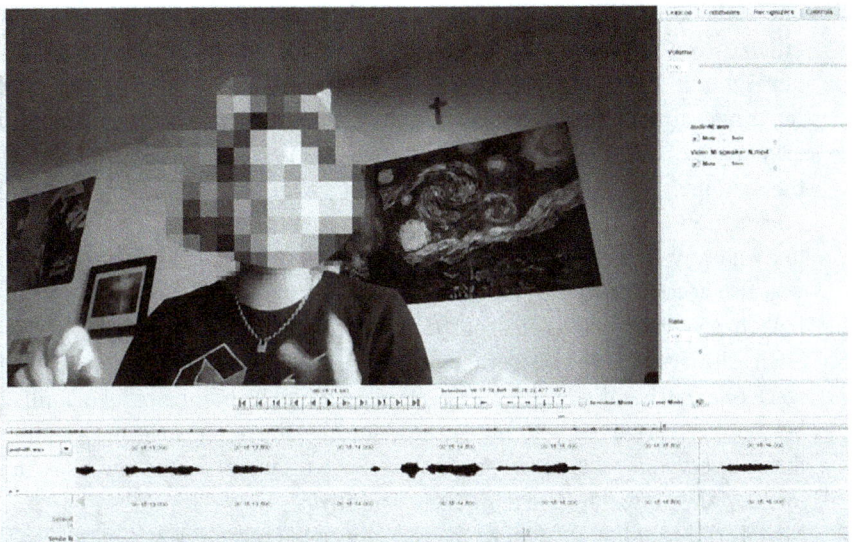

Figure 2: Sample annotation window in ELAN.

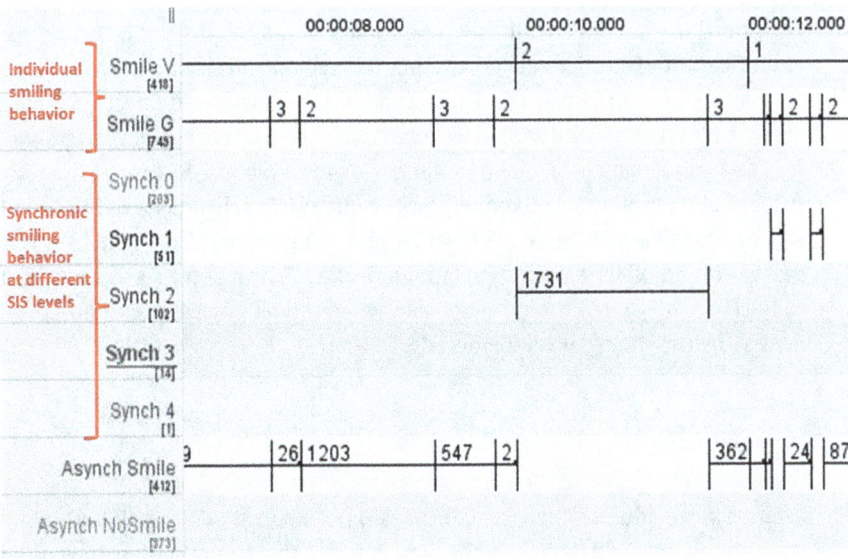

Figure 3: ELAN screen showing all smiling annotation tiers.

one of the interlocutors interpreted a given utterance as humorous. All annotations were 5 seconds long surrounding the last element of the humorous phrase, unless participants produced several instances of humor one after the other, in which case the annotations duration varied, making sure they all started 2.5 second before the first humorous phrase and 2.5 seconds after the last one. When coding for the presence of humor, no smiling or visual information was available to the researcher during the humor marking stage to avoid any bias. However, laughter, whenever it was present in the data was also accessible to the researcher during this phase and could have potentially been considered as an acoustic cue to humor.
6. Then, all tiers and videos were made visible and humor and smiling coding were analyzed and compared to determine whether humor-related smiling behaviors co-occurred with humor produced by any of the speakers – that is, if these served a reliable cue for the presence of humor in the corpus – and identify any potential false negatives or positives.
7. Next, further humor related behaviors were coded for in the attempt of replicating previous results, that is, finding whether a localized increase in smiling intensity per speaker is typical of humorous but not non-humorous portions of conversation.
8. Last, portions of conversations where humor could be present based on the identification of humor-related smiling behaviors, were annotated in a new tier called *Humor (Estimated)*. These annotations were based on the presence of smiling synchronicity at SIS 2 or higher and were 5 seconds long surrounding the smiling synchronicity annotation (or multiple of 5 in case of multiple subsequent annotations of smiling synchronicity). Synchronicity at SIS level 1 was not considered since a SIS level 1 smiling corresponds to a polite smiling that is not distinctive of conversational humor (Gironzetti, 2022), that is, it can occur with and without humor and when it does co-occur with humor, it does so below chance level (below 50%).

3.2 Participants

Participants were adult (+18 years old) speakers of English or Spanish with a native or native-like proficiency in the language of the conversation, recruited among the student population at a large university in the northeast of the United States. Following Institutional Review Board approval and procedures, they all gave their consent to be audio and video recorded and for their image to be employed in scholarly publications, provided that their identity is protected. After initial recruiting of participants, dyads were created based on availability, proficiency in the language of the conversation, and to control for the level of familiarity between speakers (i.e., no close friends were assigned to the same dyad).

4 Results

4.1 Increased individual smiling intensity as a cue for conversational humor

The methodology applied to this study led to a set of promising results for the identification and study of conversational humor. The first of these results concerns whether a localized increase of smiling intensity by individual participants serves as a cue to conversational humor. To do so, the time (in seconds as well as a percentage) participants displayed each SIS behavior with and without humor was calculated. It should be noted that, in contrast with previous studies that only considered a sample of non-humorous parts of conversation, these numbers reflect participants behavior for all non-humorous and humorous parts conversation. Table 1 and 2 summarize the percentages of each SIS behavior displayed by each speaker in the two conversations analyzed with and without humor, and Figures 4 and 5 illustrate the distribution of each SIS behavior with and without humor per each participant and conversation.

Table 1: Percentage of SIS behaviors displayed with and without humor in conversation NI.

	I no humor	N no humor	I humor	N humor
SIS 0	72%	91%	30%	57%
SIS 1	7%	2%	9%	2%
SIS 2	11%	1%	28% (+154%)	4% (+300%)
SIS 3	10%	6%	33% (+230%)	35% (+483%)
SIS 4	0%	0%	1%	1%

The data in Tables 1 and 2 and Figures 4 and 5 show that the distribution of each SIS behavior differs with and without humor, as shown in prior studies. While in the absence of humor participants rarely smile or display a SIS level 4 behavior, in the presence of humor participants are generally smiling at SIS level 2 or 3 at much higher rates than in the absence of humor and do display SIS level 4 behaviors. The presence of these behaviors, then, was initially identified as a potentially relevant

Table 2: Percentage of SIS behaviors displayed with and without humor in conversation GV.

	G no humor	V no humor	G humor	V humor
SIS 0	82%	75%	22%	20%
SIS 1	3%	17%	11%	20%
SIS 2	10%	8%	25% (+150%)	46% (+475%)
SIS 3	5%	1%	29% (+480%)	12% (+1100%)
SIS 4	0%	0%	13%	3%

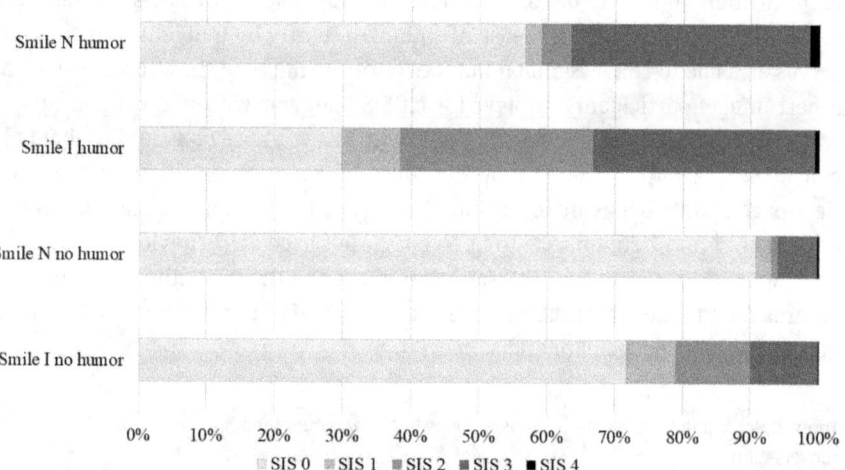

Figure 4: Distribution of SIS behaviors with and without humor in conversation NI.

cue to identify the presence of humor in conversation (but see below, as it was eventually rejected). Because a SIS level 4 behavior, a jaw-dropping laughing smile, tends to appear almost exclusively with humor, then the presence of this behavior could be employed as an *index* of humor (that is, an element that is not essential to the humor, not always co-occurring with it, and not intentionally signaling humor; see Gironzetti, 2017), but should be complemented by other cues to avoid cases of false negatives. In fact, this behavior characterizes only 8 out of 19 instances of humor in each conversation; if it were to be employed as the sole criterion to identify humor in a conversational corpus (that is, when there is SIS level 4, there is humor), half of the humor instances would not be identified as such. This poses a similar problem to the one the field is currently facing when laughter is selected as the sole criterion for the detection of humor in a corpus, since humor also exceeds laughter.

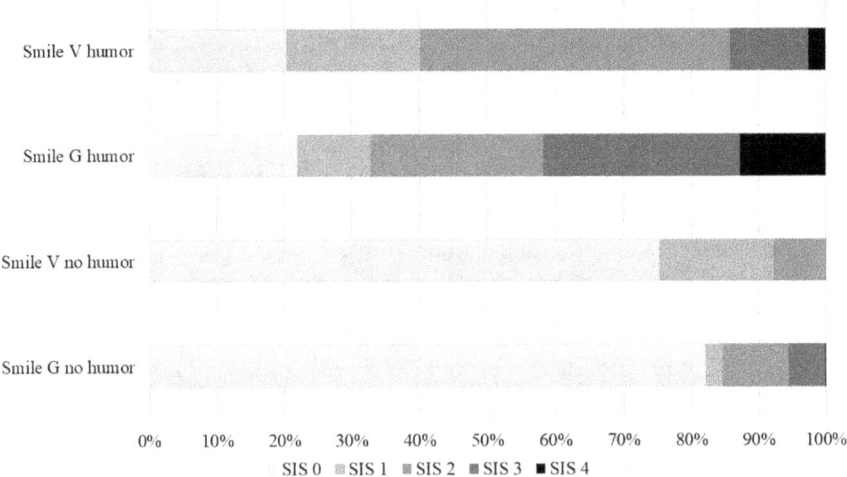

Figure 5: Distribution of SIS behaviors with and without humor in conversation GV.

An ideal candidate to be considered to complement or substitute SIS level 4 as a cue for conversational humor is the presence of SIS level 3 and SIS 2, as these behaviors co-occurred with humor more frequently than without humor (see Tables 1 and 2). To test whether each of these behaviors, independently or in combination, would be useful to identify humor in a conversational corpus, the annotations for SIS level 2, 3, and 4, and observed humor were compared. This initial analysis showed that using the presence of SIS level 4 behavior and either SIS level 2 or 3 behavior would lead to a large number of results that exceeded the number of humor instances in the corpus. Therefore, we can conclude that none of these individual smiling behaviors is, just by virtue of their presence, a reliable cue to identify humorous instances in a conversational corpus.

4.2 Smiling intensity matching as a cue for conversational humor

As a follow-up analysis, this study seeks to determine whether smiling intensity matching, a specific dyadic smiling behavior in which two speakers synchronize their smiling behavior at the same SIS level and at the same time (Gironzetti et al., 2016) can serve as a cue to identify humor in a conversation. The synchronicity data were employed to determine if it is possible to rely on smiling intensity matching by participants to identify humorous moments in the conversation. That is, since conversational partners tend to co-construct a humorous frame, which may last a few seconds, by means of synchronizing their smiling intensity and displaying the same smiling intensity at the same time, then this behavior could be employed to identify the presence of humor in a conversational corpus. Smiling matching intensity at SIS level 2 or higher was coded in a new, single tied called *Humor (Est.)*, to facilitate the comparison between observed instances of humor and estimated ones based on these smiling behaviors. Figures 6 and 7 represent the annotation density plots that illustrate the occurrence of instances of observed humor (based on the analysis of what participants said) and estimated humor (based on the presence of smiling intensity matching at SIS level 2 or higher).

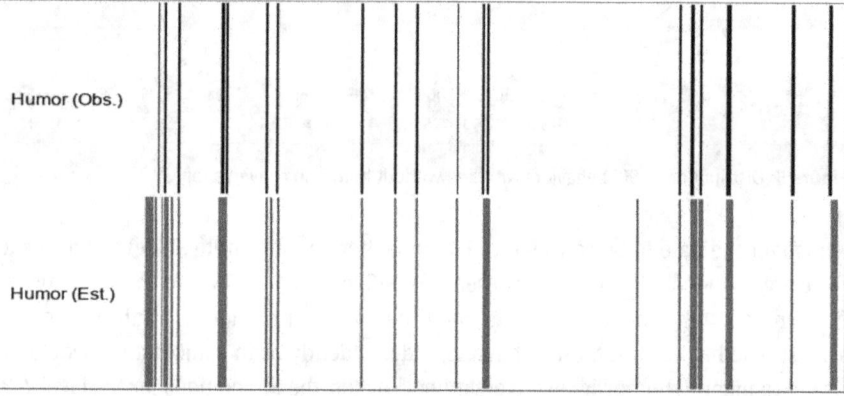

Figure 6: Density plot of annotations for humor (observed and estimated) in conversation GV.

As shown in Figure 6, all but one observed humorous instance in conversation GV correspond to and could be correctly estimated by relying on the presence of smiling intensity matching. The one false negative found when comparing the two annotations correspond to the first punchline told by one participant. In this case, the two interlocutors displayed a delayed increase of individual smiling intensity and matching that was not captured in the 5-second time window employed in this study. On the other hand, this method also led to some instances of false positives, that is, cases in which humor was estimated based on the smiling behavior of participants but was not observed based on the analysis of what was said. These were found at two moments during the conversation: at the very beginning of the conversation, before telling the first joke, when participants were getting acquainted with each other; and while discussing serious topics related to their life in the US. On both occasions, the two participants were displaying a lot of affiliative behaviors, including smiling.

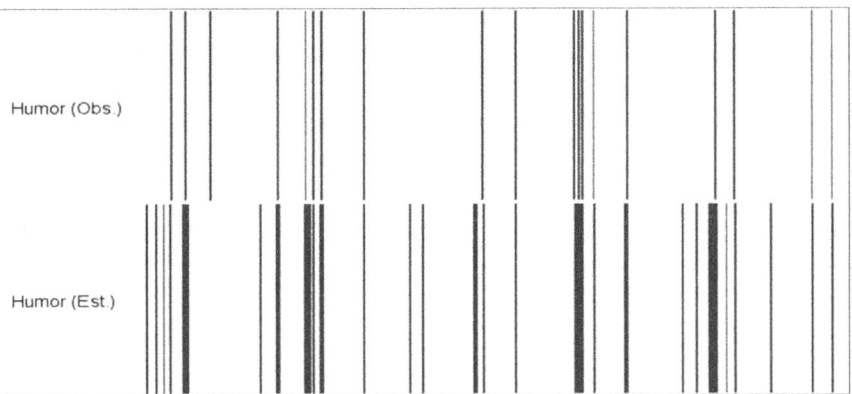

Figure 7: Density plot of annotations for humor (observed and estimated) in conversation NI.

When looking at the data for conversation NI in Figure 7, however, we see that there were more instances of false positive, and one instance of false negative. The latter, an instance of false negative in which no humor was estimated based on participants' smiling behavior, but was in fact present, represent a case of failed humor. In this particular example, one of the participants told the joke they were given as an ice breaker but none of the two participants recognized it was a joke (they interpreted it as a story with symbolism linked to myths and legends). Additionally, right after the delivery of the punchline, and likely due to her misinterpretation of the joke, the speaker continued talking about not humorous topics related to their interpretation of the joke / story, leaving virtually no time for the listener to act upon the humorous potential of the utterance.

The cases of false positive in conversation NI appeared at moments in the conversation that match what observed in conversation GV: when participants were smiling either in anticipation of or as a delayed response to an instance of humor; at the very beginning of the conversation, before telling the first joke, when participants were getting acquainted with each other, and while discussing non-humorous topics, when both participants were displaying affiliative behaviors, including smiling.

A follow-up analysis considered smiling intensity matching at SIS level 2 and 3 separately for each conversation since these appeared to be the two most relevant behaviors displayed by participants (Tables 1 and 2). This analysis was then complemented with an exploration of individual behavior at SIS 4, since this was found to be characteristic of conversational humor in the corpus, as summarized in Table 3. The data in Table 3 highlight the importance of smiling intensity matching at SIS level 2 and 3 over the contribution of SIS level 4 behaviors, while also underscoring dyadic differences that characterize each conversation. Regarding the first point, smiling intensity matching alone characterizes all but 2 instances of humor, but SIS level 4 alone only characterizes one instance of humor (GV 7), while in all other cases it co-occurs with smiling intensity matching. The two instances not marked by any of these behaviors (NI 3 and GV 1) represent one case of delayed smiling behavior (GV 1) and one case of failed humor (NI 3), as previously discussed. Regarding the second point, the data in Table 3 also show how each dyad is different from the other: the humorous interactions in conversation NI are generally characterized by intensity matching at SIS level 3 (17 out of 19 instances, or 89.5%), while in conversation GV humorous interactions are characterized by intensity matching at SIS 2 (14 out of 19, or 73.7%).

Table 3: Intensity matching and SIS 4 co-occurrences with humor.

Humor instances (keywords x 5000 msec)	Intensity Matching SIS level 2 (msec)	Intensity Matching SIS level 3 (msec)	Individual SIS level 4 (msec)
NI 1 (pocket)	153	288	–
NI 2 (cool)	591	978	268
NI 3 (donkey)	–	–	–
NI 4 (read)	–	1327	31
NI 5 (papers)	170	1104	302
NI 6 (book)	–	768	250
NI 7 (people)	–	2183	–
NI 8 (lockscreen)	–	1184	–
NI 9 (Guatemala)	331	551	–
NI 10 (yeah)	225	810	–
NI 11 (2019)	33	–	108
NI 12 (exist)	86	2319	212
NI 13 (passports)	2	862	–
NI 14 (that)	–	526	–
NI 15 (worst)	283	1330	–
NI 16 (cold)	–	385	565
NI 17 (place)	–	737	40
NI 18 (Korean)	–	1282	–

Table 3 (continued)

Humor instances (keywords x 5000 msec)	Intensity Matching SIS level 2 (msec)	Intensity Matching SIS level 3 (msec)	Individual SIS level 4 (msec)
NI 19 (Spanish)	–	899	–
GV 1 (burro)	–	–	–
GV 2 (princesa)	2464	–	–
GV 3 (mejor)	1949	–	–
GV 4 (escribir / decisiones)	1021	–	1733
GV 5 (letras)	786	–	–
GV 6 (cuentito)	108	54	–
GV 7 (lejano)	574	–	1033
GV 8 (vida)	–	–	298
GV 9 (caos)	–	847	584
GV 10 (mismo)	–	71	819
GV 11 (claramente)	378	–	–
GV 12 (igual)	55	510	–
GV 13 (mal)	2220	–	–
GV 14 (qué)	636	–	–
GV 15 (conociéndolo / gringo)	1138	431	453
GV 16 (molestaría)	692	1275	590
GV 17 (James / greencard) [x2]	–	778	8347
GV 18 (greencard)	2343	–	–
GV 19 (laboral)	1113	–	–

Note: all humor instances with one keyword correspond to 5000 msec segments of conversation. Those with more than one keyword represent cases in which several instances of humor were produced in close temporal proximity. Each segment duration is equal to 5000 msec per each keyword (e.g., GV 19 has three keywords and lasted 15000 msec).

5 Conclusions, limitations, and implications

The findings presented in the previous sections contribute to highlight the ways in which smiling can be employed as a multimodal cue to identify humor in a conversational corpus, as well as problematize the study of conversational humor and humor cues. The first set of findings related to each speaker's individual smiling intensity as a potential cue for conversational humor. This cue was found to be only marginally effective. In terms of ratio of occurrence of different smiling behaviors on the SIS, it looks like behaviors at SIS level 2, 3, and 4 are characteristic of conversational humor as these occur more frequently with humor than without humor in a conversation. In the same vein, behaviors at SIS level 0 (and less consistently at SIS level 1) occur more without humor than with humor and so can be interpreted to characterize non-humorous conversation. However, this positive result should be interpreted with caution because the presence of each of these behaviors alone, while it does characterize humor versus non-humor conversation, was not found to be a reliable cue to identify the presence of humor in the conversational corpus analyzed here. A SIS level 4 behavior is nearly exclusively occurring with humor in the corpus, but in about only half of all instances of humor identified through a pragmatic-semantic analysis, and therefore its use as the default humor cue is as problematic as the use of laughter, since humor exceeds SIS level 4 as it exceeds laughter. SIS level 3 and 2 behaviors are not exclusive of humor but also occur in non-humorous parts of conversation, which is why none of these behaviors by itself was found to be a reliable cue for conversational humor. In contrast to the results led by SIS level 4 behavior alone, however, all instances of humor could be identified by the presence of SIS level 2 or 3 behaviors, while also leading to a number of false positives. All these behaviors, then, were confirmed to serve as *humor markers* in the sense outlined in Gironzetti (2017), that is, as non-essential, not always co-occurring, and (potentially) intentional cues for conversational humor.

The analysis of smiling synchronicity and, more specifically, intensity matching, led to more positive and reliable results in contrast to the use of an increase in the individual SIS value as a cue for conversational humor. Using smiling intensity matching at SIS level 2 or 3, rather than simple the presence of SIS level 2 or 3 behaviors, added a constrain on the portions of conversation that could be identified as humorous, making the scope of the instrument narrower and so, potentially, limiting the number of false positives. In fact, in both conversations, the use of SIS level 2 or 3 intensity matching as a humor cue led to the correct identification of all successful humor instances and a limited number of false positives. Additionally, the comparative analysis of smiling intensity matching at SIS level 2 and 3, and individual smiling behavior at SIS level 4, highlighted the predictive power of smiling intensity matching over SIS level 4, as well as the importance of considering the degree of individual and dyadic differences: dyad NI relied mostly on smiling intensity matching at SIS level 3, while dyad GV relied more on smiling intensity matching at SIS level 2.

Regarding the first result, that is, that intensity matching at SIS level 2 or 3 led to no false negatives, the only instances of humor that could be identified by a pragmatic-semantic analysis but not by the presence of smiling intensity matching were instances of failed humor (in conversation NI) and one instance of successful humor with a delayed response that was not captured by the time window set up for the study (conversation GV). Future studies could then further explore the validity of this humor cue by employing time windows of different length to capture delayed responses as well as early displays. This initial positive result seems to indicate that smiling intensity matching at SIS level 2 or 3 could serve as a *humor indicator* in the sense described in Gironzetti (2017), that is, as a non-essential but always co-occurring and intentional cue for (successful) conversational humor. As such, this behavior has the potential to be employed to identify instances of successful humor in a conversational corpus. On the other hand, it is also worth considering the one case of failed humor as well as the (limited) number of false positives. In both conversations, false positives were identified at the very beginning of each conversation or when speakers were discussing personal and serious information. In all these cases, participants were displaying a large number of affiliative behaviors, verbally and non-verbally, such as nodding, repeating each other's words, agreeing with each other verbally, and so on. It is possible, then, that smiling intensity matching is a reliable humor cue in the case of successful and affiliative humor, but not disaffiliative humor, which was not present in the corpus analyzed here, or failed humor. Based on the findings, we could also hypothesize that affiliative social intentions trump conversational humor when it comes to displaying smiling intensity matching. That is, the primary function of smiling intensity matching could be affiliative, and it could also serve as a humor cue as a byproduct of its primary function in those cases in which humor is in fact affiliative.

Last, non-verbal behaviors convey multiple social meanings, and their use varies a lot depending on the people involved in the communication, their cultures, the setting (e.g., face-to-face or virtual), the topics being discussed, etc. For example, a recent study that looked at the display of affiliative behaviors such as smiling in face-to-face and video-mediated communication found that the virtual setting affects the display of smiling, with speakers smiling at a higher intensity (more animatedly), possibly emphasizing their behavior to reduce the distance between them that is exacerbated by the virtual setting of the conversations (Croes et al., 2019). Therefore, future research should also compare the value of smiling intensity matchings a humor cue across settings, topics (e.g., coding for the target or theme of humorous instances by applying the knowledge resources of Attardo and Raskin's GTVH, 1991), and the cultures to which speakers ascribe.

References

Abel, Ernest & Michael Kruger. 2010. Smile intensity in photographs predicts longevity. *Psychological Science* 21(4), 542–544.

Amoyal, Mary & Béatrice Priego-Valverde. 2019, September. Smiling for negotiating topic transitions in French conversation. In *GESPIN-Gesture and Speech in Interaction*. https://hal.science/hal-02321693.

Amoyal, Mary, Béatrice Priego-Valverde & Stephane Rauzy. 2020. PACO: A corpus to analyze the impact of common ground in spontaneous face-to-face interaction. In *Proceedings of the Twelfth Language Resources and Evaluation Conference*, 628–633, Marseille, France. European Language Resources Association.

Attardo, Salvatore. 2019. Humor and mirth: Emotions, embodied cognition, and sustained humor. In J. Lachlan Mackenzie & Laura Alba-Juez (eds.), *Emotion in Discourse*, 189–211. Amsterdam: John Benjamins.

Attardo, Salvatore & Lucy Pickering. 2011. Timing in the performance of jokes. *HUMOR – International Journal of Humor Research* 24(2), 233–250.

Attardo, Salvatore & Victor Raskin. 1991. Script theory revis(it)ed: Joke similarity and joke representation model. *HUMOR – International Journal of Humor Research* 4(3–4), 293–347. https://doi.org/10.1515/humr.1991.4.3-4.293.

Birdwhistell, Ray. 1970. *Kinesic and Context: Essays on Body Motion Communication*. Philadelphia: University of Pennsylvania Press.

Blurton Jones, Nicholas. 1971. Criteria for use in describing facial expressions of children. *Human Biology*, 365–413.

Croes, Emmelyn, Marjolijn Antheunis, Alexander Schouten & Emiel Krahmer. 2019. Social attraction in video-mediated communication: The role of nonverbal affiliative behavior. *Journal of Social and Personal Relationships* 36(4), 1210–1232. https://doi.org/10.1177/0265407518757382.

Ekman, Paul & Wallace Friesen. 1976. Measuring facial movement. *Environmental Psychology & Nonverbal Behavior* 1, 56–75. https://doi.org/10.1007/BF01115465.

Ekman, Paul & Wallace Friesen. 1978. *Facial Action Coding System: A Technique for the Measurement of Facial Movement*. Palo Alto: Consulting Psychologists Press.

Ekman, Paul, Richard Davidson & Wallace Friesen. 1990. The Duchenne smile: Emotional expression and brain physiology II. *Journal of Personality and Social Psychology* 58, 342–353.

Ekman, Paul, Wallace Friesen & Joseph Hager (eds.). 2002. *Facial Action Coding System*. Salt Lake City: Research Nexus.

Freese, Jeremy, Sheri Meland & William Irwin. 2006. Expressions of positive emotion in photographs, personality, and later-life marital and health outcomes. *Journal of Research in Personality* 41, 488–497. https://doi.org/10.1016/j.jrp.2006.05.006.

Gironzetti, Elisa. 2017. Prosodic and multimodal markers of humor. In Salvatore Attardo (ed.), *The Routledge Handbook of Language and Humor*, 400–413. New York/London: Routledge.

Gironzetti, Elisa 2021. Multimodal resources in the co-construction of humorous discourse. In Lori Czerwionka, Rachel Showstack & Judy Liskin-Gasparro (eds.), *Contexts of Co-Constructed Discourse: Interaction, Pragmatics, and Second Language Applications*, 115–135. New York/London: Routledge.

Gironzetti, Elisa. 2022. *The Multimodal Performance of Conversational Humor*. John Benjamins.

Gironzetti, Elisa, Lucy Pickering, Meichan Huang, Ying Zhang, Shigehito Menjo & Salvatore Attardo. 2016. Smiling synchronicity and gaze patterns in dyadic humorous conversations. *HUMOR – International Journal of Humor Research* 29(2), 301–324.

Gironzetti, Elisa, Salvatore Attardo & Lucy Pickering. 2019. Smiling and the negotiation of humor in conversation. *Discourse Processes* 56(7), 496–512.

Grant, Ewan. 1969. Human facial expression. *Man* 4, 525–536. https://doi.org/10.2307/2798193

Harker, LeeAnne and Dachner Keltner. 2001. Expressions of positive emotion in women's college yearbook pictures and their relationship to personality and life outcomes across adulthood. *Journal of Personality and Social Psychology* 80(1), 112–124. https://doi.org/10.1037/0022-3514.80.1.112.

Hertenstein, Mathew, Carrie Hansel, Alissa Butts & Sarah Hile. 2009. Smile intensity in photographs predicts divorce later in life. *Motivation and Emotion* 33(2), 99–105.

Kaczmarek, Lukasz, Maciej Behnke, Todd Kashdan, Aleksandra Kusiak, Katarzyna Marzec, Martyna Mistrzak & Magdalena Włodarczyk. 2018. Smile intensity in social networking profile photographs is related to greater scientific achievements. *The Journal of Positive Psychology* 13(5), 435–439.

Kaukomaa, Timo, Anssi Peräkylä & Johanna Ruusuvuori. 2013. Turn-opening smiles: Facial expression constructing emotional transition in conversation. *Journal of Pragmatics* 55, 21–42.

Kawulok, Michal, Jakub Nalepa, Jolanta Kawulok & Bogdan Smolka. 2021. Dynamics of facial actions for assessing smile genuineness. *PloSone* 16(1), e0244647. https://doi.org/10.1371/journal.pone.0244647

Lynn, John. 1940. An apparatus and method for stimulating, recording and measuring facial expression. *Journal of Experimental Psychology* 27(1), 81–88. https://doi.org/10.1037/h0058093

Pickering, Lucy, Marcela Corduas, Jody Eisterhold, Brenna Seifried, Alyson Eggleston & Salvatore Attardo. 2009. Prosodic markers of saliency in humorous narratives. *Discourse Processes* 46(6), 517–540. https://doi.org/10.1080/01638530902959604.

Priego-Valverde, Béatrice, Brigitte Bigi, Salvatore Attardo, Lucy Pickering & Elisa Gironzetti. 2018. Is smiling during humor so obvious? A cross-cultural comparison of smiling behavior in humorous sequences in American English and French interactions. *Intercultural Pragmatics* 15(4), 563–591.

Priego-Valverde, Béatrice, Brigitte Bigi & Mary Amoyal. 2020. "Cheese!": a Corpus of Face-to-face French Interactions. A Case Study for Analyzing Smiling and Conversational Humor. In *Proceedings of the 12th Language Resources and Evaluation Conference*, 467–475. Marseille, France: European Language Resource Association.

Rychlowska, Magdalena, Rachael Jack, Oliver Garrod, Philippe Schyns, Jared Martin & Paula Niedenthal. 2017. Functional smiles: Tools for love, sympathy, and war. *Psychological science* 28(9), 1259–1270.

Stewart, Patrick, Erik Bucy & Marc Mehu. 2015. Strengthening bonds and connecting with followers: A biobehavioral inventory of political smiles. *Politics and the Life Sciences* 34(1), 73–92. https://doi.org/10.1017/pls.2015.5.

Young, Gerald & Therese Décarie. 1977. An ethology-based catalogue of facial/vocal behaviour in infancy. *Animal Behaviour* 25(1), 95–107. https://psycnet.apa.org/doi/10.1016/0003-3472(77)90071-9.

Wittenburg, Peter, Hennie Brugman, Albert Russel, Alex Klassmann & Han Sloetjes. 2006. ELAN: a Professional Framework for Multimodality Research. In *Proceedings of the Fifth International Conference on Language Resources and Evaluation*. Genoa, Italy: European Language Resources Association.

Hilal Ergül, Shelby Miller, Salvatore Attardo and Kevin Kramer
4 Alternative conceptualizations of the Smiling Intensity Scale (SIS) and their applications to the identification of humor

Abstract: In this paper we discuss two development of the smiling intensity scale (SIS), a scale developed to assess the intensity of smiling (with laughter as the upper end of the scale). SIS has several advantages, vis-à-vis using the Facial Action Coding System (FACS), including being simpler and faster to implement and notably cheaper, while being equally detailed. Two new versions of SIS, which are considerably simpler to implement than the original SIS (SIS-1) are presented. SIS-1 was implemented training in FACS judges who then ranked the smiles using the holistic SIS choices. SIS-2 presents a visual scale of smiling persons which is used for ranking. SIS-3 is based on a set of yes/no questions, such as "is this person's mouth open?" Thus, both SIS-2 and SIS-3 require minimal training. Both SIS-2 and SIS-3 were tested and found to be very reliable. Use of a training video before rating using SIS-3 did not improve performance, thus showing that training judges for SIS-3 is unnecessary. SIS-2 and SIS-3 are freely available.

Keywords: smiling, laughter, Smiling Intensity Scale, SIS, Facial Action Coding System (FACS)

The Smiling Intensity Scale (SIS; Gironzetti, Attardo, and Pickering 2016; 2019) was developed to allow a quick and simplified coding of the intensity of smiles. Smiling is a very common facial expression. In fact, Calvo et al. (2014) and Girard et al. (2015b) claim it is the most frequent facial expression (with considerable individual and cultural variation, needless to say; Fang et al. 2020). Intuitively, smiles come in different levels of intensity. From a linguistic standpoint, the intensity of a smile (as well as its synchrony) may function as a humor marker (e.g., Gironzetti et al. 2019). From a psychological perspective, how intensely a person smiles in photos may even determine various life outcomes such as personal wellbeing (Harker and Keltner 2001), marital success (Hertenstein et al. 2009), life satisfaction (Seder and Oishi 2012), and longevity (Abel and Kruger 2010).

Generally, smiling and its intensity are described using the Facial Action Coding System (FACS; Ekman and Friesen 1978). FACS is an anatomically based rating system that breaks down facial expressions based on the muscles and contractions involved in them. Each of these individual muscle contractions are called an action unit (AU). FACS is the standard for measuring facial expressions especially in the field of psychology. However, FACS requires weeks of training (50 to 100 hours of self-training: https://www.paulekman.com/facial-action-coding-system/), and certification is relatively expensive: the training is followed by a paid certification process (the test by itself costs $50), for example, one study reports "80 hours of study and passing a reliability test" (Oveis et al. 2009: 3). An online course, endorsed by Ekman, is available for the cost of $990 (https://www.erikarosenberg.com/facs-training). Moreover, one needs more than a single rater, thus increasing the cost. Working with FACS also requires high quality images and videos for raters to be able to spot the sometimes minute actions in the face and can otherwise result in loss of data (e.g., Cross and Pressman 2020). AU 6, for instance, called the cheek raiser and lid compressor, denotes the movement of the orbicularis oculi, which in a simplified sense gives the impression of crow's feet around the eyes when activated. It accounts for the genuineness of the smile if accompanied by AU 12, the lip corner puller (i.e., a Duchenne smile e.g., Ekman et al. 1990). AU 6 is quite difficult to rate without a baseline for the subject's skin creases (if any) around the eyes in their natural state (e.g., Abel and Kruger 2010), and requires the absence of any physical or digital obstructions (e.g., Freese et al. 2007).

Research that uses smiling intensity as a measure in empirical studies reveals the need for a new system of measurement that is simpler, less expensive, and less time consuming while being equally (if not more) reliable and, ideally, detailed.

1 Literature Review

The need for a less complex rating system is shown for example in Tidd and Lockard (1978). In their experiment into whether different degrees of smiling could turn a monetary profit in terms of drinks ordered and larger tips (the tips were larger, but not the drink orders!), used only a 'minimal' and a 'maximal' smile, which they respectively defined as "mouth corners noticeably turned up but no teeth showing" (344) and "mouth corners turned up to extensively expose the closed front teeth in a 'natural' appearing broad smile" (344). The accuracy and consistency of the measurement seemingly depended solely on the participant observer's (a 23-year old female server) performance of the two smiles. Barger and Grandey (2006) expanded on this methodology for service encounters by dubbing these smiles levels 1 and 2 respectively, and adding a rating of 0 for no smiling. They provided their 40 coders a 75–minute training session and gave them four weeks to complete a norming procedure which involved 10–12 visits to campus establishments. Similarly yet independently, Abel and Kruger (2010) employed a relatively simple classification: no smile, partial smile (AU 12 only), or full (Duchenne) smile (AUs 6 and 12), therefore putting non-genuine smiles on a continuum with genuine smiles. While there was no mention of any FACS training other than using FACS terminology in their methodology, they did train their raters on how to classify the smiles. The duration of the training was not mentioned. The significant findings of Abel and Kruger (2010), and perhaps their methodology as well, were later contested when a replication study (i.e., Dufner et al. 2018) using the same database failed to reach similar results. Abel and Kruger's methodology has also been used in other studies as a measure of smiling intensity (e.g., Kaczmarek et al. 2018; Cross and Pressman 2020).

Harker and Keltner (2001) added the intensity scores (on a 5-point scale) of FACS AUs 6 and 12 together in order to create "a continuous measure of positive emotional expression" (115). This yields a scale ranging from 2 (if both AU are at the minimum intensity of 1) to 10 (if both AU are at maximum intensity). Intensity is scored using letters A through E in FACS, but transformation in numerical scores is trivial.

This meant that an AU of 12 with the weakest intensity (one) on the 5-point scale (barely a smile) with an extremely intense AU 6 would be scored equally intense as a level three intensity smile with a level three intensity raising of the cheeks. The latter would look like a regular and moderate warm smile while the former would look like a nearsighted person trying to read a sign half a mile away. As such, while trying to duplicate this study, Freese et al. (2007) tried this additive continuous measure of AUs 6 and 12, and upon failing to reach interrater reliability despite extensive training and the supervision of a certified FACS coder, they resolved to focus instead on whether the participants smiled and whether it was a Duchenne smile. Similarly to Freese et al. (2007), in a test of smiling intensity in relation to physical dominance and the perception thereof, Kraus and Chen (2013) changed the Harker and Keltner (2001) system as they needed to focus exclusively on AU 12 because "the fighters primarily displayed smiles using the lips (zygomatic major muscle) and rarely using the muscles surrounding the eyes (obicularis [sic] oculi muscles)" (272). Their smiling intensity scale therefore consisted of 0 (neutral face), 1 (moderate pulling up of lip corners with no teeth), and 2 (full contraction of the lip corner puller muscle, showing teeth). Despite its practical challenges, the Harker and Keltner (2001) methodology for measuring smiling intensity to predict success (or lack thereof) in different areas of life became the norm for a number of studies (e.g., Hertenstein et al. 2009; Oveis et al. 2009; Seder and Oishi 2012).

Other research uses different approaches to incorporating FACS into their own systems. Wang et al. (2015) also adopted FACS to determine smiling intensity, but the intensity of the AUs as per FACS played a minimal role, mainly to distinguish between 3 of the 6 intensity levels identified. Instead, their smiling intensity scale consisted of a combination of AUs 6, 12, and 25 (i.e., lips parted). More specifically, the six levels were: "no AU activation (neutral expression), AU12 (level 1), AU12 + AU25 (level 2), AU6 + AU12 + AU25 (level 3), AU6 + AU12B + AU25 (level 4), and AU6 + AU12C + AU25 (maximal smile)." The capital letters B and C that follow the AU numbers mark the intensity level of the AU. This is much like SIS, except SIS is more detailed in how many of the AUs from FACS it takes into account (see Appendix A). In a later study, focused on participant perceptions of smiles, Wang et al. (2016) only used level 2 (slight) and level 5 (broad) smiles from the scale they developed, thus reducing the capacity to discriminate between degrees of intensity. Fang et al. (2020), took a completely different approach to determining the intensity of smiles that displayed AUs 6 and 12; they asked untrained individuals to rate the intensity to classify their stimuli for use in a test of cultural perceptions of smiling.

Considering the difficulties discussed in the literature review, the cost of the training in FACS (especially in time), and the difficulty of applying intensity scoring to less-than-high-quality video data, we propose two versions of SIS that do not require any training and can therefore be employed more easily in any type of research that needs to determine the intensity of smiles.

2 The Smiling Intensity Scale (SIS)

SIS is largely based on FACS (Ekman and Friesen 1978). It has been successfully deployed in a number of published studies (Gironzetti et al. 2016; Priego-Valverde et al. 2018; Amoyal and Priego-Valverde 2019; Rauzy and Amoyal 2020; Rauzy et al. 2022) and in a few unpublished ones. In this chapter, we introduce alternative conceptualizations for SIS (henceforth SIS-1), which is a 5-point scale with verbal descriptions. The alternatives that we introduce, which we refer to as SIS-2 and SIS-3, are an image scale and feature breakdown sequence respectively. We use SIS to refer to the underlying system regardless of its application paradigm. SIS-1 was developed originally in 2013 as an in-house tool in the Applied Linguistics lab, at Texas A&M-Commerce, to address the concern of low-quality video recording, which made FACS analysis very difficult, since it was quite hard to discern fine muscular features, and the additive nature of the intensity measure developed in (Harker and Keltner 2001) requires being able to determine the intensity of AU 6 and AU 12.

It should be noted in passing that none of the SIS scales aim to account directly for Duchenne displays (i.e., whether the smile is felt or social) as smiling intensity is independent from its sincerity. From a communicative standpoint, it matters little whether the person means the smile (Attardo 2019), and untrained speakers presumably lack the capability of distinguishing between a genuine and non-genuine smile, at least consciously. However, there is some evidence that intensity may determine judgments of sincerity of the smile (Fang et al. 2020). It should be noted that one could, if so desired, reconstruct the Duchenne status of the smile in SIS-3, which contains a question about the orbicularis oculi contraction (AU 6).

One of the problems of the deployment of SIS-1 as it was originally delineated is that it is worded and presented in terms of FACS action units (AU) and thus requires intensive training in FACS. This has not been an issue if the raters were trained in (or at least aware of) FACS, but it obviously makes the learning curve that much steeper. In our experience, training a rater requires several days of intensive work and testing, at a bare minimum. One could argue that it is not necessary to learn all the AUs of FACS to code for SIS-1, since only seven of them (AU6, AU7, AU12, AU14, AU25, AU26, AU27) are used (see Gironzetti et al. 2016), but the bulk of the learning is obviously understanding how FACS works. Not having to remember AU 19 ("tongue show") does not really decrease the effort of learning FACS. To the best of our knowledge, SIS-1 has been used only by researchers who were certified, or had ample opportunity to familiarize themselves with FACS and with SIS-1 and had read the relevant literature.

The purpose of this chapter is to document two attempts at creating a version of SIS that could be administered to participants without any prior FACS training and ideally any training at all. In our study, the written description of smiling levels derived by Gironzetti et al. (2016; 2019) are referred to as SIS-1. The two versions of SIS we developed and describe in this paper are referred to as SIS-2 and SIS-3.

In SIS-2, we replace AU training with the presentation of a sample visual scale with the five levels of SIS exemplified by five different people. In SIS-3, we use simple yes/no questions that correspond to the diagnostic aspects of the facial expressions, such as "Is the mouth open?", "Are the bottom teeth visible?". SIS-2 does not require any training at all. SIS-3 does require a minimal amount of training, which will be described below. In particular, in order to streamline the data collection task, we wanted to develop a version of SIS that could be used in a context similar to that of Amazon's Mechanical Turk (henceforth MTurk), in which participants are recruited online and they perform the rating tasks from their devices.

MTurk has been found to be a reliable and valid crowdsourcing platform for research (Sheehan 2018). While validity questions have been raised as to the use of MTurk for psychological research, Chmielewski and Kucker (2020) concluded that response validity indicators as well as screening the answers can compensate for these concerns.

We developed SIS-2 and SIS-3 to meet these requirements and ran a few pilot studies to refine the selection of images and the wording of the questions. We also had to develop a set of attention checkers: since the MTurk participants are not physically present in a laboratory and are mercenaries, we cannot assume that they are invested, even minimally, in the success of the experiment (as most experimental research does, implicitly). We found that by inserting a small number (>5%) of attention checkers, we were able to reject those users who "clicked through" the questions without really paying attention. We also rejected all incomplete submissions (missing answers). Overall, we rejected a fairly large number of submissions (up to 61% of the raw responses collected) but given the relatively low cost of collecting data on MTurk, this was not a problem. We describe these processes in some detail below.

The chapter presents some preliminary results about the reliability of SIS-2 and SIS-3 that show encouraging results on both approaches. We should clarify, as Artstein and Poesio (2008) remind us, that reliability (in this case agreement of the coders) is a prerequisite for validity but not a guarantee of it (after all, the coders could be consistently wrong). So, we make no claim, in this context, of internal, external, or construct validity (Trochim 2022) of SIS, but merely of its reliability, i.e., its capacity to produce the same results. To be clear, external validity is the generalizability of the experiment and its tools to other situations, samples, or populations. In our case, we may want to test the external validity of the SIS by using it in a different culture/language (e.g., Priego-Valverde et al. 2018). Internal validity generally refers to how well-constructed a study is. i.e., whether it eliminates or accounts for spurious variables. Construct validity refers to whether SIS accurately describes the intensity of smiling and not of something else (for example, we may be describing the degree of opening of the mouth, rather than smiling). The way one would go about showing the construct validity of SIS would most likely be through convergent validity, i.e., we would show that SIS matches real-world perceptions of smiling intensity, or through predictive validity, i.e., SIS makes predictions about ratings that match the actual ratings collected by naive participants.

3 The development of SIS-2

SIS-1 contained a set of photographs, taken from actual data, of one speaker producing exemplars of the facial expressions we targeted. This was provided as a help for the raters, but the images had no theoretical or practical status. In SIS-2 we took full advantage of the idea of a visual scale.

We created a photo scale representing the SIS-1 descriptions by taking photos of individuals producing each of the five SIS levels to (see Figure 1).

Figure 1: SIS photo scale.

This photo scale was then used as an instrument in our first study, SIS-2. For this study, a photo of a person would be displayed in conjunction with the photo scale and participants would be asked: "Consider the large image above; which of the row of images [which image from the scale] does it best match in terms of the size of the smile?". We collected images to be judged from various stock photo websites (e.g., pexels.com, pixabay.com). The stock photos had to meet the following parameters. First, the people in the images had to be adults. No images of children were used or of seniors. People in the images had nothing obstructing their face (e.g., glasses, hands, heavy facial hair), to make the features easier to assess. The individuals also had to be facing the camera, meaning no extreme side views. The second author collected the images, and then the images were reviewed by the other researchers for quality (i.e., whether they met the SIS level criteria). Twenty-eight images were identified, five representing each SIS level and three representing other emotional states (sadness, anger, and surprise) to serve as attention checkers (see Appendix B). Images were cropped, adjusted for head tilting, and resized to a square canvas (7.5x7.5 in inches). The photos were zoomed in so that the person's philtrum (medial cleft) was roughly the center of the canvas, and the face measured at 6 inches tall (chin to hairline) in each photo. The canvas was then expanded to 7.5x8.5 in inches, leaving room underneath each photo for the photo scale.

The survey information was then compiled in Qualtrics (this is also true of all the following surveys discussed) and consisted of an informed consent form, short demographic survey, and the 28 photos to be rated on a one question scale per photo. The informed consent stated that the task would take approximately 10 minutes to complete (based on data from pilots), and that participants in this study would receive $0.25 for their participation (paid through MTurk). This is an average compensation on MTurk (Hara et al. 2018). The demographic survey (which was used throughout all of the following studies) asked for age range, gender, ethnicity, and languages spoken. The photos were randomized and evenly presented. In order to optimize the Qualtrics survey for mobile device use as well as for computers, both the image to be rated and the visual scale displayed together on the screen, while scrolling down would reveal the SIS level options (see Figure 2). Only one photo and question were displayed on the screen at a time. A different scale and question were used for the three attention checkers (also see Figure 2).

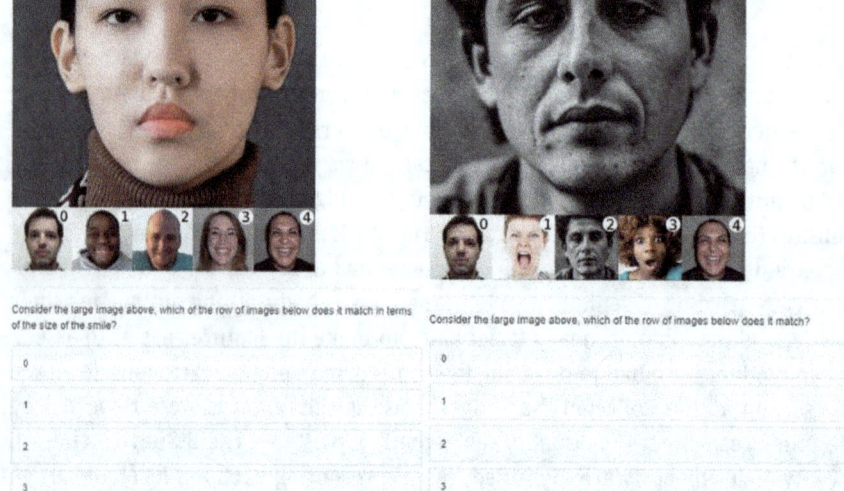

Figure 2: Example of SIS-2 screen display and attention checker photo scale.

The survey was then distributed via MTurk. The survey (as well as the following MTurk surveys) was only visible and open to MTurk workers that had previously completed 100 HITs (i.e. Human Intelligence Tasks, as "jobs" are called on MTurk) with at least a 95% approval rating by requesters like ourselves. For IRB purposes, the workers also needed to be located in the U.S. Moreover, we included a requirement for normal to corrected vision in the informed consent form so any visually impaired MTurk participants would be aware that technology such as screen readers would not be helpful for this particular HIT. This survey collected 2203 responses, of which 1,276 (58%) were used in the data analysis (i.e., 928 surveys were either incomplete or failed at least one attention checker). It should be noted that in every survey we discuss, the protocol was to remove surveys that failed even one attention checker. The data analysis (discussed elsewhere in this chapter) showed nine images performed poorly in this survey.

Based on this information, we made several strategic changes to the SIS-2 survey, many of which were for the purpose of improving the accessibility of the images on mobile devices. First, we zoomed each of the 28 photos and on the SIS photo scale (see Figure 3 for comparison). Secondly, the data collected from the first survey indicated that participants struggled to accurately identify Level 2 (L2) images, so we changed the L2 SIS photo scale image to an image that would be more discernible on a mobile device and also reflected a similar smile intensity as our other L2 photos (scale difference also reflected in Figure 3).

Figure 3: Comparison of photos from the first SIS-2 survey and the second SIS-2 survey.

Next, we replaced one L3 image (Image BB) with a different photo because facial aspects of the original image (specifically the lower teeth) may have been hard to discern on smaller devices. Before we ran the survey for the second time, we ran several pilot studies to test various aspects of our instrument, specifically working to refine the bank of 28 photos. We replaced several images of our prior 28 photos, specifically L3 images E and Z, all five L2 images (B, D, H, U, V), and L1 images Q, S, and T (see Appendix C). Apart from these changes, the survey format and questions remained identical to the first SIS-2 survey (i.e., "size of the smile"). The informed consent procedures information was updated to state that the task should take approximately 7 minutes to complete, but participants would have up to 15 minutes to complete it, and that participants would receive $0.20 for their participation. The survey ran again on MTurk and collected 2,144 responses, of which 1,228 (57%) were used in the data analysis (i.e., 43% were either incomplete or failed at least one attention checker).

4 The development of SIS-3

Concurrently, we began developing a third survey, labeled as SIS-3. SIS-3 itself consisted of two studies.

4.1 The first SIS-3 study

The first study was an exploration of how well people could analyze diagnostic aspects of facial expressions pertaining to the scale without being given explicit instruction on the SIS scale. Since this survey was being devised during the first version of SIS-2, this first version of SIS-3 utilized the original 28 photos (see Appendix B) from SIS-2 (minus the photo scale). Apart from the three attention checkers, each of the 25 primary photos were presented alongside nine questions that pertained to the various SIS levels (see Table 1). The three attention checkers were only accompanied with Q1 and Q9.

Table 1: Original SIS-3 Survey Questions.

Survey Question	L0	L1	L2	L3	L4
Q1. Is this person smiling?	No	Yes	Yes	Yes	Yes
Q2. Are one or both corners of the mouth of this person pulled back?	No	Yes	Yes	Yes	Yes
Q3. Are there wrinkles at the outer corner of this person's eyes (crow's feet)?	Can Be	Can Be	Can Be	Yes	Yes
Q4. Is this person's mouth open?	Can Be	No	Yes	Yes	Yes

Table 1 (continued)

Survey Question	L0	L1	L2	L3	L4
Q5. Are this person's upper teeth visible?	No	No	Yes	Yes	Yes
Q6. Are both this person's upper and lower teeth visible?	No	No	No	Can Be	Yes
Q7. Is this person's jaw dropped?	No	No	No	No	Yes
Q8. Is there a gap between this person's lower and upper teeth?	No	No	No	Can Be	Yes
Q9. Is this person laughing?	No	No	No	No	Yes

Much like SIS-2, only one photo and one question were presented on the screen at a time, which meant that apart from the introduction, demographic survey, and informed consent pages, the survey images/questions totaled 231 pages. We piloted the instrument and made adjustments to the wording of Q4, Q7, Q8, and Q9 (see Table 2).

Table 2: Updated SIS-3 Survey Questions.

Survey Question	L0	L1	L2	L3	L4
Q1. Is this person smiling?	No	Yes	Yes	Yes	Yes
Q2. Are one or both corners of the mouth of this person pulled back?	No	Yes	Yes	Yes	Yes
Q3. Are there wrinkles at the outer corner of this person's eyes (crow's feet)?	Can Be	Can Be	Can Be	Yes	Yes
Q4. Are this person's lips parted?	Can Be	No	Yes	Yes	Yes
Q5. Are this person's upper teeth visible?	No	No	Yes	Yes	Yes
Q6. Are both this person's upper and lower teeth visible?	No	No	No	Can Be	Yes
Q7. Is this person's jaw dropped / mouth gaping open?	No	No	No	No	Yes
Q8. Is there a gap between this person's lower and upper teeth?	No	No	No	Can Be	Yes
Q9. Is this among the biggest laughs that this person could produce?	No	No	No	No	Yes

Again, since the SIS-3 study was taking place concurrently with the SIS-2 studies, before we ran SIS-3 a second time, the 28 images were updated to match the final set of images being used in SIS-2 (see Appendix C). The informed consent stated that the task would take approximately 35 minutes to complete, but participants would have up to 45 minutes to complete it, and that participants in this study would receive $0.50 for their participation.

This second run of SIS-3 collected 1,577 responses, of which 611 (39%) were used in the data analysis (i.e., 61% were either incomplete or failed at least one attention checker).

As stated above, SIS-3 consisted of two studies. We now turn to the second study.

4.2 The SIS-3 conversational data analysis

The second SIS-3 survey was made up of only ten images (2 images reflecting each SIS level; see Appendix D) and a SIS training video. In this experiment, we analyzed stills from dyadic conversational data, in which participants engaged in a joint task (to assemble a puzzle), but then continued with open conversation. The purpose of the experiment was to deploy SIS-3 in a naturalistic environment, using a very small number of raters (two groups of two raters; n = 4) who rated independently the same set of data. One group was asked to watch an 18-minute training video on SIS-3. The raters were graduate students of Linguistics, and so could be assumed to have some basic aptitude at scoring data, but had no training in SIS, except in the case of the video training group.

The original data from which the 10 images were drawn were collected by one of the authors during her dissertation research (Miller, 2019) but are here re-analyzed from the angle of the smiling behavior of the participants. Her data consisted of 16 dyadic conversations (32 different participants), each lasting about 10 minutes. The speakers were all native speakers of English and evenly distributed for gender. Thirty out of 36 participants are under the age of 44, but only 44% of all participants are students or associated with the university. The still images captured from this data set only had to meet the parameters of having the speakers in the video facing the camera or at least in a profile view (in other words, the participants' faces were not angled away from the camera). Since the still images were pulled from live interactions (rather than posed photos), the parameters were different from the parameters we used for selecting images for SIS-2 (e.g., no extreme side views). One researcher (Author 2) extracted the images, which were then reviewed by the other researchers to confirm whether they met the SIS level criteria. The images were resized and zoomed in on a 6x6 canvas. These ten images were situated in Qualtrics in the same format and alongside the same questions from the first SIS-3 survey. The informed consent stated that the task would take approximately 20–40 minutes depending on whether or not the participant was assigned to watch the training video. Participants in this study did not receive compensation.

5 Reliability statistics

5.1 SIS-2 reliability testing

The SIS-2 questionnaire required respondents to match an image to one of five increasing degrees of smiling. A partial credit model was used in which the correct answer was assigned two points. If the participant's selection was off by one level either above or below the correct answer, one point was given. No points were given for answers greater than one level from the correct answer. There were 1228 subjects, and there were no missing data.

Again, WINSTEPS® software was used to fit the data to a partial credit Rasch model. Two images were found to be misfit using the ZSTD criteria—image R with a ZSTD of 3.89 and image B with a ZSTD of 2.10. The Andrich thresholds between partial credit points were −.62 and 62. Cronbach's alpha for internal reliability was 90.

5.2 SIS-3 reliability testing

The SIS-3 MTurk survey consisted of nine dichotomously scored questions (yes/no) for each of the 25 images. It was noted after the survey that an image had been improperly labeled and therefore, it was removed from further analysis. There were no missing data for the remaining images, and there were 611 subjects.

Using the software, WINSTEPS® (Version 4.7.1, Winsteps.com, Beaverton, OR USA), the questionnaire was evaluated for misfitting items and reliability. The analysis of item fit statistics was based on the WINSTEPS® standardized fit index, outfit ZSTD, which is thought to be the better choice for assessing fit (Smith 2004). The cutoff chosen for misfit was greater than 2.0 for outfit ZSTD.

A Rasch dichotomous model was used since the items all had yes/no response sets. Twenty-six out of the 216 items were misfit based on ZSTD. Four of nine questions were misfitting for image W, while three of nine questions were misfitting for images F and M. Cronbach's alpha for internal reliability was measured at 93.

In summary, both SIS-1 and SIS-2 were found to have items with good fit to the relevant Rasch model and were very reliable.

5.3 SIS-3 Experiment 2 reliability testing

As we saw, in this experiment, we analyzed stills from dyadic conversational data, in a naturalistic environment, using only two groups of two raters (n = 4). Rating was done independently. One group was asked to watch an 18-minute training video on SIS-3 whereas the control group had no video and no other training in SIS.

We calculated two Cronbach alpha scores, using the cronbach.alpha function in the package "ltm" in R (Rizopoulos 2006): the training video condition yielded an alpha of 0.81, while the group that had not seen the training video had an alpha of 0.84. Thus both groups achieved a good level of internal consistency. The difference between the two alphas, calculated using the cocron package (Diedenhofen 2016) was not significant (p = 0.95), hence we conclude that the training video had no impact on the performance. We also tested inter rater reliability, using the kappa2 function in the irr R package (Gamer 2012) within each group: the group who watched the training video had a kappa of 0.68, whereas the group with no training video had a kappa of 0.73 (both had significant p values).

Hence, we conclude that even when deployed in a more naturalistic environment (small number of raters; graduate students; conversational data) SIS-3 performed reasonably well, albeit less well than in the MTurk data. The use of a short training video had no significant effect on the performance of the graduate students raters and thus is probably unnecessary. This reinforces our conclusion that SIS-3 can be successfully deployed with untrained raters.

6 Discussion

We have explained in some detail the various steps we undertook to develop a satisfactory alternative to SIS-1 that would not require the extensive and expensive training required for SIS-1. The results of the first two experiments show that 1) using a visual comparison scale (SIS-2) is an effective tool for ratings of smiling intensity using untrained personnel; 2) using simple yes/no questions (SIS-3) can substitute the visual scale with minimal loss of reliability. The third experiment shows that using SIS-3 in a naturalistic setting (i.e., having untrained graduate students rate still images from a conversational video) still results in good internal consistency.

We believe that SIS-2 and SIS-3 can thus be useful tools for researchers wishing to explore smiling intensity using raters. The tools will be made available for free to any interested researchers. Further research is being planned. For example, it would be interesting to see whether, when SIS-2 and SIS-3 are applied to the same set of naturalistic data, the results are convergent. Further refinements of the tools may also be envisaged.

One of the uses that SIS can be put to is the identification of humor in interaction. There is growing evidence that, while smiling per se is not a reliable marker of the presence of humor, the matching (synchrony) of smiling intensity is a much better indicator (Gironzetti 2022; [this volume]). Assuming that this correlation is definitely proven, the presence of smiling intensity "agreement" could be used as a factor in the triangulation process of identifying humor (Attardo, 2012). For example, the researcher may flag all suspected instances of humor and then hire a number of raters to score the smiling intensity of all the participants. The use of Krippendorff' alpha measure (Krippendorff 2004) would allow treating data sets with missing responses and any number of raters and thus to determine if there is a sufficient agreement that two or more speakers are smiling at the same level of intensity. We are planning to explore the feasibility of such an approach in further research.

7 Conclusions

We have demonstrated that it is possible to construct easily implemented, low-cost alternatives to SIS-1 that are reliable and consistent. This is a desideratum for scholars wishing to validate their analyses of smiling intensity using groups of raters, either in environments like MTurk or in more traditional settings in which one's students/assistants are recruited to do so. Furthermore, we have demonstrated that it is possible to achieve high levels of reliability in the assessment of smiling intensity without any training whatsoever (in fact, watching the 18-minute training video *worsened* the performance of the raters, albeit not significantly).

In this article we did not address a completely different approach to smiling intensity rating, which consists of using facial analysis software to perform the task, thus largely bypassing human raters (Girard et al. 2015a/b; Lee et al. 2015; Rauzy and Amoyal 2020), albeit not entirely, as the systems have to be trained using manually annotated samples. While arguably cheaper and as easily implemented as SIS-2 or SIS-3, software-based processing has its own set of issues, starting with the fact that implementing this method requires significant computational expertise. Another issue that is not addressed in SIS (nor in any of the other methods of assessing smiling intensity discussed in the paper) is the relative speed of onset of the smile (Krumhuber and Kappas 2005) which have been shown to have an impact on the perception of authenticity (Krumhuber and Manstead 2009) and hence may have an impact on the perception of intensity (e.g., Hess et al. 1989). Conversely, there is research that shows that intensity is a strong clue of authenticity (see a review in Fang et al. 2020: 296) with more intense smiles being perceived as more authentic.

Appendix A

List of AUs considered in SIS-1

Level	Description	AUs considered in SIS-1
0	No smile	6, 7, 12, 14, 25, 26
1	Closed mouth smile	6, 7, 12, 14
2	Open mouth smile	6, 7, 12, 14, 25
3	Wide open mouth smile	6, 7, 12, 14, 25, 26
4	Laughing smile	6, 7, 12, 14, 25, 26, 27

Appendix B

Summary of Images, 1st Edition

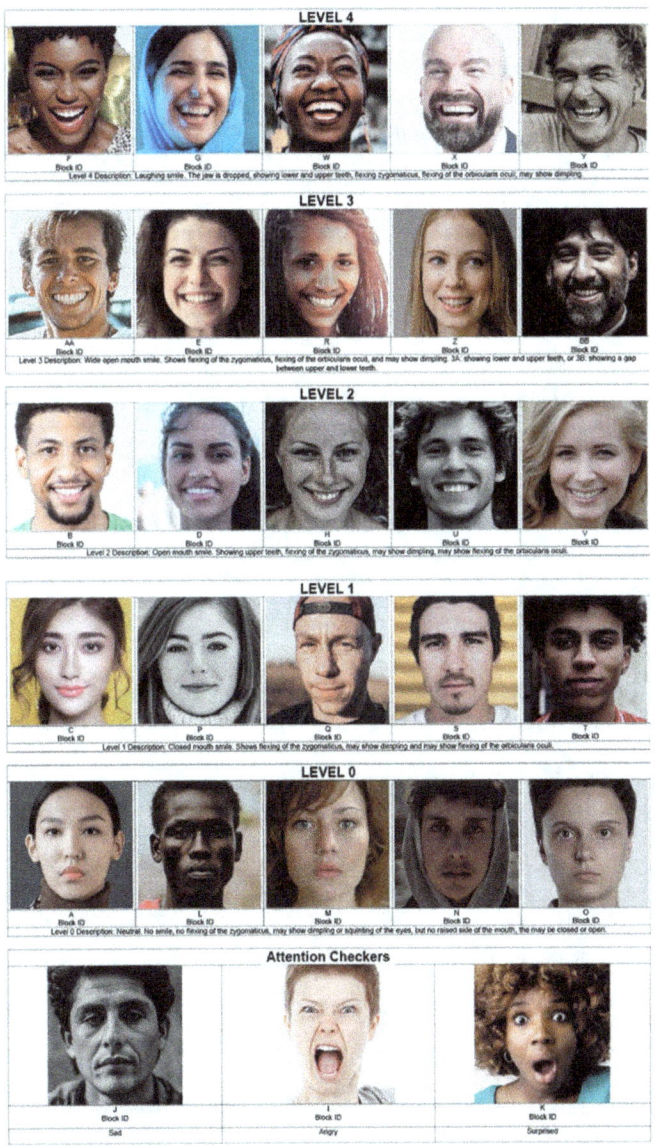

Appendix C

Summary of Images, Final Edition

Appendix D

Second SIS-3 Survey Images

References

Abel, Ernest L. & Michael L. Kruger. 2010. Smile intensity in photographs predicts longevity. *Psychological Science* 21(4). 542–544. https://doi.org/10.1177/0956797610363775

Amoyal, Mary & Béatrice Priego-Valverde. 2019. Smiling for negotiating topic transitions in French conversation. Paper presented at the Gesture and Speech in Interaction (GeSpIn) meeting. Paderborn, 11–13 September, 2019.

Artstein, Ron., & Poesio, Massimo. (2008). Inter-coder agreement for computational linguistics. *Computational linguistics*, 34(4), 555–596.

Attardo, Salvatore. 2012. Smiling, laughter and humor. In Paolo Santarcangelo (ed.), *Laughing in Chinese*, 421–436. Rome: Aracne.

Attardo, Salvatore. 2019. Humor and mirth: Emotions, embodied cognition, and sustained humor. In J. Lachlan Mackenzie & Laura Alba-Juez (eds.), *Emotion in discourse*, 189–212. Amsterdam, NL: John Benjamins Publishing Company.

Barger, Patricia B. & Alicia A. Grandey. 2006. Service with a smile and encounter satisfaction: Emotional contagion and appraisal mechanisms. *Academy of Management Journal* 49(6). 1229–1238. https://doi.org/10.5465/amj.2006.23478695

Calvo, Manuel Gutiérrez, Aida Gutiérrez-García, Andrés Fernández-Martín & Lauri Nummenmaa. 2014. Recognition of facial expressions of emotion is related to their frequency in everyday life. *Journal of Nonverbal Behavior* 38(4). 549–567. https://doi.org/10.1007/s10919-014-0191-3

Chmielewski, Michael & Sarah C. Kucker. 2020. An MTurk Crisis? Shifts in Data Quality and the Impact on Study Results. *Social Psychological and Personality Science* 11(4). 464–473. https://doi.org/10.1177/1948550619875149

Cross, Marie P. & Sarah D. Pressman. 2020. Say cheese? The connections between positive facial expressions in student identification photographs and health care seeking behavior. *Journal of Health Psychology* 25(13–14). 2511–2519. https://doi.org/10.1177/1359105318790066

Diedenhofen, Birk. 2016. The cocron package. http://comparingcronbachalphas.org

Dufner, Michael, Martin Brümmer, Joanne M. Chung, Pia M. Drewke, Christophe Blaison & Stefan C. Schmukle. 2018. Does Smile Intensity in Photographs Really Predict Longevity? A Replication and Extension of Abel and Kruger (2010). *Psychological Science* 29(1). 147–153. https://doi.org/10.1177/0956797617734315

Fang, Xia, Disa A. Sauter & Gerben A. van Kleef. 2020. Unmasking smiles: The influence of culture and intensity on interpretations of smiling expressions. *Journal of Cultural Cognitive Science* 4(3). 293–308. https://doi.org/10.1007/s41809-019-00053-1

Freese, Jeremy, Sheri Meland & William Irwin. 2007. Expressions of positive emotion in photographs, personality, and later-life marital and health outcomes. *Journal of Research in Personality* 41(2). 488–497. https://doi.org/10.1016/j.jrp.2006.05.006

Gamer, Matthias. 2012. Various coefficients of interrater reliability and agreement. https://www.r-project.org

Girard, Jeffrey M., Jeffrey F. Cohn, Laszlo A. Jeni, Michael A. Sayette & Fernando De la Torre. 2015a. Spontaneous facial expression in unscripted social interactions can be measured automatically. *Behavior Research Methods* 47(4). 1136–1147. https://doi.org/10.3758/s13428-014-0536-1

Girard, Jeffrey M., Jeffrey F. Cohn & Fernando De la Torre. 2015b. Estimating smile intensity: A better way. *Pattern Recognition Letters* (Pattern Recognition in Human Computer Interaction) 66. 13–21. https://doi.org/10.1016/j.patrec.2014.10.004

Gliem, Joseph A. & Rosemary R. Gliem. 2003. Calculating, interpreting, and reporting Cronbach's alpha reliability coefficient for Likert-type scales. Paper presented at the Midwest Research-to-Practice Conference in Adult, Continuing, and Community Education. Columbus, 8–10 October, 2003.

Ekman, Paul, Richard J. Davidson & Wallace V. Friesen. 1990. The Duchenne smile: Emotional expression and brain physiology II. *Journal of Personality and Social Psychology* 58(2). 342–353. https://doi.org/10.1037/0022-3514.58.2.342

Ekman, Paul & Wallace V. Friesen. 1978. *Facial action coding system*. Palo Alto: Consulting Psychologists Press.

Gironzetti, Elisa. 2022. *The multimodal performance of conversational humor*. Amsterdam: John Benjamins Publishing Company.

Gironzetti, Elisa, Salvatore Attardo & Lucy Pickering. 2016. Smiling, gaze, and humor in conversation. In Leonor Ruiz-Gurillo (ed.), *Metapragmatics of humor: Current research trends*, 235–254. Amsterdam: John Benjamins Publishing Company.

Gironzetti, Elisa, Salvatore Attardo & Lucy Pickering. 2019. Smiling and the negotiation of humor in conversation. *Discourse Processes* 56(7). 496–512. https://doi.org/10.1080/0163853X.2018.1512247

Gironzetti, Elisa, Lucy Pickering, Meichan Huang, Ying Zhang, Shigehito Menjo & Salvatore Attardo. 2016. Smiling synchronicity and gaze patterns in dyadic humorous conversations. *Humor* 29(2). 301–324. https://doi.org/10.1515/humor-2016-0005

Hara, Kotaro, Abigail Adams, Kristy Milland, Saiph Savage, Chris Callison-Burch & Jeffrey P. Bigham. 2018. A data-driven analysis of workers' earnings on Amazon Mechanical Turk. In *Proceedings of the 2018 CHI conference on human factors in computing systems, Montreal, Canada, April 21–26, 2018*, 1–14. New York: Association for Computing Machinery.

Harker, LeeAnne & Dacher Keltner. 2001. Expressions of positive emotion in women's college yearbook pictures and their relationship to personality and life outcomes across adulthood. *Journal of Personality and Social Psychology* 80(1). 112–124. https://doi.org/10.1037/0022-3514.80.1.112

Hertenstein, Matthew J., Carrie A. Hansel, Alissa M. Butts & Sarah N. Hile. 2009. Smile intensity in photographs predicts divorce later in life. *Motivation and Emotion* 33(2). 99–105. https://doi.org/10.1007/s11031-009-9124-6

Hess, Ursula, Arvid Kappas, Gregory J. McHugo, Robert E. Kleck & John T. Lanzetta. 1989. An analysis of the encoding and decoding of spontaneous and posed smiles: The use of facial electromyography. *Journal of Nonverbal Behavior* 13(2). 121–137. https://doi.org/10.1007/BF00990794

Kaczmarek, Lukasz D., Maciej Behnke, Todd B. Kashdan, Aleksandra Kusiak, Katarzyna Marzec, Martyna Mistrzak & Magdalena Włodarczyk. 2018. Smile intensity in social networking profile photographs is related to greater scientific achievements. *The Journal of Positive Psychology* 13(5). 435–439. https://doi.org/10.1080/17439760.2017.1326519

Kraus, Michael W. & Teh-Way David Chen. 2013. A winning smile? Smile intensity, physical dominance, and fighter performance. *Emotion* 13(2). 270–279. https://doi.org/10.1037/a0030745

Krippendorff, Klaus. (2004). *Content Analysis: An Introduction to its Methodology* (2nd ed.). Thousand Oaks, CA: Sage.

Krumhuber, Eva G., & Kappas, Arvid. (2005). Moving smiles: The role of dynamic components for the perception of the genuineness of smiles. *Journal of Nonverbal Behavior* 29. 3–24.

Krumhuber, Eva G., & Manstead, Anthony, S. R. (2009). Can Duchenne smiles be feigned? New evidence on felt and false smiles. *Emotion* 9(6). 807–820.

Lee, Juhun, Irene Teo, Michele Guindani, Gregory P. Reece, Mia K. Markey & Michelle Cororve Fingeret. 2015. Associations between psychosocial functioning and smiling intensity in patients with head and neck cancer. *Psychology, Health & Medicine* 20(4). 469–476. https://doi.org/10.1080/13548506.2014.95137

Miller, Shelby. 2019. Lexicosemantic features, speech acts, and indirect speech: The influence of personality on linguistic production. Commerce: Texas A&M University-Commerce dissertation.

Oveis, Christopher, June Gruber, Dacher Keltner, Juliet L. Stamper & W. Thomas Boyce. 2009. Smile intensity and warm touch as thin slices of child and family affective style. *Emotion* 9(4). 544–548. https://doi.org/10.1037/a0016300

Priego-Valverde, Béatrice, Brigitte Bigi, Salvatore Attardo, Lucy Pickering & Elisa Gironzetti. 2018. Is smiling during humor so obvious? a cross-cultural comparison of smiling behavior in humorous sequences in American English and French interactions. *Intercultural Pragmatics* 15(4). 563–591. https://doi.org/10.1515/ip-2018-0020

Rauzy, Stéphane & Mary Amoyal. 2020. SMAD: A tool for automatically annotating the smile intensity along a video record. Paper presented at the 10th Humour Research Conference (HRC2020), Commerce, 20 March, 2020.

Rauzy, Stéphane, Mary Amoyal & Béatrice Priego-Valverde. 2022. A Measure of the smiling synchrony in the conversational face-to-face interaction corpus PACO-CHEESE. Paper presented at the Workshop SmiLa, Language Resources and Evaluation Conference (LREC), Marseille, 20–25 June, 2022.

Rizopoulos, Dimitris. 2006. ltm: An R package for latent variable modeling and item response theory analyses. *Journal of Statistical Software* 17(5). 1–25. https://doi.org/10.18637/jss.v017.i05

Seder, J. Patrick & Shigehiro Oishi. 2012. Intensity of smiling in Facebook photos predicts future life satisfaction. *Social Psychological and Personality Science* 3(4). 407–413. https://doi.org/10.1177/1948550611424968

Sheehan, Kim Bartel. 2018. Crowdsourcing research: Data collection with Amazon's Mechanical Turk. *Communication Monographs* 85(1). 140–156. https://doi.org/10.1080/03637751.2017.1342043

Smith, Richard. M. 2004. Fit analysis in latent trait measurement models. In Everett V. Smith & Richard M. Smith (eds.), *Introduction to Rasch Measurement: Theory, models and applications*, 73–92. Maple Grove: JAM Press.

Tidd, Kathi L. & Joan S. Lockard. 1978. Monetary significance of the affiliative smile: A case for reciprocal altruism. *Bulletin of the Psychonomic Society* 11(6). 344–346. https://doi.org/10.3758/BF03336849

Trochim, William M. K. 2022. https://conjointly.com/kb/construct-validity/

Wang, Ze, Mao, Huifang, Li, Yexin J., & Liu, Fan. (2016). Smile big or not? Effects of smile intensity on perceptions of warmth and competence. *Journal of Consumer Research* 43(5). 787–805.

Wang, Ze, Xin He & Fan Liu. 2015. Examining the effect of smile intensity on age perceptions. *Psychological Reports* 117(1). 188–205. https://doi.org/10.2466/07.PR0.117c10z7

Wang, Ze, Huifang Mao, Yexin Jessica Li & Fan Liu. 2017. Smile big or not? Effects of smile intensity on perceptions of warmth and competence. *Journal of Consumer Research* 43(5). 787–805. https://doi.org/10.1093/jcr/ucw062

Béatrice Priego-Valverde and Stéphane Rauzy

5 Facial gestures and laughter as a resource for negotiating humor in conversation

Abstract: This chapter focuses on interactional humor in dyadic face-to-face conversations in French. Adopting an expanded version of the Smiling Intensity Scale (Gironzetti et al. 2016; Gironzetti, Attardo, and Pickering 2016), this chapter focuses on participants' facial gestures (i.e., neutral facial expressions and smiles) and laughter in the 11 interactions of the "Cheese!" corpus. The aim of this article is to investigate *the way both the speaker's and the recipient's multimodal behaviors are used as a resource for producing, reacting to, and negotiating humorous utterances.*

Using a mixed approach, the aim of this chapter is twofold: (1) to provide a statistical analysis based on the whole corpus which highlights general trends about the way neutral facial expressions, smiles, and laughter are displayed in humorous segments; (2) to provide a deeper understanding of the multimodal achievement of humor in conversation through a sequential analysis of three examples. With these complementary quantitative and qualitative approaches, we will show that while a quantitative analysis can illustrate the way humor is *accompanied* by nonverbal behaviors, only a sequential analysis allows us to consider them as *a resource* used by participants to produce, react to, and negotiate humor.

Keywords: interactional humor, negotiation, Smile Intensity Scale, neutral face, smile, laughter, statistical analysis, sequential analysis

Acknowledgments: We thank the CEP (*Centre d'Expérimentation de la Parole*, Laboratoire Parole et Langage), for its help in the recording of the "Cheese!" corpus.
  We thank Mary Amoyal for her facial annotations and our discussions.
  We thank Manon Meaume for her annotations of the humorous sequences.
  We are very grateful to Oriana Collins for her proofreading of the present chapter, as well as very helpful comments and suggestions from the anonymous reviewers.

Note: The video files can be accessed via the following link: https://www.degruyter.com/document/isbn/9783110983128/html

https://doi.org/10.1515/9783110983128-006

1 Theoretical background

1.1 Negotiation of interactional humor

This chapter adopts Tsakona and Chovanec's term *interactional humor* (2018). According to the authors, interactional humor is characterized by three features: (1) it appears in interaction, whether face-to-face, written or computer-mediated; (2) it is sequentially constructed, i.e., humor includes not only the humorous utterance per se but also participants' reaction(s) to it; and (3) consequently, humor involves more than one person, i.e., a necessary "co-participation" (Tsakona and Chovanec 2018: 9). Henceforth, at least in the broad field of discourse analysis (including Conversation Analysis, interactional linguistics, and sociopragmatics), which considers an interaction to be fundamentally "collaborative" (Sacks, Schegloff, and Jefferson 1974) or a "joint activity" (Clark 1996), there is a consensus: *from the moment it appears in an interaction, humor, just like any other action, is negotiated and interactionally achieved*. In other words, whether humor is analyzed via its production or via its resulting reactions, these two aspects of humor represent two sides of the same coin.

Starting from this premise, all studies on interactional humor can be read or re-read through the prism of negotiation. Studies focusing on the linguistic and discursive devices of humor could thus be logically categorized as *studies on humor production*. However, they can also be seen in two different ways which take into account the recipient(s) and the sequential organization of the interaction in which humor appears. On the one hand, the analysis of discursive devices such as rebound (Norrick 1993), other repetition and pinning (Tannen 1989; Bertrand and Priego-Valverde 2011; Guardiola et al. 2012; Priego-Valverde 2016) or (fictitious) reported speech (Tannen 2010; Chovanec 2015; Guardiola and Bertrand 2013; Bertrand and Priego-Valverde 2011; Priego-Valverde 2016) show that humor, while physically produced by a single person, is often built on the other's discourse. On the other hand, the analysis of linguistic devices such as prosody, phonetics, or lexicon (see Haugh 2014 for an overview) raises the question not only of how humor is designed but also – and maybe above all – for whom (and consequently why) humor is designed.

A possible answer can be found in the literature about humor markers and the way humor can be framed (see Haugh 2014; Burgers and van Mulken 2017; Gironzetti 2017; Attardo 2020). These studies may appear to focus solely on humor production. However, regardless of whether they employ the term "markers," "contextualization cues" (Gumperz 1982), humorous "frame" (Bateson 1955/1972), or humorous "keying"

(Hymes 1972),[1] the question remains, by essence, interactional. Because humor is necessarily interactionally achieved, it must be negotiated by the participants in order to succeed. As such, various markers, cues, or framing devices are all tools that can be used by the speaker to incite the other participant(s) to accept or at least recognize the speaker's humor. Thus, they are all potential tools for negotiation.

Henceforth, studies focusing on *humor reactions* can be seen as studies about the way the negotiation of humor is conducted and what the outcome is. As mentioned above, *"[. . .] the audience plays a vital role in the construction of humorous discourse."* (Hay 2001: 56). Some studies – though less numerous than those on humor production – have focused on reactions to humor, and more precisely on reactions to failed humor. For instance, while identifying certain strategies of "humor support" Hay (2001) also identifies potential reasons for humor to fail due both to the speaker and to the recipient. More recently, emphasizing the "shared responsibility" of both interlocutors in the failure of humor, Bell (2015), refines the notion of failed humor as a type of *miscommunication* between the participants. Finally, building on studies on the disruptiveness of humor (Sherzer 1978; Norrick 1993; Chiaro 1992; Hay 1995) and the notions of "frame" (Bateson 1955/1972), "keying" (Hymes 1972), or non-bona-fide communication (Raskin 1985), the disruptiveness of humor has been presented as a cause of failed humor because humor is considered as an attempt to either change the topic, keep or hold the floor, or introduce a play frame (Bell 2015). Introducing a play frame is thought to be *"[. . .] one of the most common reasons that humor fails in conversation"* (Bell 2015: 83) and can lead to a conflict between serious and humorous frames (Priego-Valverde 2003; 2020). Negotiating humor is (especially) crucial because it can lead to a frame switch of the whole conversation. This last point has been recently investigated through the analysis of failed humor when it is disaligned (with respect to the structural organization of the conversation) and/or disaffiliated (with respect to the ongoing frame) (Priego-Valverde 2021). Going further, Gironzetti (2022) introduces the term "misalignment" to encompass both disalignment and disaffiliation, and analyzes multimodal cues of failed humor displayed by both the speaker and the recipient.

Finally, the interactional achievement of humor has also been demonstrated by studies focusing on joint fantasizing humorous sequences,[2] where more than one participant collaborate in an *"incremental elaboration"* (Stallone and Haugh 2017) of humor, in *"a form of escalation where a word or utterance is a springboard for the next"* (Priego-Valverde 2018).

---

[1] See Tsakona and Chovanec (2018) and Attardo (2020) for a more complete overview of the various terminology.
[2] For a broader terminology review, see Stallone and Haugh (2017), Priego-Valverde (2018).

1.2 Functions of smiling and laughter in interaction

Studies on smiling in interaction involve both its emotional and interactional dimensions. When analyzed *in relation to emotions*, smiling appears as an ambivalent phenomenon. On the one hand, it is mainly seen as the expression of joy (Birdwhistell 1968; Ekman, Sorenson, and Friesen 1969; Ekman 1984; Izard 1997; Elfenbein and Ambady 2002; Ekman 2007) which can be displayed after positive affect (Niedenthal et al. 2001). Smiling can also convey positive emotions such as pleasure (Ambadar, Cohn, and Reed 2009). On the other hand, smiling can be triggered by embarrassment (Keltner 1995; Ambadar, Cohn, and Reed 2009).

When analyzed through its *interpersonal and interactional dimensions*, smiling is considered a *"conversational facial gesture"* (Bavelas et al. 1991) which conveys various interpersonal and interactive functions (Argyle 1988; Bavelas, Gerwing, and Healing 2014). Focusing on its interpersonal functions, smiling can be both affiliative (Niedenthal, Krauth-Gruber, and Ric 2006) and disaffiliative i.e., displaying both agreement and disagreement between participants (Bousmalis et al. 2009). It can also be seen as the expression of politeness in conversational opening sequences (Cosnier 1996). The interactive functions of smiling have also been demonstrated in teaching contexts. Smiling can allow a professor to change activities (Tellier 2010), ask questions and answer students, tell a story, underline important points, or display his/her attention (Theonas, Hobbs, and Rigas 2008). Some of these interactive functions have also been found in everyday interactions. Smiling can be a backchannel signal (Brunner 1979; Duncan, Brunner, and Fiske 1979; Argyle 1988; Bousmalis et al. 2009; Jensen 2015; Boudin et al. 2021) or a resource to punctuate narratives (Chovil 1991/1992) or display a stance toward what it is being discussed (Ruusuvuori and Peräkylä 2009; Prepin, Ochs, and Pélachaud 2012). Smiling can also frame a discourse in different ways, for example, as sensitive (Haakana 2010).

In comparison to smiling, laughter has received far more attention. However, smiling and laughter appear to share certain common functions, whether they are emotional, interpersonal, or interactional. For instance, laughter, like smiling, can be linked to positive emotions such as joy (Trouvain and Phuong Truong 2017) and can also display embarrassment (Haakana 2001).

Moreover, like smiling, laughter can have ambivalent interpersonal functions. For instance, whether or not it is shared by participants, laughter can be both affiliative (Jefferson, Sacks and Schegloff 1987; O'Donnell-Trujillo and Adams 1983; Haakana 2002; Osvaldsson 2004; Mehu and Dunbar 2008) and disaffiliative (Romaniuk 2013), which has been synthesized by Glenn's distinction between *"laughing with and laughing at"* (Glenn 2003). According to which person produces laughter in multiparty interactions, laughter can also be affiliative and disaffiliative at the same time (Clift 2016).

Finally, analyzing laughter according to the institutional and interactional roles of the participants (Glenn 2003; 2010) can reveal some of its functions. For instance, laughter plays an important role in the construction of reported speech (Clift 2012). Laughter can also serve to mitigate a sensitive action (Glenn and Holt, 2013; Shaw, Hepburn, and Potter 2013) such as complaints (Voge 2010, Clift 2012), or to manage topic and floor (Holt 2010).

1.3 Smiling and laughter in relation to humor

While the links between smiling and humor seem obvious at first sight, the way smiling can frame a discourse as humorous was initially only briefly mentioned in research (Coates 1991, Haakana 2010), before being studied in more depth more recently. One study revealed that smiling can initiate an emotional shift from a neutral or serious emotion to a positive or humorous one when produced in an opening turn (Kaukomaa, Peräkylä, and Ruusuvuari 2013). Research comparing smiling behavior during humorous and non-humorous sequences has shown that participants not only smile more during humor, but also before humorous segments, which tends to confirm the role of smiling in framing discourse as humorous (Gironzetti et al. 2016; Gironzetti, Attardo, and Pickering 2016; Gironzetti 2017; Priego-Valverde et al. 2018). Furthermore, smiling has been shown to participate in the negotiation of humor (Gironzetti, Attardo, and Pickering 2018). However, despite its role in framing, not only does smiling fail to prevent humor from failing (Priego-Valverde, Bigi, and Amoyal 2020), but it can also be a type of response to failed humor (Bell 2009; Gironzetti 2022).

Since Jefferson's early work on laughter (Jefferson 1979; 1984; 1985; 2004), the links between laughter and humor and the way laughter can frame a discourse as humorous have been more regularly explored. However, they have been also treated as much more questionable. Earlier studies considered that laughter and humor were a sort of adjacency pair (Norrick 1993), but this claim has since been disproven (Provine 2000) for at least two reasons. The first is that the link between laughter and humor is far from systematic: humor does not necessarily trigger laughter, and laughter is not always provoked by humor (see Attardo 1994; Chapman, and Foot 1996; Morreall 2001; Priego-Valverde 2003). In the same way, laughter can be a response to failed humor (Bell 2009), but a lack of laughter does not necessarily mean that humor has failed either. Laughter can also be used as a support strategy (Hay 2001) but the link between the two is tenuous *"[c]ounting instances of laughter is a misleading approach to investigating levels of support"* (Hay 2001: 76), because laughter is far from being the only possible reaction to humor (Attardo 2008[3]). The second reason involves the term "humor" per se, at least in Conversation Analysis. As humor is considered too abstract and *"insufficiently specific for describing social actions and sequences or the visible orientations of the participants"* (Glenn and Holt 2017: 295), "humor" has been replaced by the term "laughable" in order to avoid any presupposition concerning the nature of the discourse treated with or by laughter.[4] Crucially grounding on the assumption that laughter is always related to a laughable within a specific context (whether humorous or not), Mazzocconi et al. (2020) consider laughter as having propositional content predicating about the laughable. They analyse in depth the laughable laughter can be related to and propose a taxonomy of laughter's pragmatic functions on the basis of conversational corpus data. They distinguish four main classes of laughables: pleasant incongruity (which can be instances of humor), social incongruity (when an incongruity with the ideal flow of an interaction occurs), pragmatic incongruity (when there is a clash between what is meant and what is uttered) and pleasantness (events not involving any incongruity, but appraised as pleasant, towards which laugher shows a positive disposition).

In line with Conversational Analysis (Sacks, Schegloff and Jefferson 1974) and interactional linguistics frameworks (Couper-Kuhlen and Selting 2018), in this chapter, we highlight the way humor is multimodally negotiated and interactionally achieved by both participants in dyads. In this respect, we will use the notions of "alignment" and "affiliation" as defined by Stivers (2008) to analyze the way humor, moment-by-moment, is inserted in the ongoing interaction. These notions refer to structural and relational constraints that the recipient's response(s) must respect for the ongoing activity to develop. While an aligned answer respects the structure of the ongoing activity (e.g., producing positive feedback after a confirmation request), an affiliative answer is more relational since it occurs through affiliation *"[. . .] the hearer displays support of and endorses the teller's conveyed stance"* (Stivers 2008: 35). We also adopt a multimodal approach to interactional humor in which the term "resources," or *"substance-based linguistic (or other) forms or entities that can be described with respect to their structure and use"* (Couper-Kuhlen and Selting 2018: 29), will refer both to verbal and nonverbal behaviors displayed by the participants. In this respect, their facial gestures (neutral facial expression and smile) and laughter will be analyzed as follows: (1) by relying on a rigorous annotation of the humorous sequences (see Subsection 2.3.2), participants' nonverbal behaviors will be analyzed in relation to humor identified

---

[3] For a more extensive presentation, see Attardo 2020.
[4] The authors note that the notion of laughable can overlap with humor (Glenn 2003, Glenn and Holt 2013).

as such; (2) when they are displayed by both participants, i.e., during the production of humor and reaction(s) to it; (3) not as simply triggered by humor, but as a resource used by both participants to *design* and *negotiate* humor.

Using a mixed approach, we combine a statistical and a sequential analysis of both the humorous sequences and the nonverbal behaviors produced. Assuming the complementarity of the two approaches, the aim of this chapter is twofold. Through a quantitative analysis based on the whole corpus, this chapter will first focus on general trends about the way ("neutral face", smiling, and laughter are displayed in humorous segments. We will also show through a sequential analysis of three examples that although certain general tendencies can be quantitatively retrieved, an in-depth understanding of the relationship between humor and these three nonverbal behaviors requires a detailed analysis of the data. While a quantitative analysis can illustrate the way humor is *accompanied* by nonverbal behaviors, only a sequential analysis allows us to consider them as *a resource* used by participants to produce, react to, and negotiate humor.

2 Corpus and methodology

"Cheese!" (Priego-Valverde, Bigi, and Amoyal 2020) is an audio-video conversational corpus recorded in 2016 at the Laboratoire Parole et Langage (LPL) in Aix-en-Provence, France.[5] The corpus consists of 11 mixed and non-mixed dyadic interactions, lasting approximately 15 minutes each. "Cheese!" was first collected in order to conduct a cross-cultural comparison of smiling during humorous productions between American English and French speakers (Priego-Valverde et al. 2018). Consequently, the corpus was recorded following the protocol adopted in Texas, as closely as possible, especially involving the tasks given to the participants (see below).

2.1 The participants

The 22 participants in the corpus were all students studying linguistics at Aix-Marseille University. Each interaction involved two participants who were in the same class and were also friends outside the university. All the participants were French natives between 20 and 40 years old. They were all informed of the purpose of the data collection at the end of the task and signed a written consent form before the recordings.

---

5 At the Centre for Speech Experimentation (CEP).

2.2 Experimental protocol

Two tasks were given to the participants. First, they were asked to read a canned joke to each other given to them by the researchers.[6] Second, they were asked to speak as freely as they wished until the end of the interaction.

The participants were recorded in a soundproof room sitting face to face. They were fitted with two headset microphones optimally positioned so as not to hide their mouths. Two cameras were positioned in such a way that each participant was shown from the front. A video editing program was used to merge the two videos into a single one (see Figure 1) and to embed the high-quality sound of the microphones.

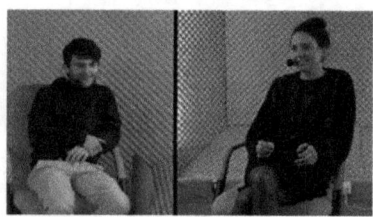

Figure 1: Experimental design of "Cheese!".

2.3 Annotation of the data

An analysis the whole corpus (3 hours of interaction) provided a total of 3899 intervals annotated as "neutral face," "smile" (3 intensities), and "laughter". Within the 339 humorous segments extracted, 210 humorous sequences were identified.

2.3.1 Annotation of the audio signal

Using SPPAS (Bigi 2015), each audio signal was automatically segmented into Inter-Pausal Units (IPUs), or blocks of speech bounded by silent pauses of over 200 ms and time-aligned to the speech signal. An orthographic transcription was provided at the IPU level to include phenomena occurring in spontaneous speech (such as hesitations, repetitions, etc.). Vocal laughter was also annotated based on the audio signal during this stage. The annotation was based on Enriched Orthographic Transcription conventions (Bertrand et al. 2008).

---

6 This part of the recordings will not be analyzed here.

2.3.2 Annotation of humor

The protocol of annotation and analysis applied here is not linear. As interactional humor cannot be annotated or analyzed without taking into account the interaction in which it appears or its sequential organization which necessarily shapes its forms (Priego-Valverde 2020; 2021), our protocol involved going back and forth between the annotation and the analysis stages. This protocol was selected in order to provide both a sequential analysis of interactional humor and a statistical analysis of the participants' multimodal resources.

At this stage, all the humorous instances were manually annotated by one of the authors with Praat (Boersma and Weenink 2018) using only the audio files. As the canned jokes (see Subsection 3.2) were left aside from the analyses, only the instances of conversational humor were annotated, following this chronological order:

(1) Each humorous item was pre-selected using various cues such as laughter – although the link between humor and laughter has proven to be tenuous (see Subsection 2.3), sing-song intonation, smiling voice, or metacommunicative comments (such as "this was a funny thing" to introduce a humorous utterance). Although this step seems quite intuitive, it was taken as an insufficient but necessary point of departure signaling to the analyst that "something was happening here."

(2) Because humor is interactional, the second step was to annotate participants' reactions to the pre-selected items. Two kinds of reactions were distinguished based on various multimodal cues: positive reactions (such as laughter, positive feedback, or metacommunicative comments) and negative reactions (such as negative feedback or metacommunicative comments). This classification of participants' various reactions enabled us to add or exclude some items initially considered humorous, for example due to the sole presence of laughter.

(3) At this step, a double coding was carried out for each item and Cohen's Kappa (Cohen 1960) was calculated. The inter-annotator agreement rates ranged from 0.22 to 0.94 according to the interactions.

(4) This step involved a joint analysis during which the two judges went over each item that they had both selected in steps 1 and 2. The judges jointly identified and categorized the devices used in each humorous item. In the present study, following Mullan and Béal (2018), the features that were detected can be classified into two broad categories: linguistic features and discursive features. The former involves various linguistic levels such as prosody, phonetics, lexicon, syntax, or gestures.[7] The latter are broader. They refer to various "strategies" (Mul-

---

[7] Prosody was not analyzed here, and as mentioned above, gestures were excluded from the annotation phase of the audio file.

lan and Béal 2018) with which participants organize and stage their discourse, such as reported speech, fictionalization, allusion to shared knowledge, or "local logic" (Koestler 1980; Ziv 1984), also called "internal logic" (Mullan and Béal 2018). The categorization of the humorous devices was useful because it enabled us to reject an item selected as humorous when no device was identified, which allowed us to distinguish humor from "non-seriousness" (Chafe 2007). This process also enabled us to add some items which one of the two annotators had not selected but where a device was identified after all. Only the items which were agreed upon by both judges were retained for analysis.

In order to perform the statistical measures of each participant's multimodal resources, whether they were displayed during humorous or non-humorous moments (see Section 3), the humorous items were annotated as follows:

(1) The boundaries of each humorous item produced by one participant were aligned to the time boundaries of the IPU where humor appeared. This means that each participant's humor was annotated independently from the other's. Thus, Participants 1 and 2 of a given interaction were each attributed their own series of humorous item intervals. Consequently, a humorous item time interval from Participant 1 can overlap with a humorous item time interval from Participant 2 if both of them produced humor simultaneously.

(2) In a second stage, humorous segments for each participant were formed by clustering the individual humorous items when they were separated by fewer than five seconds. Thus, similarly to the items, humorous segments could also overlap when both participants were producing humor. In total, 339 humorous segments were retained.

(3) In a final stage, we delineated the humorous sequences by merging the contiguous or overlapping humorous segments of the two participants. This step allowed us to distinguish the production of humor from a reaction to humor when the latter was also humorous. 210 humorous sequences were extracted.

2.3.3 Annotation of facial gestures

In order to annotate the participants' facial gestures, i.e., their smiles and neutral facial expressions ("neutral face"), we used an *expanded and multimodal version* of the Smiling Intensity Scale (SIS) (Gironzetti et al. 2016; Gironzetti, Attardo, and Pickering 2016; Gironzetti, this volume; Ergül, Miller, Kramer, and Attardo, this volume).

The original SIS measures the intensity of smiling progressively on a scale from 0 (neutral face) to 4 (laughing smile), based on Action Units (AUs) detailed by the Facial Action Coding System (FACS) (Ekman and Friesen 1978). As such, the SIS focuses entirely on the participant's face. However, facial expressions alone do not always allow us to distinguish smiles from laughter because both can involve common AUs (such as AU6 or 7; AU12; or AU14; see Hofmann, Platt, and Ruch 2017; Lynch and Trivers 2012). However, certain differences between smiling and laughter have been identified: they have a different mean duration (Ruch and Ekman 2001) and appear in different contexts in interaction (Haakana 2002) with different functions (Haakana 2002). In addition, in contrast to smiles, laughter involves other body parts, such as movements of the shoulders (Niewiedomski et al. 2013; Haddad, Tits, and Dutoit 2018). Consequently, following the latter authors, we consider in this chapter that *"laughter and smiles cannot overlap: a laughter is not a smile and a smile with one of the movements mentioned above is a laugh."* (Haddad, Tits, and Dutoit 2018: 56). For this reason, we also took into account participants' body movements in addition to their facial expressions to identify their facial gestures, i.e., neutral face, smiles (and their intensities), or laughter. For the same reason, we also added the participants' vocalizations using the audio files, as detailed below.

The whole procedure leading to the SIS annotation of "Cheese!" is fully described in Amoyal 2022 (see also Amoyal, Priego-Valverde, and Rauzy 2020). After a manual annotation of smiles which we used to build the SMAD tool[8] (Rauzy and Amoyal 2020),we applied SMAD to the whole "Cheese!" corpus and to another corpus, "PACO"[9] (Amoyal, Priego-Valverde, and Rauzy 2020). After the entire procedure was conducted with SMAD, we manually corrected the automatic inputs from SMAD using ELAN, and we also took into account the annotations of participants' shoulder movements and vocalized laughter transcribed with Praat during the transcription phase. This led us to *refine* the label S4 in our use of the SIS. Consequently, following our methodology, S4 corresponds to laughter, which also means that the participants' smiles are displayed through only 3 different intensities (S1, S2, S3), as illustrated by Table 1.

Finally, this stage of the annotation process was performed by an annotator with expertise in the SIS system. We found that manually correcting the labels and interval boundaries of the automatic outputs for the two corpora reduced the annotation time by a factor of 10 as compared with the time spent manually annotating expanded SIS levels without pretreatment (Amoyal 2022). A double correction, also starting from the automatic outputs, was performed by a second annotator on 4 interactions of "Cheese!" and 5 interactions of "PACO." The inter-rater agreement is satisfying (0.64 for "Cheese!" and 0.57 for "PACO") and validates the whole procedure

---

[8] SMAD: Smile Movement Automatic Detection.
[9] « PACO » was recorded in 2018 following the same protocol as "Cheese!", except that the participants met each other for the first time in the soundproof room on the day of the recordings. This corpus is thus constituted of initial interactions.

Table 1: Smiling Intensity Scale (Gironzetti et al. 2016; Gironzetti, Attardo, and Pickering 2016), illustrated with "Cheese!".

| Neutral face | Smile S1 | Smile S2 | Smile S3 | Laughter |

(Amoyal 2022). The expanded SIS annotations retained for the current study are the ones corrected by the SIS expert annotator for the 11 interactions of "Cheese!".

3 Quantitative results

The main characteristics of the 5 levels of the scale are summarized in Table 2 presented below. A total of 3899 intervals were annotated for the 11 conversations of "Cheese!" (22 participants). The annotations are distributed by intensity ("Level" column in Table 2) according to the number of intervals ("Nbr of intervals" column in Table 2). Each labeled interval has its own duration. For each level, we computed the distribution of the interval durations. The "MID" and "SDID" columns respectively display the mean (i.e., Mean Interval Duration) and the standard deviation (i.e., Standard Deviation Interval Duration) of these distributions. The S0 neutral face level intervals have an average duration of 13.54 seconds with a high level of variability in their durations (i.e., a standard deviation of 18.60 seconds). By comparison, the 3 smile intensities (S1, S2, and S3) and laughter (S4) have a shorter average duration and a narrower dispersion of their interval durations (e.g., an average of 3.12 seconds and a standard deviation of 2.81 seconds for the S2 level). The total time the 22 participants spent in each intensity level is provided in the "Duration" column and its corresponding "Proportion" column. For example, the S0 neutral face level was produced by the participants for 13664.92 seconds which represents a proportion of 60.1% of the total duration of the participants' productions (22725.69 seconds, or 6 hours and 19 minutes).

These characteristics reveal a high level of variability between participants. The proportion of S0 neutral face is 86.1% for participant CM while it falls to 29.7% for participant AC. The average proportion of S1 smile intensity varies from 25.5% (AG) to 2.6% (OR); S2 ranges from 30.6% (OR) to 5.8% (CM); and S3 ranges from

14.8% (AC) to 1.4% (CM). The average proportion of laughter (S4) varies from 28.8% (MZ) to 1.3% (OR).

Table 2: The main characteristics of the 5 SIS levels for "Cheese!". Each category ("Level" column) includes the number of intervals ("Nbr of intervals"), the mean of the distribution of interval durations ("MID", in seconds), the standard deviation of this distribution ("SDID" in seconds), the total time at each level ("Duration", in seconds) and the corresponding proportion ("Proportion").

Level	Nbr of intervals	MID (s)	SDID (s)	Duration (s)	Proportion
S0	1009	13.54	18.60	13664.92	0.601
S1	710	3.17	3.66	2250.34	0.099
S2	910	3.12	2.81	2842.34	0.125
S3	595	2.85	2.45	1698.19	0.075
S4	675	3.36	2.89	2269.90	0.100
All	3899	5.82	10.81	22725.69	1.000

In order to illustrate the major difference between our adopted annotation scheme and the SIS system, we quantified the multimodal aspect of the scale by focusing on S4 laughter. In particular, we focus on the link between the S4 level and the manually annotated vocal laughter during the speech transcription of the corpus and aligned using SPPAS (Bigi 2015).

"Cheese!" contains 975 manual annotations of vocal laughter produced by the 22 participants which represents about 3.2% of the duration of the whole corpus (a total of 747 seconds). 90% of the vocal laughter annotations are S4, 3.7% are S3, 3.4% are S2, 1.9% are S1, and 1% are S0. Roughly speaking, each occurrence of vocal laughter is thus associated with an S4 annotation in our expanded scale. The remaining 10% matching the S0 neutral face or the 3 smile intensities (S1, S2 and S3) are explained by annotation mistakes or by a imprecise temporal alignment of the laughter in the audio signal.

Our S4 annotations include many more features than just vocal laughter (2269 seconds of S4 on "Cheese!" compared to 747 seconds of vocal laughter). The S4 annotation areas are associated with vocal laughter (28.6%), but also with silence (43.8%) and speech activity (27.6%). This discrepancy is mainly explained by the annotation strategy we adopted. In our scheme, short time intervals between two consecutive occurrences of vocal laughter were annotated as S4 even in the absence of corresponding laughter in the acoustic signal. This was also the case when shoulder movements occurred during this interval, for example. Therefore, a short time interval separating two occurrences of vocal laughter (which were both annotated S4) received a S4 label and was merged with its two neighboring vocal laughs to form a larger S4 area. For example, almost half of the annotated

S4 areas (49%) correspond with silence or speech intervals separating two consecutive events of vocal laughter.

"Cheese!" contains 339 humorous segments of variable duration. Humorous segments are formed by one or several humorous items separated by fewer than 5 seconds (which were aligned with IPUs). The durations of humorous segments span from 0.32 to 71.72 seconds, with a mean of 5.76 seconds, a median of 3.04 seconds, and a standard deviation of 7.98 seconds. As explained in Section 2.3.2, for each interaction, the humorous segments produced by the two participants can potentially overlap, i.e., when both participants produce instances of humor simultaneously. Figure 2 illustrates such a case. The graph shows the variation of the intensity levels (in ordinates) along the timeline (in abscissa) for the interaction between MA and PC (the blue curve of the top panel for MA and the red curve of the bottom panel for PC). The light blue areas represent the humorous segments produced by MA and the light red ones the humorous segments produced by PC. Two overlapping humorous segments occur between 400 and 450 seconds (in light purple on the graph). There are 87 humorous instances produced in overlap (i.e., 25.6% of all the instances).

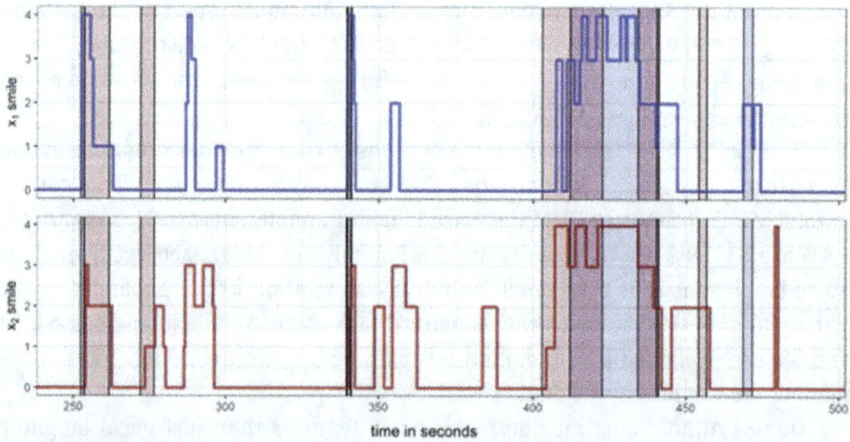

Figure 2: Illustration of the Expanded SIS encoding for an extract of the MAPC interaction in "Cheese!". The variation of the intensities (level 0 for neutral face, level 1, 2 and 3 for the 3 smile intensities and level 4 for laughter, in ordinates) along the timeline in abscissa is shown for Participants 1 (MA) and 2 (PC) (top and bottom panel). Light blue and light red areas respectively indicate the locations of humorous segments produced by Participants 1 and 2.

The most straightforward way to investigate the relationship between humor and smiling or laughter is to compare smiling behavior during humorous and non-humorous segments. However, several studies have shown that changes in smiling behavior are not restricted to the time interval spanned by the humorous segment but also involve the areas before and after the segment boundaries (Gironzetti et al. 2016; Gironzetti, Attardo, and Pickering 2016; Gironzetti 2017; Gironzetti, Attardo, and Pickering 2018; Priego-Valverde et al. 2018).

Hereafter we investigate how the proportions of the different smile intensities evolved in the neighborhood of humorous instances with 2 subsets of humorous segments that we selected from the corpus. The first subset contains the humorous segments which are not preceded by another humorous segment (produced by the speaker or the recipient) within a time window of 5 seconds. There are 147 occurrences (i.e., around 43%) of such isolated humorous segments in "Cheese!". This subset allowed us to study the evolution of the SIS levels before the start of humorous segments. We verified that the 5-second time window preceding each humorous segment was a non-humorous segment.

Similarly, the second subset contains humorous segments not overlapping with another segment within the 5 seconds following the segment. This second selection includes 148 occurrences and was used to investigate the evolution of Expanded SIS level proportions after the end of humorous segments.

With this in mind, we computed the proportions of the expanded SIS levels within time intervals of 1 second (i.e., "bins") with varying locations relative to the start of the humorous segment for the 147 selected segments of the first subset. In Figure 3, the bin locations are the abscissa of the graphs on the left panel. The first bin is the time interval between -6 and -5 seconds preceding the start of the humorous segment. The 0 abscissa stands for the start of the humorous segment, and positive bin locations indicate that the bin is inside the humorous area. In the current analysis we merged the 3 smile levels (S1, S2, and S3) together in order to obtain more robust trends. Therefore, we used 3 main categories of the expanded scale: neutral face (S0), smiling (S1, S2, S3), and laughter (S4). For each category and for each bin, we computed each participant's proportion of the category in the bin averaged on all the participant's selected humorous segments produced in the interaction. We also distinguished whether the participant was the speaker (i.e., the producer of the humorous segment) or the recipient. The results are shown for the 3 categories at the top, center, and bottom graphs of Figure 3. For each bin indicating the relative time location with respect to the start of the humorous segments (the abscissa of the graph), the values plotted in ordinate are the means of the distribution of these proportions for the 22 participants. Participant role is marked in red for the speaker and in blue for the recipient. We also computed the standard deviation of the distribution and the standard error associated with the estimate of this mean proportion, which corresponds to the 1-sigma error bars plotted on Figure 3. The right panels show the evolution of the mean proportions after the end of the humorous segments. They were obtained using the second subset of 148 segments mentioned above.

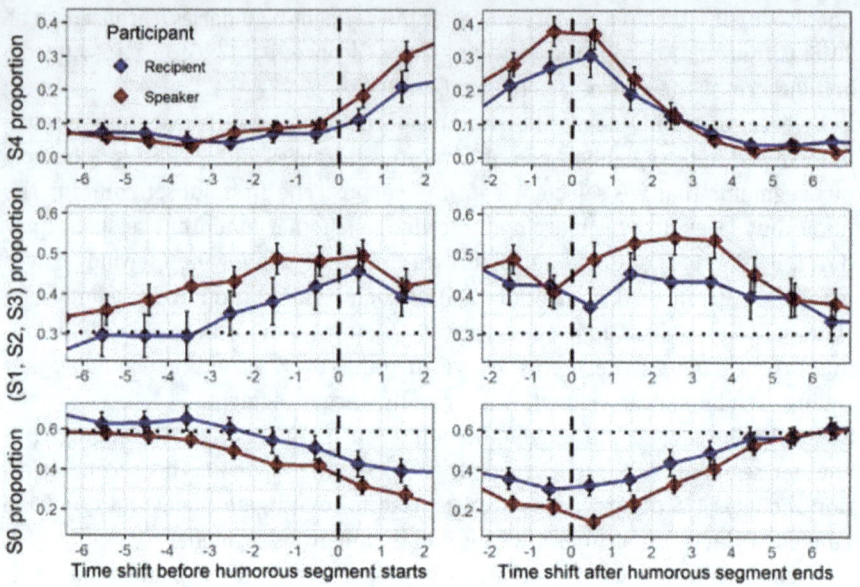

Figure 3: Variation of the mean proportions of each smile intensity preceding (left panels, 147 segments) and following (right panels, 148 segments) humorous segments.

The top left and right panels of Figure 3 depict the evolution of the mean proportion of S4 (laughter). The horizontal dotted line indicates the mean value of the S4 proportion over the interaction (including humorous and non-humorous areas but excluding canned joke areas). The mean proportion of S4 remains stable (between 5% and 10%) until the start of the humorous segment (indicated by the vertical dashed line at 0 abscissa on the left panel). It increases during the humorous segment and reaches an apex at the end of the humorous segment (the vertical dashed line at 0 abscissa on the right panel). The proportion then returns to 5% between the 3 and 4 second marks. This trend occurred for both the speaker and the recipient but was more marked for the speaker who produced the humorous segment (at the apex, the proportion was about 40% for the speaker versus 30% for the recipient for the 148 segments).

The mean proportion of the smiling group (S1, S2 and S3) is presented on the 2 middle panels of Figure 3. Here again, the dotted horizontal line is the average value of the proportion over the whole interaction except for the canned joke areas. For the speaker, the (S1, S2, S3) mean proportion starts to increase 6 seconds before the start of the humorous segment, increasing from 30% at 6 seconds to 50% at the start of the humorous segment. It reaches a plateau inside the humorous area, and this plateau remains present until 4 seconds after the end of the humorous segment.

The proportion decreases after that and returns to normal 6 seconds after the end of the humorous segment. The recipient's behavior is similar, with one major difference. Before the start of the humorous segment, the smooth increase of the recipient's proportion of smiles is delayed by about 2 seconds when compared to the speaker's increase. The recipient's mean value of the plateau after the end of the humorous segment is also slightly lower than the speaker's (45% vs. 55%).

Our quantitative study revealed three main trends. Firstly, the proportion of laughter starts to increase at the beginning of a humorous segment, reaches an apex at the very end of the segment and decreases afterward. This trend can be observed for both the speaker and the recipient. However, although this behavior is produced on average, it does not characterize all of the humorous instances. At the end of the humorous segments, the proportion of laughter is approximately 30% for the recipient and 40% for the speaker, which means that 70% and 60% of the instances do not end with laughter.

The second observed trend is the evolution of the proportion of smiles for the smiling group (S1, S2, S3). The speaker's proportion of smiles starts to increase at about 6 seconds before the beginning of the humorous segment and reaches a plateau that lasts throughout the segment and until 4 seconds after the end of the segment. Interestingly, the recipient adopts the same behavior on average, but the recipient's smooth increase is delayed by about 2 seconds with respect to the speaker.

Here again, the trend is real, but it does not occur in all of the humorous segments produced, which leads to the third trend: around half of the humorous segments start with participants exhibiting a neutral face (45% for the recipient and 50% for the speaker).

We now focus only on the 43% of humorous segments which were produced in isolation (i.e., without a second humorous occurrence within a 5 second window). The remaining cases, which are composed of alternate humorous segments between the speaker and the recipient, can potentially give rise to more complex smiling or laughter patterns. These results suggest that, even though some general tendencies can be quantitatively retrieved, an in-depth understanding of the relationship between humor and smiling or laughter requires a detailed analysis of the data.

4 Sequential analyses of three examples

The videos of the three excerpts analyzed here are available at: https://www.degruyter.com/document/isbn/9783110983128/html.

4.1 Example 1. MAPC: "Did you listen?"

```
MAPC: "Did you listen?"
PC 79: it changes absolutely nothing though
     PC : S0
     MA : S0
MA 77: class last week ↑
     MA : S0
     PC : S0
PC 80: hm
     PC : S0
     MA : S0
MA 78: hm it was ok actually class last week was ok
     MA : S0
     PC : S0
MA 79: {smiling voice} did you listen [in class] @
     MA :                                          S4
     PC :                                          S0
PC 81: yes + oh yes
     PC : S0      S3
     MA : S4
PC 82: no wait last week {smiling voice} I did listen
     PC : S2
     MA : S3
PC 83: I was even totally into it
     PC : S2
     MA : S1
PC 84: remember
     PC : S2
     MA : S1
MA 81: (sigh) yeah
     MA : S1
     PC : S2
PC 85: I rarely am but [last week] I was totally into it
     PC : S2
     MA : S1
MA 82: it depends / actually it depends on the weeks though there are some weeks where
     MA : S0
     PC : S0
MA 83: it's very clear
     MA : S0
     PC : S0
MA 84: well where it's ok actually
     MA : S0
     PC : S0
[...]
```

Figure 4: Transcript MAPC.

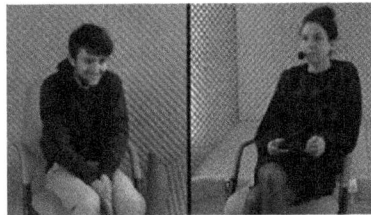

Figure 5: "did you listen".

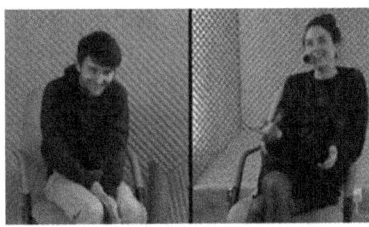

Figure 6: "oh yes".

The participants are students in the same year at university (2nd year), and they are also friends. In this excerpt (figure 4), they are talking about a class they are taking. While MA has good grades and PC does not, neither of them like the class. One minute and 22 seconds before the excerpt (non-transcribed lines), PC complains about their class and adds that she does not really listen in this class. In (PC 79), she says that, even when she reads over her notes, she does not understand the class better. In (MA 78), MA disagrees with PC, saying that the last session of the class was understandable. Aligning with her, he thus disaffiliates in not sharing her complaint. From the beginning until (MA 78), both participants display a neutral face while talking about their class. But in the next line (MA 79), MA, keeping the floor, asks if PC really listened in the last class that she has been complaining about (figure 5). At first glance, his question could be serious, aligned, and affiliated. He could really be asking this question to understand why PC is struggling with this class. But instead, with this question, he initiates a humorous frame to tease PC. Firstly, he disaffiliates with PC, switching from a neutral face to sudden laughter. As such, he frames his utterance as humorous instead of sharing the stance she is displaying. Secondly, and more interestingly, he also disaligns. His question is produced while he already has the floor and as such, it could be seen as an expression of interest. However, the device MA uses to produce his humor shows another picture. His teasing is based on a *rebound*, which has been characterized as a device used in conversational humor (Norrick 1993). What is remarkable here is the fact that the teasing is based on a rebound not of something which has just been said, but of something which was uttered one minute and 22 seconds earlier.

MA then backtracks and doing so, he disrupts PC's ongoing complaint and disaligns with her. Thus, while MA both disaligns and disaffiliates with PC, his rebound allows him to play both on their shared knowledge about their attitudes in class in general and on what was mentioned previously in the ongoing interaction, even in passing. Both laughter and the discursive strategy (the rebound) MA uses to produce teasing work together to highlight all the ambivalence of his teasing. While laughter allows MA to *"combin[e] elements of (ostensible) provocation and (ostensible) playfulness"* (Haugh 2017:77), the rebound on their shared knowledge allows him to "bond while biting" (Boxer and Cortés-Conde 1997) and deepen their relationship.

This last aspect of MA's teasing is retained by PC who plays along with the teasing (from PC 81 to PC 85) (figure 6). She thus aligns and affiliates with MA and, like him, she reacts both to their shared past (PC 85) and to the last class they mentioned (PC 83). She also directly appeals to MA ("remember," PC 84), as they know how each of them behaves in class. As for MA's teasing, the facial and discursive resources used in PC's first reaction (PC 83) are congruent with one another. While she first acknowledges (first "yes") MA's question seriously with a neutral face, her second positive answer, produced with a S3 smile, initiates her self-deprecating utterances. From then on, all her utterances are produced and answered while smiling (from S1 to S3), even if MA, the recipient, displays a less intense smile.

Finally, MA, who has the floor when he initiates the teasing sequence, keeps the floor to end it (MA 82). His return to seriousness is concomitant with a neutral face both participants display simultaneously.

Focusing on facial expressions, this example shows that the entire humorous sequence, from its very beginning to its end, is bounded by neutral faces displayed by both participants. Moreover, in this example, the participants do not begin to smile before the first humorous item. Smiling thus does not frame humor here as is sometimes the case (Gironzetti et al., 2016; Gironzetti, Attardo, and Picketing 2016; Priego-Valverde et al. 2018). Switching directly from a neutral face to laughter, MA, the speaker, laughs after the first humorous item, framing it *afterwards* as humorous. As for the recipient, PC seems to need more time and smiles (S3) after having acknowledged MA's teasing with a neutral face. Finally, both participants display a simultaneous neutral face when they go back both to being serious and to the previous conversational topic they were developing before MA's humorous insert (the class they were talking about).

4.2 Example 2. ERAG: "a decade"

```
AG 215: but when we met we were really young and
   AG: S1
   ER: S0
AG 216: and it was so great you know to say that we were seeing each other
   AG: S1                       S2
   ER: S0
again in another town uh which was totally different from where we grew up
   AG: S2                  S0
   ER: S0
AG 217: years uh
   AG: S0
   ER: S0
AG 218: actually a decade later
   AG: S0
   ER: S0
AG 219: and uh
   AG: S0
   ER: S1
ER 150: a decade that sounds BAD huh
   ER: S3
   AG: S2
AG 220: yeah @@really bad@@ @ + having said it [out loud] yeah
   AG:      S2     S4
   ER:      S3     S4
ER 151: @
   ER: S4
   AG: S4
AG 221: right + {smiling voice} a few years later
   AG: S3
   ER: S4
AG 222: but uh yeah no no it was
   AG: S2
   ER: S4                        S3
AG 223: nice
   AG: S1
   ER: S3
ER 152: yeah i can imagine but
   ER: S3
   AG: S1
AG 224: to see people again uh
   AG: S2
   ER: S3
[…]
```

Figure 7: Transcript ERAG.

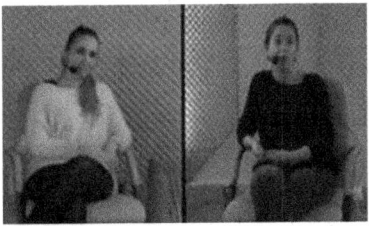

Figure 8: Just before "a decade that sounds bad".

Figure 9: "a decade that sounds bad".

The two participants are PhD students. From the beginning of the excerpt (figure 7) to (AG 218), AG is talking about an old acquaintance she met by chance in the city where she is currently living, while the two of them grew up in a different city, and she is pondering the fact that their high school days are far behind them. During her narration, she first displays some smiles (S1 and S2) and suppresses them to display a neutral face. The recipient, ER, displays a neutral face throughout this passage. However, just after having heard "a decade," ER displays a small smile (S1) (figure 8) while AG maintains a neutral face (AG 219). Then, in (ER 150) ER pins (Traverso, 1999; Guardiola et al., 2012; Priego-Valverde, 2016) the word "decade" to initiate a humorous utterance while increasing her smile (up to S3) (figure 9). Insisting on the word "bad" produced in a louder voice, not only she exaggerates what one can feel realizing that ten years have passed, but also the suddenness of this realization. In doing so, she both disaligns and disaffiliates with AG: not only does she disrupt the ongoing storytelling, but she also switches into a humorous frame while AG was in a serious one. This humorous disruption is accepted by AG; she both aligns and affiliates with ER. AG affiliates by switching from a neutral face to a smile (S2) while ER is producing her humorous utterance (ER 150), and then she aligns with ER, playing along with the humorous utterance (AG 220). While AG is laughing, she rebounds on the word "bad" and exaggerates even more through the interjection "really bad". She also plays along with the sudden realization implied by ER ("having said it [out loud] yeah"). Both participants jointly laugh until AG goes back to her story progressively. In (AG 221), AG, while smiling (S3), rephases her previous serious utterance which was humorously pinned, as if her mitigation could also lessen the number of the years that had gone by, and her smile progressively subsides as she continues her story. At the same time, ER, the recipient, producing a bigger smile than AG – which could be seen as an affiliative smile, see Gironzetti, this volume – finally aligns with AG (ER 152) by producing positive feedback to AG's comments (AG 223), and AG can continue her story.

In both of the previous examples, the humor produced is accepted and played along with. Both participants' smiles and/or laughter in each example appear around the humorous sequences and disappear after them. The distribution of smiles and laughter displayed by both participants is thus consistent with the quantitative results shown in the previous section. However, the sequential analysis of these examples shows that the interactional negotiation of humor by the participants is more complex than the quantitative analysis of their nonverbal behavior suggests. For instance, in Example 1 the humor is produced by the participant who currently has the floor, while it is produced by the recipient in Example 2. This appears to show that when humor is produced by the current speaker, laughter frames humor afterwards, whereas when it is produced by the recipient, humor is framed before being produced, and is done so by a smile. In other words, participants act as if humor is legitimate to a greater or lesser extent according to their interactional role and as such, as if humor should be more or less announced and prepared.

The way the humorous sequence ends also differs according to the participants' interactional role. In both cases the humorous sequences are closed by both participants displaying a neutral face, thus marking their agreement, but in Example 1, the speaker who has already the floor when producing humor both initiates and ends the humorous sequence. On the contrary, in Example 2, the humorous sequence is ended by the participant who had the floor before being humorously disrupted. Here again, the way the humorous sequence is closed raises the question of the legitimacy of the humor. In Example 1, the humor seems to be more legitimate, but it is ended by the participant who introduced it. In contrast, in Example 2 the legitimacy of the humor can be seen as more questionable, but it is closed by the participant who was disrupted.

4.3 Example 3. JSCL: « content and form »

This excerpt appears during the last few minutes of the interaction between the two participants. The participants, who take the same classes with the same professors, are talking about one of their classmates who, a few days after the recording, will take an oral exam with a professor whom neither of them really likes (CL 362 to JS 341). This is why JS (340) produces a confirmation request about the members of the jury of the oral exam after this professor is mentioned by name. While the name of the problematic professor is pronounced with a neutral face, both participants then simultaneously display a small smile (in S1) until (JS 241) during which JS produces a deprecating comment about the professor, wishing the student "good luck." This negative comment, produced with a small smile displayed by both participants, shows their agreement about the professor. The smile is then followed by a long silence (3.20) during which CL purses her lips and Figure 10 is the transcript of the example. JS looks at the camera. In doing so, they both show that they realize simultaneously that they are not only being recorded,

```
CL 362: he told me that MH would definitely be on his jury
    CL: S1              ──S0
    JS: S0
JS 340: on his own jury
    JS: S0           S1
    CL: S0        S1
CL 363: yeah
    CL: S1
    JS: S1
(2.05 seconds of silence)
JS: 341: good luck
    JS: S1
    CL: S1
(3.20 of silence; CL purses her lips and JS looks over at the camera)
CL 364: yeah I just @@ thought of that @@ @
    CL: S2                    S4
    JS: S2   S3          S4
JS 342: @
    JS: S4
    CL: S4
(3.37 seconds of silence)
CL 365: @
    CL: S4
    JS: S4
CL 366: @
       CL: S4
    JS: S4
CL 367: @
       CL: S4
    JS: S4
(Shared laughter for 8.18 seconds)
CL 368: but no pf $it's the it's the + the content + the form$ @@I'm telling
you@@ @
    CL: S4       S0                                                  S4
    JS: S4                                          S2      S4
JS: 343: @
    JS: S4
    CL: S4
CL 369: @
    CL: S4
    JS: S4
CL 370: @
       CL: S4
    JS: S4
CL 371: @@shit so yesterday I called my grandfather
    CL: S3            S0
    JS: S2           S1
CL 372: to tell him how well it was the 24th
    CL: S0
    JS: S0
[…]
```

Figure 10: Transcript JSCL.

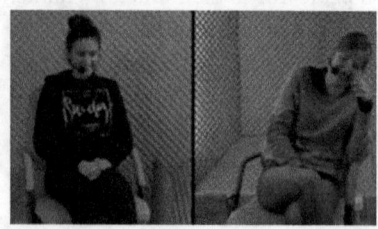

Figure 11: Before "the content".

Figure 12: During "the content".

Figure 13: After "the content".

but also that the experimenter outside the room is a colleague of the professor they mentioned. Their mutual silence is ended by increased smiles and laughter both displayed when CL verbalizes that they made a mistake (CL 364). Their shared laughter lasts for more than 8 seconds (figure 11). Sharing laughter for such a long interval is probably multipurpose. It can mark their embarrassment (Chafe 2007) as well as their bonding. But when they realize their blunder, instead of minimizing it, CL stands by it (CL 368) by quoting one of the professor's language tics ("it's the content, the form") (figure 12). She thus produces reported speech, making the professor talk. What marks this utterance as teasing the professor is the fact that, previously in the ongoing interaction, CL has said it before, also to tease the professor. This utterance thus constitutes a kind of inside joke between the two participants, which is accepted as such by JS who laughs (figure 13).

Focusing on the nonverbal behavior CL displays while producing her teasing is interesting. On the one hand, her reported speech is produced with a sudden neutral face. Neutral face thus appears to function as a humorous device. While CL is repeating one of the professor's language tics, she also mimics her irritated stance when she corrects students in class. Thus, CL's neutral face, far from being surprising or even paradoxical when it is displayed during a teasing sequence, is, on the contrary, *part of the teasing sequence* because it is an integral part of the reported speech CL is producing. The reported speech constituting the teasing is preceded by laughter and ends with CL's final laugh. While the sudden switch from neutral face to laughter could be seen as paradoxical, it can, on the contrary, be explained interactionally: as shown by the transcript (CL 368), the recipient (JS) begins to laugh before the speaker. By doing so, not only does she show her understanding and appreciation of the teasing, but she also may have caused CL to laugh who thus finishes her reported speech laughing and with a final laugh.

CL's neutral face during her teasing sequence is thus not incongruous with the activity: it is essential to her teasing in which she reports both speech and the facial expression of her professor. While it is successful, this teasing is only answered by the recipient's laughter and is not further developed. In the end, it is CL herself who closes the humorous sequence she has initiated, changing the conversational topic (CL 371).

5 Concluding remarks

Our study reports on interactional humor in face-to-face interactions using a mixed approach. Our quantitative analysis of the whole corpus uncovers three main trends. *The first trend involves laughter* and highlights two results. On the one hand, the proportion of laughter starts to increase at the beginning of a humorous segment, reaches an apex at the very end of the segment and decreases afterward. But on the other hand, this result concerns only 30% of the recipient's productions and 40% of the speaker's (see Section 3), which means that most humorous instances are produced without generating laughter. In addition to showing that there is not a one-to-one relationship between laughter and humor (see Section 1.3), the sequential analysis of the examples can provide some answers. Indeed, none of the three examples analyzed show the trend where laughter increases before humor until reaching an apex, and decreases afterward. On the contrary, in Examples 1 and 2, laughter appears only *after* the humorous instances. But while both examples have the same humorous device in common, a "rebound" (Norrick 1993) on what was said previously, the speaker's facial expression preceding the humorous utterance is different. In Example 1, MA displays a neutral face. As he rebounds on the other's words produced in a serious voice, MA adopts a serious voice as well to then signal, only afterwards, with laughter, that he has switched into a humorous mode of communication. Using a rebound as a discursive device to produce humor can explain this fact. Rebounding on something the other person has said, is, in some ways, putting oneself in the other's shoes, apparent seriousness included. It is up to the recipient to understand the rebound and to uncover the humorous dimension of it. In other words, it appears that both humorous discursive devices and nonverbal behaviors may be used by participants in a complementary way in order to produce humor. Example 2 is different: although ER uses the same humorous device (a rebound) and also produces laughter afterwards, ER produces a small smile (S1) before her humorous utterance and increases it (S3) during her production of humor.

Example 2 leads to the *second observed trend, i.e., the evolution of the mean proportion of each smile intensity* (S1, S2, S3). For both the speaker and the recipient, smiles increase in proportion starting at about 6 seconds before the beginning of a humorous segment and reach a plateau that remains present throughout the segment and only starts to decrease 4 seconds after the end of the segment. The same trend is observed for the recipient but delayed by about 2 seconds with respect to the speaker. Here again, however, our sequential analysis of the examples shows another picture. In Example 2, ER displays an S1 smile before the humorous utterance and increases it to S3 during the utterance, while in the other two examples the participants have neutral facial expressions before and during the humorous sequence. In other words, Example 2 is consistent with this trend and previous studies (see Gironzetti et al. 2016; Gironzetti, Attardo, and Pickering 2016; Gironzetti 2017; Gironzetti et al. 2018; Priego-Valverde et al. 2018), while the other examples show that this trend is not systematic. Moreover, since the same discursive device (a rebound) is used in Examples 1 and 2, ER's smile could be explained by her role as recipient and not as current speaker (as in Example 1), as if the question of the legitimacy of the humor produced were at stake. In this case, smiling could facilitate its acceptance.

Furthermore, our sequential analysis can provide some explanations as to why the recipient's behavior mirrors the speaker's but is delayed. Beyond the obvious fact that the recipient needs time to listen to the utterance before reacting to it, s/he also needs time to uncover the humorous dimension of the utterance before reacting. For instance, in Example 1, PC, the recipient, who displayed a neutral face during MA's humorous sequence, begins to smile only after MA laughs. In other words, PC's reaction was likely produced after she understood that MA's utterance was humor and not a reproach for not having listened to the class she did not understand. In Example 2, AG, the recipient, displays an S2 smile when ER, the speaker, is producing an S3, before they end up laughing together. These examples thus show that the recipient needs time not only to listen to an utterance, but also to find out the potential humorous dimension of the utterance before reacting to it. In other words, smiles and laughter are resources for both the speaker and the recipient for negotiating humor: while smiles and laughter are used by the speaker to show (even afterwards) that s/he is producing humor, they are used by the recipient to show his/her acceptance, or at least recognition.

The final trend highlighted by the quantitative analysis involves neutral face: about half of the humorous segments start with participants exhibiting a neutral face (45% for the recipient and 50% for the speaker). This result is exemplified in Example 1 where both participants display a neutral face before and during the humorous utterance. However, neutral face cannot be only analyzed in terms of framing or a comprehension cue and as such, Example 3 is remarkable. Before the production of the humorous utterance in this example, both participants are laughing together. They have just realized they have probably made a mistake when they overtly made fun of a professor and said her name. But instead of changing the topic, one of the participants (CL) pushes it further and stages this professor using reported speech. Not only does she repeat a phrase that the professor always uses in class, but she also imitates the professor's facial expression and attitude. Here, the neutral face CL displays during her humorous reported speech (contrasting with her laughing just before), can be seen both as a humorous device per se and a resource to show she is switching into humor.

In this chapter, assuming their complementarity, we have provided a mixed analysis – both quantitative and qualitative – of three nonverbal behaviors (neutral face, smiles, and laughter) displayed by participants before, during, and after humorous sequences. Although a quantitative analysis is necessary to give a comprehensive picture of the whole corpus and identifies general trends, we have shown that only a sequential analysis (necessarily of smaller parts of the corpus) allows us to analyze the different participants' nonverbal behaviors as a *resource* to produce humor, to react to it, and then to negotiate it. It is only by analyzing, moment-by-moment, the way these nonverbal behaviors are displayed, that one can understand how integral they are to the negotiation of humor. If some general trends highlighted by the quantitative analysis can appear surprising (e.g., the frequency of neutral face preceding a humorous utterance), the sequential analysis shows that none of these nonverbal behaviors appear randomly. While a neutral face can function as a humorous device per se (Example 3), another humorous device (the rebound) can also explain why some humorous utterances are framed *afterwards* by laughter, and not beforehand, and how this strategy is successful since the recipients end up smiling and accepting the humor after it is produced (Example 1).

This preliminary study must be followed up with a more in-depth analysis. Considering that a conversation is a very organized interaction (Sacks, Schegloff, and Jefferson 1974) structured into different activities (such as storytelling, explanation, or argumentation), and where, according to the activity, the participants are attributed the roles of main speaker and recipient with correlative actions (see Stivers 2008; Guardiola and Bertrand 2013; Priego-Valverde 2020; 2021), further analyses should integrate these elements. While this point was only mentioned for Examples 1 and 2, we would like to investigate more systematically the way these nonverbal resources are used depending on whether the producer of humor is the main speaker or the recipient. Similarly, it would be useful to analyze the way (both verbally and nonverbally) the humorous sequence is ended and by whom.

Finally, all the examples sequentially analyzed were of successful humor. Further analyses are needed to investigate the role of these nonverbal behaviors in cases of failed humor.

Annexes

Transcription conventions

@	laughter
{smiling voice}	applied to the following segments
:	vocalic extension
+	silent pause
↑	rising tone
a-	truncated word
§word§	reported speech
it HURTS	emphasized word or syllable
underlined word	overlap
/	self-interruption
✷	undetermined noise
In bold	occurrence of humor

French transcriptions

Example 1 : MAPC, « tu avais écouté ? »

```
PC 79 : ça change absolument rien quoi
   PC : S0
   MA : S0
MA 77 : le quoi le cours de la s(e)maine dernière↑
   MA : S0
   PC : S0
PC 80 : hm
   PC : S0
   MA : S0
MA 78 : hm ça va encore celui de la s(e)maine dernière ça va
   MA : S0
   PC : S0
MA 79 : t(u) avais écouté @
   MA :    S0            S4
   PC :    S0            S0
PC 81 : oui + ah oui
   PC : S0       S3
   MA : S4
PC 82 : non attends la- la s(e)maine dernière {voix souriante} j'ai écouté
   PC : S2
   MA : S3
PC 83 : j'étais à fond même
   PC : S2
   MA : S1
PC 84 : rappelle-toi
   PC : S2
   MA : S1
MA 80 : (soupir) ouais
   MA : S1
   PC : S2
PC 85 : rarement j€ le suis mais là j'(é)tais à fond
   PC : S2
   MA : S1
MA 81 : ça dépend / en fait ça dépend des s(e)maines quoi (il) y a des semaines où
   MA : S0
   PC : S0
MA 82 : c'est super clair super
   MA : S0
   PC : S0
MA 83 : (en)fin où ça va en fait
   MA : S0
   PC : S0
[…]
```

Example 2: ERAG, « une décennie »

```
AG 215 : et pourtant on s'est connues on était toute petite et
    AG : S1
    ER : S0
AG 216 : et c'était vachement bien tu vois de se dire qu'on + se recroisait
    AG : S1                        S2
       ER : S0
dans une aut(re) ville euh ~ qui avait rien à voir de là où on avait grandi
       AG: S2        S0
       ER : S0
AG 217 : des années euh
    AG : S0
    ER : S0
AG 218 : une décennie même après
    AG : S0
    ER : S0
AG 219 : et euh
    AG : S0
    ER : S1
ER 150 : ça fait MAL une décennie hein
    ER : S3
    AG : S2
AG 220 : @@ ouais grave @@ @ + de l'avoir dit ouais
    AG : S4
    ER : S4
ER 151 : @
    ER : S4 :
    AG : S4
AG 221 : bon + {voix souriante} quelques années après
    AG : S3
    ER : S4
AG 222 : mais euh ouais non non c'était
    AG : S2
    ER : S4                        S3
AG 223 : sympa
    AG : S1
    ER : S3
ER 152 : ouais j'imagine mais
    ER : S3
    AG : S1
AG 224 : de retrouver des gens euh
    AG : S2
    ER : S3
[…]
```

Example 3: JSCL, « le fond et la forme »

```
CL 362 : I il m'a dit que forcément dans son jury il y aurait MH
   CL : S1                    S0
   JS : S0
JS 340 : dans son jury à lui
   JS : S0         S1
   CL : S0 S1
CL 363 : ouais
   CL: S1
   JS: S1
(silence de 2.05 secondes)
JS : 341 : courage
   JS : S1
   CL : S1
(silence de 3.20 ; moue rieuse de CL et regard caméra de JS)
CL 364 : ouais je viens @@ d'y penser @@ @
   CL : S2                         S4
   JS : S2 S3                   S4
JS 342 : @
   JS: S4
   CL: S4
(silence de 3.37 secondes)
CL : 365 : @
   CL : S4
   JS : S4
CL 366 : @
      CL : S4
   JS : S4
CL 367 : @
      CL : S4
   JS : S4
(Rire commun pendant 8.18 secondes)
CL 368 : mais non pf c'est le c'est la + le fond + la forme @@ je te dis @@
@
   CL : S4     S0                                              S4
   JS: S4                                          S2     S4
JS : 343 : @
   JS: S4
   CL: S4
CL 369 : @
   CL : S4
   JS : S4
CL 370 : @
      CL : S4
   JS : S4
CL 371 : @@putain hier j'ai appelé mon@@ grand-père du coup
   CL : S3            S0
   JS : S2            S1
CL 372 : pour lui dire comment ça enfin euh c'était le vingt-quatre
   CL : S0
   JS : S0
[…]
```

References

Ambadar, Zara, Jeffrey Cohn & Lawrence Ian Reed. 2009. All smiles are not created equal: Morphology and timing of smiles perceived as amused, polite, and embarrassed/nervous. *Journal of nonverbal behavior 33*(1). 17–34.

Amoyal Mary, Béatrice Priego-Valverde & Stéphane Rauzy. 2020. PACO: A corpus to analyze the impact of common ground in spontaneous face-to-face interaction. *Language Resources and Evaluation Conference, LREC2020*, Marseille, France, May 2020.

Amoyal, Mary. 2022. *Le sourire dans les transitions thématiques: analyse multimodale d'interactions conversationnelles en fonction de la relation des interactants*. Aix-en-Provence: Aix Marseille Université Dissertation.

Argyle, Michael. 1988. [1975]. *Bodily communication*. London: Methuen.

Attardo, Salvatore. 1994. *Linguistic Theories of Humor*. Berlin/Boston: De Gruyter Mouton.

Attardo, Salvatore. 2008. Semantics and pragmatics of humor. Language and Linguistics *Compass* 2/6. 1203–1215.

Attardo, Salvatore. 2020. *The linguistics of humor. An introduction*. Oxford: Oxford University Press.

Bateson, Gregory. 1955/1972. The position of humor in human communication. In Heinz von Foerster (ed.), *Cybernetics, Ninth Conference*, 1–47. New York: Josiah Macey Jr Foundation.

Bavelas, Janet Beavin, Nicole Chovil, Linda Coates & Lori Roe. 1991. Gestures specialized for dialogue. *Personnality and Social Psychology Bulletin* 21. 394–405.

Bavelas, Janet, Jennifer Gerwing & Sara Healing. 2014. Including facial gestures in gesture speech ensembles. In Mandana Seyfeddinipur and Marianne Gullberg (eds.), *From Gesture in Conversation to Visible Action as Utterance: Essay in honor of Adam Kendon*, 15–34. Philadelphia: John Benjamins.

Bell, Nancy. 2009. Responses to failed humor. *Journal of Pragmatics* 41.1825–1836.

Bell, Nancy. 2015. *We are not amused. Failed humor in interaction*. Berlin/Boston: De Gruyter Mouton.

Bertrand, Roxane, Philippe Blache, Robert Espesser, Gaëlle Ferré, Christine Meunier, Béatrice Priego-Valverde & Stephane Rauzy. 2008. 'Le CID—Corpus of Interactional Data-Annotation et Exploitation Multimodale de Parole Conversationnelle. *Traitement Automatique des Langues* 49. 105–134.

Bertrand, Roxane & Béatrice Priego-Valverde. 2011. Does prosody play a specific role in conversational humor? *Pragmatics and Cognition* 19. 333–356.

Bigi, Brigitte. 2015. SPPAS – Multi-lingual Approaches to the Automatic Annotation of Speech. *The Phonetician – International Society of Phonetic Sciences*, 111–112. 54–69.

Birdwhistell, Ray. 1968. L'analyse kinésique. *Langages* (10). 101–106.

Boersma, Paul & David Weenink. 2009. *Praat:Doing Phonetics by Computer*. (Version5.1.05) [Computer program]. Available online: http://www.praat.org/

Boudin, Auriane, Roxane Bertrand, Stéphane Rauzy, Magali Ochs & Philippe Blache. 2021. A Multimodal Model for Predicting Conversational Feedbacks, In *International Conference on Text, Speech, and Dialogue*. Springer.

Bousmalis, Konstantinos, Marc Mehu & Maja Pantic. 2009. Spotting Agreement and Disagreement: A Survey of Nonverbal Audiovisual Cues and Tools. Proceedings Vol. II *Workshop on Affective Brain-Computer Interfaces and IEEE International Workshop on Social Signal Processing, International Conference on ACII 2009*: Affective Computing and Intelligent Interaction September 2009, Amsterdam, The Netherlands, 121–129.

Boxer, Diana & Florencia Cortés-Conde. 1997. From bonding to biting: Conversational joking and identity display. Journal of Pragmatics, 27(3). 275–294.

Brunner, Lawrence J. 1979. Smiles can be back channels. *Journal of Personality and Social Psychology* 37(5). 728–734.

Burgers, Christian & Margot Van Mulken. 2017. Humor markers. In Salvatore Attardo (ed.), *The Routledge handbook of language and humor*, 385–399. London, UK: Routledge.

Chafe, Wallace. 2007. *The importance of not being earnest. The feeling behind laughter and humor*. Amsterdam/Philadelphia: John Benjamins Publishing Company.

Chapman, Anthony J. & Hugh Corrie Foot. 1996. *Humour and Laughter: Theory, research and applications*. London: Wiley.

Chiaro, Delia. 1992. *The Language of Jokes: Analyzing Verbal Play*. London/New-York: Routledge.

Chovanec, Jan. 2015. Participant roles and embedded interactions in online sports broadcasts. In Marta Dynel & Jan Chovanec (eds.) *Participation in Public and Social Media Interactions*, 67–95. Amsterdam/Philadelphia: John Benjamins.

Chovil, Nicole. 1991. Social determinants of facial displays. *Journal of Nonverbal Behavior* 15(6). 141–154.

Clark, Herbert. H. 1996. *Using language*. Cambridge: Cambridge University Press.

Clift, Rebecca. 2012. Identifying action: Laughter in non-humorous reported speech, *Journal of Pragmatics* 44. 1303–1312.

Clift, Rebecca. 2016. Don't make me laugh: Responsive laughter in (dis)affiliation, *Journal of Pragmatics* 100. 73–88.

Coates, Linda. 1991. *A collaborative theory of inversion: irony in dialogue*. Victoria: University of Victoria dissertation.

Cohen, Jacob. 1960. A coefficient of agreement for nominal scales. *Educational and psychological measurement*, 20(1). 37–46.

Cosnier, Jacques. 1996. Les gestes du dialogue, la communication non verbale. *Psychologie de la motivation* 21. 129–138.

Couper-Kuhlen, Elisabeth & Margret Selting. 2018. *Interactional Linguistics. Studying Language in Social Interaction*. Cambridge: Cambridge University Press.

Duncan, Starkey, Lawrence J. Brunner & Donald W. Fiske. 1979. Strategy signals in face-to-face interaction. *Journal of Personality and Social Psychology* 37(2). 301–313.

Ekman, Paul. 1984. Expression and the nature of emotion. *Approaches to emotion*. 3.19–344.

Ekman, Paul. 2007. *Emotions Revealed*. New York: Henry Holt.

Ekman, Paul & Wallace Friesen. 1978. *Manual for the Facial Action Code*. Palo Alto, CA: Consulting Psychologist Press.

Ekman, Paul, Richard Sorenson & Wallace Friesen. 1969. Pan-cultural elements in facial displays of emotion. *Science* 164 (3875). 86–88.

Elfenbein, Hillary Anger & Nalini Ambady. 2002. On the universality and cultural specificity of emotion recognition: A meta-analysis. *Psychology Bulletin* 128(2). 203–235.

Ergül, Hilal, Shelby Miller, Kevin Kramer & Salvatore Attardo. This volume. Alternative conceptualizations of the Smiling Intensity Scale (SIS) and their applications to the identification of humor. In Béatrice Priego-Valverde (ed.), *Interactional humor: multimodal design and negotiation*, Berlin/Boston: De Gruyter Mouton.

Gironzetti, Elisa. 2017. *Multimodal and eye-tracking evidence in the negotiation of Pragmatic intentions in dyadic conversations: The case of humorous discourse*. Commerce: Texas A & M University-Commerce dissertation.

Gironzetti, Elisa, Lucy Pickering, Meichan Huang, Ying Zhang, Shigehito Menjo & Salvatore Attardo. 2016. Smiling synchronicity and gaze patterns in dyadic humorous conversations. *Humor: International Journal of Humor Research* 29(2). 301–324.

Gironzetti, Elisa, Salvatore Attardo & Lucy Pickering. 2016. Smiling, gaze, and humor in conversation. In Leonor Ruiz-Gurillo (ed.), *Metapragmatics of Humor: Current research trends*, 235–254. Amsterdam/Philadelphia: John Benjamins Publishing.

Gironzetti, Elisa, Salvatore Attardo & Lucy Pickering. 2018. Smiling and the negotiation on humor in conversation, *Discourse Processes*. https://doi.org/10.1080/0163853X.2018.1512247

Gironzetti, Elisa. 2022. *The multimodal performance of conversational humor*. Philadelphia: John Benjamins.

Gironzetti, Elisa. This volume. Humorous Smiling: A Reverse Cross-Validation of the Smiling Intensity Scale for the Identification of Conversational Humor and its Cues. In Béatrice Priego-Valverde (ed.), *Interactional humor: multimodal design and negotiation*, Berlin/Boston: De Gruyter Mouton.

Glenn, Phillip. 2003. *Laughter in interaction*. Cambridge: Cambridge University Press.

Glenn, Phillip. 2010. Interviewer laughs: Shared laughter and asymmetries in employment Interviews, *Journal of Pragmatics* 42. 1485–1498.

Glenn, Phillip & Elisabeth Holt (eds.). 2013. *Studies of laughter in interaction*. London, UK: Bloomsbury Academic Press.

Glenn, Phillip & Elisabeth Holt. 2017. Conversation analysis and humor. In Salvatore Attardo (ed.), *The Routledge handbook of language and humor*. 295–308. London: Routledge.

Guardiola, Mathilde, Roxane Bertrand, Sylvie Bruxelles, Carole Etienne, Emilie, Jouin-Jardon, Florence Oloff, Beatrice Priego-Valverde & Véronique Traverso. 2012. Other-repetition: displaying others' lexical choices as "commentable", In *ISICS: International Symposium on Imitation and Convergence in Speech 1*, Aix-en-Provence, France.

Guardiola, Mathilde & Roxane Bertrand. 2013. Interactional convergence in conversational storytelling: when reported speech is a cue of alignment and/or affiliation. *Frontiers in Psychology* 4. 1–17.

Gumperz, John. 1982. The linguistic bases of communicative competence, In *Analyzing discourse: Text and talk*. Georgetown University Press: Washington DC.

Haakana, Markku. 2001. Laughter as a patient's resource: Dealing with delicate aspects of medical interaction, *Text* 21(1/2). 187–219.

Haakana, Markku. 2002. Laughter in medical interaction: From quantification to analysis, and back. *Journal of sociolinguistics* 6(2). 207–235.

Haakana, Markku. 2010. Laughter and smiling: Notes on co-occurrences. *Journal of Pragmatics* 42(6). 1499–1512.

Haddad, Kevin, Noé Tits & Thierry Dutoit. 2018. Annotating Nonverbal Conversation Expressions in Interaction Datasets. In Jonathan Ginzburg & Catherine Pélachaud (eds.), *Proceedings of Laughter Workshop*, 54–57. France: Sorbonne Université.

Haugh, Michael. 2014. Jocular Mockery as interactional practice in everyday Anglo-Australian conversation. *Australian Journal of Linguistics* 34(1). 76–99.

Haugh, Michael. 2017. Teasing. In Salvatore Attardo (ed.), *Handbook of language and humour*. 204–218. London: Routledge.

Hay, Jennifer. 1995. *Gender and humour: beyond a joke*. New Zealand: Victoria University of Wellington Master thesis.

Hay, Jennifer. 2001. The pragmatics of humor support. *Humor* 14(1). 55–82.

Heritage, John. 1984. A change-of-state token and aspects of its sequential placement. In J. Maxwell Atkinson & John Heritage (eds.), *Structures of Social Action*. Cambridge University Press, Cambridge.

Hofmann, Jennifer, Tracey Platt & Willibald Ruch. 2017. Laughter and Smiling in 16 Positive Emotions. *IEEE Transactions On Affective Computing*. 1–14.

Holt, Elisabeth. 2010. The last laugh: Shared laughter and topic termination. *Journal of Pragmatics* 42(6). 1513–1525.

Hymes, Dell. 1972. Models of the interaction of language and social life. In John Gumperz & Dell Hymes (eds.), *Directions in sociolinguistics: The ethnography of communication*, 35–71. New York: Holt, Rinehart and Winston.

Izard, Carroll E. 1997. Emotions and facial Expressions. A Perspective from Differential Emotions Theory. In James A. Russell & José Miguel Fernández-Dols (eds.), *The Psychology of Facial Expression*, 57–76. Cambridge, UK: Cambridge University Press.

Jefferson, Gail, Harvey Sacks & Emanuel Schegloff. 1987. Notes on laughter in pursuit of intimacy. In Graham Button, Graham & John Lee (eds.), *Talk and Social Organization*, 152–205. Multilingual Matters, Clevedon.

Jefferson, Gail. 1979. A technique for inviting laughter and its subsequent acceptance declination. In George Psathas (ed.), *Everyday language: Studies in ethnomethodology*, 79–96. New York: Irvington.

Jefferson, Gail. 1984. On the organization of laughter in talk about troubles. In J. Maxwell Atkinson & John Heritage (eds.), *Structures of Social Action: Studies In Conversation Analysis*, 346–369. Cambridge, UK: Cambridge University Press.

Jefferson, Gail. 1985. An exercise in the transcription and analysis of laughter. In Teun Van Dijk (ed.), *Handbook of discourse analysis. Discourse and dialogue*, 25–34. London, UK: Academic Press.

Jefferson, Gail. 2004. A note on laughter in 'male-female' interaction. *Discourse Studies*, 6(1). 117–133.

Jensen, Mikael. 2015. Smile as Feedback Expressions in Interpersonal Interaction. *International Journal of Psychological Studies*. 7(4). 95–105.

Kaukomaa, Timo, Anssi Peräkylä & Johanna Ruusuvuori 2013. Turn-opening smiles: Facial expression constructing emotional transition in conversation. *Journal of Pragmatics* 55. 21–42.

Keltner, Dacher. 1995. Signs of appeasement: evidence for the distinct displays of embarrassment, amusement, and shame. *Journal of Personality and Social Psychology*, 68. 441–454. doi:10.1037/0022-3514.68.3.441

Koestler, Arthur. 1964. *Le cri d'Archimède*, Paris: Calmann-Levy.

Lynch, Robert F. & Robert L. Trivers. 2012. Self-deception inhibits laughter. *Personality and Individual Differences* 53. 491–495.

Mazzocconi, Chiara, Ye Tian & Jonathan Ginzburg. 2020. What's your laughter doing there? A taxonomy of the pragmatic functions of laughter, *IEEE Transactions on Affective Computing*. 13 (3). 1302–1321.

Mehu, Marc & Robin Denbar. 2008. Relationship between Smiling and Laughter in Humans *(Homo sapiens)*: Testing the Power Asymmetry Hypothesis. *Folia Primatologica* 79(5). 269–280.

Morreall, John. 2001. Sarcasm, irony, wordplay, and humor in the Hebrew bible: A response to Hershey Friedman. *Humor* 14(3): 293–302.

Mullan, Kerry & Christine Béal. 2018. Conversational humor in French and Australian English: What makes an utterance (un)funny? *Intercultural Pragmatics* 15(4). 457–485.

Niedenthal, Paula M, Markus Brauer, Jamin Halberstadt & Ase Innes-Ker. 2001. When did her smile drop? Facial mimicry and the influences of emotional state on the detection of change in emotional expression, *Cognition and Emotion* 15 (6). 853–86.

Niedenthal, Paula, Silvia Krauth-Gruber & François Ric. 2006. *Psychology of Emotion: Interpersonal, Experiential, and Cognitive Approaches*. New York: Psychology Press.

Niewiadomski, Radoslaw, Maurizio Mancini, Tobias Baur, Giovanna Varni, Harry Griffin & Min S. H. Aung. 2013. MMLI: Multimodal Multiperson Corpus of Laughter in Interaction. In Albert Ali Salah, Theo Gevers, Nicu Sebe & Alessandro Vinciarelli (eds.), *Proceedings of Human Behavior Understanding*, 184–195. Switzerland: Springer International Publishing.

Norrick, Neal R. 1993. *Conversational Joking*. Bloomington: Indiana University Press.
Nick O'Donnell-Trujillo & Katherine Adams. 1983. Hehe in conversation: some coordination accomplishments of laughter. *Western Journal of Speech Communication* 47. 175–191.
Osvaldsson, Karin. 2004. On laughter and disagreement in multiparty assessment talk. *Text* 24. 517–545.
Prepin, Ken, Magalie Ochs & Catherine Pelachaud. 2012. Mutual stance building in dyad of virtual agents: Smile alignment and synchronisation, In *International Conference on Privacy, Security, Risk and Trust and International Conference on Social Computing*. IEEE.
Priego-Valverde, Béatrice. 2003. *L'humour dans la conversation familière: description et analyse linguistiques*, France: L'harmattan.
Priego-Valverde, Béatrice. 2016. Teasing in casual conversations: An opportunistic discursive strategy. In Leonor Ruiz-Gurillo (ed.), *Metapragmatics of humor*, 215–233. Amsterdam: John Benjamins.
Priego-Valverde, Béatrice. 2018. Sharing a laugh at others: Humorous convergence in French conversation. *European Journal of Humour Research* 6 (3). 68–93.
Priego-Valverde, Béatrice. 2020. 'Stop kidding, I'm serious': Failed humor in French conversations. In Salvatore Attardo (ed.), *Script-based semantics. Foundations and applications. Essays in honor of Victor Raskin*, 191–225. Berlin/Boston: De Gruyter Mouton.
Priego-Valverde, Béatrice. 2021. Failed humor in conversation: disalignment and (dis)affiliation as a type of interactional failure. *Humor* 34 (4). 613–636.
Priego-Valverde, Béatrice, Brigitte Bigi, Salvatore Attardo, Lucy Pickering & Elisa Gironzetti. 2018. Is smiling during humor so obvious? A cross-cultural comparison of smiling behavior in humorous sequences in American English and French interactions. *Intercultural Pragmatics* 15(4). 563–591.
Priego-Valverde, Béatrice, Brigitte Bigi & Mary Amoyal. 2020. Cheese!: A corpus of face-to-face French interactions. A case study for analyzing smiling and conversational humor. *Language Resources and Evaluation Conference*. 460–468. LREC2020, May 2020, Marseille, France.
Provine, Robert. 2000. *Laughter: A scientific investigation*. New York, NY: Viking.
Raskin, Victor. 1985. *Semantic Mechanisms of Humor*. Dordrecht, Holland: D. Reidel Publishing Company.
Rauzy, Stéphane & Mary Amoyal. 2020. SMAD: A tool for automatically annotating the smile intensity along a video record. *HRC2020, 10th Humour Research Conference*, March 2020, Commerce, Texas, United States.
Romaniuk, Tanya. 2013. Interviewee laughter and disaffiliation in broadcast news interviews. In Philip Glenn & Elizabeth Holt (eds.), *Studies of laughter in interaction*, 201–220. London: Bloomsbury.
Ruch, Willibald & Paul Ekman. 2001. The Expressive Pattern of Laughter. In Alfred W. Kaszniak (ed.), *Emotions, qualia, and consciousness*, 426–443. Singapore: World Scientific.
Ruusuvuori, Johanna & Anssi Peräkylä. 2009. Facial and verbal expressions in assessing stories and topics. *Research on Language and Social Interaction*, *42*(4). 377–394.
Sacks, Harvey, Emanuel Schegloff & Gail Jefferson. 1974. A Simplest Systematic for The Organization of Turn Taking for Conversation. *Language* 50 (3). 696–735.
Shaw, Chloë, Alexa Hepburn & Jonathan Potter. 2013. Having the last laugh: On post-completion laughter particles, in Phillip Glenn & Elisabeth Holt (eds.), *Studies of Laughter in Interaction*, 91–106. London: Bloomsbury.
Sherzer, Joel. 1978. Oh! That's a pun and I didn't mean it. *Semiotica*. 22-3/4. 335–350.
Stallone, Letícia & Michael Haugh. 2017. Joint fantasizing as relational practice in Brazilian Portuguese interactions. *Language and Communication* 55. 10–23.

Stivers, Tanya. 2008. Stance, Alignment, and Affiliation During Storytelling: When Nodding Is a Token of Affiliation. *Research on Language and Social Interaction* 41(1). 31–57.

Tannen, Deborah. 1989. *Talking voices. Repetition, Dialogue, and Imagery in Conversational Discourse*, Cambridge: Cambridge University Press.

Tannen, Deborah. 2010. Abduction and identity in family interaction: Ventriloquizing as indirectness, *Journal of Pragmatics*. 42 (2). 307–316.

Tellier, Marion. 2010. Faire un geste pour l'apprentissage: le geste pédagogique dans l'enseignement précoce. In Colette Corblin & Jérémy Sauvage (eds.), *L'enseignement des langues vivantes étrangères à l'école. Impact sur le développement de la langue maternelle*, 31–54. Paris: L'Harmattan.

Theonas, G., Dave Hobbs & Dimitrios Rigas. 2008. Employing Virtual Lecturers' Facial Expressions in Virtual Educational Environments. *The International Journal of Virtual Reality*. 7(1), 31–44.

Traverso, Véronique 1999. *L'analyse des conversations*. Paris: Armand Colin.

Trouvain, Jürgen & Khiet Phuong Truong. 2017. Laughter. In Salvatore Attardo (ed.), *The Routledge handbook of language and humor*, 340–355. New York/London: Routledge.

Tsakona, Villy & Chovanec (eds.). 2018. *The Dynamics of Interactional Humour*. 229–255. Amsterdam: John Benjamins.

Vöge, Monika. 2010. Local identity processes in business meetings displayed through laughter in complaint sequences. *Journal of Pragmatics* 42. 1556–1576.

Ziv, Avner. 1984. *Personality and Sense of Humor*. New York: Springer Publishing Company.

Thomas Kiderle, Hannes Ritschel, Silvan Mertes
and Elisabeth André

6 Multimodal humor in human-robot interaction

Abstract: Over the last decade, humor has been of increasing interest in human-robot interaction research. Most research focuses on entertainment, whereas the use of humor in human-robot dialog, such as small talk, is still scarce. Meanwhile, robots are envisioned to be part of our everyday work and domestic environments of the future. Thus, robot humor is a thankful opportunity for making everyday human-robot interactions more pleasant and equipping robots with social intelligence.

The process of creating and presenting robot humor encompasses different building blocks. First, the humor must be scripted in advance or generated dynamically based on the interaction context. Next, the presentation of humor with a social robot requires synchronized verbal and non-verbal behaviors, such as vocal gestures, adjusted prosody, facial expression, gaze and gestures. Since humor is a subject of taste, finally, the robot should also be able to consider the individual user's preferences and personalize its presentation based on human feedback.

This chapter provides a structured overview of the building blocks involved in creating and communicating robot humor. Since robot humor is inspired by human communication, we (1) give a short overview of the most commonly used humor types (canned humor, irony) and how they are communicated by humans. The humor signals reported in the literature are the foundation for a structured implementation of multimodal humor for social robots. Next, we (2) give an overview of state-of-the-art robots performing humor, including scenarios, contents and adaptation approaches. Afterwards, we (3) present selected computational approaches from the literature for generating verbal humor. They serve as basis for a (4) step by step guide for augmenting verbal humor with verbal and non-verbal humor signals, which is applicable to humanoid robots. Finally, we (5) illustrate challenges for robot humor using the example of domestic human-robot interaction. This includes recognizing the dialog context, appropriateness and predictability of the humorous effect, limitations resulting from robot embodiment, salience of different modalities and adaptation of humor to individual users.

Keywords: human-robot interaction, canned joke, irony, multimodal humor, humor marker, implementation

1 Motivation

Humor belongs to one of the most sophisticated cognitive resources of the human mind, which helps in fostering interpersonal attraction, trust, reduction of stress, tension and more. The use of humor by robots is one opportunity to equip the machine with socially intelligent behaviors, to enhance the interaction experience for the user and ultimately to benefit from resulting positive effects. *Social* robots are predestined for communicating humor. They typically have a humanoid or zoomorphic embodiment and benefit from verbal and non-verbal communication channels (see Figure 1), including speech, sound, gaze and facial expression, gestures and posture, movement, as well as LED lights and displays.

In the last decades, robot humor has been investigated primarily for the purpose of entertainment in the context of standup comedy, involving one or two robots performing a show for an audience. Besides this domain, the use of humor in everyday and future HRI, such as in the user's domestic environment, is by no means the norm. This is due to the complexity of implementing humor in interactions with fully autonomous robots. First of all, the machine should be aware of the context or dialog topic of the interaction and estimate whether the use of humor is reasonable. Then, it must generate thematically linked humor or select appropriate prepared content and finally present it to the human with the aid of the available modalities. This situation is aggravated by the fact that humor preferences might differ between users, since sense of humor depends on a person's culture, age, gender and personality.

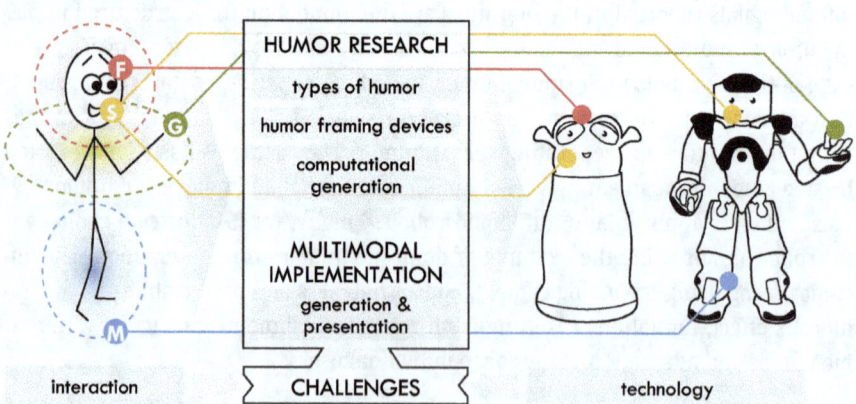

Figure 1: Insights from humor research are the basis of generating and presenting robot humor. F: facial expression/gaze. S: speech/prosody. G: gestures. M: movement/posture.

This chapter focuses on implementing robot humor by transferring the findings from human interaction to the machine. First, different types of humor (section 2) and their verbal and non-verbal human communication (section 3) are outlined in order to identify a set of characteristics and cues suitable for technical implementation. The aggregated observations from the humor literature serve as a basis for embedding, generating and communicating humor in HRI. Then, section 4 gives an overview of the literature with regard to robots presenting humor and humor generation approaches. Subsequently, it presents a structured approach for generating and communicating multimodal robot humor by transferring the findings from human interaction to a social robot. Finally, section 5 outlines several challenges, which must be taken in the future for embedding generative and scripted robot humor in everyday HRI with fully autonomous robots.

2 Types of humor

In human interaction and daily life, humor is usually communicated through *verbal* or *non-verbal* channels. Non-verbal humor consists of non-verbal behaviors, such as facial expressions, gestures, or non-verbal sounds (Norrick 2004). In contrast, verbal humor is manifested either through language in the form of verbal utterances or in textual form.

To be able to transfer human aspects of humor to a robot, first it is necessary to know, which types of humor in interpersonal interaction exist and how they are constituted. Therefore this section gives an overview of the types of humor, which will serve as potential starting points for implementing humor with a robot (see section 4). While the literature provides more in-depth details about specific types and subtypes, we focus on a high-level overview on verbal humor, since this is one of the most prominent modalities of a social robot.

Dynel (2009) classifies verbal humor among others according to the main categories: *canned* humor and *conversational* humor.[1] Although the boundaries may blur with respect to the degree of contextualization (Zajdman 1991), we decided to destinguish the humor types similar to Dynel's taxonomy. Thereby, the humor classification and implementing an humorous interaction is more straightforward. Since verbal humor and its augmentation with multimodal robot behaviors is the main subject of this chapter, the following sections present the theoretical basis.

---

[1] See also Martin et al. (2003) for humor styles.

2.1 Canned humor

Canned jokes are either delivered orally during a dialogue or presented textually. They are often described as a conversational component that is mainly decoupled from the rest of a conversation and thus independent of its context. However, detachment interrupts the conversational flow, if a speaker tells the joke without prior announcement. Therefore, jokes are usually introduced by verbal explicit statements, such as "Do you know this joke?" Jokes are composed of a *setup* and a *punchline*. (Dynel 2009, Attardo, Pickering and Baker 2013)

"A joke is a short humorous piece of oral literature in which the funniness culminates in the final sentence, called the *punchline*." (Hetzron 1991: 65–66). The first part, the setup, consists of a narrative, which is usually told monologically by the speaker in a longer conversational sequence. After the end of the narrative follows the punchline. It reveals information that leads to incongruence with the setup: the expectation built up in the listener during the setup is crossed by an unexpected turn in the end. The listener is triggered to reinterpret certain aspects from the narrative, and this is where the actual hilariousness of a joke resides.

Canned jokes can, among others, be subdivided into the special forms of riddles and oneliners. Both can be considered as a separate category (next to canned jokes) because of their distinct structure. Riddles involve asking a question, which serve as the setup, followed by a funny answer (e.g., "What is red and smells like blue paint? Red paint."). Oneliners are jokes where the setup and punchline consist of just a few words (e.g., "Chuck Norris tells Simon what to do."). Oneliners interrupt the conversational flow less than a conventional joke because of their reduced decoupling from the rest of the conversation. Therefore, they tend to be used contextually as well, which leads to be perceived similar to witticisms (see section 2.2).

2.2 Conversational humor

Conversational humor is defined as a humorous conversational component that is incorporated at any point into the surrounding conversation without humor. This conversational component has semantically the same function as the punchline for canned humor and is called *conversational punchline* or *jabline*. It is uttered spontaneously or is previously prepared for the respective context. Often, these utterances are shorter than a canned joke. Hence, conversational humor preserves the conversation flow. It does not usually need to be introduced by any preceding announcement by the speaker. However, this makes the humor highly context dependent and requires reference to the previous conversation's content. Thus, the humorous sequence represents an important element that often affects the development of the conversation. (Dynel 2009, Attardo, Pickering and Baker 2013)

One essential manifestation of conversational humor is witticism (e.g., "As little chance as a snowball in hell." Norrick 1984: 196). It is defined as an intelligent, humorous conversational component, which is closely connected with a not necessarily humorous conversation and usually refers to conventional topics of conversation (e.g., politics). Formally, witticisms look like one-liners, but usually rather communicate meanings outside the humorous component (e.g., other intentions). Depending on the communication goal, they may occur as a spontaneously uttered comment or previously accepted utterance of a social group. Other manifestations of conversational humor, such as lexemes, phrasemes, retorts, teasing, banter, putdowns, self-denigrating humor or anecdotes can be found in Dynel (2009).

2.3 Humor techniques

Alternatively to the previously introduced types of humor, Dynel (2009: 1288) distinguishes verbal humor regarding the "semantic phenomena or stylistic figures on which they operate." Other authors similarly use the term "humor techniques" (Buijzen and Valkenburg 2004, Juckel, Bellman and Varan 2016), on which we will also rely in this chapter.

There is no unified definition of *irony*, but the literature has identified several characteristics about its nature, comprehension and usage (Colston 2017). According to the relevance-theoretic claims in Yus (2016) there are several interpretations on irony: An utterance expressing a belief echoing implicitly the speaker's attitude and the echoed attitude dissociates from the utterance. Attardo (2000a) characterizes irony, i.a., by the following properties: (1) it is contextually inappropriate, (2) at the same time relevant, (3) used intentionally with awareness of the contextual inappropriateness, (4) the speaker intends that the audience recognizes the points (1)-(3). As a result, irony *may*, but need not, result in humor. There is no clear-cut differentiation between irony and sarcasm; Attardo (2000a) describes sarcasm as an "overtly aggressive type of irony".

Another humor technique is the *pun*, which is defined a humorous expression with intentional ambiguity in one or more words. These occur in one shape and communicate multiple meanings among others through the multiple sematics of the utterance itself or an allusion to an utterance with similar phonetics (e.g.,"The man who invented knock-knock jokes should get a no bell prize."). Examples for other well-known humor techniques as hyperboles/exaggeration, metaphors, paradoxes, allusions (distortions, quotations) or register clashes can be found in Buijzen and Valkenburg (2004), Dynel (2009), and Juckel, Bellman and Varan (2016).

According to Dynel (2009) there is no clear-cut border between different types of conversational humor. Additionally, each type can be combined with humor techniques. For instance, irony can coincide with witticism resulting in an ironic witticism (e.g., "As clear as mud.", see Norrick 1984: 196) or puns may be combined with riddles resulting in a punning riddle (e.g., "If Apple made a car, what would be missing? " "Windows.").

3 Humor framing devices

Besides knowledge about the structure of different humor types (see section 2), transferring human humor to social robots requires to present it appropriately to interlocutors. Therefore, we give an overview of how multimodal presentation of canned, conversational humor and irony are communicated in human interactions. This overview aggregates and lists multimodal humor signals to build a rich set of humor signals that could be implemented technically. We are aware that some of the signals were observed only raringly in the literature and some studies cannot easily be compared.

Verbal humor without any additional hints can be difficult to comprehend or not apparent at all to the listener in interpersonal conversations. Sometimes, humorous information can hardly be distinguished from non-humorous information and the humor may fail to achieve its desired effect. According to Chovanec and Tsakona (2018), the understanding of comical sections can be faciliated by applying additional *framing devices* via different modalities (e.g., speech, facial expressions, prosody, etc.), which communicate the message "this has been funny" on a meta-level. A shift between serious and humorous interaction modes is signaled with *code switches* (Georgalidou and Kaili 2018) or *metalinguistic devices* (Shilikhina 2018). Alternatively *explicit statements* and *humor signals* (Gironzetti 2017) can be used to signal that the current conversational unit has to be interpreted humorously.

Humor framing devices are not necessarily restricted to the role of the speaker, listeners can also share and negotiate with others their own evaluation of the current context (Dore 2018, Chovanec 2018, Cain 2018, Karachaliou and Archakis 2018). Independently from the speaker's intention this behavior can even lead to an unintended contribution of humor at all. Some signals do not only fall under the definition of humor support (Hay 2001), they can also work as a framing device (e.g., laughter).

In the following subsections, the literature about signalling canned humor, conversational humor and irony is presented. Thereby, the focus is on humor signals and explicit statements as humor framing devices. Since sometimes there is no clear distinction between the speaker and listener, such as when framing devices are co-developed, these special cases are excluded. At the end of each literature review, a table will be provided, which summarizes the state of the art on the humor framing devices for the corresponding humor in interpersonal interactions. This will serve as a blueprint for implementing robot humor.

3.1 Canned and conversational humor

Literature on canned and conversational humor signals is presented in the following and summarized in Table 3.

3.1.1 Explicit statements

Canestrari (2010: 339) introduces the *Meta-Knowledge Resource* for verbal humor, which "refers to humorous intention expressed by signals." It includes communicating the intention of applying humor through explicit statements like "I'll tell you a joke" (Canestrari 2010: 339) before or afterwards. Sometimes, neologisms occur, too, such as is the case with Sheldon's "Bazinga" known from "Big Bang Theory". These explicit statements can be alternatively subsumed as a reference to different parts of humor, for example by referencing parts of the joke or repeating the punchline. Furthermore, the specific type of humor is sometimes announced (e.g. "I'll tell you a joke/riddle", see Canestrari 2010: 340) or mentioned afterwards (e.g., "that's a dirty joke", see Canestrari 2010: 340). Canestrari also observe that jokes may be announced by an auditive signal, such as the "rimshot" percussion technique known from standup comedy in the USA. This is in line with the sound design of comedy films and, in particular, animated cartoon videos, where these signals are either directly played or imitated through a character's voice. Auditive signals include the chirping of a cricket, the carnival fanfare and effects with musical instruments (e.g., french horn, trombone glissando).

Another reference signal of the Meta-Knowledge Resource determines, that the humorous situation itself can be indicated by comments, such as e.g., "just kidding" (Canestrari 2010: 340) "I didn't like that one" (Canestrari 2010: 339)or "what a laugh" (Canestrari 2010: 340). The latter two fall into the category of evaluating the quality of humor (see Chovanec and Tsakona 2018).

Attardo, Pickering and Baker (2013) mention that canned humor is introduced by so-called "negotiation sequences", whereas conversational humor usually is not introduced. Altogether these signals for humor fall into Chovanec's category of explicit statements as humor framing device, which indicate humor or its quality explicitly. Since Canestrari introduced the Meta-Knowledge Resource for verbal humor, these explicit statements are not exclusive for canned humor, although this is rather uncommon (see Attardo, Pickering and Baker 2013). According to Chovanec and Tsakona (2018: 3) "such cues are also used by addressees signal to signal their own humorous interpretation of discourse, whether this interpretation was the one intended by the speaker or not", which indicates that explicit statments can be used by speakers and listeners alike.

3.1.2 Humor signals

The following sections rely on the terminology by Gironzetti (2017). A *factor* is an unintentional humor signal, which can't be omitted without annihilating the humorous effect. Hence, it is *essential* and *always co-occurs* with the humor. In contrast, *markers* announce humor with full intention, but they are neither essential nor always co-occurring with the humor. Although markers, such as laughter, can be omitted without comprising the punchline, their exclusion can affect the listener's perception and the resulting interpretation of humor negatively. In addition, there are *indicators*, which are communicated intentionally and always co-occur, but are not essential. If none of these characteristics apply, the humor signal is classified as an *index*.

The following overview is based on the work by Gironzetti (2017) with additional references and discussions, since there is no consensus in literature yet.

Setup According to Bird (2013) the humor in a riddle is signaled by the verbal syntax and the content of the riddle's setup (question and answer, e.g., "What is red and smells like blue paint?"). According to Douglas this also applies for canned jokes in general (e.g., "There were three men, an Irishman, etc.", see Douglas 1968: 365). Bird mentions that speakers use restricted pitch range, slight pitch changes on syllable and utterance level in the riddle setup. Table 1 summarizes the humor signals for canned joke setups.

Table 1: Humor signals for joke setups.

References	Context	Humor signal
Bird (2013)	Riddles	Combination of restricted pitch range, slight pitch changes (syllable and utterance internal), verbal syntax and content
Douglas (1968)	Jokes	Verbal syntax and content

Prosody of Humor Generally, there is not much literature about prosody of humor. Both non-empirical and empirical findings are presented in the following. The most important and salient units are not only part of a punchline, but also of a narrative's climax. Hence, verbal humor can be interpreted as a short story with a climax, whose position determines whether the narrative is classified as canned or conversational humor. Therefore, the overview on prosodic humor signals for canned and conversational humor in Table 2 also includes signals for climaxes of narratives in general. (Pickering et al. 2009, Attardo and Pickering 2011, Gironzetti 2017)

Table 2: Prosodic humor signals for joke punchlines/jablines. (no entry = uninvestigated, ✗ = no signal, ✓ = signal, ↑ = increased feature, ↓ = decreased feature, ↕ = both possible).

References (non-empirical)	Context	Pitch	Volume	Speech rate	Break
Folk theory, comedians (Pickering et al. 2009, Attardo and Pickering 2011, Gironzetti 2017)	Verbal Humor	↑	↑	↕	✓
Bauman (1986)	Narrative	↑	↑		✓
Chafe (1994)	Narrative	↑	↑		✓
Audrieth (1998)	Jokes				✓
Norrick (2001)	Jokes	↕		↑	
Wennerstrom (2001)	Narrative	↑	↑	↕	
Wennerstrom (2001)	Conv. Humor	↓			

References (empirical)	Context	Pitch	Volume	Speech rate	Break
Pickering et al. (2009), Attardo and Pickering (2011)	Jokes	↓	✗	↓	✗
Purandare and Litman (2006)	Conv. Humor	↑	↑	↑	
Archakis et al. (2010)	Conv. Humor		↑	↑	✓
Flamson, Bryant and Barrett (2013)	Conv. Humor	✗	✗	✗	✗
Urios-Aparisi and Wagner (2013)	Conv. Humor	↕			✓
Attardo, Pickering and Baker (2013) and Attardo et al. (2013)	Conv. Humor	✗	✗	✗	✗
Buján (2019, 2020)	Conv. Humor	✗	✗		

A majority of non-empirical research agrees with the folk theory and professional comedians, that canned and conversational humor are likewise signaled with increased pitch, volume, speech rate, and distinct pauses.

In contrast, Pickering et al. (2009) and Attardo and Pickering (2011) report empirical research with respect to punchlines of canned humor. The prosody of the punchline is less determined by the salience of the conversational phrase, but rather by its position in the narrative. This position affects pitch, volume, and speech rate. These results are important because The results of Chafe (1994) also confirm a correlation between pitch, volume, and position in the narrative. Since the empirical results are contrasted by the non-empirical research and comedians, there is still the tendency to signal canned humor through increased pitch, volume, speech rate, and distinct pauses.

With respect to conversational humor, the empirical research is not in consensus. According to Attardo, Pickering and Baker (2013), Attardo et al. (2013), Flamson, Bryant and Barrett (2013), and Buján (2019, 2020) conversational humor generally seems to lack prosodic humor signals. The results by Archakis et al. (2010) are in opposition to this hypothesis, suggesting that the speaker uses higher volume, speech rate, and distinct pauses. Similarly, Purandare and Litman (2006) confirm these findings for pitch, energy and speech rate. This is complemented by Urios-Aparisi and Wagner (2013), who report a difference in pitch and a break for jablines.

However, these results should not be considered solely by their results, but also by their criticism: the data lacks mostly variance regarding age, cultural background, geographical origin or humor type (Purandare and Litman 2006, Archakis et al. 2010, Attardo, Pickering and Baker 2013, Flamson, Bryant and Barrett 2013, Urios-Aparisi and Wagner 2013, Attardo et al. 2013, Buján 2019, 2020). Additionally the analysing criteria of the experiments can be problematic. Some (Archakis et al. 2010, Attardo, Pickering and Baker 2013, Attardo et al. 2013) defined the break length unusually and investigated punchlines, which are per definition emphasized phrases. Such utterances are normally surrounded by breaks, which can also bias the results.

This critique weakens the results of empirical research (Attardo, Pickering and Baker 2013, Flamson, Bryant and Barrett 2013, Attardo et al. 2013, Buján 2019, 2020) that conversational humor is generally not signalled by humor markers. Additionally, some empirical results (Archakis et al. 2010, Urios-Aparisi and Wagner 2013) support the non-empirical results of markering punchlines. Hence, there seems to be also a tendency for conversational humor to be indicated using pitch, volume, speaking rate, and significant pauses.

Generally, as punchlines and jablines are told by speakers, prosody cannot be used by listeners. In contrast to the multimodal markers, that will be addressed in the following, no clues were found that prosodic humor signals have to be combined to increase their saliency and perceivability during interaction. As a result, we assume that these signals contain a strong expressivity even in isolated usage.

Multimodality of Humor Laughter is an audible signal which should be combined with other multimodal humor signals (e.g., smile Attardo, Pickering and Baker 2013, Attardo et al. 2013). Otherwise it can fail to be perceived when it is used inexpressively or when the viewing conditions of the interlocutors are bad (Attardo, Wagner and Urios-Aparisi 2013, Gironzetti 2017). Additionally, it should be applied context-sensitively, because in some situations (e.g., in case of humor applied during a serious talk) it is criticized as an inadequate response (Hay 2001). Humorous sequences may not only be signaled by the speaker (Jefferson 1979, O'Donnell-Trujillo and Adams 1983), but also by the listener's laughter (Jefferson, Sacks and Schegloff 1977, Norrick 1993).

According to some researchers (Aubouin 1948, Olbrechts-Tyteca 1974, Provine 2004) laughter has not always to co-occur with humor, because it may serve a different function and thus have a different origin than humor (e.g., social cue). In contrast, the vast majority of research provokes laughter as a necessary response to successful humor (Sacks 1989, Jefferson, Sacks and Schegloff 1977, Jefferson 1979, O'Donnell-Trujillo and Adams 1983, Norrick 1993, Hay 2001), even it may be not the only one (Hay 2001). There is also empirical, but not significant evidence, where laughter is observed during presentation of conversational humor jablines (Attardo, Pickering and Baker 2013, Attardo et al. 2013). Similarly, Pickering et al. (2009) observes *smiling voice* or *laughing voice* during the presentation of canned humor punchlines. They define it as an "impressionistic label describing some effects of the latitudinal adjustment of the vocal tract in smiling, which has clear effects on the acoustics of speech". Although different combinations of laughing and smiling voice occurred for a majority, due to the small number of participants significance tests have not been conducted.

Concluding on the research, laughter can serve as a canned and conversational humor marker if it is used multimodally to increase its perceivability. Next to other humor responses (see Hay 2001) there is also evidence to use a smiling/laughing voice to indicate humorous units.

Similar to laughing, smiling in isolation can also fail to be perceived. Although it is used more intensely as a humor signal as opposed to its occurrence in non-humorous utterances (Gironzetti and Menjo 2014, Gironzetti et al. 2015b), it is sometimes difficult to perceive (Pickering et al. 2009, Attardo, Pickering and Baker 2013). The low saliency may result from the synchronous characteristic of smiling (Gironzetti and Menjo 2014, Priego-Valverde et al. 2018), which is adapted to the intensity of the interlocutors (Gironzetti and Menjo 2014, Gironzetti et al. 2015a,b). Another hypothesis could be a low expressivity (Riggio and Riggio 2002) for smiling. It can be multimodally combined with laughter for canned (Pickering et al. 2009) and conversational humor (Attardo, Pickering and Baker 2013, Attardo et al. 2013, Ikeda and Bysouth 2013), whereas smiling also can be applied by listening interlocutors (Ikeda and Bysouth 2013, Priego-Valverde et al. 2018). Another possibility to combine smiling multimodally is gazing at each other during humor (Gironzetti et al. 2015b), which especially concerns the facial parts of an interlocutor involved in the smile like eyes and mouth (Gironzetti, Attardo and Pickering 2016, Gironzetti et al. 2016). Combining smiling with gaze also applies to canned humor. If the audience consists of several persons, the punchline is tendentially accompanied by a change of the speaker's gaze (Gardair, Healey and Welton 2011, Katevas, Healey and Harris 2015). However, smiling has not necessarily to be a response to humor. Analogical to laughing, it can also serve other communicative functions (Ikeda and Bysouth 2013), such as signaling positive mood in conversations.

All in all, laughter, smile, and gaze are used as signals of canned and conversational humor, both by speakers and listeners. Although most empirical results are not statistically significant and require further investigations regarding variety of the data (see critique on the prosody), the overall research results tend to advocate this. However, due to the multimodal nature, these signals should not be used as a standalone humor signal, otherwise the humor might not be perceived. (Gironzetti, Attardo and Pickering 2016, Gironzetti et al. 2016, Gironzetti 2017)

3.1.3 Summary

Explicit statements, prosodic and multimodal humor signals are applied for both canned and conversational humor in interpersonal interactions and mostly for both the speaker and the listener. Table 3 summarizes the findings from interpersonal communication research, which aims to serve as a blueprint for the implementation of robot humor in section 4.

3.2 Irony

Dynel (2014) gives an overview of different types of irony, including *ideational reversal irony*, which is based on the "negation of a chosen element of the literally expressed meaning or the pragmatic import of the entire utterance" (Dynel 2014: 624). In the work at hand, the negation of one element is particularly interesting because it can be realized computationally to a certain extent (see section 4.3.2).

Table 3: Multimodal humor framing devices. User: **S**peaker/**L**istener/**A**udio. Modality: **Sp**eech/**A**udio/**Pro**sody/**Fac**ial expression/**Gaz**e. Device type: **F**actor, **M**arker, **I**nde**x**, **E**xplicit **S**tatement.

Humor	User	Modality	Device type	Framing device
Verbal	S/L	Sp	ES	Utterances before or afterwards (also own creations, e.g., "Bazinga"): referencing humorous intention or parts/type/quality of humor
Verbal	S/L/A	Sp, A	ES	Sound afterwards: cricket, carnival fanfare, effects with musical instruments (e.g., french horn, trombone glissando, drum hits followed by cymbal hit, also imitated through human voice, e.g., "Badumm tzz")
Verbal	S	Pro	M, Ix	Pitch ↑, speech volume ↑, speech rate ↑, break before punchline
Verbal	S/(L)	Pro	M, Ix	Laughter, laughing voice
Verbal	S/(L)	Fac, Pro	M, Ix	Smiling, smiling voice
Verbal	S/L	Gaz	M	Gaze at facial areas involved in smiling (eyes, mouth), mutual gaze
Verbal	S	Gaz	M	Gaze shift to other person
Riddle	S	Pro, Sp	M, F	Combination of limited pitch range, low pitch change (syllables, utterance), syntax and content in the setup of riddles.

Irony factor

In ideational reversal irony, the negation of an element may result for example in saying "I love being stressed every Monday" while meaning "I hate being stressed every Monday". The resulting utterance is contextually inappropriate, but at the same time still relevant (see section 2.3). The linguistic negation constitutes the irony factor. Removing the factor would destroy the irony. (Attardo 2000b)

Irony markers

Similar to the framing devices presented previously in the context of canned and conversational humor, the use of multimodal framing devices supports the listener in identifying the ironic intention of the speaker. Table 4 gives an overview of reported irony markers in the literature. Typical linguistic markers include exaggerations and understatments (e.g., "barely", "almost") and positive and negative interjections (e.g., "Great!", "Super!", "Damn it!", etc.). With regard to prosody, atypical speaking behavior is often used, which contrasts normal speech modulations

Table 4: Multimodal irony framing devices.

Modality	Markers
Language	Exaggeration and understatement (Attardo 2000b), positive and negative interjections, onomatopoeic expressions for laughter (Carvalho et al. 2009, Frenda 2016), quotation and heavy punctuation marks (Attardo 2000b, Carvalho et al. 2009, Frenda 2016), ellipsis (Attardo 2000b), hashtags (Valitutti and Veale 2015, Hee, Lefever and Hoste 2018, Cignarella et al. 2018), emojis (Hee, Lefever and Hoste 2018, Cignarella et al. 2018)
Facial expr.	Gaze aversion (Williams, Burns and Harmon 2009), wink (Attardo 2000b, Attardo et al. 2003), rolling eyes, wide open eyes and smiling (Attardo et al. 2003)
Prosody	Intonation and nasalization (Attardo 2000b, Attardo et al. 2003), stress patterns (Attardo 2000b), speech rate, extra-long pauses and exaggerated intonational patterns (Attardo et al. 2003)
Gestures	Nudges (Attardo 2000b)

in terms of pitch, rhythm and speech rate. The *compressed pitch pattern* is characterized by a "flat" intonation, causing very little pitch movement while pronouncing the utterance. In contrast, *pronounced pitch accents* exaggerate the intonation by accentuating words throughout the whole sentence, certain words or multiple syllables of the same word. Often, they are combined with elongations and stilted pauses. Facial expression includes wide open eyes, raised or lowered eyebrows, squinting or rolling, winking, smiling or a so-called *blank face*, which is perceived as "expressionless", "emotionless" and "motionless". (Attardo et al. 2003) In addition, gaze aversion is a typical signal accompanying sarcastic statements. (Williams, Burns and Harmon 2009)

4 Implementing multimodal robot humor

As illustrated in Figure 1, humor research provides an important basis and guidance for implementing robot humor in HRI. So far literature has explored primarily specific types of humor and use cases in isolation. While these experiments say little about the comprehension of humour in other naturally occurring and highly context-dependent scenarios, it demonstrates, that robots are able to sucessfully deliver humor. Moreover, it provides a good starting point for implementing generative approaches to robot humor.

Given the type of humor and linguistic content, verbal and non-verbal human humor signals can be transferred to social robots, depending on their embodiment, hardware actuators and software. In addition, computational generation or transformation approaches are of central interest for generating humor dynamically.

Embedding robot humor in HRI relies on two basic elements (see Figure 2): (1) the multimodal generation, communication of the humor itself and (2) an optional feedback loop, which allows the robot to take the user's reactions into account. The former is realized by augmenting verbal scripted or dynamically generated humor with additional (non-)verbal, artificial social signals, including speech, prosody, facial expression, gaze, sounds, gestures, posture, movements and more. The latter relies on humor support, which includes the user's smile, laughter, comments and more as contemporary reactions to the robot's humor. This feedback is acquired by processing human social signals during the interaction. It is a key element for the adaptation and personalization of the content selection and generation process (see also section 5).

Building on the insights from humor research, this section gives an overview of robot humor and computational humor in the literature. Subsequently, a guideline is given for implementing scripted and generative multimodal canned humor, as well as irony with a social robot. It focuses on linguistic content, prosody, gaze and facial expression and is based on the insights from the literature presented in section 3.

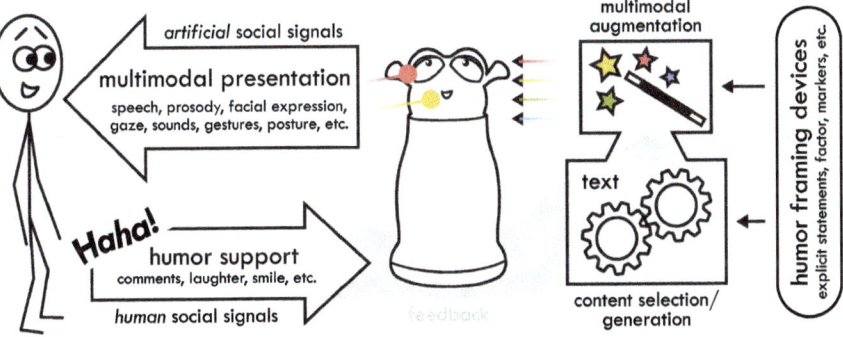

Figure 2: Verbal and non-verbal humor framing devices from humor research serve as a basis for implementing multimodal robot humor. Sometimes, human feedback is used for adapting content selection and humor performance (see section 5).

4.1 Humorous robots

Table 5 gives an overview of robots presenting humor in research. More Systems can be found in Oliveira et al. (2020). Oliveira et al. (2020). focus on the characteristics of

Table 5: Comedy robots in research. DGC = Dynamically Generated Content.

References	Humor	DGC	Actors	Audience	Input signals	Audience adaptation
Tosa and Nadatsu (2002)	Manzai	✗	PC, human	Arbitrarily	Sound	✗
Hayashi et al. (2008)	Manzai	✗	Robovie, Robovie	Arbitrarily	Sound	Timing: actions, speech
Umetani, Nadamoto and Kitamura (2017)	Manzai	✓	Ai-Chan, Gonta	Arbitrarily	Topic	Skript with respect to topic
Knight et al. (2011) and Knight (2011)	Jokes	✗	Nao, human	Arbitrarily	Sound, card colour (feedback)	Type of jokes
Katevas, Healey and Harris (2014) and Katevas, Healey and Harria (2015)	Jokes	✗	RoboThespian	50 persons	Sound, facial expressions	Gestures, gaze, type / timing of response
Weber et al. (2018a, b)	Jokes, grimaces, sounds	✗	Reeti	1 person	Laughter, smiling	humorous content
Ritschel et al. (2019)	Irony	✓	Reeti	1 Person	Sound	✗
Ritschel et al. (2020a, b)	Punning Riddle	✓	Reeti	1 person	Laughter, smiling	✓
Vilk and Fitter (2020)	Jokes	✗	Nao	10–20 Persons	Audio	Joke timing, funny remark wrt. audience feedback Joke type
Swaminathan and Fitter (2021) Swaminathan et al. (2021)	Standup-Comedy	✗	Blossom	Arbitrarily	✗	✗

(robot) humor and resulting human perceptions. In contrast, the work at hand focuses on the multimodal implementation of robot humor and its performance.

Manzai is a Janapese standup comedy show, where the *Boke* is rebuked (sometimes through slapping) by the *Tsukkomi* for its stupid actions. Tosa and Nakatsu (2002) develop a Manzai system, where the user acts as the Boke and the computer as the Tsukkomi. Emotions and content are inferred from the user's speech input. The computer uses both to generate a facial expression on screen and appropriately offensive replies via speech. There is no adaptation to the audience. An explicit number of spectators is not mentioned, but is assumed to be unrestricted. The system runs on a computer, but can also be tailored to robots. Another Manzai system has been introduced by Hayashi et al. (2008), where both roles are played by a Robovie robot. The spectator's audio is tracked using a sound-level meter, which is used to time the robots' contributions to the audience. The corresponding speech and movements of the robots are scripted. The performance is intended for any size audience. Umetani, Nadamoto and Kitamura (2017) also implement Japanese Manzai using a Gonta robot as the Boke and Ai-Chan robot as the Tsukkomi. The Manzai show is intended for an audience of arbitrary size. The system tracks the keywords from the audience, extracts the topic and dynamically generates the Manzai dialog based on matching online news. The script schedules each robot's movement, facial expressions (via displays of eyes) and synthesized voice. There is no other audience adaptation than topics.

Knight et al. (2011) and Knight (2011) perform traditional standup comedy in a human-robot duo, where a Nao robot is the comedy sidekick of the human. The jokes are scripted, labeled with a type and linked with a scripted animation. Using convex programming the robot learns the spectator's preference for joke types and adapts the content over the time. Based on the learned model a joke is selected and presented by the robot using scripted animations linked to the joke. The feedback comes from an on-stage microphone measuring the applause and laughter intensity. Additionally, a camera tracks the audience preference from green and red cards, which are hold up for positive and negative feedback. After updating the model, the next joke or a simple question is selected. The show takes place in a lecture hall, hence, the size of the audience depends on the room.

As opposed to previous projects, Katevas, Healey and Harris (2014) and Katevas, Healey and Harris (2015) use a single standup comedy actor: a RoboThespian robot tells a series of jokes in front of about 50 people. The stage is equipped with a camera, whose recordings are passed to the SHORE system (Ruf, Ernst and Küblbeck 2011) shore. This analysis tool extracts different faces from the video and computes features for each face in real-time, including position, rotation and facial expression. This allows the humanoid robot to adapt its gestures (e.g., pointing at a specific participant) and gaze behavior to the audience during the show. Additionally, three directional microphones track the audience's laughter and applause. Depending on the acoustic feedback a positive or negative response is selected from a list, which is associated with each joke. Also, the robot's timing is adapted to the sensor data. The content is scripted by a professional comedian.

Weber et al. (2018a,b) use Reeti robot to present different combinations of scripted jokes, grimaces and comical sounds. These combinations are adapted to the listener's preferences with reinforcement learning. The user's social signals in terms of laughter and smile are tracked with a microphone and webcam in real-time. Both serve as feedback for the adaptation process (see also section 5.4). Ritschel et al. (2020a,b) present a prototype for communicating and personalizing dynamically generated humor with a Reeti robot. More details on their work is presented in section 4.3. The same applies for the irony generation approach by Ritschel et al. (2019).

Vilk and Fitter (2020) let a single Nao robot perform a standup-comedy show in front of a 10–20 people. The Nao's speakers are used for presenting prerecorded speech (Amazon Polly), the internal microphone is used to record the performance and react to the acoustic audience feedback. The robot's builtin sound peak detection is the basis for timing the next joke: it captures the audience feedback (e.g., laughter, clapping) and prevents overlaps with the audience's reactions. The type of feedback (positive or negative) also determines, whether the robot tells a witty post-joke utterance and its type. The jokes, accompanying gestures and after-joke quips are scripted by professional comedians.

The feedback prediction of Vilk and Fitter is enhanced by Srivastava and Fitter (2021), using Naive Bayes, SVM and a neural network. These algorithms are trained with recordings from their previous work (Vilk and Fitter 2020) and predict the success of the delivered joke. They suggest using the prediction to tell a similar joke on success and attempting to recover from the bad performance by telling a quip on failure. Otherwise, the robot should proceed with the original joke sequence.

Swaminathan et al. (2021) present a robot comedy duo in a portable theater at local farmers markets and festivals. Their in-the-wild street studies focus on attracting bystanders to watch the show. Two Blossom robots present scripted jokes and query the audience during and at the end of each show in order to get feedback about their performance in terms of performer capability and joke quality. The audience is invited to give feedback via a show of hands. Scripted jokes and movements are prepared in several variations, recorded by human speakers and played back with two speakers. The show is recorded and analyzed afterwards.

4.2 Computational humor generation

As illustrated in the last section, the majority of robot humor is based on scripted humor, such as selecting static content from a joke compilation or Manzai scripts. However, it is desirable to generate robot humor dynamically in HRI in order to produce humor during runtime of an interaction. With language and speech being a very important humor communication channel, this section gives an overview of computational generation approaches, extending the work by Amin and Burghardt (2020). Since neural network based approaches (Ren and Yang

2017, Yu, Tan and Wan 2018, Chippada and Saha 2018, He, Peng and Liang 2019, Luo et al. 2019, Zhang et al. 2020, Kazi et al. 2021) report problems with the resulting humor, the work at hand is focused on template-based approaches. Table 6 visualizes the input variables to these approaches and the resulting output.

Table 6: Template-based humor generators.

References	Input	Output
Mnemonic Sentence Generator (McDonough 2001)	8 alpha-numeric characters	Humorous topic related sentence
WISCRAIC (McKay 2002)	personal description (profession, name, adjective)	Punning witticism Punning riddle
Scalar Humor Generator (Binsted, Bergen and MaKay 2003)		Scalar Humor
Song Parody Generator (Gatti et al. 2017)	Concepts	parodied song (melody and vocals)
STANDUP (Ritchie et al. 2006, Manurung et al 2008, Ritchie and Masthoff 2011)	Joke type, topic, lexeme	Punning riddle

One of the earlier humor generating systems is the template-based "Mnemonic sentence generator" of McDonough (2001), which generates a humorous quote from a cryptic password. Each character in the alphanumeric password is attributed to a word, where the initial character either equals or is associated with the corresponding character (e.g., numbers). This substitution encompasses the insertion of opposing verb forms and a name originating from a particular topic (e.g., politics). One disadvantage of the generator is its restricted capability of referring other topics than politics. Additionally, the generation is currently limited to passwords with a fixed length. The downsides can presumably be solved by using more sophisticated templates and databases. (McDonough 2001, Mulder and Nijholt 2002)

WISCRAIC (Witty Idiomatic Sentence Creation Revealing Ambiguity In Context) by McKay (2002) generates jokes. The system accepts personal descriptions referring to name, job or an adjective as input, which the systems tries to refer to in the generation process. A common idiom is reconstructed using phonetic ambiguity and database entries. This results in a punning witticism or a punning riddle referring to the input. One advantage of WISCRAIC is that it retrieves semantic information from the keyword context and lexical database entries. In contrast to STANDUP (see below) it works independently of syntactic and semantic categories and requires less structured information. Additionally, the generation process can be easily configured to deal with every input sentence containing a verb and is therefore not restricted to idioms.

Binsted, Bergen and McKay (2003) implement a generator for scalar humor, which outputs jokes, such as "X is so Y, Z". In contrast to most of the other generators, the reader's expectation is not crossed by a pun. The first part X stands for an active actor (e.g., a person), who is attributed a strong manifestation of characteristic Y. X is expected to be found in a situation, where it has the property Y to a realistic degree. This expectation is crossed by Z. The generation requires knowledge about underlying semantic properties, which are retrieved from OpenCyc and primarily handcrafted knowledge resources. One advantage of the system is the potential for extension to the various available joke mechanisms for the future, once the handcrafted knowledge can be replaced by a scalable knowledge resource.

Gatti et al. (2017) generate lyrics parodies from predetermined concepts. In the prototype, these are extracted from online news via Natural Language Processing (NLP) and extended to related concepts from the daily news. These concepts are used to substitute words in a prominent passage of the original song (e.g., refrain) considering lexical, metrical rules and rhymes. In another step, this result is melodized by additional processing of the words using MIDI music files. Finally, the system outputs a parody version of the original song containing new vocals and the original melody. One advantage of the system is its modularity, which enables future extensions in several areas. For instance, other input than news could be provided or another underlying elicitation mechanism than just referring to news could be developed (e.g., irony).

The STANDUP joke generator (Ritchie et al. 2006, Manurung et al. 2008, Ritchie and Masthoff 2011), is based on JAPE (Binsted and Ritchie 1994, Binsted 1996, Binsted and Ritchie 1997) and produces punning riddles. The generation process can be influenced by specifying a user profile for basic generation characteristics (duplicate check, phonetic similarity, available joke types, etc.), a topic, lexeme or joke type. Alternatively, jokes can be generated randomly. The generation process is similar to JAPE and uses schemas, description rules and text templates. Its implementation uses WordNet (Fellbaum 1998) and Unisyn (The Centre for Speech Technology Research 2001). Despite the similar generation process, STANDUP has been enhanced in different ways. Among others, it attempts to bypass the generation of bad jokes and uses better phonetic comparisons, which results in reduced generation time, increased joke quality and an increased repertoire of different jokes.

4.3 Multimodal augmentation of verbal humor

This section presents a guideline for the implementation of robot humor. In specific, it illustrates how to generate and present canned jokes and irony with a social robot. For the implementation of robotic humor, expert knowledge from professional comedians how to present an individual type of humor would be necessary. Since to our knowledge no guideline for canned humor and irony exists, the implementation follows findings from the literature about the presentation of these types of humor (see section 3). As a result, the implementation focuses on the modalities speech/prosody, gaze and facial expression.

The general approach is to augment scripted or dynamically generated verbal humor (i.e., text) with multimodal humor signals in order to enrich the performance, to help the user to identify the robot's behaviors as humor and to provide a more compelling interaction. Most robot humor experiments so far (see section 4.1) use scripted humor by professional comedians for the purpose of entertainment with scripted texts, animations, sounds, and so on. In contrast, the following rule-based approaches aim to be embedded in HRI (in specific the use of irony) and explain how multimodal humor framing devices can be dynamically applied alongside with canned humor and irony. The techniques are exemplified based on the *Reeti* robot and the *Cerevoice* Text-To-Speech (TTS) system with Speech Synthesis Markup Language (SSML) support, which allows for controlling the robot's prosody.

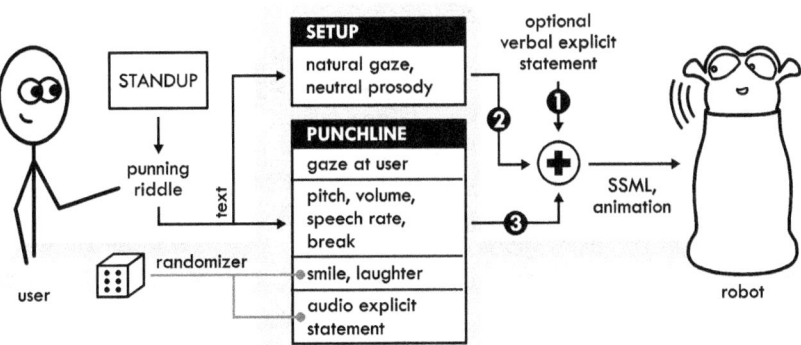

Figure 3: Approach for generating multimodal canned humor.

4.3.1 Canned humor

The overall generation process for a robot's multimodal presentation of canned humor is illustrated in Figure 3. To maintain variability in the robot's multimodal behaviors, several aspects of the humor framing device generation are randomized to a certain degree. All applied humor framing devices refer to Table 3.

Canned humor can be scripted or generated, such as with the software packages listed in section 4.2. The work at hand generates punning riddles, consisting of a setup and a punchline. The prosodic signals, laughter and explicit statements (utterances and sounds) are implemented with SSML. Non-verbal humor signals (i.e., gazing, smiling) for setup and punchline are generated and sent to the robot before the speech output starts.

Text Generation First, an utterance is selected from a prepared list of introductory sentences, since the literature suggests to indicate canned humor with a verbal explicit statement (see section 3.1.1). This list include "Do you know this firecracker?", "This one is a real perl of comedy" and the like. This framing device sets the frame and signals that the following or preceding utterance (if it's inserted after the punchline) should not be taken seriously. It may also serve a transition purposes between several jokes. In practice, the use of an explicit statement can be randomized, both in terms of the specific utterance and frequency (e.g., 10 %). A higher frequency can be chosen if humor occurs rarely. If the joke is strongly interwoven in the surrounding utterances, it might be reasonable to use an explicit statement everytime the humor occurs.

In the next step, the text is generated. Any generator can be used as long as it outputs the setup and punchline separately (even a database with scripted jokes). Due to the advantages discussed in the last section, the example at hand generates canned humor with the STANDUP (Manurung et al. 2008) generator during runtime. It uses the type-based generation process and outputs a punning riddle in the form of one of the following STANDUP types: *call* (e.g., "What do you call X that has Y?"), *cross* (e.g., "What do you get when you cross X with Y?"), *difference* (e.g., "How is X different from Y?"), *similarity* (e.g., "Why is X like Y?") and *type* (e.g., "What kind of X is Y?"). For more details about the types and their instantiations, see Ritschel et al. (2020a).

Prosodic Signals and Auditive Explicit Statements According to Table 3 a punning riddle is indicated by riddle specific syntax and content in the setup. Since the generation process of STANDUP already underlies these linguistic constraints, the resulting output satisfies this humor signal. In terms of prosody, limited pitch range and low pitch change between syllables are typical signals used during the setup. This accounts also for the utterance level. Due to technical constraints of Cerevoice TTS, these two prosodic humor signals can't be realized. Neither experiments with the emphasis tag nor the pitch range attribute revealed perceivable results. Therefore, the setup is translated to SSML without modifications (see Figure 4a), which results in neutral speech.

```
ⓐ  <speak><s>What do you get when you cross a choice with a meal?</s></speak>
ⓑ  <speak>
       <break time="1500ms"/>
       <s><prosody pitch="high" rate="fast" volume="loud">A pick-nic.</prosody></s>
       <spurt audio="g0001_019"></spurt>
       <audio src="path\badum.wav"></audio>
    </speak>
ⓒ  <emphasis level="strong">Great!</emphasis>
    <prosody volume="x-soft">
       <emphasis level="none">I absolutely love having stress every Monday.</emphasis>
    </prosody>
ⓓ  <prosody rate="x-slow">
       <emphasis level="strong">Great!</emphasis> I <emphasis level="strong"> absolutely
       <break strength="medium"/> love <break strength="medium"/></emphasis>
       having <emphasis level="strong"> stress <break strength="medium"/> every
       <break strength="medium"/> Monday</emphasis>.
    </prosody>
```

Figure 4: SSML sample code.

The literature suggests prosodic humor signals preceeding, during and succeeding the punchline (see Table 3). Some speakers make a break before the punchline. This can be realized by inserting an SSML *break* tag, which specifies the duration in milliseconds. The current research does not suggest a concrete break duration. The example at hand uses a random value between 1.5 and 2.0 seconds. Afterwards, the punchline is usually presented using contrasting pitch, speech rate and speech volume as opposed to the setup. This can be realized with the SSML *prosody* tag, which allows to specify pitch, speech rate and volume with corresponding tags. For Cerevoice TTS, the predefined pitch values *low*, *medium* and *high* produce the most natural variations. Similarly, *slow*, *medium* and *fast* speech rate and *soft*, *medium* and *loud* speech volume work best. Modifying the corresponding attributes more extremely (e.g., *x-slow*, *x-fast*) results in worse comprehensibility and naturalness, because some parts are not uttered clearly. An example is illustrated by Figure 4b.

Another important humor signal for presenting canned humor is vocal laughter after the punchline. In Cerevoice, laughter can be realized with so-called *vocal gestures*, which are specified within the *spurt* tag. Vocal gestures include several variations with different intensity and length (e.g., short giggling or longer laughter). Since the amount of laughter samples is limited and research suggests, that not every joke is followed by laughter, the probability of playing back laughter is set to 30%, which is in line with the findings of Attardo, Pickering and Baker (2013).

Research and comedy suggest to use sounds as an explicit statement indicating canned humor (see Table 3). Technically, this can be implemented by playing back a prerecorded sound after the laughing sequence using the SSML *audio* tag. Similar to the vocal gestures mentioned above, frequent repetitions of the same sounds might be noticed quickly, if there are not enough variations. Thus, their usage is randomized and they are applied with a probability of 15 %. Either one of two drum sounds, a french horn effect, the chirping of a cricket, a carneval fanfare or an effect with a musical instrument is played back. Figure 4b includes an example with laughter and subsequent playback of a drum sound after the punchline.

Non-verbal Signals During the joke setup, the robot performs natural gaze behavior with saccades in order to contrast the gazing humor signal in the subsequent punchline. Saccades are implemented by focussing random points near the spectator, so that the robot is not looking at the listener all the time (see figure 5).

Figure 5: Left: natural gaze during the setup. Middle: center head and gaze on the spectator before telling the punchline. Right: smiling is supported with the ears in order to reinforce the smile during the punchline.

As can be derived from in Table 3, joking speakers focus facial areas responsible for the listeners smile during the punchline (e.g., mouth and eyes). This humor signal is realized by centering both the robot's head and gaze on the spectator (see Figure 5). In addition, the punchline could also be signaled by gaze changes between different listeners, if the audience consists of more than one spectator. The literature also reports the combined use of gaze and smile during the punchline. However, Attardo, Pickering and Baker (2013) suggested for this signal not to be applied everytime. Based on these results, the concurrent use of smile and gaze is implemented with a probability of 80%. To be even more salient, the ears of the Reeti are raised while smiling (see Figure 5). After the punchline, the robot returns to its neutral pose without smiling in order to contrast the markers from the rest of the conversation.

4.3.2 Irony

The use of humor techniques (see section 2.3), such as irony, is one option to enrich human-robot interaction with humor. Again, the robot's verbal and non-verbal behaviors are the building blocks for communicating the humorous intention successfully. The irony generation approach at hand uses NLP and Natural Language Generation (NLG) for transforming an input sentence into an ironic version of the same sentence. In addition, the robot augments the text with typical prosody and facial expression according to the literature. It implements ideational reversal irony: the approach does not create ironic utterances from scratch, but uses a non-ironic text utterance and transforms it into an ironic version by inverting the polarity of one element of the sentence. The robot's non-verbal behaviors are used to reinforce the ironic intention. See Figure 6 for an overview of the generation process.

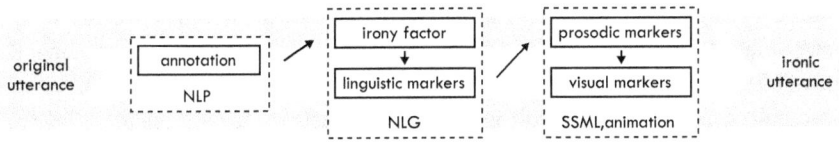

Figure 6: Approach for generating multimodal irony.

Irony Factor The first step analyzes the input utterance with sentiment analysis and identifies verbs, adjectives and nouns with strong polarity, such as "hate" in "I hate being stressed every Monday." After annotating these candidates with NLP techniques one candidate is replaced with the corresponding antonym based on a dictionary lookup, resulting e.g., in "I love being stressed every Monday." The replacement is prioritized as follows: (1) verbs, (2) adjectives and (3) nouns. NLG techniques are used for preserving the conjugation of verbs, comparative and superlative of adjectives and number of nouns. In case no suitable antonym can be found, the main verb is negated using the word "not". If the original sentence already contains a negated verb, not is removed to create the irony factor. Subsequently, verbal and non-verbal markers of irony (see Table 4) are used to make the human aware of the ironic intention.

Linguistic Signals Exaggerations, understatements, as well as positive or negative interjections are inserted into the utterance containing the irony factor. For example, the previous example is prefixed with the positive interjection "Great!", resulting in *Great! I love being stressed every Monday.* In addition, the intensity of the irony factor can be increased by adding, removing or replacing adjectives and adverbs, which strengthen or weaken the meaning of the sentence. For the given example, this results in "I *absolutely* love being stressed every Monday." One or more linguistic markers can be applied at the same time to emphasize the use of irony, for example "*Great!* I *absolutely* love being stressed every Monday." Onomatopoeic expressions of laughter, acronyms, emoticons, quotation and heavy punctuation marks, as well as ellipsis are not used, since they occur in written language and cannot be rendered by TTS systems adequately. Instead, the robot uses prosody, facial expression and animation as follows.

Prosodic Signals Prosodic markers for irony include two acoustic parameter modulations: the compressed pitch pattern and pronounced pitch accents (see Table 4). These atypical speaking behaviors are realized based on SSML by imitating pitch, rhythm, speech rate and accents in order to contrast the robot's normal speech modulations. The "flat" intonation of the compressed pitch pattern is implemented with the *x-soft* prosody variant. It is used to prevent emphasis and emotion in the resulting speech (see Listing 4c). In contrast, the exaggerated intonation of the pronounced pitch accents is realized in SSML by reducing the overall speech rate and encapsulating the main verb, adjectives, adverbs and nouns in *emphasis* elements, as well as *break* tags for accentuated timing (see Figure 4d). For the example above, pronounced pitch accents result in putting emphasis on "I *absolutely* . . . *love* . . . having *stress* . . . *every* . . . *Monday*." Interjections are emphasized independently of the applied pattern in order to highlight the emotional intensity.

Non-verbal Signals The Reeti robot's abilities for facial expression are predestined for highlighting the ironic intention. All of the reported markers with regard to facial expression (see Table 4) can be implemented with the robot's face and actuators by animating the head, mouth, eyes, eye lids and ears. Figure 7 illustrates a set of implemented irony markers. Gaze aversion is the opposite of the robot's gaze behavior during punchlines in section 4.3.1. Here, the robot avoids mutual gaze and looks away intentionally for the duration of the ironic utterance. Animations include rolling eyes and winking. Wide open eyes are implemented by lifting the eyelids. Only one, randomly selected marker is shown for the duration of the ironic utterance. Afterwards, the robot returns to its neutral facial expression, which centers on the spectator.

Figure 7: Visual humor signals of irony are implemented with facial expression and animations.

5 Challenges for multimodal humor in interaction

So far, robot humor experiments focused to a large extent on stand-up comedy, where the robot's task is to entertain the audience with scripted, multimodal humor. However, embedding robot humor in HRI with bidirectional communication, such as in dialog scenarios, involves several challenges, as soon as the robot acts autonomously. Only few experiments so far investigated generative approaches for robot humor, which take user input into account (see section 4.1). In general, conversational humor will be even more important for future every day HRI. Robots already today serve as first point in contact, such as in selected malls or restaurants. Most likely, these machines will also be part of our domestic environments of the future, similar to smart home and speech assistants. Thus, this section gives an overview of important challenges, which need to be overcome in order to generate and embed robot humor in HRI.

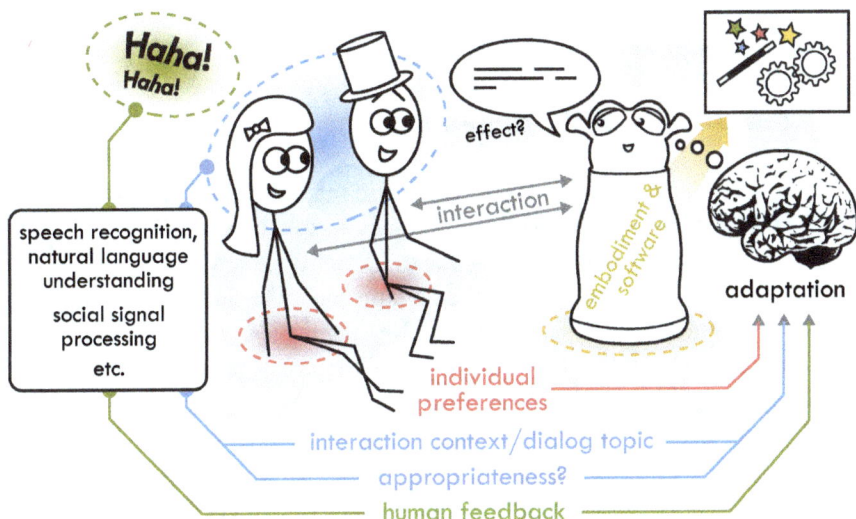

Figure 8: An autonomous robot is faced with several challenges when embedding humor in interactions with human users.

5.1 Task, dialog context and appropriateness

Humor often emerges from human interaction. One challenge for robots is to extract the current context. Therefore, spoken dialog systems, speech-to-text and NLP techniques are essential to sense the interaction partners' spoken input, derive context information from keywords. In case of social signals being relevant for the context, an additional social signal tracking and inferencing system is needed. Including those technical components introduces additional technical challenges (e.g., noise, see Figure 8).

Another challenge is the evaluation of the extracted context. Given different situations, a robot's use of humor should be preceded by a decision process about its appropriateness and potential violations of social norms, decency and respect: joking in a small talk scenario or a wild party might be a welcome contribution, which is not necessarily the case in a work environment, public speaking or a private, serious conversation. Additionally, some interlocutors require a preselection of the humorous content to prevent the application of inappropriate humor (e.g., inappropriate jokes for children). Even the type of humor can be not suitable, if applied in the wrong situation (e.g., irony). In addition of generating appropriate content, the context awareness also can be used to generate humor matching the current topic (e.g., joke about sports).

5.2 Predictability of the humorous effect

In contrast to scripted humor, which is prepared manually and can be tweaked in advance with regard to all modalities, dynamic generation of humor is technically challenging and does not necessarily result in humor. For example, the irony generation approach from section 4.3.2 relies on a dictionary for looking up antonyms. The system cannot check whether the resulting utterance is perceived as irony or sarcasm. Although study results in a small talk scenario show that participants were able to correctly identify the robot's use of irony and a better user experience was associated with it (Ritschel et al. 2019), there is no guarantee on a humorous outcome, as long as the machine cannot "understand" the humor it is producing.

In addition, the robot's embodiment, verbal and non-verbal behaviors also contribute to the communication of humor. The synchronization of verbal and non-verbal content is essential, which becomes another hard challenge as soon as one or both of them are generated dynamically.

5.3 Multimodal humor performance

Non-empirical and especially empirical interpersonal communication research on humor framing devices are still scarce, which leads to the challenge of an appropriate usage of humor signals in a certain situation. In this context, it is still underexplored, whether and how age, nationality, familiarity between interlocutors and professionalism regarding comedy influence the humor signals to be applied. Another challenge resulting from the lack of research is to signal a certain humor type precisely. Current research only provides signals for the coarse grained categories irony, conversational and canned humor. It is desirable for future experiments to also investigate more specific types (e.g., witticism). This will presumably enable a higher variability in signalling humor (in case of overlapping categories) as well as to indicate a specific humor type more precisely and credibly.

One more challenge is to combine humor signals of different modalities appropriately according to findings of interpersonal research (e.g., combined smiling and gazing). Currently, there are just few insights whether humor should be signaled by prosody, even less for laughter, smile, laughing voice and none for gestures, postures and other facial expression next to smiling. Therefore, research has to explore each humor signal modality more deeply in isolation. This will shed additionally light on framing devices, which signal humor reliably even without multimodal usage. Since some humor signals are sometimes only perceivable in combination (e.g., in poor visibility conditions), these findings will have to be extended with the exploration of additional combinations.

Another challenge is to implement these isolated signals or signal combinations from communication research in a robot without loosing perceivability. The perceivability of isolated modalities depends on the technical implementation of these in the robot and can therefore change how modalities should be combined to still result in a salient humor presentation. Many prosodic humor signals can be realized with modern TTS systems supporting SSML for an isolated usage, even though only selected parameter configurations produce pleasing results. If smiling should be combined with other signals also depends on the embodiment of the robot. For example, the Reeti robot's smile is not very expressive due to the small size of the mouth and thus should be combined with laughter and gaze.

The implementation of humor framing devices depends on the embodiment of the corresponding robots (see Figure 8) and is a challenge on its own, because different hardware supports different communication modalities (see Figure 1). For instance, the Reeti robot supports speech, gaze, smile and head movements, whereas the NAO robot does not support gaze, but supports gestures, posture and walking. As a result, humor framing devices from non-supported modalities can not be implemented for the humorous performance (e.g., NAO cannot smile).

Another challenge is the believability and appeal of the robot's humor signals. On the one hand there should be enough variability in the generated behaviors, for example by randomizing parts of the generation process, so that the robot's behaviors do not use the same signals all the time. On the other hand the humor presentation has to be consistent across all involved modalities (e.g., speech has to fit the robot).

5.4 Personalizing robot humor

The sense of humor strongly depends on a person's culture, age, gender, mood and personality. For example, offensive humor is more favoured in the Asian region, especially in Singapore, than in America (Nevo, Nevo and Yin 2001). For example, the preference of the Asians is also reflected in Japanese Manzai (see section 4.1). Hence, in an interactive HRI, one challenge for robots is to choose humorous content that matches the individual users' preferences. One way to realize this is to adapt the robot's humor to the user based on explicit feedback and human social signals, such as laughter and smile, as done e.g., in Knight et al. (2011), Weber et al. (2018a), and Ritschel et al. (2020a). Algorithmically speaking, real-time adaptation to the audience has been implemented in the literature, e.g., based on convex programming and reinforcement learning.

As illustrated in Figure 8, several aspects of HRI can be relevant for the challenge of adapting and personalizing the humor of robots. First, there are individual user preferences regarding the sense of humor (see above). Second, the interaction or task context (see section 5.1) may influence the type and appropriateness of robot humor, too. During the interaction, the users' reactions can serve as indicators of the robot's humor success. For example, user smile and laughter has been applied as reward signal for reinforcement learning, which allows the robot to learn when its humor performance is successful (Weber et al. 2018a, Ritschel et al. 2020a). Personalization may be used for filtering and preselecting humorous content, selecting topics for a dynamic humor generation process or optimizing the employed humor framing devices for the robot's multimodal presentation (e.g., timing, prosody, facial expression, gestures and animations).

6 Conclusion

Humor research in human interaction is a valuable source of insights with regard to the communication of humor with social robots. The classification of different humor types, canned humor, conversational humor and stylistic devices, as well as associated humor framing devices, which signal the presence of humor and reinforce it with multimodal behaviors, provide a solid basis for the implementation of robot humor in interactions with humans. Many humor signals, which include linguistic and prosodic features, gaze, facial expression and gestures can be transferred to modern social robots with humanoid embodiments. In addition, several computational approaches have been presented over time for generating verbal humor with the typical structure of jokes, riddles, irony and more. However, research so far has investigated the implementation of robot humor primarily for entertainment with scripted contents by professional comedians.

For the first time, this chapter presented a structured overview and implementation guideline for applying the insights from humor research for dynamic generation and multimodal presentation of canned and conversational robot humor. The robot's embodiment plays a key role in this process and at the same time is one of the biggest challenges, since each robot platform provides its own set of hardware actuators and software, which is the limiting technical factor with regard to the use of multimodal humor signals. In addition, several challenges have been outlined for embedding robot humor in HRI, which go beyond its generation and technical limitations. Appropriateness of humor, its dependence on the interaction context and adaptation to the individual users' preferences will be important aspects to consider when developing fully autonomous robots, which contribute humor in interactions with humans. In addition, the knowledge about humor theories has to be refined. Traditional computational humor generators were based on rule-based construction mechanisms and focused on selected types of humor. More insights from humor research and theory in combination with answers for basic problems of artificial intelligence (e.g., knowledge representation, logical attribute inference) are essential for implementing more sophisticated computational methods of humor generation for social robots in the future. Additionally, insights about the multimodal human communication of humor should be refined in future experiments, which should at least address the following aspects: culture, age, gender, mood, personality, humor types, interpersonal familiarity, humor signal modality combinations and their perceivability. To be able to make use of all findings from interpersonal communication research robots have to improve their expressive capabilities.

Bibliography

Amin, Miriam & Manuel Burghardt. 2020. A survey on approaches to computational humor generation. In Stefania Degaetano-Ortlieb, Anna Kazantseva, Nils Reiter & Stan Szpakowicz (eds.), *Joint sighum workshop on computational linguistics for cultural heritage, social sciences, humanities and literature*, 29–41. International Committee on Computational Linguistics.

Archakis, Argiris, Maria Giakoumelou, Dimitris Papazachariou & Villy Tsakona. 2010. The prosodic framing of humour in conversational narratives: evidence from greek data. *Journal of Greek Linguistics* 10(2). 187–212.

Attardo, Salvatore. 2000a. Irony as relevant inappropriateness. *Journal of Pragmatics* 32(6). 793–826.

Attardo, Salvatore. 2000b. Irony markers and functions: towards a goal-oriented theory of irony and its processing. *Rask* 12(1). 3–20.

Attardo, Salvatore, Jodi Eisterhold, Jennifer Hay & Isabella Poggi. 2003. Multimodal markers of irony and sarcasm. *Humor: International Journal of Humor Research* 16(2). 243–260.

Attardo, Salvatore & Lucy Pickering. 2011. Timing in the performance of jokes. *Humor: International Journal of Humor Research* 24(2). 233–250.

Attardo, Salvatore, Lucy Pickering & Amanda Baker. 2013. Prosodic and multimodal markers of humor in conversation. In Salvatore Attardo, Manuela Maria Wagner & Eduardo Urios-Aparisi (eds.), *Prosody and humor*, 37–60. Amsterdam, Philadelphia: John Benjamins.

Attardo, Salvatore, Lucy Pickering, Fofo Lomotey & Shigehito Menjo. 2013. Multimodality in conversational humor. *Review of Cognitive Linguistics* 11(2). 402–416.

Attardo, Salvatore, Manuela Maria Wagner & Eduardo Urios-Aparisi. 2013. Prosody and humor. In Salvatore Attardo, Manuela Maria Wagner & Eduardo Urios-Aparisi (eds.), *Prosody and Humor*, 189–201. Amsterdam, Philadelphia: John Benjamins.

Aubouin, Elie. 1948. *Les genres du risible: ridicule, comique, esprit, humour [the genres of the laughable: ridicule, comedy, wit, humor]*. France: Ofep.

Audrieth, Anthony. 1998. *The art of using humor in public speaking*. https://www.squaresail.com/auh.html (accessed June 27 2023).

Bauman, Richard. 1986. *Story, performance, and event: contextual studies of oral narrative*. Vol. 10 (Cambridge Studies in Oral and Literate Culture). Cambridge: Cambridge University Press.

Binsted, Kim. 1996. *Machine humour: an implemented model of puns*. Edinburgh: The University of Edinburgh: College of Science & Engineering dissertation.

Binsted, Kim, Benjamin Bergen & Justin McKay. 2003. Pun and non-pun humour in second-language learning. In *Conference on human factors in computing systems*.

Binsted, Kim & Graeme Ritchie. 1994. An implemented model of punning riddles. In 633–638. Seattle: AAAI Press.

Binsted, Kim & Graeme Ritchie. 1997. Computational rules for generating punning riddles. *Humor: International Journal of Humor Research* 10(1). 25–76.

Bird, Christy. 2013. Formulaic jokes in interaction: the prosody of riddle openings. In Salvatore Attardo, Manuela Maria Wagner & Eduardo Urios-Aparisi (eds.), *Prosody and humor*, 81–102. Amsterdam, Philadelphia: John Benjamins.

Buijzen, Moniek & Patti Valkenburg. 2004. Developing a typology of humor in audiovisual media. *Media psychology* 6(2). 147–167.

Buján, Marta. 2019. Gesture and speech coordination to frame utterances as humorous. In (Gesture and Speech in Interaction – GESPIN 6), 15–20. Germany: Universitätsbibliothek Paderborn.

Buján, Marta. 2020. Prosodic contrast in non-scripted humorous communication. *Language design: journal of theoretical and experimental linguistics* (Special Issue). 67–91.

Cain, Sarah. 2018. Teasing as audience engagement: setting up the unexpected during television comedy monologues. In Villy Tsakona & Jan Chovanec (eds.), *The dynamics of interactional humor: creating and negotiating humor in everyday encounters*, vol. 7, 127–152. Amsterdam, Philadelphia: John Benjamins.

Canestrari, Carla. 2010. Meta-communicative signals and humorous verbal interchanges: a case study. *Humor: International Journal of Humor Research* 23(3). 327–349.

Carvalho, Paula, Luís Sarmento, Mário Silva & Eugénio de Oliveira. 2009. Clues for detecting irony in user-generated contents: oh . . . !! it's "so easy";-). In *Workshop on topicsentiment analysis for mass opinion*, 53–56. Hong Kong: Association for Computing Machinery.

Chafe, Wallace. 1994. *Discourse, consciousness, and time: the flow and displacement of conscious experience in speaking and writing*. University of Chicago Press.

Chippada, Bhargav & Shubajit Saha. 2018. Knowledge amalgam: generating jokes and quotes together. *CoRR* abs/1806.04387.

Chovanec, Jan. 2018. Laughter and non-humorous situations in TV documentaries. In Villy Tsakona & Jan Chovanec (eds.), *The Dynamics of Interactional Humor: Creating and negotiating humor in everyday encounters*, vol. 7, 155–180. Amsterdam, Philadelphia: John Benjamins.

Chovanec, Jan &Villy Tsakona. 2018. Investigating the dynamics of humor: Towards a theory of interactional humor. In Villy Tsakona & Jan Chovanec (eds.), *The Dynamics of Interactional Humor: Creating and negotiating humor in everyday encounters*, vol. 7. Amsterdam, Philadelphia: John Benjamins.

Cignarella, Alessandra Teresa, Simona Frenda, Valerio Basile, Cristina Bosco, Viviana Patti & Paolo Rosso. 2018. Overview of the EVALITA 2018 task on irony detection in italian tweets (ironita). In Tommaso Caselli, Nicole Novielli, Viviana Patti & Paolo Rosso (eds.), *Evaluation campaign of natural language processing and speech tools for italian. final workshop (EVALITA 2018) co-located with the fifth italian conference on computational linguistics*, vol. 2263. Turin: CEUR-WS.org.

Colston, Herbert. 2017. Irony and sarcasm. In Attardo Salvatore (ed.), *The routledge handbook of language and humor*, 234–249. New York: Taylor & Francis.

Dore, Margherita. 2018. Laughing at you or laughing with you? In Villy Tsakona & Jan Chovanec (eds.), *The dynamics of interactional humor: creating and negotiating humor in everyday encounters*, 105–126. Amsterdam, Philadelphia: John Benjamins.

Douglas, Mary. 1968. The social control of cognition: some factors in joke perception. *Man* 3(3). 361–376.

Dynel, Marta. 2009. Beyond a joke: types of conversational humour. *Language and Linguistics Compass* 3(5). 1284–1299.

Dynel, Marta. 2014. Isn't it ironic? Defining the scope of humorous irony. *Humor: International Journal of Humor Research* 27(4). 619–639.

Fellbaum, Christiane. 1998. Wordnet: an electronic lexical database. Cambridge: MIT Press.

Flamson, Thomas,Gregory Bryant & Clark Barrett. 2013. Prosody in spontaneous humor: evidence for encryption. In Salvatore Attardo, Manuela Maria Wagner & Eduardo Urios- Aparisi (eds.), *Prosody and humor*, 61–80. Amsterdam, Philadelphia: John Benjamins.

Frenda, Simona. 2016. Computational rule-based model for irony detection in italian tweets. In Pierpaolo Basile, Anna Corazza, Francesco Cutugno, Simonetta Montemagni, Malvina Nissim, Viviana Patti, Giovanni Semeraro & Rachele Sprugnoli (eds.), *Italian conference on computational linguistics & fifth evaluation campaign of natural language processing and speech tools for italian*. Vol. 1749. Napoli: CEUR-WS.

Gardair, Colombine, Patrick Healey & Martin Welton. 2011. Performing places. In *Acm conference on creativity and cognition*, 51–60. Atlanta: Association for Computing Machinery

Gatti, Lorenzo, Gözde Özbal, Oliviero Stock & Carlo Strapparava. 2017. Automatic generation of lyrics parodies. In *Acm international conference on multimedia*, 485–491. Mountain View: Association for Computing Machinery.

Georgalidou, Marianthi & Hasan Kaili. 2018. The pragmatics of humour in bilingual conversations. In Villy Tsakona & Jan Chovanec (eds.), *The dynamics of interactional humor: creating and negotiating humor in everyday encounters*, 77–104. Amsterdam, Philadelphia: John Benjamins.

Gironzetti, Elisa. 2017. Prosodic and multimodal markers of humor. In Salvatore Attardo (ed.), *The Routledge handbook of language and humor*, 400–413. Routledge.

Gironzetti, Elisa, Salvatore Attardo & Lucy Pickering. 2016. Smiling, gaze, and humor in conversation: a pilot study. In *Metapragmatics of humor: current research trends*, 235–254. Amsterdam, Philadelphia: John Benjamins.

Gironzetti, Elisa, Salvatore Attardo, Lucy Pickering, Meichan Huang, Shigehito Menjo & Ying Zhang. 2015a. Multimodal analysis of humor in conversation. In *Conference of the international society of humor studies (ishs)*. Oakland.

Gironzetti, Elisa, Meichan Huang, Lucy Pickering & Salvatore Attardo. 2015b. *The Role of Eye Gaze and Smiling in Humorous Dyadic Conversations*. Toronto.

Gironzetti, Elisa & Shigehito Menjo. 2014. Smiling as a discourse marker of humor. In *2nd conference of the american pragmatics association (ampra)*. Los Angeles.

Gironzetti, Elisa, Lucy Pickering, Meichan Huang, Ying Zhang, Shigehito Menjo & Salvatore Attardo. 2016. Smiling synchronicity and gaze patterns in dyadic humorous conversations. *Humor: International Journal of Humor Research* 29(2). 301–324.

Hay, Jennifer. 2001. *The pragmatics of humor support*.

Hayashi, Kotaro, Takayuki Kanda, Takahiro Miyashita, Hiroshi Ishiguro & Norihiro Hagita. 2008. Robot manzai: robot conversation as a passive-social medium. *International Journal of Humanoid Robotics* 5(01). 67–86.

He, He, Nanyun Peng & Percy Liang. 2019. Pun generation with surprise. In Jill Burstein, Christy Doran & Thamar Solorio (eds.), *Conference of the north american chapter of the association for computational linguistics: human language technologies*, vol. 1, 1734–1744. Minneapolis: Association for Computational Linguistics.

Hee, Cynthia Van, Els Lefever & Véronique Hoste. 2018. Semeval-2018 task 3: irony detection in english tweets. In Marianna Apidianaki, Saif M. Mohammad, Jonathan May, Ekaterina Shutova, Steven Bethard & Marine Carpuat (eds.), *International workshop on semantic evaluation*, 39–50. New Orleans: Association for Computational Linguistics.

Hetzron, Robert. 1991. On the structure of punchlines. *Humor: International Journal of Humor Research* 4(1). 61–108.

Ikeda, Keiko & Don Bysouth. 2013. Laughter and turn-taking: warranting next speakership in multiparty interactions. *Studies of laughter in interaction*. 39–64.

Jefferson, Gail. 1979. A technique for inviting laughter and its subsequent acceptance/declination. *Everyday language: Studies in ethnomethodology*. 79–96.

Jefferson, Gail, Harvey Sacks & Emanuel Schegloff. 1977. Preliminary notes on the sequential organization of laughter. *Pragmatics Microfiche* 1.

Juckel, Jennifer, Steven Bellman & Duane Varan. 2016. A humor typology to identify humor styles used in sitcoms. *Humor: International Journal of Humor Research* 29(4). 583–603.

Karachaliou, Rania & Argiris Archakis. 2018. Reactions to jab lines in conversational storytelling. In Villy Tsakona & Jan Chovanec (eds.), *The dynamics of interactional humor: creating and negotiating humor in everyday encounters*, 29–56. Amsterdam, Philadelphia: John Benjamins.

Katevas, Kleomenis, Patrick Healey & Matthew Harris. 2015. Robot comedy lab: experimenting with the social dynamics of live performance. *Frontiers in psychology* 6. 1253.

Katevas, Kleomenis, Patrick GT Healey & Matthew Tobias Harris. 2014. Robot stand-up: engineering a comic performance. In *Humanoid robots and creativity at the ieee-ras international conference on humanoid robots humanoids*. Madrid.

Kazi, Taaha, Sameer Joshi, Steeve Kaitharath & Imran Mirza. 2021. Transformer based neural joke generator. *International Journal of Computer Applications* 975. 8887.

Knight, Heather. 2011. Eight lessons learned about non-verbal interactions through robot theater. In Bilge Mutlu, Christoph Bartneck, Jaap Ham, Vanessa Evers & Takayuki Kanda (eds.), *International conference on social robotics*, 42–51. Berlin, Heidelberg: Springer.

Knight, Heather, Scott Satkin, Varun Ramakrishna & Santosh Divvala. 2011. A savvy robot standup comic: online learning through audience tracking. In *Conference on tangible, embedded and embodied interaction*. Funchal.

Luo, Fuli,Shunyao Li, Pengcheng Yang, Lei Li, Baobao Chang, Zhifang Sui & Xu Sun. 2019. Pun-GAN: generative adversarial network for pun generation. In Kentaro Inui, Jing Jiang, Vincent Ng & Xiaojun Wan (eds.), *Conference on empirical methods in natural language processing and the 9th international joint conference on natural language processing*, 3386–3391. Hong Kong: Association for Computational Linguistics.

Manurung, Ruli, Graeme Ritchie, Helen Pain, Annalu Waller, Dave O'Mara & Rolf Black. 2008. The construction of a pun generator for language skills development. *Applied Artificial Intelligence* 22(9). 841–869.

Martin, Rod, Patricia Puhlik-Doris, Gwen Larsen, Jeanette Gray & Kelly Weir. 2003. Individual differences in uses of humor and their relation to psychological well-being: development of the humor styles questionnaire. *Journal of research in personality* 37(1). 48–75.

McDonough, Craig. 2001. *Mnemonic String Generator: Software to aid memory of random passwords*. Tech. rep. West Lafayette: CERIAS Technical report.

McKay, Justin. 2002. Generation of idiom-based witticisms to aid second language learning. In Carlo Strapparava Oliviero Stock & Anton Nijholt (eds.), *The april fools' day workshop on computational humor*, 77–87. Netherlands: University of Twente.

Mulder, Matthijs & Anton Nijholt. 2002. *Humour research: state of art*. Netherlands: Centre for Telematics & Information Technology (CTIT).

Nevo, Ofra, Baruch Nevo & Janie Yin. 2001. Singaporean humor: a cross-cultural, crossgender comparison. *The Journal of General Psychology* 128(2). 143–156.

Norrick, Neal. 1984. Stock conversational witticisms. *Journal of Pragmatics* 8(2). 195–209.

Norrick, Neal. 1993. *Conversational joking: humor in everyday talk*. Indiana University Press.

Norrick, Neal. 2001. On the conversational performance of narrative jokes: toward an account of timing. *Humor: International Journal of Humor Research* 14(3). 255–274.

Norrick, Neal. 2004. Non-verbal humor and joke performance. *Humor: International Journal of Humor Research* 17(4). 401–409.

O'Donnell-Trujillo, Nick & Katherine Adams. 1983. Heheh in conversation: some coordinating accomplishments of laughter. *Western Journal of Communication* 47(2). 175–191.

Olbrechts-Tyteca, Lucie. 1974. *Le comique du discours [the comedy of speech]*. Université de Bruxelles.

Oliveira, Raquel, Patrícia Arriaga, Minja Axelsson & Ana Paiva. 2020. Humor–robot interaction: a scoping review of the literature and future directions. *International Journal of Social Robotics*. 1–15.

Pickering, Lucy, Marcella Corduas, Jodi Eisterhold, Brenna Seifried, Alyson Eggleston & Salvatore Attardo. 2009. Prosodic markers of saliency in humorous narratives. *Discourse processes* 46(6). 517–540.

Priego-Valverde, Béatrice, Brigitte Bigi, Salvatore Attardo, Lucy Pickering & Elisa Gironzetti. 2018. Is smiling during humor so obvious? A cross-cultural comparison of smiling behavior in humorous sequences in american english and french interactions. *Intercultural Pragmatics* 15(4). 563–591.

Provine, Robert. 2004. Laughing, tickling, and the evolution of speech and self. *Current Directions in Psychological Science* 13(6). 215–218.

Purandare, Amruta & Diane Litman. 2006. Humor: prosody analysis and automatic recognition for f*r*i*e*n*d*s. In *Conference on empirical methods in natural language processing* (EMNLP '06), 208–215. USA: Association for Computational Linguistics.

Ren, He & Quan Yang. 2017. Neural joke generation. *Final Project Reports of Course CS224n*.

Riggio, Heidi & Ronald Riggio. 2002. Emotional expressiveness, extraversion, and neuroticism: a meta-analysis. *Journal of Nonverbal Behavior* 26(4). 195–218.

Ritchie, Graeme, Ruli Manurung, Helen Pain, Annalu Waller & Dave O'Mara. 2006. The standup interactive riddle builder. *IEEE Intelligent Systems* 21(2). 67–69.

Ritchie, Graeme & Judith Masthoff. 2011. The standup 2 interactive riddle builder. In *International conference on computational creativity*. Mexico City.

Ritschel, Hannes, Ilhan Aslan, David Sedlbauer & Elisabeth André. 2019. Irony man: augmenting a social robot with the ability to use irony in multimodal communication with humans. In *Conference on autonomous agents and multiagent systems*, 86–94. Richland: International Foundation for Autonomous Agents & Multiagent Systems.

Ritschel, Hannes, Thomas Kiderle, Klaus Weber & Elisabeth André. 2020a. Multimodal joke presentation for social robots based on natural-language generation and nonverbal behaviors.

Ritschel, Hannes, Thomas Kiderle, Klaus Weber, Florian Lingenfelser, Tobias Baur & Elisabeth André. 2020b. Multimodal joke generation and paralinguistic personalization for a socially-aware robot. In Yves Demazeau, Tom Holvoet, Juan M. Corchado & Stefania Costantini (eds.), *Advances in practical applications of agents, multi-agent systems, and trustworthiness*, 278–290. Cham: Springer.

Ruf, Tobias, Andreas Ernst & Christian Küblbeck. 2011. Face detection with the sophisticated high-speed object recognition engine (shore). In Albert Heuberger, Günter Elst & Randolf Hanke (eds.), *Microelectronic systems: circuits, systems and applications*, 243–252. Berlin, Heidelberg: Springer.

Sacks, Harvey. 1989. An analysis of the course of a joke's telling in conversation. Studies in the Social and Cultural Foundations of Language. 337–353.

Shilikhina, Ksenia. 2018. Discourse markers as guides to understanding spontaneous humor and irony. In Villy Tsakona & Jan Chovanec (eds.), *The dynamics of interactional humor*, 57–75. Amsterdam, Philadelphia: John Benjamins.

Srivastava, Ajitesh & Naomi Fitter. 2021. A robot walks into a bar: automatic robot joke success assessment. In *International conference on robotics and automation*, 2710–2716. Xi'an.

Swaminathan, Janani, Jane Akintoye, Marlena Fraune & Heather Knight. 2021. Robots that run their own human experiments: exploring relational humor with multi-robot comedy. In *International conference on robot & human interactive communication*, 1262–1268. Vancouver: IEEE.

The Centre for Speech Technology Research. 2001. *Unisyn Lexicon, version 1.3*. https://www.cstr.ed.ac.uk/projects/unisyn/ (accessed June 27 2023).

Tosa, Naoko & Ryohei Nakatsu. 2002. Interactive comedy: laughter as the next intelligence system. In *International symposium on micromechatronics and human science*, 135–138.

Umetani, Tomohiro, Akiyo Nadamoto & Tatsuya Kitamura. 2017. Manzai robots: entertainment robots as passive media based on autocreated manzai scripts from web news articles. *Handbook of Digital Games and Entertainment Technologies*. 1041–1068.

Urios-Aparisi, Eduardo & Manuela Maria Wagner. 2013. Prosody of humor in Sex and the City. In Salvatore Attardo, Manuela Maria Wagner & Eduardo Urios-Aparisi (eds.), *Prosody and Humor*, 167–188. Amsterdam, Philadelphia: John Benjamins.

Valitutti, Alessandro & Tony Veale. 2015. Inducing an ironic effect in automated tweets. In *International conference on affective computing and intelligent interaction*, 153–159. Xi'an: IEEE.

Vilk, John & Naomi Fitter. 2020. Comedians in cafes getting data: evaluating timing and adaptivity in real-world robot comedy performance. In *International conference on human-robot interaction*, 223–231. Cambridge: Association for Computing Machinery.

Weber, Klaus, Hannes Ritschel, Ilhan Aslan, Florian Lingenfelser & Elisabeth André. 2018a. How to shape the humor of a robot – social behavior adaptation based on reinforcement learning. In *International conference on multimodal interaction*, 154–162. Boulder: ACM.

Weber, Klaus, Hannes Ritschel, Florian Lingenfelser & Elisabeth André. 2018b. Real-time adaptation of a robotic joke teller based on human social signals. In Elisabeth André, Sven Koenig, Mehdi Dastani & Gita Sukthankar (eds.), *International conference on autonomous agents and multiagent systems*, 2259–2261. Stockholm: International Foundation for Autonomous Agents & Multiagent Systems Richland, SC, USA / ACM.

Wennerstrom, Ann. 2001. *The music of everyday speech: prosody and discourse analysis*. New York: Oxford University Press. 592–595.

Williams, Jason, Erin Burns & Elizabeth Harmon. 2009. Insincere utterances and gaze: eye contact during sarcastic statements. *Perceptual and motor skills* 108(2). 565–572.

Yu, Zhiwei, Jiwei Tan & Xiaojun Wan. 2018. A neural approach to pun generation. In Iryna Gurevych & Yusuke Miyao (eds.), *Annual meeting of the association for computational linguistics*, vol. 1, 1650–1660. Melbourne: Association for Computational Linguistics.

Yus, Francisco. 2016. Relevance theory and contextual sources-centred analysis of irony: current research and compatibility. *Relevance Theory: Recent developments, current challenges and future directions* 268. 147–171.

Zajdman, Anat. 1991. Contextualization of canned jokes in discourse. *Humor: International Journal of Humor Research* 4(1). 23–40.

Zhang, Hang, Dayiheng Liu, Jiancheng Lv & Cheng Luo. 2020. Let's be humorous: knowledge enhanced humor generation. In Shruti Rijhwani, Jiangming Liu, Yizhong Wang & Rotem Dror (eds.), *Annual meeting of the association for computational linguistics*: *student research workshop*, 156–161. Association for Computational Linguistics.

Part 2: **Mediated interactions**

Sabina Tabacaru
7 Facial expressions as multimodal markers of humor: More evidence from scripted and non-scripted interactions

Abstract: Previous studies (Tabacaru and Lemmens 2014; Tabacaru 2019) have shown that facial expressions, specifically brow movements (see also eye-roll in Colston 2020), play a role in making the speaker's humorous intention known to the hearer. These *gestural triggers* have been explored in TV series as well as political debates (Tabacaru 2020) to examine their role in interaction, highlighting the fact that the speaker wants their message to be interpreted as humorous by the interlocutor/s or the audience. As such, they are considered markers of humor that allow the switch between different frames of meaning (Fauconnier 1994; Coulson 2005).

Drawing on previous findings, this chapter deals with multimodality and sarcasm in interaction, focusing on the facial expressions used by the speaker/s in different contexts. The examples presented come from various sources (TV shows, political/cultural shows, TV series, stand-up comedy) in order to analyze the frequency and the use of such facial expressions for humorous purposes. Raised eyebrows are known to play an accentuation role in speech (Rockwell 2000; Krahmer *et al.* 2002).; in the case of humor, these facial expressions represent gestural triggers allowing the switch from a discourse base space to a pretense space (Brône 2008).

Sarcasm is particularly compelling to analyze in these types of interactions since it includes a target that is mocked/criticized (Tabacaru 2018). As such, the speaker's intention will be accentuated through the use of nonverbal elements as well as verbal ones. These nonverbal elements play a crucial role in intersubjectivity as the speakers need to constantly coordinate their meanings and expectations (Schelling 1960).

Keywords: sarcasm, facial expressions, brow movement, raised eyebrows, interaction

1 Introduction

It has long been explained that the secret to humorous discourse is incongruity: speakers play on different readings of their message to create humorous meanings (Koestler 1964; Raskin 1985; Attardo 1997, and many others). If two (or more)

meanings are possible, then the hearer first accesses the more salient[1] one (see Giora 1999, for example), and then switches to another one (in the case of a joke, this would happen after the punchline has been uttered). Consider the following joke:

Q: Why do the English drink so much tea?

A: Because tea leaves.

The incongruity here is possible because of the two meanings of the word *leaves*: (1a) as a noun in the plural form and (1b) as a verb in the 3rd person singular, as shown below:

(1a) Because [$_{NP}$ *tea leaves*]

(1b) Because [$_{NP}$ *tea*] [$_{VP}$ *leaves*]

The hearers are able to access these different meanings at the same time, and able to switch between them to make sense of the joke. In Cognitive Linguistics, this incongruity has been explored using mental spaces (Fauconnier 1994) and layering (Clark 1996). While mental spaces refer to the way human beings categorize information, Clark (1996) explains language and communication using layers of meaning: Layer 2 (imagined as construed on Layer 1) depends on Layer 1, which is the communicative act that speakers share. Brône (2008) proposed an account of humor that combines both Clark's (1996) layering model and mental spaces (see Figure 1 below). Referring back to example (1), the joke has to be compared against the background of shared knowledge, thus accessing the context of Brexit and the UK leaving the European Union. The switch between the two meanings is possible because hearers are aware of the UK *leaving* the EU: the first meaning of *tea leaves* as NP is replaced by the action of leaving while the English are metonymically referred to by the noun *tea* (PART FOR WHOLE),[2] which would be the most salient element in the frame ENGLISH. In order for the joke to work, hearers need background information and to access different mental spaces. The link between the two men-

---

[1] According to Giora (1999: 921), "if a word has two meanings retrievable directly from the lexicon the meaning which is more popular, or more prototypical, or more frequently used in a certain community is more salient."

[2] For more on metonymy and humor, see Brône and Feyaerts (2003), who explain that the most salient element of a frame will be used to access the whole frame. In this case, *tea leaves* (as in 'the English drinking tea') would be considered the most salient element to give access to the frame ENGLISH.

tal spaces will be done through layering, as seen in Figure 1 below, and made possible because of the two interpretations of the same form *tea leaves*.

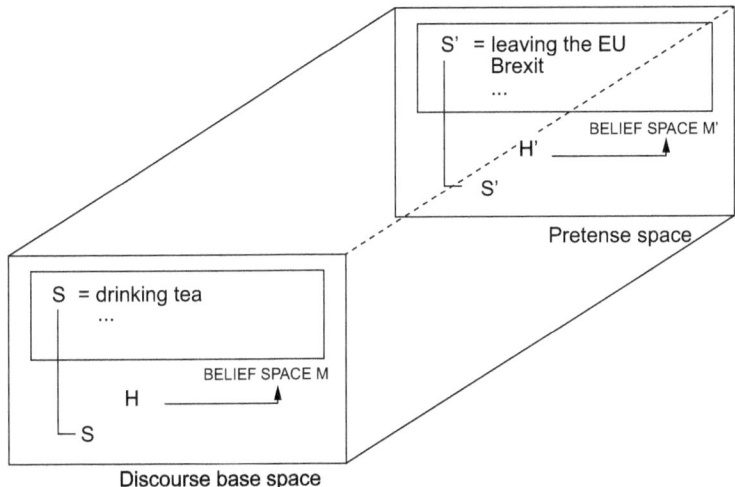

Figure 1: Mental configuration for the joke (based on Brône 2008: 2031).

Hence, the element that humor plays on is surprise: the hearer is "tricked" into accessing one meaning, which is then replaced by another.

This joke depends on verbal interpretations of the same words, but human interactions are more complex and depend on a number of things. As such, in conversations, people are able to enrich the common ground they share, adding new meanings and implications when talking. The associations they can make are therefore far richer than for narrative jokes. Human interactions also play on tone of voice, pitch, facial expressions, gestures, posture, gaze, etc. These past few years, researchers have underlined the importance different modes have on communication (see, for example, Norris 2011). Norris (2004: 2) notes:

Previously, language has been viewed as constituting the central channel in interaction, and nonverbal channels have been viewed as being subordinated to it. While much valuable work on the interplay between the verbal and nonverbal has been established, I believe that the view which unquestionably positions language at the center limits our understanding of the complexity of interaction.

Norris (2004: 2) further notes that "gesture, gaze, and head movement also may take the superior position in a given interaction, while language may be subordinated or absent altogether." Since narrative jokes are not the only means of creating humorous implications, taking into account all these elements is crucial for the understanding of humorous communication, which is, as Raskin (1985: 2) put it, "a universal human trait." This cognitive ability to make such complex associations between elements that (often times) may have nothing in common (like the joke in example [1]) deserves to be analyzed from a multimodal perspective, focusing not only on the verbal, but also on the non-verbal factors at play in any human conversation (even when they are not face-to-face, for example, in a phone conversation).

Furthermore, Raskin (1985: 2) notes that "the ability to appreciate and enjoy humor is universal and shared by all people, even if the kinds of humor they favor differ widely." While there are different types of humor, it is safe to assume that most humorous exchanges play on incongruity and surprise and the shift that takes place in interpretation will be marked by the speakers through different modes.

The present paper explores such uses of non-verbal elements with humor in order to emphasize the role they play in human interactions. I focus on facial expressions in particular and their use as gestural triggers in humorous interactions in order to help the switch between different mental spaces: a discourse base space and a pretense space (as shown in Figure 1 above), using mainly Brône's (2008) account of humor, which combines interaction, layering, and mental spaces. The examples presented here come from different types of media (stand-up comedy, television shows, talk shows), which further emphasizes how pervasive these uses are and how they help interpret the messages as humorous.

2 What's in a face?

Since all interactions are multimodal (Norris 2004), many recent studies have focused on the non-verbal aspects of human communication. But what does that tell us about the way humor is created? If participants are able to imply much more than what they explicitly say, where does that leave humorous exchanges?

Different approaches and studies on multimodality in humor include prosodic analyses (Urios-Aparisi and Wagner 2011; Bertrand and Priego-Valverde 2011; Attardo et al. 2013a, among others), but also facial expressions. For example, Attardo et al. (2013b) and Gironzetti (2017) discuss the role of smiling as a marker for humor and Attardo (2003) mentions laughter (from the part of the speaker, not the hearer) as a marker of humor. Studies by Tabacaru and Lemmens (2014) and Tabacaru (2019) emphasize the role of eyebrows in humorous exchanges: speakers use them to mark the switch between the different meanings and mental spaces. Tabacaru and Lemmens (2014: 20) name such marker a *gestural trigger* which would be used as "the gesture that guides the hearer to interpret the utterance as humorous." Such markers would be used with parts of the message that are important to help switch between the different interpretations. Specifically, these studies use Ekman's (1979) theory of emotion and facial expressions, focusing on the interpretation of raised eyebrows as a marker of surprise/interest.[3]

Researchers have also pointed out the accentuation role raised eyebrows have in communication. Birdwhistell (1970: 166) links raised eyebrows to the expression of question and doubt (similar to Ekman 1979), but for very short durations; he notes (1970: 166):

> If we ignore the duration of the action and attend only to the spatial movement of the brows, an identical movement of the brows may be seen in the circumvocal behavior of speakers who select the brows for kinesic stress functions.

Using an experiment with a Talking Head, Krahmer et al. (2002: 4) conclude that both auditory and visual elements "can have a significant effect on the perception of focus."

In the following, several examples are discussed, taken from both scripted and non-scripted humor. Even though data for scripted humor is much easier to find and analyze, the results show that such markers are also used in more spontaneous uses of humor (see Tabacaru 2020, for example, for spontaneous uses of humor in French election debates). The examples presented below, which come from various languages and media, show that facial expressions are an integral part of the humorous message and they will behave as gestural triggers for the hearers.

2.1 Scripted humor

Tabacaru and Lemmens (2014) and Tabacaru (2019) propose studies that explore the use of facial expressions with scripted, non-spontaneous humor. Indeed, such studies can include more data that is more easily available for research (and/or annotation). The studies above focused on the use of gestural triggers in television series (*House M.D.* and *The Big Bang Theory*), showing how even different genres (a drama and a sitcom) make use of facial expressions with humorous meanings. These uses and results can also be compared to other types of data (different television shows, etc.) and different languages, as will be shown in more detail below.

---

[3] Ekman (1979: 182) also notes that raised eyebrows with eyes wide open will also be used with actions that use surprise/interest, such as questioning, doubting, greeting, emphasizing.

The examples presented here involve sarcasm. If humor generally plays on two (or more) different interpretations of the same message, sarcasm adds something else to the interaction: it involves a criticism towards something or someone. A sarcastic occurrence has been defined as "instantiated by statements that are inconsistent or incompatible with the actual situation presented by the discourse, and which target someone or something specifically, be they present or not" (Tabacaru 2018: 188). Rockwell (2000) states that the use of sarcasm comes with a specific intonation and hearers are able to recognize a sarcastic tone of voice. Sarcasm is particularly interesting because it is built on criticism, mockery or a hostile attitude towards something or someone (Tabacaru 2018; see also Colston 1997, Lee and Katz 1998, Mesing, Williams, and Blasko 2012).

Consider the following example, taken from iUmor,[4] a Romanian talent show where contestants and guests present their humorous bits (i.e., music, dance, magic, a stand-up routine, etc.). Teo, a well-known stand-up comedian in Romania, was invited as a guest on the show in 2020, when Romania was in a state of emergency due to the Covid19 pandemic. Raised eyebrows (in bold in the example), as shown in Figure 2 below, are adopted when he makes use of onomatopoeia for the element of surprise/fear present in the discourse about the pandemic:

(2) Teo: Starting on a serious note, we live in difficult times, these are uncertain times. It's normal to be scared because we are in a state of emergency, but the enemy is invisible. Where is the enemy? Inside. **Ihh!** A metaphor.[5] [H[6] laughter] (iUmor, S09)[7]

Raised eyebrows are used after an introduction by the comedian where he actually insists on the seriousness of the context of the pandemic. The switch to the joke and the pretense space is done also through the raised eyebrows which are used with his expression of both fear and surprise (the tone of his voice also goes up as if startled). Sarcasm here is targeted at the discourse around the Covid19 pandemic, which was filled with metaphors of war[8] (*state of emergency*, *enemy* in this instance). The onomatopoeia is used with the element of surprise and fear,

---

[4] The name of the TV show is a pun: based on the English pronunciation, /aɪ/ is also the 2nd person singular for the verb *to have* (= *you have*), which would then mean *You are humorous/funny*.
[5] Translation from Romanian by ST. Original: "Începând într-o notă serioasă, trăim niște vremuri dificile, sunt niște vremuri tulburi. E normal să ne fie frică pentru că suntem în stare de război, dar dușmanul e invizibil. Unde e dușmanul? În noi. Îhhh ! Metaforă."
[6] H is used for when the hearer or hearers laugh, whereas S is used if the speaker laughs.
[7] ©Antena 1; the video can be accessed here: https://www.youtube.com/watch?v=ySlikFRu818.
[8] See, for instance, Musolff 2022.

on a serious note

ihh

Figure 2: Raised eyebrows in example (2), via YouTube (©Antena1, iUmor).

because it is exactly what the government was trying to achieve by using such strong expressions. The incongruity here comes from the fact that the *enemy* presented by the government is not real, but metaphorical, and the comedian raises his eyebrows exactly as he switches through these two meanings. The gestural trigger is used here as he goes from one mental space—the frame of WAR as used by the government—to a pretense space where he mocks these metaphors as they do not give 'real' solutions to the Covid pandemic.

Another example from stand-up comedy is the following extract presented by Blanche Gardin at the Montreux Comedy Festival. Raised eyebrows are marked in bold, and, in italics and bold, the raise of one single eyebrow, as opposed to the rest of their uses in this context:

(3) Blanche Gardin: I read, so I read a lot, eh. When I **get bored**, I read. I am captivated by **feminist** writers, Simone de Beauvoir and all that, I didn't know [them]. **It's** very **comforting, eh**, to see that there are women who **had** rich lives without actually having a husband and children. And, **by the way**, it's funny because that's when I realized that my beliefs are **very fragile**, actually, and that I was very easily influenced because before, I didn't like feminism at all, it even annoyed me a little bit, and I read two books and

now I'm hooked. **That's why I think** I shouldn't probably read *Mein Kampf*.[9] [H laughter][10]

There are several layers to the sarcastic punchline delivered by Gardin here: one is, evidently, as mentioned by herself, a criticism towards herself (as a person who can be easily influenced by anything) and a second one that targets feminism, which is compared to Hitler's *Mein Kampf*. Raised eyebrows are used by her for different elements in the speech[11] that are then highlighted to reach these meanings:

bored→feminism→by the way→comforting→fragile.

These elements seem to build up to the punchline and the frame created by Gardin which emphasizes her as a fragile individual that can be easily hooked on something (i.e., after reading only two books) that she quite disliked before. Now, interestingly, she uses raised eyebrows for longer when she introduces the punchline *That's why I think*, and only one eyebrow is raised (right eye) with the use of the title *Mein Kampf*, as shown in Figure 3 below:

So, even though raised eyebrows are used throughout this example, their uses seem to (i) underline elements that create the frame she is building and (ii) differ with the use of the punchline: by the introduction of the punchline, for which the use is longer, and by the name of the book that she should not read. This sarcastic implication is based on reasoning (Tabacaru, 2019), and the criticism understood through entailment:

If P If she reads feminist books = If she reads Mein Kampf
Then Q →She gets hooked = →She will be hooked

---

[9] Translation from French by ST. Original: "Je lis, je lis beaucoup en ce moment, du coup, hein. Quand je m'emmerde, je lis. Je suis tombée dans les écrivains féministes : Simone de Beauvoir tout ça, je connaissais pas. Ça console beaucoup, hein, de lire des écrivains féministes, de voir qu'y a des femmes qui ont eu des vies riches, hein, sans pour autant avoir ni de mari ni d'enfant. Et d'ailleurs c'est marrant parce qu'à cette occasion je me suis rendu compte que mes croyances étaient très fragiles, en fait, que j'étais très influençable parce qu'avant je n'aimais pas du tout le féminisme, ça m'énervait même un petit peu et j'ai lu deux bouquins et maintenant je suis à fond. C'est pour ça que je me dis qu'il faut peut-être pas que je lise Mein Kampf."

[10] ©Montreux Comedy. The video can be accessed here: https://www.youtube.com/watch?v=IeUtQsHCit8.

[11] It is possible that raised eyebrows were used more in this context, but some frames are given from too far and it is not possible to see the comedian's face at all times.

That's why I think   Kampf

Figure 3: Raised eyebrows for example (3), via YouTube (©Montreux Comedy).

Similar to the example above, these facial expressions help switch between the two meanings: the discourse base space, which Gardin constructs as her reading feminist books, and a pretense space in which she would read *Mein Kampf*. If she got 'hooked' on something she actually disliked before, then this could also be true of this imagined scenario.

Another example where the raised eyebrows differ in duration and complexity is example (4) that comes from the television series Fleabag (2016–2019),[12] a British comedy-drama, created by Phoebe Waller-Bridge. In this scene, the main character goes to therapy and talks about her issues regarding men and sex; the scene takes place after the therapist asked her not to use humor or, if she did, to make it very obvious so that nothing gets lost in "humorous translation." Raised eyebrows are marked in bold:

(4) Fleabag: "I've just . . . Sex didn't bring anything **good**. So, I'm trying **not** to but I've . . .
Therapist: And what have you found in your abstinence?
Fleabag: Well, I'm very **horny** and **your little scarf isn't** helping." (Fleabag S02E02)[13]

This example presents several instances of raised eyebrows as well, all with the same purpose: accentuating elements of the message that are important to the speaker. The words *good* and *not* make sense with this type of accentuation and focus on the negative sides of sex on her life and they differ also from the way raised eyebrows are used with the humorous meaning in the last line, as shown in Figure 4:

---

12 ©BBC Three.
13 The video is available here: https://www.youtube.com/watch?v=Yy6kbVptkRY.

Anything   your little scarf

Figure 4: Raised eyebrows for example (3), via YouTube (©BBC Three).

Furthermore, the humorous message is far richer from a kinesic perspective: the character smiles (see Gironzetti 2017 for the role of smiling for humor), and points to the scarf the therapist is wearing (second frame), while also raising her eyebrows more often and on larger chunks of speech: *horny* and *your little scarf isn't*. Hence, the switch from the two meanings is made clear. The humor is aimed at herself (just like Gardin's example above), but in a more playful tone, made evident through the use of smiling as well. The implied meaning here is that she is even sexually attracted by her therapist (a middle-aged woman) and it is used in this case to go from a serious discourse (i.e., therapy) to a non-serious discourse space.

These scripted examples are, in a certain way, easier to analyze and spot, because, as they are known beforehand, actors and comedians are able to make the shift to the pretense space more obvious to an audience (especially in such cases when the humorous meaning depends on the correct interpretations of these switches). In the following, a few examples are presented from non-scripted humor, taken from various sources, for comparison.

2.2 Non-scripted humor

The following example is taken from Would I Lie to You,[14] a British panel show where guests read a statement while the opposing team has to decide whether it is true or false. Even though the lies/truths presented by the guests are prepared in advance and the show edited, the exchanges among the speakers seem to be

---

14 ©BBC One.

genuine.[15] In the following, Stephan Mangan reads out an unbelievable statement about himself, which is enriched by Lee Mack's comments and reactions. Raised eyebrows are depicted in bold:

(5) 1 Stephan Mangan: "Whenever I eat beans-on-toast, I always imagine I'm **a rescue helicopter,**
 2 **and with every forkful I'm airlifting tiny bald men on a raft to safety**. [H laughter]
 3 [. . .]
 4 Lee Mack: Any reason you do this apart from just keeping yourself **amu**sed or . . . ?
 5 Stephan Mangan: **It's that my auntie Bridget, who used to live with us** . . .
 6 Lee Mack: Yes, is **this going to be a tragic story**? She's **bald** . . . **She was on a raft** [H laughter]
 7 she never survived and it's our way of remembering her.
 8 Stephan Mangan: She was on a raft with **400 bald men** who needed rescuing.
 9 Lee Mack: Trust me, **we all know your auntie** [H laughter]. You say raft, you mean mattress."
 10 [H laughter]
(Would I Lie to You S07E02)[16]

The speakers use raised eyebrows several times in this exchange; what is noteworthy is that the purpose of their use seems to be different. The two longer uses by Mangan seem to be compatible with the element of surprise (Ekman and Friesen 2003). It is revealed at the end that the statement is indeed false, so it might be right to assume that raised eyebrows were used here to mark the surprise of the speaker when reading out the statement for the first time. In line number 5, it is also possible that Mangan was starting to use humor, but the story was interrupted by Mack, who uses humor to build up another frame, that of the James Cameron 1997 movie "Titanic" (mentioning the raft). In line 8, Mangan picks up on the elements provided and enriches the common ground with the element *400 bald men,* for which he uses raised eyebrows (which aren't used with the rest of his line), as shown in Figure 5.

---

15 According to an article in radiotimes: https://www.radiotimes.com/tv/entertainment/the-secrets-of-would-i-lie-to-you/, retrieved March 2022.
16 The video is available here: https://www.youtube.com/watch?v=Zdxa9wkmNdA.

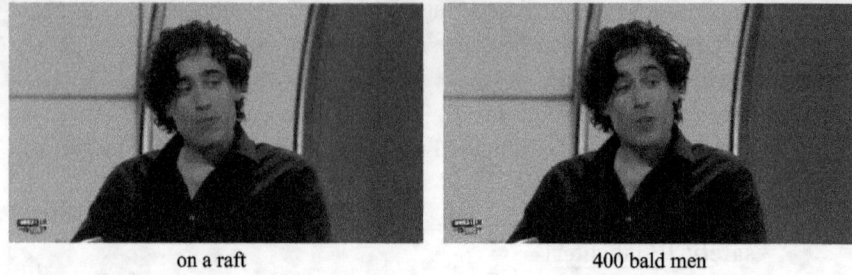

Figure 5: Raised eyebrows used by Stephan Mangan (line 8), via YouTube (©BBC One).

The *Titanic* frame is once again mentioned by Mack (line 9) with *We all know your auntie* (Figure 6 below for raised eyebrows). Appealing to the frame of the movie, we are all familiar with Rose, the survivor telling the story in the movie, who manages to float on a piece of paneling. Even after the audience and participants laugh, Mack adds *You say raft, you mean mattress*, once more making the frame obvious to everyone. The frame AUNTIE here is used to mean *old female* and therefore switched to a *famous old female* in the pretense space created by Mack. Here, it would be Rose from Titanic, telling the story.

Figure 6: Raised eyebrows used by Lee Mack, via YouTube (©BBC One).

Similar to the examples presented with scripted humor, facial expressions are used with elements that help build the frame of TITANIC, and particularly with longer chunks of speech (*she was on a raft* or *we all know your auntie*, for example). Given the movie frame built in this exchange, sarcasm is layered and targeted at the story that Mangan wants the others to believe (lines 1 and 2), the film Titanic (lines 9 and 10), and even the frame of TRAGIC STORY (line 6). It is also the concept of the show (two opposing teams) that makes sarcasm more frequent because the teams will be critical of each other.

Another example is taken from Profesioniştii (The Professionals)[17] a cultural show on TVR1, a Romanian public broadcast service. The guest on the show was Cristian Tudor Popescu,[18] a well-known Romanian journalist and political commentator, who is asked about his main defect, to which he replies being Romanian. He argues in favor of this answer, as opposed to any other country of origin, with the link to the frame of ALCOHOL and the deep conversations people have in pubs in Romania. Raised eyebrows are marked in bold:

(6) Cristian Tudor Popescu: [. . .] Utopias built at the pub, in bars [H smiles]. What outbursts of intelligence, what glimmers, **but even now, go to Bucharest pubs to see, there are all sorts of characters that define themselves there, only in the pub**. I had to fight hard against this urge, mine too, to not do, only to speak. What fascinating conversations I had in my life, if those had **ever** been **filmed, those [that took place] at 1am**, in the pub with different people throughout my life.
Eugenia Vodă: What would **the title** have been? Not The Professionals, but The Voyeurals [S laughter].
Cristian Tudor Popescu: **The Amateurs! No, sir,**[19] **The Amateurs, because there's amateurism there**.
Eugenia Vodă: [S laughter] **The Amateurals!**[20]

Raised eyebrows are used here with the frame alcohol that is built to define what it is to be Romanian. Popescu creates this scene where being Romanian means having deep conversations in the pub with different people. He places himself in this universe where he himself had very profound conversations late at night with such people and that it would have been interesting to film them. His facial expressions accompany the scenario in which you can still verify what he is saying (*even now, go to Bucharest pubs . . .*) as well as the pretense space in which

---

17 ©TVR.
18 The video is available here: https://www.youtube.com/watch?v=EkFv7LI3KtI.
19 The word "dom'le" (abbreviated from the word *domnule*, in the vocative), literally *mister*, is generally used with exclamations in Romanian.
20 Translation from Romanian by ST. Original: « [. . .] Utopii construite la cârciumă, în bodegi. Ce dezlănţuiri de inteligenţă, ce sclipiri, da' şi acuma, du-te prin cârciumile bucureştene să vezi, sunt tot felul de personaje care acolo se definesc, numai în cârciumă. A trebuit să lupt din greu cu această tendinţă şi a mea de a nu face, ci de a vorbi doar. Ce discuţii fascinante am avut in viaţa mea, dacă ălea ar fi fost filmate vreodată, ălea de la 1 noaptea, la cârciumă cu diverse persoane de-a lungul vieţii. Eugenia Vodă : Cu ce titlu ar fi fost ? Nu Profesioniştii, ci Voyeuriştii . . . CTP : Amatorii ! Nu, dom'le, amatorii, pentru că acolo ăla este amatorism. Eugenia Vodă : Amatoriştii! ».

such conversations would have been filmed. His interlocutor enriches his words by asking about the title of such a show. Given the title of this show is *The Professionals*, she proposes the title The Voyeurals (in Romanian, *voyeuriștii*), to make a play on words between the two scenarios. Popescu, again using raised eyebrows, proposed the title *The Amateurs*, the sarcasm here being targeted at himself and his interlocutors from the past, discussing things in the pub without any plan to make things happen. The last line here also constitutes humor and is used with raised eyebrows and a raised finger (as shown in Figure 7 below) because Vodă still creates a title with the same suffix as the title of the current show, namely The Amateurals (in Romanian, the suffix -*st*[21] is used for all three titles, here *amatoriștii*).

Therefore, there are two scenarios here based on the common ground between interlocutors and the audience watching the show: the discourse base space is the show The Professionals taking place, while the pretense space is a show that would be called The Amateurals and would include improbable conversations with strangers in pubs. In Romanian, the past conditional (i.e., *ar fi fost*) is used for *had [ever] been filmed* and *would [the title] have been*, which underlines the imagined scenario.[22]

The Amateurs   The Amateurals

Figure 7: Raised eyebrows for example (6), via YouTube (©TVR).

The following excerpt was broadcast in 2005 and comes from Tout le monde en parle,[23] a French talk show presented by Thierry Ardisson and produced by Catherine Barma. The talk show host asks a few questions about real life (literally called 'Real life interview') to his guest Laurent Ruquier, a TV presenter himself. The raised eyebrows are marked in bold:

---

21 Here, in the plural with the determiner, hence -*ştii*.
22 In terms of humor, the sarcasm here is combined with joint fantasy (Feyaerts 2013).
23 ©France 2, @INA, Institut National de l'Audiovisuel. The video is available here: https://www.youtube.com/watch?v=BQxTQi0ZNEY.

(7a) Thierry Ardisson: So, Laurent, in real life, **do you go out with make up on**?
Laurent Ruquier: [S laughter] **Well** yeah, because there are **cameras when I go to the bank** [H laughter], there are cameras in the there are cameras in the bus aisles
Ardisson: // **in parking lots**
Magloire: Oh, so you live in Neuilly as well? [S laughter]
Laurent Ruquier: . . . there are cameras in **parking lots**, so there you go, **I have as much respect for security guards as I do for my audience** [H laughter; S laughter]
[. . .]

(7b) Thierry Ardisson: In real life, do you have **a prompter, you never know**, when people come to dine at your house?
Laurent Ruquier: [pretends to read slowly from a prompter] **there is no prompter in real life and there is** [H laughter] **no prompter on televi . . . sion either** there you go[24]

The questions asked by the talk show host revolve around Ruquier's life as a TV presenter and its similarity with his TV persona. Interestingly, the raised eyebrows are used by Ardisson for questions, which is compatible with findings regarding Sign Language (see for instance Coerts 1992, or Weast 2008).[25] This example is very similar to the previous examples, where both S and H bring elements which enrich the common ground (the TITANIC reference picked up by H in example [5]). For instance, in (7a), when Ardisson understands where Ruquier is going with the answer (i.e., there are cameras present in the public space), he adds *parking lots* to add to his enumeration. This element is uttered with raised eyebrows by both speakers.

The *camera* (see Figure 8) is the element linking Ruquier's different lives: the TV persona and what is called here his 'real life.' The humor is thus created through the understanding that as long as there is a camera present, he should be wearing make-up. There is also a comparison between his audience and the secu-

---

24 Translation from French by ST. Original version: "Ardisson : Alors, Laurent, est-ce que dans la vraie vie, tu sors maquillé ? Ruquier : Bah oui, parce qu'il y a des caméras quand je vais à la banque, y a des caméras dans les y a des caméras dans les couloirs de bus Ardisson : dans les parkings // Magloire : Ah, vous habitez Neuilly aussi ? Ruquier : Y a des caméras dans les parkings, donc voilà j'ai autant de respect pour les vigiles que pour mon public [. . .] Ardisson : Est-ce que dans la vraie vie t'as un prompteur, on sait jamais, quand les gens viennent dîner chez toi ? Ruquier : Il n'y a pas de prompteur dans la vraie vie et il n'y en a pas non plus à la télévi . . . sion voilà ».
25 According to Weast (2008), for example, in American Sign Language, the height of raised eyebrows marks the distinction between questions and statements.

cameras

Figure 8: Raised eyebrows for example (7), via YouTube (©INA, ©INA Arditube).

rity guards that would be present in parking lots or at the bank, which creates two different frames whose common element is Ruquier himself: TELEVISION and REAL LIFE. In (7b), he is asked about a prompter, which TV presenters use, to which Ruquier replies by pretending to read from a prompter. He pretends to read the answer slowly from a prompter which elicits laughter, and once again compares the two frames built in (7a): TELEVISION and REAL LIFE. The humorous implications here are more complex because they build on the exchange in (7a): if there are cameras on set, there are also cameras in 'real life'; if there is no prompter in 'real life', there is no prompter on television either. This is particularly marked since he pretends to read the answer out from a prompter and so the incongruity, specific to humor, would add a layer of humor to his answer. Other gestures are used in these exchanges: when enumerating places that have cameras, Ruquier starts counting on his fingers, when pretending to read out from a prompter in (7b), he squints as if he was not able to see clearly what the prompter says, thus making his humorous reply more prominent.

The spontaneous nature of these exchanges is made clear by the interruptions (*the parking lots* remark added by Ardisson, the question asked by Magloire, which interrupts his enumeration and to which he gives no reply), the repetition (in [7a]), *there are cameras in the there are cameras in the bus aisles*).

In the following section, these uses are analyzed in more detail in order to highlight the role facial expressions play in these humorous exchanges.

3 Discussion

It has been said (Tabacaru 2019) that the use of facial expressions for humor can be seen through a semantic-pragmatic approach: they are either used as underliners (Ekman 1979) in order to put emphasis on a word or structure (see Lee Mack' *we all know your auntie* in example (5) or they would be used to mark surprise. Ekman (1979) describes raised eyebrows as expressions of surprise/astonishment. The interesting thing is that, as shown in the examples above, with humor, they would not be used by the hearers/audience, but by the speakers themselves. These uses are very similar for both scripted and non-scripted humor as they can be used with smaller and longer parts of speech, depending on the contexts of use. We can compare the Fleabag example in (4) to Ruquier's reactions in (7), where what is underlined by facial expressions is also made more prominent with the use of other gestures (hand gestures and smiles are used in both examples). The difference is enriching the common ground, which happens in non-scripted examples, as both speakers add layers of meaning. The examples presented here all contain humor from both speakers: in example (6), both interlocutors create humorous meanings regarding the imagined scenario of conversations in Romanian pubs; in example (7), the interlocutor is able to add a place that has a camera to the enumeration started by the speaker; and in example (5), the TITANIC frame starts to be used by the interlocutor as well.

The question remains whether these markers are correctly understood by the hearers.

In order to answer this question, take, for example, the excerpt below, that took place in 2017 and in which Trump gives a speech regarding the National Space Council.[26] Buzz Aldrin, the Apollo 11 astronaut, present during the speech, reacts using different facial expressions (especially raised eyebrows, see Figure 9)[27] to the words used by president Trump. The use of raised eyebrows is marked in bold, but they are not used by the speaker (like the previous examples discussed in this article), but by the hearer (Buzz Aldrin)—hence H is used when they occur:

(8) Donald Trump: "I used to say, before doing what I did, I used to say 'What happened? Why are[n't] we moving forward?' Today's announcement sends a clear signal to the world that we are restoring [**H raised eyebrows**] America's proud legacy of leadership in space [. . .] At some point in the future, we'll look back and say 'How did we do it without space?' [**H raised eye-**

---
26 ©wh.gov, ©Trump White House Archived.
27 The video is available here: https://www.youtube.com/watch?v=TAUqcBc0hYI.

brows] [. . .] The privatization of certain aspects is going to be very is going to play a very crucial role, don't you think? [**H raised eyebrows**] [. . .]"

Figure 9: Depiction of raised eyebrows from the hearer in example (8), via YouTube (©Trump White House Archived).

What is interesting about this example is that, despite no intention on the part of the hearer to be sarcastic/humorous, these facial expressions have been interpreted as both humorous and an expression of surprise. These are some of the headlines following the video, which became viral and was especially discussed on Twitter:

"Buzz Aldrin's Reaction To Donald Trump Talking About Space Is Priceless" (huffingtonpost.co.uk)[28]

"Donald Trump talked about space and Buzz Aldrin's face says it all" (news.yahoo.com)[29]

"Buzz Aldrin's facial expressions while listening to Donald Trump speak about space are incredible" (thenationalstudent.com)[30]

"Buzz Aldrin's hilarious expressions on Donald Trump's speech on space have left Twitterati in splits" (indianexpress.com)[31]

Other publications have focused on the emotion of surprise:

"Astronaut's baffled reactions to strange Trump comments on infinity win the internet" (miamiherald.com)[32]

---

[28] https://www.huffingtonpost.co.uk/entry/buzz-aldrins-reaction-to-donald-trump-speaking-about-space-is-all-of-us_uk_595b72b1e4b05c37bb800d45.
[29] https://news.yahoo.com/donald-trump-talked-space-buzz-092556759.html.
[30] https://www.thenationalstudent.com/International/2017-07-05/buzz_aldrins_facial_expressions_while_listening_to_donald_trump_speak_about_space_are_incredible.html.
[31] https://indianexpress.com/article/trending/trending-globally/buzz-aldrin-face-donald-trump-speech-on-space-twitter-reactions-4734416/.
[32] https://www.miamiherald.com/news/nation-world/national/article159329879.html.

"Apollo 11 hero Buzz Aldrin looks bemused as Donald Trump gives speech about space" (standard.co.uk)[33]

Therefore, the semantic-pragmatic approach proposed for these types of interactions and uses should still be taken into account. Raised eyebrows are part of the frame of surprise, and they will be used as such even in somatic idioms, for example. Consider the following example, discussed in Langlotz (2006):

(9) The deputy leader, Roy Hattersley, raised Labour eyebrows (Nicolas 1995: 243, quoted in Langlotz 2006: 33).

Langlotz (2006: 33) notes: "This idiom is transparent in the sense that the bodily reaction described in the idiom stands for the emotional cause of surprise." In my view, such somatic expressions have ambiguous uses, but they are relevant to the frame of emotion[34] and will be used metonymically to refer to certain emotions, especially that of surprise. Pragmatically, raised eyebrows underline elements that are central to the message conveyed by the speaker and can be used to show that the speaker intends to be humorous.

Therefore, it is hard to differentiate between these uses: we, humans, are used to raising our eyebrows when surprised, but we also raise eyebrows to accentuate words when interacting with our peers. The headlines regarding Buzz Aldrin's facial expressions point exactly to that: we interpret them as either humorous ("hilarious") or as a sign of surprise, even confusion ("baffled", "bemused"), regardless of the user's intended meaning. It is therefore safe to assume that, in a context in which the speakers intend to be humorous, such markers will also be used, as human communication is "a fundamentally cooperative enterprise" (Tomasello 2008: 6). We do want the others to understand our implied meanings, which takes us back to Grice (1975) and the cooperative principle (see also Priego-Valverde 2006). We will make our intentions clear to an audience (in the case of stand-up comedy, or a show) or to our interlocutors (in face-to-face conversations, similar to the ones presented here).

---

33 https://www.standard.co.uk/news/world/apollo-11-hero-buzz-aldrin-looks-bemused-as-donald-trump-gives-speech-about-space-a3578556.html.
34 A quick search on the COCA/BNC corpus reveals hundreds of uses for the expression *raised eyebrows*.

4 Conclusion

Humor has received more and more attention these past years, with research focusing specifically on markers of meaning and facial expressions and/or prosody (Attardo *et al.* 2003; Tsakona 2009; Gerhardt 2009, and others). It is more difficult to research non-scripted, spontaneous uses of humor/sarcasm because these uses are more complex and less frequent (as opposed to stand-up comedy shows or television shows that are meant to be humorous). Sarcasm, as a means of criticizing the interlocutor or themself (see example [6], for instance) will be used more frequently even though the result is not intended to make a big audience laugh. For the same reasons, sarcasm will also be more prominent than other types of humor used in similar exchanges.

Multimodality in such interactions is more complex as it draws from different means: the speakers use different facial expressions (although raised eyebrows seem to be the most frequent ones), smiling, hand gestures and head gestures (going from nods to shakes and tilts, etc.), shrugs, and so on. Implied meaning also goes through prosody, and speakers make use of different intonations to either make something sound not serious or to put emphasis on different parts that play a role in the intended meaning. What is noteworthy is that scripted and non-scripted uses of humor seem to be very similar, as the same facial expressions are used to mark the switch between incongruous meanings and implications, and to enrich the common ground that interlocutors share. The links between these various meanings is apparent enough because the speakers (this is particularly clear with non-scripted humor) manage to pick on these meanings and add something to the same pretense space (for example, [6] above).

To sum up, facial expressions and their uses represent complex ways of human communication (from emotion, to humor, and even somatic idioms) and their meaning, even if correctly understood in conversation, is still underexplored. Evidently, more data from different types of exchanges is needed to fully grasp all the implications of these facial expressions. It might be that by exploring bigger and various types of data we will see that there is more to facial expressions than meets the eye.

References

Attardo, Salvatore. 1997. The semantic foundations of cognitive theories of humor. *Humor: International Journal of Humor Research* 10(4). 395–420.
Attardo, Salvatore. 2003. Introduction: The Pragmatics of humor. *Journal of Pragmatics* 35(9). 1287–1294.

Attardo, Salvatore, Jodi Eisterhold, Jennifer Hay & Isabella Poggi. 2003. Multimodal markers of irony and sarcasm. *Humor: International Journal of Humor Research* 16(2). 243–260.
Attardo, Salvatore, Lucy Pickering & Amanda Baker. 2013a. Prosodic and multimodal markers of humor in conversation. In Salvatore Attardo, Manuela Maria Wagner & Eduardo Urios-Aparisi (eds.), *Prosody and humor*, 37–60. Amsterdam: John Benjamins.
Attardo, Salvatore, Pickering, Lucy, Lomotey, Fofo & Menjo, Shigehito. 2013b. Multimodality in conversational humor. *Review of Cognitive Linguistics* 11(2). 400–414.
Bertrand, Roxane & Béatrice Priego-Valverde. 2011. Does prosody play a specific role in conversational humor? *Pragmatics & Cognition* 19(2). 333–356.
Birdwhistell, Ray L. 1970. *Kinesics and Context. Essays on body motion communication*. Philadelphia: University of Pennsylvania Press.
Brône, Geert. 2008. Hyper and misunderstanding in interactional humor. *Journal of Pragmatics* 40. 2027–2061.
Brône, Geert & Feyaerts Kurt. 2003. The cognitive linguistics of incongruity resolution: Marked reference-point structures in humor. University of Leuven, Department of *Linguistics preprint* no. 205.
Coerts, Jane. 1992. *Nonmanual Grammatical Markers: An Analysis of Interrogatives, Negations and Topicalisations in Sign Language of the Netherlands: Academisch Proefschrift*. Amsterdam: Universiteit van Amsterdam Dissertation.
Colston, Herbert L. 1997. Salting a wound or sugaring a pill: The pragmatic functions of ironic criticism. *Discourse Processes* 23. 23–45.
Colston, Herbert. 2020. Eye-rolling, irony and embodiment. In Angeliki Athanasiadou & Herbert L. Colston (eds.), *The Diversity of Irony*, 211–235. Berlin/Boston: Mouton de Gruyter.
Coulson, Seana. 2005. Sarcasm and the space structuring model. In Seana Coulson & Barbara Lewandowska-Tomasczyk (eds.), *The literal and the nonliteral in language and thought*, 129–144. Berlin: Lang.
Clark, Herbert H. 1996. *Using language*. Cambridge: Cambridge University Press.
Ekman, Paul. 1979. About brows—emotional and conversational signals. In Mario von Cranach, Klaus Foppa, Wolf Lepenies & Detlev Ploog (eds.), *Human Ethology*, 169–248. Cambridge: Cambridge University Press.
Ekman, Paul & Wallace V. Friesen. 2003. *Unmasking the face. A guide to recognizing emotions from facial expressions*. Cambridge, Massachusetts: Malor Books.
Fauconnier, Gilles. 1994. *Mental spaces: Aspects of meaning construction in natural language*. Cambridge: Cambridge University Press.
Feyaerts, Kurt. 2013. Tackling the complexity of spontaneous humorous interaction. An integrated classroom-modeled corpus approach. In Leonor Ruiz-Gurillo & Maria Belén Alvarado Ortega (eds.), *Irony and humor*, 243–268. Amsterdam/Philadelphia: John Benjamins Publishing.
Gerhardt, Cornelia. 2009. Multimodal and intertextual humor in the media reception situation: The case of watching football on TV. In Neal R Norrick. & Delia Chiaro (eds.), *Humor in Interaction*, 79–98. Amsterdam/Philadelphia: John Benjamins.
Giora, Rachel. 1999. On the priority of salient meanings: Studies of literal and figurative language. *Journal of Pragmatics* 31(7). 919–929.
Gironzetti, Elisa. 2017. Prosodic and multimodal markers of humor. In Salvatore Attardo (ed.), *The Routledge Handbook of Language and Humor*, 400–413. New York: Routledge.
Grice, Paul. 1975. Logic and conversation. In Peter Cole & Jerry L. Morgan (ed.), *Syntax and semantics, Vol. 3: Speech Acts*, 41–58. New York: Academic Press.
Koestler, Arthur. 1964. *The art of creation*. London: Hutchinson & Co.

Krahmer, Emiel, Zsofia Ruttkay, Marc Swerts & Wieger Wesselink. 2002. Pitch, eyebrows, and the perception of focus. *ISCA Archive* https://www.isca-speech.org/archive_open/sp2002/sp02_443.pdf

Langlotz, Andreas. 2006. *Idiomatic creativity: A cognitive-linguistic model of idiom-representation and idiom-variation in English*. Amsterdam/Philadelphia: John Benjamins.

Lee, Christopher J. & Albert N. Katz. 1998. The differential role of ridicule in sarcasm and irony. *Metaphor and Symbol* 13(1). 1–15.

Mesing, Joslyn, Danielle Williams & Dawn Blasko. 2012. Sarcasm in relationships: Hurtful or humorous? *International Journal of Psychology* 47. 724–724.

Musolff, Andreas. 2022. "War against COVID-19": Is the pandemic as war metaphor helpful or hurtful?" In Andreas Musolff, Ruth Breeze, Kayo Kondo & Sara Vilar-Lluch (eds.), *Pandemic and Crisis Discourse: Communicating COVID-19 and Public Health Strategy*, 307–320. Great Britain: Bloomsbury.

Nicolas, Tim. 1995. Semantics of idiom modification. In Martin Everaert, Erik-Jan van der Linden, Andr Schenk & Rob Schreuder (eds.), *Idioms: Structural and psychological perspectives*, 233–252. Hillsdale, NJ: Lawrence Erlbaum Associates.

Norris, Sigrid. 2004. *Analyzing multimodal interaction: A methodological framework*. New York/ London: Routledge.

Norris, Sigrid. 2011. *Identity in (inter)action: introducing multimodal (inter)action analysis*. Germany: Mouton de Gruyter.

Priego-Valverde, Béatrice. 2006. How funny it is when everybody gets going! A case of co-construction of humor in conversation. *Círculo de lingüística aplicada a la communicación* 27. 72–100.

Raskin, Victor. 1985. *Semantic mechanisms of humor*. Dordrecht: D. Reidel.

Rockwell, Patricia. 2000. Lower, slower, louder: vocal cues to sarcasm. *Journal of Psycholinguistic Research* 29(5). 483–495.

Schelling, Thomas C. 1960. *The strategy of conflict*. Cambridge: Harvard University Press.

Tabacaru, Sabina. 2018. When language bites. A corpus-based taxonomy of sarcastic utterances in American television series. *Pragmatics & Cognition* 24(2).186–211.

Tabacaru, Sabina. 2019. *A Multimodal Study of Sarcasm in Interactional Humor*. Berlin: De Gruyter Mouton.

Tabacaru, Sabina. 2020. Faces of sarcasm. Exploring raised eyebrows with sarcasm in French political debates. Dans Angeliki Athanasiadou & Herbert L. Colston (eds.), *Diversity of irony*, 256–277. Berlin/Boston: Mouton de Gruyter.

Tabacaru, Sabina & Maarten Lemmens. 2014. Raised eyebrows as gestural triggers in humor: The case of sarcasm and hyper-understanding. *European Journal of Humor Research* 2(2). 18–31.

Tomasello, Michael. 2008. *Origins of human communication*. Cambridge, Massachusetts: The MIT Press.

Tsakona, Villy. 2009. Language and image interaction in cartoons: Towards a multimodal theory of humor. *Journal of Pragmatics* 41(6). 1171–1188.

Urios-Aparisi, Eduardo & Manuela Maria Wagner. 2011. Prosody of humor in *Sex and the City*. *Pragmatics & Cognition* 19(3). 507–529.

Weast, Traci Patricia. 2008. *Questions in American Sign Language: A quantitative analysis of raised and lowered eyebrows*. The University of Texas at Arlington dissertation.

Jia Qiu, Xinren Chen and Michael Haugh
8 Emojis and jocular flattery in Chinese instant messaging interactions

Abstract: While emojis are traditionally understood to be a means of expressing emotion and politeness in text-based forms of digitally-mediated communication, recent work has demonstrated that emojis play an important role in the interactional accomplishment of conversational humour as well. In this chapter, we focus on the role of emojis in the joint accomplishment of jocular flattery in multi-party instant messaging interactions in (Mandarin) Chinese. In the course of this study, we draw particular attention to how emojis are involved in different stages of performing jocular flattery, and how they are employed by participants in these sequences to accomplish particular footings with respect to instances of it. We conclude by considering the implications of our study for understanding the roles played by emojis in co-constructing conversational humour more broadly.

Keywords: teasing, emojis, instant messaging, interactional pragmatics, digital CA, Mandarin Chinese

1 Introduction

Conversational humour is broadly defined as (sequences of) utterances that are designed to 'amuse' participants, or are treated as 'amusing' by participants, across various different kinds of social interaction (Dynel, 2009; Haugh & Priego-Valverde, forthcoming). This means it is inherently dialogic in nature, as it necessarily involves the use of various kinds of cues by which participants frame or respond to an utterance (or series of utterances) as being meant, ostensibly at least, to be taken as 'playful' or in 'jest', rather than as straightforwardly 'seriously'. Conversational humour has traditionally been studied in the context of everyday face-to-face interactions amongst friends or family members (Kotthoff,

Acknowledgements: This study is supported by a project titled "An Interpersonal Pragmatic Study of Teasing in Online Interactions" (21NDJC119YB) financed by Zhejiang Federation of Humanities and Social Sciences Circles; China Scholarship Council (201806190081), and a major project titled "Language Issues in the Social Management of Cyberspace" funded by National Social Science Fund of China (20&ZD299). The authors would like to thank anonymous reviewers for their helpful feedback on an earlier version of this chapter.

https://doi.org/10.1515/9783110983128-009

2006; Norrick, 1993). In recent years, however, scholars have also increasingly focused on the ways in which conversational humour can also arise in various kinds of computer-mediated or digitally-mediated communication (Weitz, 2017; Yus, 2021), reflecting the rapid upsurge in the use of various forms or modes of technology-mediated communication in our daily lives.

Mirroring developments in the field of computer-mediated communication more generally (Herring, 2019), early work on humour initially focused on text-based forms of computer-mediated communication (CMC), such as email (e.g. Hübler & Bell, 2003; Schnurr & Rowe, 2008), or online discussion boards (e.g. Chovanec, 2011; North, 2007). With the rise of social media platforms and various kinds of instant messaging applications, however, there has been increasing attention paid to multimodal dimensions of humour across other forms of technology-mediated communication (TMC), as such platforms and apps readily support multimodal enrichment of text-based communications (e.g. Mullan, 2020; Vásquez et al., 2021; Zhang & Cassany, 2021).[1] A growing body of research on multimodal dimensions of conversational humour has illustrated how extra-linguistic or non-verbal features of interaction, such as prosody, facial expressions (including smiles), gaze, gestures, and touch, systematically shape the design and uptake of conversational humour practices in face-to-face interaction (e.g. Attardo et al., 2013; Bertrand & Priego-Valverde, 2011; Brône, 2021; Buján, 2019; Gironzetti, 2022; Li, 2020). Scholars have also recently started to demonstrate the ways in which graphical elements of communication, such as emojis, GIFs, image memes, photos and avatars, or what Herring and Dainas (2017) collectively refer to as 'graphicons', can shape the interactional accomplishment of conversational humour across different forms of TMC (Cruz-Moya & Sánchez-Moya, 2021; König, 2019; Sampietro, 2021a, 2021b). Amongst this assortment of different kinds of graphicons, emojis have emerged as one of the most frequently used multimodal resources in sequences of conversational humour in TMC (Sampietro, 2020).

In this chapter, we focus on the role of emojis in sequences of jocular flattery in instant messaging interactions in (Mandarin) Chinese. Jocular flattery is a relatively understudied conversational humour practice that involves ostensibly elevating others in a playful, teasing manner, often in the context of multiparty interactions (Qiu, Chen & Haugh, 2021). Our objectives in this study are twofold. On the one hand, we aim to contribute to the growing body of research that focuses on multimodal

---

[1] We use the term, technology-mediated communication (TMC) in this chapter as an umbrella term to cover computer-mediated, digitally-mediated, electronically-mediated or Internet-based communication (CMC, DMC, EMC, IBC, respectively), as text-based forms of communication in which emojis can be deployed are now available not only through computers, but also smartphones, and other devices.

dimensions of conversational humour across different modes of communication. On the other hand, we also aim to contribute to a better understanding of the role played by emojis in co-constructing conversational humour across different linguistic and sociocultural contexts.

We begin, in the following section of the chapter, by briefly reviewing relevant literature on the pragmatic functions of emojis, in general, and their role in conversational humour in technology-mediated communication settings, in particular. We then outline, in section three, our dataset and methodological approach, before moving on, in section four, to analyse the contribution of emojis to the joint accomplishment of jocular flattery in multi-party instant messaging interactions. In the course of this analysis, we draw particular attention to how emojis are involved in different stages of performing jocular flattery, and how they are employed by participants in these sequences to accomplish particular footings with respect to instances of it. We conclude by briefly outlining the implications of our study for understanding the roles played by emojis in co-constructing conversational humour more broadly.

2 Emojis and technology-mediated communication

2.1 The pragmatic functions of emojis

The use of emojis in various forms of technology-mediated communication (TMC) has attracted scholarly attention across a range of different disciplines, but in linguistics research has largely focused on the functions of emojis (Li & Yang, 2018; Sampetro, 2020). Emojis are sometimes regarded as primarily indicators of emotion (e.g. Riordan, 2017), similar to their text-based precursors, emoticons (Wolf, 2000), and are designed to stand for the facial expressions that are otherwise present in face-to-face interaction. However, subsequent research has shown that emojis can actually perform a range of different pragmatic functions beyond simply expressing emotion. Semantically, emojis can be used to encode lexical meanings (Aull, 2019; cf. Dürscheid & Siever, 2017), or to embody an action or depict verbal elements (Herring & Dainas, 2017). At the discourse level, they may help to structure interactive exchanges and organize conversational discourse (Al Rashdi, 2018; König, 2019). Emojis can also carry out rhetorical functions, such as emphasizing particular elements of text (Gibson et al., 2018), as well as indexing registers or signaling speech genres (Sampietro, 2019).

Among the various labels attached to the functions of emojis recorded by researchers to date, however, the majority of them seem to be largely interpersonal in nature. Within this broad category, research has demonstrated that emojis can not only signal the illocutionary force or modify the tone of the utterance (Herring & Dainas, 2017), but may also be used as upgraders or downgraders to strengthen or mitigate different speech acts (Sampietro, 2019), thereby signaling politeness or rapport (Al Rashdi, 2018; Aull, 2019; Sampietro, 2019), as well as in claiming or attributing identities within and across online communities (Graham, 2019; Parkwell, 2019; Togans et al., 2021). The nuanced ways in which emojis can be used to signal playfulness or humour have also been increasingly noted by researchers (König, 2019; Messerli & Locher, 2021; Qiu, Chen & Haugh, 2021; Sampietro, 2021a; Zhang, Wang & Li, 2021). However, while the latter function of emojis is arguably of particular note here, indexing a playful or jocular stance through emojis overlaps with some of the functions mentioned above, such as structuring interactive exchanges (e.g. initiating or closing a playful interaction), modifying the illocutionary force or tone of speech acts (e.g. signaling certain speech acts as non-serious), and creating alignment and rapport, and so cannot be considered in isolation from those other functions.

2.2 Emojis and conversational humour in instant messaging interactions

Early work on humour in text-based forms of computer-mediated communication suggested that it can be difficult to recognise in such contexts due to the lack of paralinguistic or non-linguistic cues, such as prosody, facial expressions and gestures (Hancock, 2004; Hübler & Bell, 2003). Vandergriff and Fuchs (2012), for instance, argue that the most frequent response to conversational humour in text-based forms of CMC is further humour. Recent work on instant messaging via social media platforms and messaging apps, however, has demonstrated that emojis, alongside "transcribed" laughter (e.g. 'hahaha', 'hehe') (Petitjean & Morel, 2017), play an important role in signaling and managing conversational humour across a range of different languages and cultural settings, including English as a lingua franca (Messerli & Locher, 2021), German (König, 2019), (Mandarin) Chinese (Qiu, Chen & Haugh, 2021), (Omani) Arabic (Al Rashdi, 2018), and Spanish (Sampietro, 2021a, 2021b).

Research on the relationship between emojis and conversational humour in Spanish WhatsApp dyadic chats, for instance, has shown how emojis can be used to signal the opening and closing of the play frame, respond to instances of humour, graphically reproduce laughter, and as a form of play in their own right

(Sampietro, 2021a, 2021b). Their employment as contextualization cues to frame verbal utterances as joking or teasing is also supported in Omani WhatsApp group chats (Al Rashdi, 2018) and Chinese WeChat group chats (Qiu, Chen & Haugh, 2021), albeit such functions are only mentioned in passing. Drawing on analysis of German WhatsApp chats, König (2019) finds that emojis are closely connected with "laugh" particles and can help to distinguish between different laughing stances such as "laughing with" and "laughing at" the target(s). Studies also indicate that emojis frequent encode humour support in online communication. Messerli and Locher (2021), for instance, report that emojis account for the largest percentage of the range of humour support indicators they identified in online viewers' timed comments about Korean TV drama series.

While the use of emojis as a non-verbal marker or index of humour has been observed in different technology-mediated communication contexts, with the exception of important work by Sampietro (2021a), few studies in pragmatics to date have been solely devoted to exploring the role emojis play in performing humour in different cultural contexts, in spite of research emerging that demonstrates the use and interpretation of emojis can vary across cultures (Sampietro, Felder & Siebenhaar, 2022), and that the seemingly 'playful' or even 'subversive' stances instantiated by emojis can mask an underlying orientation to social conformity (Zhang, Wang & Li, 2021). This chapter aims to explore how emojis contribute to the multimodal co-construction of jocular flattery (Qiu, Chen & Haugh, 2021), a form of conversational humour identified in the literature recently which serves as a vehicle for accomplishing interactional rapport (in the Chinese sociocultural context at least). In so doing, it attempts to further our understanding of the relation of emojis to conversational humour across different linguistic and sociocultural contexts.

3 Data and method

3.1 Data

Examples of jocular flattery were collected from instant messages exchanged in text-based WeChat group chats. Approximately 70% of the total population in China use instant messaging applications, with WeChat being one of the most popular apps used for this purpose (Xie and Li, 2021). Alongside enabling private dyadic chats, WeChat also allows users to set up or join a group chat, where all group members can share messages, pictures, links and other types of files. It is thus fairly similar in its functionality to instant messaging in WhatsApp, and is also accessible through computers, smart phones and other devices.[2] Compared to private dyadic exchanges between individuals, multi-party chats are open to larger groups of participants and arguably are semi-public, since users know whatever appears in the group chat is visible to all the group members and could be spread to others outside the group. While voice chat and video chat have both been recently made available to WeChat users, we only focused on text-based chat, because the latter is the most typical way in which *multi-party* interactions occur in WeChat (Xie & Li, 2021).

Our dataset consists of 29 episodes of multi–party instant messaging interactions involving 89 individual instances of jocular flattery, which in turn were identified within a larger dataset of 156 sequences involving conversational humour. These instances of jocular flattery were collected with prior consent from 11 WeChat groups where at least one of the first two authors was a member of the group over the period between June 2018 through to December 2019.[3] These different WeChat group chats consist of interactions among people having various relationships, including among colleagues, old classmates, fellow PhD students of adjacent grades and the same supervisor, relatives and acquaintances. A more detailed description of this dataset, as well as the procedure for identifying instances of jocular flattery, can be found in Qiu, Chen and Haugh (2021: 229–230).

Examining instances of jocular flattery occurring in authentic naturally occurring multi-party interactions provides us with valuable opportunities to observe and investigate Chinese people's daily online communications, including their use of conversational humour. This is important for at least two reasons. First, multi-party chat among relatives, classmates, colleagues and other familiar ones arguably reflect how Chinese people communicate online in an 'acquaintance society' (*shuren shehui*, 熟人社会).[4] Second, conversational humour, and teasing in particular, seems to be more likely with increasing familiarity (Keltner et al., 2001) in the context of an 'acquaintance society'.

---

[2] The similarity in technological affordances of WeChat and WhatsApp also enables potential comparison of the role of emojis in relation to humour across different linguistic contexts (König, 2019; Sampietro, 2021a, 2021b).

[3] Membership of multi-party chats is very useful for providing valuable ethnographic knowledge of the interactions (e.g. interactional context, relational history etc.). We do not include any examples in our analysis, however, where any of the authors directly participated in the jocular flattery sequence in question.

[4] According to Fei Xiaotong (1948/2019), a leading Chinese sociologist and anthropologist, Chinese society is a typical society of acquaintances and kinships (instead of being 'stranger society', *moshengren shehui*, 陌生人社会). In this society, 'relations' or 'connection' (*guanxi*, 关系) between people are particularly important for one's social flourishing or even survival.

Emojis were used in all of the 29 episodes of jocular flattery. Moreover, in many cases, one single turn simultaneously employs more than one types of emojis or/and duplicates the same emoji, as can be observed in the examples discussed in Section 4. Candidate examples of jocular flattery were transcribed according to their actual occurrence in the original online interactions.[5] Pseudonyms are used for all of the participants to maintain confidentiality.

3.2 Analytical approach

The analysis of our dataset relied primarily on an interactional pragmatics approach to analysing conversational humour and teasing (Haugh, 2010, 2014, 2016; Qiu, Chen & Haugh, 2021), although also drew upon multimodal discourse analytic research (Gárces-Conejos Blitvich & Bou-Franch, 2019; Herring, 2019), and digital CA (Giles et al., 2015; Giles, Stommel & Paulus, 2017) for the analysis of emojis. One distinct advantage of CA-informed approaches to analysing TMC, such as interactional pragmatics and digital CA, is their emphasis on the importance of turn composition and sequential position in licensing the analyst's inferences about the understandings of participants. Particular attention was thus paid to the core analytical question of 'why that now?' (i.e. why are the participants using that emoji – or that set of emojis – now at this point in the interaction?) in examining the data.

Building on our initial observations of the jocular flattery dataset and research on teasing (Drew, 1987; Haugh, 2010; Haugh & Pillet-Shore, 2018), sequences involving instances of jocular flattery was divided into three different moves or stages: (1) triggering jocular flattery; (2) formulating jocular flattery; and (3) responding to jocular flattery. These stages arguably capture not only the dynamic development of jocular flattery sequences, but also the three important interrelated dimensions suggested in teasing more generally (Haugh, 2017). Recurrent patterns in the use of emojis emerged in the course of our analysis, which focused specifically on the following two research questions:
1) What roles do emojis play in the three moves of jocular flattery sequences?
2) How does the use of emojis in jocular flattery sequences vary with respect to the footing of the participant(s)?

---

[5] We provide original script in Chinese characters, followed by a translation into English. We have used italics in the translation to indicate turn–final particles in the excerpts that are difficult to translate directly into English (e.g. *la, a, o, ne*).

4 The role of emojis in jocular flattery sequences

Jocular flattery is a form of teasing that involves elevating others, while also indicating non-seriousness (Qiu, Chen & Haugh, 2021). Unlike other teasing practices that have been studied to date, where the target is ridiculed or set up to be ridiculed (Haugh, 2016, 2017), jocular flattery involves exaggerated positive evaluations of others that are designed to be responded to as playful or joking. In the Chinese sociocultural context, jocular flattery indexes a particular cultural frame in which praising or complimenting, which is highly valued, can be accomplished while at the same time leaving the relative sincerity of those positive evaluations somewhat equivocal. Notably, while instances of jocular flattery can be observed to arise in both co-present and digitally-mediated settings, in this study we examine jocular flattery sequences which arose in multiparty instant messaging interactions in Chinese, focusing, in particular on the role played by emojis in those sequences. In the course of our analysis, we illustrate how emojis play a distinct role in each of the different interactional moves through which jocular flattery sequences are interactionally accomplished, and how emojis are typically employed within such interactions with respect to the respective footings of the participant(s).[6]

4.1 Role of emojis in triggering jocular flattery

Our first observation was that the use of emojis appeared to increase the chances that a jocular flattery sequence would be triggered. A teasable, that is, what is construed as triggering the tease, is canonically the first-positioned action in a teasing sequence (Drew, 1987; Haugh & Pillet-Shore, 2018). Jocular flattery in Chinese multi-party instant messaging interaction may be triggered by three main types of teasables: (1) overdone actions, (2) unfulfilled actions, and (3) out-of-place actions (Qiu, Chen & Haugh, 2021). While emojis alone do not occasion jocular flattery in our dataset, they can nevertheless increase the chances that instances of jocular flattery will be triggered.

---

6 The trends presented in this chapter are based on our dataset. Other findings may, of course, be possible with larger, more diverse datasets.

4.1.1 Enhancing a teasable

In the case of overdone actions that are treated as teasables, emojis may enhance a teasable by amplifying the excessiveness of the action in question. This may be achieved by the target strengthening the illocutionary force of a certain speech act, or by indicating an underlying emotive attitude or stance that is in some way incongruous with what has been expressed verbally in the message in question.

Just one turn prior to the following example, which is taken from a WeChat group among 45 colleagues working in the same school of a university, a teacher, who is responsible for arranging office hours for other teachers in the group, has just shared the timetable and reminded his colleagues in the group of their respective office hours this week.

Jocular flattery is initiated by Tang when he predicts that Xin, a man in his forties of common appearance, will get appointments from students due to his "dashing" looks (turn 2). The flattery is designed to be understood as non-serious, evidenced not only by Tang's exaggeration of Xin's looks, but also by the weeping face emoji and jocular self-mockery immediately following the flattery in the same turn in which Tang pretends to pity himself for his own looks (turn 2). The target, Xin, also treats the flattery as jocular, as evidenced by his teasingly setting up Tang through fabricating information that many colleagues think they look like broth-

---

7 "Feng" here is the last character of Tang's given name (anonymized). This form of address (i.e. one's last character of given name plus "er") is quite common among close friends (e.g. peers or the elder to the younger) and family members (i.e. used only by the elders to address the youngers) in China.

ers, accompanied by duplicated emojis of beaming face with smiling eyes, and smiling face with a sidelong glance (turn 3).

In investigating the sequential environment prior to the jocular flattery in turn 2, a close examination of the composition of Xin's prior turn is crucial. Notably, while Xin apparently poses a question about whether there will be students coming during his office hours again this week, he uses ellipsis instead of the question mark, which deviates from the normal practice of posing questions in written form, thereby blurring the illocutionary force of the utterance. The emoji of smiling face with sunglasses and shining teeth in utterance-final position is therefore particularly crucial in conveying the speaker's tone and guiding the hearer's interpretation of it. The image of the emoji involves a broad smile showing shinning teeth, with a pair of black sunglasses, and is often associated with the slang sense of 'cool'. These two elements, when combined together, seem to convey a confident or even complacent attitude. In addition, the use of the word "again" in the text presupposes students have come during his office hours before, thereby implying his popularity in this context. The emoji here arguably not only clarifies the otherwise ambivalent illocutionary force of the utterance, but also strengthens the force of this (ostensible) self-flattery. Xin's utterance is then treated as showing off by Tang (at least), which, as an overdone action, and so teasable, occasions the opportunity for jocular flattery in the following turn.

The following excerpt shows how emojis may contribute to triggering jocular flattery by (unintentionally) indicating an (underlying) emotive attitude or stance that is to a certain extent incongruous with the meaning or actions delivered in the text of the message in question. It is taken from a WeChat group among 15 fellow PhD students who share the same supervisor in which a response to congratulations sets off an extended sequence of multiple instances of jocular flattery.[8] Here, we focus on the sequential environment that precedes that extended jocular flattery sequence.

(2) 'Piano competition'
    01   Yuan: 那个~西安会议我大概去不成了~~小P孩晋级了，
                    得陪着去日本参加决赛
                    'umm~ I probably cannot attend the meeting in Xi'an~~ my brat has won a competition, and I have to accompany him to Japan for the final'

---

8 For a detailed analysis of the longer sequence of jocular flattery, see Qiu, Chen and Haugh (2021: 231–232).

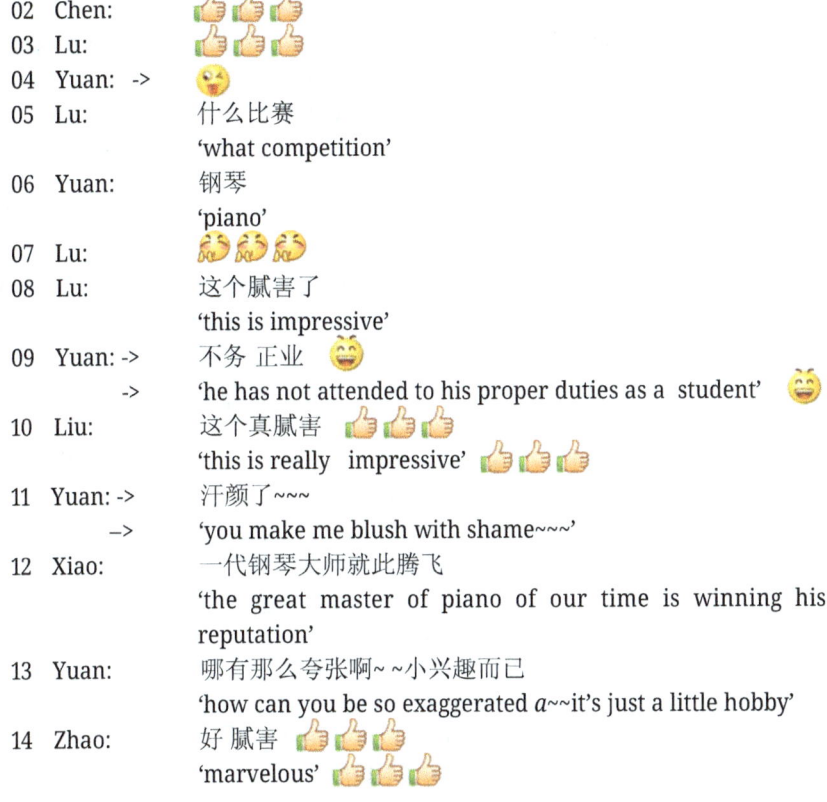

The first 11 turns involve Yuan giving an account for her absence at the forthcoming meeting in Xi'an (turn 1), as well as the other active participants showing interest (turn 5), and offering a series of felicitations (turns 2–3, 7), and compliments (turns 8, 10). Notably, Yuan's revealing information about her future absence from the meeting is not obligatory in the first place. In addition, her first turn not only contains specific details such as going to Japan for the final competition, but also employs tilde symbols ('~'), which often convey a cheerful, excited and light-hearted tone, while also indicating a slight rising-falling change of intonation in Chinese instant messaging chats.

In responding to the others' felicitations, Yuan first uses the emoji of winking face with tongue (turn 4), thereby indicating a naughty, excited tone, but rejects the compliments with criticisms of her son's under-performance as a student (turn 9), and protestations that she feels embarrassed (turn 11). However, in rejecting the compliment through belittling her son's achievements, the emoji of grinning face with smiling eyes is placed in utterance-final position (turn 9), implying Yuan's (unsaid) satisfaction with her son's performance, which is arguably incongruous with the prior belittling criticism in the same turn. Moreover, in claiming that she is embarrassed by Liu's compliment, Yuan nevertheless uses tilde symbols to act 'cute' and convey a cheerful tone (turn 11).

Considering all the above clues, we are inclined to regard Yuan's self-disclosure at the beginning of the excerpt to be primarily about sharing this good news about her son rather than informing others of her future absence from the meeting. The two emojis (turns 4, 9), together with the tilde symbols, seem to give off Yuan's underlying emotive stance (i.e. she is thrilled at the good news and very proud of her son), which is, to a certain extent, incongruous with the apparent rejections of their felicitations about his achievement (turns 9, 11). This incongruity may, in turn, increase the degree of excessiveness of Yuan's ostensible modesty, which occasions the subsequent instance of jocular flattery (turn 12), and subsequently an extended series of them (data not shown) (see Qiu, Chen and Haugh, 2021). It is apparent, then, that emojis may enhance the degree to which the action in question can be construed as overdone and thereby constitutes a teasable.

4.1.2 Indexing the delicacy of the situation

Unfulfilled actions, such as when the target fails to fulfil a promise or an appointment, or attempts to save oneself from such "unfavorable" situations through offering some seemingly elegant excuse, can be construed as teasables. In such cases, emojis may serve to suggest the delicacy of the situation among the participants through explicitly expressing the target's embarrassment and uneasiness, thereby implicitly reminding the other interlocutor(s) – in particular the party to whom the excuse is made – of the delicacy of the current situation.

The following excerpt is taken from a WeChat group among 33 parents, which was voluntarily created by Xue to enhance their children's self-confidence through offering them chances to freely perform in small-scale concerts.

(3) 'Host's speech'
01 Xue: @常 左思的曲目发给我哦
                '@Chang send me the name of the performance
                Zuo Si plans to give o'
02 Chang: 这是要干嘛
                'what is this for'
03 Xue: 排节目单，我写主持稿哦
                @常 这是我们第三次音乐会了，欢迎左思哦 🎉🎉
                'I'll write a draft of the host's speech for the

		concert programme o
		@Chang this is our third concert, welcome Zuo Si o' 🎉🎉
04	Zhan:	@薛 高晨: 跳舞: 新唐诗; 唱歌:
		你笑 起来真好看 😊😊
		'@Xue Gao Chen: dancing: "New Tang Poetry"; singing:
		"You Look So Pretty When You Smile"' 😊😊
05	Xue:	👌
06	Pan: ->	@薛 朱凯, 横笛, 曲目明天报 给你 😂😂
	->	这几天回家晚, 他都 睡了 😂😂
	->	'@Xue Zhu Kai, bamboo flute, I'll tell you the piece of music
	->	tomorrow 😂😂
	->	I went back home late these days, and he was asleep' 😂😂
07	Xue:	教授不 易啊 🤭 @潘
		'a professor's life is not easy a 🤭 @Pan'
08	Pan:	😂😂

The instance of jocular flattery in question occurs in turn 7, where Xue deliberately addresses Pan, who she knows is a lecturer, as a "professor". In the turns prior to this instance of jocular flattery (turns 1–6), Xue has told Chang, a new member of the chat group, to send her the specific information about the performance Chang's daughter plans to give, and has explained the reason for doing that (turns 1, 3). It is pertinent to mention here that just one day before the interaction, Xue, the organizer of the concert, reminded group members for a second time to let her know what their children plan to perform in the upcoming concert. While several parents immediately did what they were asked, Pan failed to do so, and only replied with an "OK" emoji (data not shown). While directed at Chang, Xue's utterances also serve as an indirect reminder to other parents who have not sent the required information yet (turns 1, 3). Zhan, for instance, responds almost immediately in the next turn, and gives the required information (turn 4).

In this context, then, Pan's repeated failure to send Xue the required information constitutes a potential impropriety, which may incur negative assessments from Xue and other participants (e.g. being evaluated as impolite and inconsiderate, etc.), thereby threatening Xue's face as an individual, and their relational face (Chang, 2016; Mao, 1994). The delicacy involved in the current interaction is arguably recognized by Pan, as evidenced by the design of her subsequent turn, in which she immediately provides some information about the performance information, promises to give full information about it tomorrow, and also offers a seemingly objective account for why she has failed to do so until now (i.e. "I went back home late these days, and he was asleep") (turn 6). Notably, Pan first employs duplicated emojis of face with tears of joy to treat her failure to fulfil her promise as both a laughable and a trouble (cf. Sampietro, 2021b), while the utterance "Zhu Kai, bamboo flute, I'll tell you the piece of music tomorrow" does not seem to involve humour per se. She then uses duplicated emojis of laughing face with tears and hand covering the eyes[9] to convey her reluctance to cause such trouble and her embarrassment about this (i.e. her failure to provide the full information as required is construed as inadvertent and unintentional). Duplicating the two types of emojis within the same turn not only highlights Pan's uneasiness, but also emphasizes the delicacy of the current situation, which is recognized by Xue, and arguably occasions her jocular flattery directed towards Pan in the subsequent turn. The latter simultaneously achieves different interactional goals, including showing (ostensible) admiration for Pan's diligence in her work, expressing sympathy and understanding, and mitigating potential embarrassment, thereby saving Pan's face.

4.1.3 Displaying humorous intent

Seemingly out-of-place actions may also trigger jocular flattery. They often involve a seemingly "nice aspect" of the target, such as some kind of talent, attractive appearance, expertise, or other socially positively valued qualities being exhibited in a context that is to a certain extent not suitable for that, thereby potentially making the target (and/or some members of the audience) feel embarrassed. Most of the out-of-place actions in our dataset are afforded by the sharing of photos and links concerning the target in the group chat, often with no extra emoji involved in the triggering stage. However, there are nevertheless some cases where emojis may increase the chances of triggering jocular flattery by indicating the speaker's awareness of the potential inappropriacy of the shared photo or link, thereby inviting humorous contributions.

In the following except taken from a WeChat group among 15 fellow PhD students who share the same supervisor, for instance, the first instance of jocular flattery occurs when Yuan expresses ostensible admiration for Lin[10] through in-

---

9 The tone conveyed by this emoji can be various. Depending on the specific context, this emoji can be used to convey the meaning of laughing to tears, not knowing whether to laugh or to cry, having no alternatives, etc. It is often used when the speaker finds something both funny and annoying, or something that is embarrassing or silly.

10 *Dàwèi* (大卫, 'David') is a nickname Yuan gave to Lin who has a good appetite. In Chinese, *Dàwèi* (大卫, 'David') and *dàwèi* (大胃, 'big stomach') are homophones. Since Yuan also has a good appetite, whenever Yuan calls Lin "David", Lin always responds by calling Yuan "king-sized David".

voking a popular Internet slang expression, which here means "you are the most admirable person in my eyes" (turn 6).[11]

(4) 'Wet kisses'
```
01  Chen:       屏幕都被你们吻湿了
                'your kisses wet the phone screen'
02  Yuan:       师兄这话,真不好接。。。
                'it's not easy to reply to academic elder brother's words...'
03  Lin:   ->   不会湿,因为不是法式热吻  😜
         ->    'no, the screen won't become wet, because those are
         ->    not French kisses'  😜
04  Lin:        祝师兄师姐一切顺利,旗开得胜~
                'wish everything goes well in academic elder brother and sister's
                doctoral defense. Succeed at the first try~'
05  Wu:         哈哈哈
                'ha ha ha'
06  Yuan:       刮风下雨, 我墙都不扶, 就服你大卫林  🙏
                'in windy and rainy days, I don't even hold the wall,
                I only admire you, David Lin'  🙏
07  Lin:        @袁 特大卫, 承让了  🙏🙏
                '@Yuan King-sized David, thanks for letting me win'  🙏🙏
```

It is pertinent to mention here that the complete log of the interaction starts when Chen, also on the behalf of other three group members who are about to give a doctoral defence (including Yuan), invites people in the group chat for a dinner after their doctoral defence, which is their tradition. While those invited express their good wishes to the four hosts, Liu, who is an academic peer of Yuan, mistakenly addresses the hosts as "academic elder brothers and sisters". This slip of the tongue (or slip of the finger) occasions extended bouts of teases (data not shown here).

The sequential environment immediately prior to the instance of jocular flattery shown here involves Chen teasing some female participants who used the red lip emoji to express their affection for each other by claiming that such behavior could end up wetting their phone screens (turn 1). While Yuan admits that

---

[11] Having many variants, this Internet slang is often used to jokingly express one's admiration when witnessing certain eye-opening events.

she does not find it easy to respond to what Chen has texted (turn 2), which arguably implies the potential difficulty involved in winning this verbal duel, Lin succeeds in beating him through jocular word play on "kiss" (*wen*, 吻), arguing that the screen would remain dry because those are not French kisses (turn 3). Lin's witty response immediately wins Wu and Yuan's appreciation (turns 5–6). Notably, in utterance-final position, Lin uses a smiling face with a sidelong glance, the emoji which is often associated with the speaker indicating he or she is harboring certain mischievous designs. Despite a rescue of the targets of Chen's tease, through her witty reply[12] Lin seems to have exhibited her expertise in kissing, which is inappropriate given the setting here is semi-public and consists of both males and females. By using a smiling face with a sidelong glance, Lin not only indicates her awareness of potential impropriety (which may incur negative evaluation from others), but also displays her non-serious intent and invites humorous contribution from other participants (thereby dissolving potential negative evaluation of her).[13] Therefore, while Yuan's jocular flattery (turn 6) seems to be occasioned by Lin's playful yet "dirty" remark (turn 3), Yuan also aligns with Lin's humorous framing of her contribution, and satisfies her expectation for a further humorous contribution, which is indicated by the emoji of smiling face with a sidelong glance.

As we can see from the analysis above, while emojis are not always used in every case where jocular flattery is triggered, and emojis alone do not necessarily occasion jocular flattery, when they are employed they can contribute to constructing a teasable. This can be achieved either by increasing the degree of excessiveness of the action in question, or by highlighting the delicacy of the situation, or by displaying the humorous framing of the contribution in question and inviting humorous responses to it.

4.2 Role of emojis in formulating instances of jocular flattery

A close examination of our dataset shows that the majority of instances of jocular flattery employ at least one emoji.[14] Various emojis are used by the teaser to indi-

---

[12] While Chen's jocular mockery arguably also involves sexual connotations, Lin's reply goes much further, as is often seen in the case of verbal duels.
[13] By 'besting' Chen in this way, Lin is arguably well aware of the possibility of becoming the target herself, as evidenced by her use of the emoji in utterance-final position in turn 3.
[14] Given that an initial instance of jocular flattery often tends to occasion further jocular flattery (Qiu, Chen & Haugh, 2021), this section includes all the instances of jocular flattery found in the dataset, rather than being limited to only the initial instance of jocular flattery in each interactional episode.

cate or intensify the jocular effect, which can be classified into two broad categories, based on their role in the second stage of jocular flattery sequences.

4.2.1 Indexing jocularity

The first category can be further divided into two sub-categories: laughing emojis and exaggerating emojis. The former refers to emojis that involve various kinds of smiles or laughing, typically including grinning face with smiling eyes (see example 2, turn 9), 😄 beaming face with smiling eyes, 😁 and smiling face with hand over mouth.[15] 🤭 The latter refers to emojis that involve exaggerated facial expressions, typical examples of which include grinning face with open eyes and rising eyebrows, 😃 squinting face with tongue, 😝 and heart-eyes with drooling mouth. 🤤 Emojis in this category are designed to mimic the facial cues participants are thought to display when overtly signaling a humorous intent, rather than delivering them in a po-faced manner (Drew, 1987), or when engaging in jocular pretence (Haugh, 2016). The use of emojis from this category explicitly frames the utterance as non–serious, in the sense that the facial expressions represented through the employment of these emojis generally indicate some kind of deviation from serious talk. Laughing emojis, on the other hand, tend to construe something as (potentially) laughable, and invite other participants to treat the teasing flattery as a laughable.

The following excerpt, which is also taken from a WeChat interaction between 44 fellow PhD graduates and PhD students, consists of three instances of jocular flattery (turns 1–3). In each case, more than one type of emoji is used in formulating the turn as an instance of jocular flattery. It is pertinent to mention here that just prior to this excerpt, Song had posted a screenshot of his senior, Sheng, from an online course he was giving, and described him as "drop-dead gorgeous".

(5) 'Drop-dead gorgeous'
01 Gao: -> 粉嫩嫩~ 🤭🤭😁😁
   -> 'fair and tender~' 🤭🤭😁😁
02 Xu: -> 万千粉黛无颜色! 😁🌷🌷🌷
   -> '((his face)) outshines hundreds and

---

15 This does not mean emojis including smiles in their design are necessarily associated with humour. The emoji of smiling face with smiling eyes, 🙂 for instance, tends to be used for conveying a lovable, amiable and friendly tone.

		->	thousands of pretty faces!' 😁 🌹🌹🌹
03	Gao:	->	师兄古文功底深厚 👍👍😝 @许
		->	'academic elder brother has solid mastery
		->	of ancient Chinese prose 👍👍😝 @Xu'
04	Xu:		@高 😊
			'@Gao'
05	Gao:		😄😄😁😁

Gao's jocular flattery initially targets Sheng (turn 1). In evaluating the target's face as "fair and tender", followed by the tilde symbol to act 'cute', Gao first displays her humorous intent through the underlying incongruity between the image of a beautiful maiden and that of a middle-aged male. Both emojis of smiling face with hand over mouth, and beaming face with smiling eyes are used twice in utterance-final position to explicitly emphasize the teaser's humorous framing of this positive assessment. Xu not only recognizes but also appreciates Gao's jocular flattery, as evidenced by his further elaborating the jocular flattery sequence through echoing Gao's turn design, in the sense that 万千粉黛无颜色 ("one's face outshines hundreds and thousands of pretty faces"), an adaptation of "Yang Yu-huan outshone in six palaces the fairest face" (六宫粉黛无颜色), is also normally used for describing beautiful young women (turn 2).[16] He also employs a beaming face with smiling eyes to show his enjoyment and construe his contribution as laughable, while using three roses simultaneously to intensify the flatterable (i.e. Sheng's good state captured in the screenshot).

Although some exaggerating emojis may also involve some form of smile in their design, they arguably differ from laughing emojis in that they foreground facial expressions that are exaggerated in an overtly conspicuous manner; for example, by rising eyebrows, sticking out tongue, and so on, to construe something as (potentially) naughty and mischievous, or funny and hilarious, thereby overtly framing the contribution as non-serious. In example (5) presented above, for instance, Xu himself later becomes the target of jocular flattery in turn 3, when Gao jocularly flatters him as having a "solid mastery of ancient Chinese prose". She also employs two emojis of thumbs-up to exaggerate the flatterable through emphasizing her admiration, and a squinting face with tongue to index a playful tone (turn 3).

---

16 This is a line from Bai Juyi's famous poem "The Everlasting Regret", which describes the romantic love between Emperor Xuan Zong of the Tang Dynasty and his favourite mistress Yang Yu-huan, who is commonly regarded as one of the Four Beauties in ancient China.

The emoji of heart-eyes with drooling mouth, when used in sequences of jocular flattery, tends to convey enthusiastic feelings and strong desire for a person, usually the target, so as to exaggerate his/her positive qualities and construe them as the flatterable in question (e.g. sexy, attractive, outstanding). In the following example, for instance, taken from a WeChat group among 26 colleagues working in the same department of a college, Chai, one of the teachers, posted a news report which details Tao's strengths and hails him, a lecturer in the department and also member in the group chat, as a model party member in the title of the report. The posting of this news report arguably occasions Fang's jocular flattery in turn 1 below.

(6) 'News report'
```
01  Fang:    ->    陶爷怎么可以那么优秀    😍😁
            ->    'How could Tao-ye be so excellent'    😍😁
02  Shao:          同为椎间盘，汝何如此突出?¹⁷
                  'being intervertebral disc, why art thou so protrusive?
                  (i.e. how can you be so outstanding among your peers?)'
03  Fang:    🤗
```

Notably, addressing the target, Tao, as 陶爷 ("Tao ye") provides a linguistic cue for a playful frame in turn 1, as 爷 ("ye") is a term traditionally used in times gone by when addressing men of high social status (e.g. bureaucrats, rich men, etc.) to show respect, but Tao is only several years older than his colleague Fang. At the end of this turn, Fang uses two emojis. The emoji of heart-eyes with drooling mouth clearly involves exaggeration as it consists of a pair of red, cartoon-styled hearts for eyes and a salivating mouth, which together emphasize strong enthusiasm, adoration and desire. This emoji is also used by males to express ostensible enthusiastic feelings for another male of similar age, thereby indicating a non-serious frame. This emoji is then followed by a laughing emoji, beaming face with smiling eyes, to explicitly display the teaser's humorous intent and construe what is said in this turn as a laughable.

---

17 This is an adaptation of the popular Internet slang, 同是腰椎间盘,为何你那么突出 (literally, "being lumbar intervertebral discs, why are you so protrusive", meaning "to be outstanding among one's peers").

4.2.2 Intensifying jocularity

The second category involves emojis that are commonly used to indicate approval or compliments. When they are used in formulating instances of jocular flattery, they can therefore intensify its degree of jocularity through emphasizing this is only ostensible approval or congratulations. Framing a non-serious tone in this case is achieved implicitly, in the sense that recognition of the teaser's humorous intent relies more on linguistic cues and background information (e.g. some kind of incongruity).[18] In terms of image design, emojis of this category are mostly gestural rather than facial. Typical emojis include thumbs-up, red rose, cupping one's fist in the other hand, and clapping-hands, with the first two emojis occurring most frequently in our dataset.

In the next example, which is taken from a WeChat group chat consisting of 44 former and current PhD students, most of whom were previously, or are currently, under the supervision of the same supervisor, we can see how the emoji of thumbs-up may intensify jocularity of the jocular flattery by emphasizing (ostensible) approval while also indicating an affiliative orientation towards the target. In the turn just prior to this excerpt, Wu posted a picture in which Xiao, the target, dressed in a red sweater and looking energetic, is talking enthusiastically to a good-looking female doctor who is his senior. While there may be other people in the room, the picture only shows two of them: Xiao concentrates on talking while fixing his eyes on his good-looking senior listener.

(7) 'Red sweater'
   01 Hua:  ((words in the picture: 'wow~'))

   02 Lin: 程哥为何如此兴奋？
            'Why is Cheng-ge[19] so excited?'
   03 Chen: 这需要解释吗

---

[18] This does not mean emojis of this category have nothing to do with indexing jocularity. Depending on the situated context, these emojis may simultaneously convey other meanings such as a slightly mild ironic tone, expressing (playful) whoops and cheers, etc., apart from echoing the flattery.

[19] The address form of using the last character of one's given name plus "ge" (哥, meaning elder brother), can be used either for self-reference when one is older or more senior than the hearer, or used to address someone who is younger than oneself. However, in this example, addressing Xiao, the target, as "Cheng ge" (程哥) by Lin is jocular, since Lin is Xiao's elder both in age and seniority (i.e. Lin is an academic elder sister of Xiao).

			'Is explanation here really necessary'
04	Lin:	->	人面桃花相映红 👍
		->	'a charming face among peach blossoms' 👍
05	Lin:		需要解释啊?
			'It needs explanation *a*?'
06	Lin:		男人的心思我不会猜啊~不懂~
			'I don't know how to read a man's mind *a*~
			I just don't understand~'
07	Wu:		😂😂
08	Xiao:	->	正在向师姐虚心请教 😂😂
		->	'I'm humbly consulting the academic elder sister' 😂😂
09	Lin:		哦，原来是这样啊 😁
			'Oh, so it is *a*' 😁
10	Lee:		

((words in the picture: 'cannot help laughing in my beard'))

After Hua expresses ostensible admiration through an animated picture of a lovely bear clapping hands and gasping "wow" (turn 1), Lin raises an apparently "innocent" question (turn 2), which is rejected by Chen implying that the answer is only too obvious (turn 3). Lin then initiates an instance of jocular flattery directed at Xiao in which she quotes a line from a well-known poem of the Tang Dynasty, "a charming face among peach blossoms" (人面桃花相映红). It is worth explaining here that 桃花 ("peach blossoms") in Chinese is often used to symbolize the beauty of young girls, as the original meaning of the line demonstrates (i.e. "a girl's pretty face and the peach flowers reflect each other's glow"), and therefore, incongruity occurs when Lin quotes this line to depict Xiao's exciting face, implying that talking to a pretty woman makes Xiao look more lively and energetic (turn 4). This incongruity, which indicates a non-serious framing here, is easily recognizable to the group members, due to shared contextual information (e.g. background knowledge concerning the understanding of the well–known poem, what is presented in the picture, and what has been implied in the ongoing interaction, etc.). This is evidenced by the responses from other participants in the subsequent turns (turns 7–8, 10). The emoji of thumbs-up in the utterance-final position is primarily used to intensify jocularity by emphasizing Lin's (ostensible) approval for Xiao's vitality (i.e. the flatterable), given that jocular flattery involves construing a certain aspect of the target as a flatterable (Qiu, Chen & Haugh, 2021).

Apart from thumbs-up, red rose (see example 5, turn 2), cupping one's fist in the other hand[20] (see example 4, turn 6), and clapping-hands can also be employed in instances of jocular flattery in similar ways, intensifying the degree of absurdity of the jocular flattery through expressing (ostensible) congratulation, approval or admiration while indicating a rapport-oriented stance.

From the analysis in this section, we can see that the roles emojis play in formulating jocular flattery may differ in systematic ways. Specifically, laughing emojis (e.g. beaming face with smiling eyes, smiling face with hand over mouth, etc.) and exaggerating emojis (e.g. grinning face with open eyes and rising eyebrows, squinting face with tongue, etc.) are used mainly for *indicating* jocularity through explicitly displaying various laughing and exaggerated facial expressions. Gestural emojis such as thumbs-up, red rose, cupping one's fist in the other hand, and clapping–hands, on the other hand, can be employed to *intensify* jocularity through emphasizing (ostensible) approval. Nevertheless, these seemingly different emojis can be employed together in formulating an instance of jocular flattery (see example 5, turns 2–3).

4.3 Role of emojis in responding to jocular flattery

The responses of the target and the co-present audience constitute an important dimension of conversational humour in multi-party interactions. While there are clear differences in the responses of the target and the audience to instances of jocular flattery (Qiu, Chen & Haugh, 2021), on the whole, emojis used in this final stage of jocular flattery sequences serve to indicate alignment through displaying recognition of the teaser's humorous intent or echoing the jocular frame initiated by the teaser.

4.3.1 Endorsing or denying jocularity by the target

Depending on their participation footings, the target, at whose expense the tease is performed, may experience different emotions from those of the teaser or other co-present parties (Keltner et al., 1998; Kowalski, 2000). Indeed, compared to the responses of the other participants, there tends to be greater variation in the responses of targets to jocular flattery. These range from playing along, show-

---

20 This is a traditional Chinese gesture for showing politeness, which may be used for greetings, farewells and congratulations.

ing (ostensible) amusement, and evading the flattery in a non-serious manner, through to non-serious rejection, showing (ostensible) modesty, or disattending the jocular flattery (Qiu, Chen & Haugh, 2021). Except for very small number of cases where there was no response from the audience to the jocular flattery, the target, despite being the butt of the tease, always seems to display recognition of the teaser's humorous intent. Notably, this is often achieved through emojis, among other resources available. Specifically, emojis are used by the target in his/her response to endorse or license jocularity by displaying recognition of the teaser's humorous intent, or to make as if the target denies its jocularity by displaying ostensible embarrassment.

a. Endorsing jocularity

In formulating an instance of jocular flattery, the teaser depends on linguistic and non-linguistic cues to display his/her humorous intent. To show alignment with the teaser and achieve interpersonal rapport, among other interactional goals of jocular flattery, the target needs to endorse the jocular frame initiated by the teaser.

One way for the target to achieve that is to play along with the jocular flattery, for instance, by reciprocating the jocular flattery, as illustrated in the final two turns of example 4 (repeated here for convenience).

(4) 'Wet kisses'
06 Yuan: 刮风下雨, 我墙都不扶, 就服你大卫林
'in windy and rainy days, I don't even hold the wall, I only admire you, David Lin'
07 Lin: -> @袁 特大卫, 承让了
-> '@Yuan King-sized David, thanks for letting me win'

In replying to jocular flattery directed at her by Yuan (turn 6), Lin performs mock thanks. By saying "thanks for letting me win", Lin implies that Yuan surpasses her in terms of the flatterable construed by Yuan (turn 7). Notably, Lin not only reciprocates the jocular flattery, but also employs the same type of emoji and a similar way of formulating jocular flattery to show alignment with Yuan. Moreover, Lin doubles the emoji of cupping one's fist in the other hand, so as to emphasize her (ostensible) admiration for Yuan and intensify its jocularity, implying that Yuan deserves this flattery more than herself.

The target may also endorse the jocular frame initiated by the teaser by showing (ostensible) amusement through emojis. Interestingly, face with tears of joy, which, based on its design, is widely used to show in an exaggerated manner that one is laughing so hard that it even brings tears to one's eyes, is overwhelmingly employed in this dataset by the target for this purpose, echoing Sampietro's (2021b) findings in analysing WhatsApp in Spanish. As illustrated in examples 3 and 7 presented above, in both cases, the target, Pan and Xiao respectively, doubles this emoji to emphasize (ostensible) amusement and endorse jocularity.

Even in cases involving displaying (ostensible) modesty, emojis may still be used to indicate the continuation of a jocular frame, as illustrated in example 8 (which is a continuation of example 2 previously discussed in section 4.1.1).

(8) 'Piano competition' (continuation)
    20 Chen: @袁 你是国际钢琴大师他妈
                      '@Yuan you're the mother of the piano master of the world'
    21 Yuan: ->   我是烦人精 他妈
                ->   'I'm the mother of an annoying demon'

While belittling her son, and casting herself as "the mother of an annoying demon", Yuan uses a laughing emoji, grinning face with smiling eyes, to indicate her non-serious stance here and endorse the jocularity developed in the prior turns by the different teasers.

In our dataset, using emojis to endorse the playful frame of jocular flattery often occurs in cases where the target's response involves playing along, showing (ostensible) amusement, non-serious rejection, or showing (ostensible) modesty.

b. <u>Ostensibly deflecting the flattery</u>
In some cases, the target responds to jocular flattery by evading the flattery in a non-serious manner. While this is often achieved by both linguistic and non-linguistic means, different types of emojis can be employed on such occasions to ostensibly deny jocularity by showing the target's (ostensible) embarrassment. The emoji of sweating face, for instance, is often used by the target to convey awkward feelings.²¹ Other emojis that may indicate similar feelings and thereby ostensibly deny jocularity include slightly frowning face, black face with tears, red face with sweat, shy face, and laughing face with tears and hand covering the eyes.

The following excerpt, which is taken from a longer sequence of more than 25 turns of jocular flattery, centres on the Dean's looks, and subsequently his love life,

---

21 The emoji of sweating face has a similar meaning to 汗 ("sweat") when the latter is used as a form of Internet slang, and commonly refers to a state of speechless embarrassment.

when he was a student at the university. The interaction occurred in a WeChat group chat among colleagues in the same school of a university. Li, one of the teachers, posted an interview with the Dean, who is currently in his late forties, about campus life when he was a college student in the group chat. A picture of the Dean that featured in the interview was posted separately in the group chat by another teacher, Gao. Notably, revealing and publicizing a superior's personal picture and love story in workplace settings (i.e. group chat among colleagues) is generally considered to be inappropriate, despite the fact this information was taken from an interview. The excerpt in question begins with an assessment of the Dean's appearance in the photo when he was a student by Zhou.

(9) 'Little Tiger'
```
01  Zhou:          小后生颜值很高
                   'this lad is very handsome'
02  Gao :          当年小虎队的赶脚    👍
                   'looks like "Little Tiger" in those years'    👍
03  Zhai:          不得了呀水嫩水嫩
                   'oh my, such tender and smooth skin'
04  Xu:            绝对的    👍👍👍👍
                   'absolutely'   👍👍👍👍
05  Wang:          superstar
06  Yang:          嫩得来    😁
                   'looks so young and vigorous'    😁
07  Wang:          @李 院长大大的爱情故事很浪漫呀    😁😁👍👍
                   '@Li Dean's love story is so romantic ya'   😁😁👍👍
08  Li:            在学生圈里发现的,疯传    😁
                   'I found this in students' moments circle, crazy'   😁
09  Zha:   ->      乃们在做什么?   😳😳😳
            ->     'what are you doing?'    😳😳😳
10  Zha:   ->      突然发现群里全是我?   😳😳😳
            ->     'all of a sudden, I become the only topic
            ->     of the group chat?'   😳😳😳
11  Zha:   ->      答辩完了再来爬楼   🤦🤦🤦
            ->     'I'll read the chat logs after the defense'   🤦🤦🤦
```

As it is evident from the photo that the Dean was "plain" looking, even when younger, Zhou's assessment of the Dean as "very handsome" (turn 1), sets off a series of turns of jocular flattery in which the Dean is teased that he was a "Little Tiger"[22] (turn 2), had "smooth and tender skin" (turn 3), was a "superstar" (turn 5), and looked "young and vigorous" (turn 6). In turn 7, the Dean's "love story" is proposed as the next target for another sequence of jocular flattery (data not shown).

Notably, while the teasers use beaming face with smiling eyes and thumbs–up, among other resources, to indicate a playful frame as well as their enjoyment of performing jocular flattery together, the dean, also the target Zha in this example, employs totally different emojis from the teasers. He first responds with mock complaints about the way in which he has become the target here (turns 9–10). In formulating these mock complaints, he deliberately uses a non-standard form of the second person plural (乃们), which was originally only used in ancient Chinese prose, but is increasingly used in informal online interactions to indicate a playful tone. He also triples the emojis of 'shy face' and 'red face with sweat' to emphasize his (ostensible) feelings of embarrassment. The above mock complaints are subsequently followed by an account as to why Zha is unable to give timely response at the moment (i.e. he is attending a defense), accompanied by triple employment of 'laughing face with tears and hand covering the eyes', which arguably indicate both recognition of the non-serious frame here (i.e. laughing face), and his embarrassment (i.e. covering eyes) at the flattery (turn 11).

It is evident from the analysis presented above, then, that emojis provide a useful means for the target of jocular flattery to achieve multiple meanings, ranging from endorsing jocularity by displaying recognition of the teaser's humorous intent, and even extending the jocular flattery sequence, to ostensibly deflecting the jocular flattery by showing embarrassment.

4.3.2 Supporting jocularity by the audience

The audience in our dataset tend to reply to instances of jocular flattery by showing appreciation and enjoyment, or/and elaborating or (partially) repeating the jocular flattery, except for very infrequent cases where the jocular flattery is disattended (Qiu, Chen & Haugh, 2021). Emojis are therefore mainly employed in these responses from the audience to indicate an extension or continuation of the playful frame, and to echo jocularity by expressing feelings of appreciation, excitement and enjoyment.

---

[22] This is an allusion to a popular Taiwanese pop idol group in the 1990s, which consisted of three handsome, young male singers.

a. Extending or continuing the jocular flattery

Close examination of the dataset indicated that an initial instance of jocular flattery tends to occasion further jocular flattery, which is usually directed at the same target to form a kind of banter sequence (Qiu, Chen & Haugh, 2021). Through contributing to the ongoing interaction with more instances of jocular flattery, the audience can change their original participation footings and become joint co-teasers. Emojis used in subsequent instances of jocular flattery performed by the audience, therefore, can indicate an extension (i.e. elaborating the prior jocular flattery), or a continuation (i.e. repeating the prior jocular flattery) of the jocular frame.

As example (9) shows, for instance, Gao, Xu, Yang and Wang, all employ emojis to indicate an extension of the jocular flattery sequence initiated by Zhou (turns 2, 4, 6–7)

b. Echoing jocularity

While the target may use emojis to ostensibly deflect the flattery by showing embarrassment, this practice is not observed in the audience's responses. Instead, the audience only use emojis to echo jocularity by expressing feelings of appreciation, excitement and enjoyment, which may also be conveyed through laugh particles 哈哈哈 ("hahaha") (e.g. see example 4, turn 5), and animated pictures in some cases (e.g. see example 7, turn 10).

Laughing emojis, such as 'grinning face with smiling eyes', 'beaming face with smiling eyes', and 'smiling face with hand over mouth', as mentioned earlier (see section 4.2.1), are employed by the audience to echo jocularity. The most commonly used emoji in this dataset, 'face with tears of joy', which is employed by the target to show (ostensible) amusement, is frequently used in the audience's responses to express appreciation and enjoyment of instances of jocular flattery in prior turns (see example 7, turn 7).

5 Conclusion

The rapidly increasing use of emojis in communications on social media platforms and messaging apps has started to attract increasing attention in digital discourse analysis and pragmatics in recent years. This chapter has examined the role of emojis in jocular flattery sequences, a specific form of conversational humour that occurs through (ostensibly) elevating others, in the context of multi-party instant messaging interactions in Chinese. We focused in our analysis on the roles emojis play in different stages of jocular flattery sequences, and the way emojis are typically employed within such interaction with respect to the footings of the participant(s). A number of key findings emerged from our study.

First, emojis may increase the likelihood of jocular flattery being triggered through enhancing the teasable, suggesting the delicacy of situation, or by displaying humorous intent. Second, emojis can be employed by the teaser to indicate or intensify jocularity in formulating jocular flattery. The former function is accomplished mainly through laughing emojis and exaggerated emojis, which may indicate a playful frame by construing something as (potentially) laughable, mischievous, or hilarious. The latter function can be accomplished through employing emojis commonly used to indicate approval, thereby emphasizing (ostensible) approval for the flatterable while indicating a rapport-oriented stance. Third, the role emojis play in responses to jocular flattery varies according to the footings of the participants. Emojis can be employed by the target to endorse the playful frame set by the teaser or sometimes to ostensibly deflect the jocular flattery by expressing (ostensible) embarrassment. On the other hand, emojis can be employed by the audience to indicate an extension or continuation of the playful frame, and to echo jocularity by expressing feelings of appreciation, excitement and enjoyment.

There remains, however, more to be done to further our understanding of the roles emojis play in co-constructing conversational humour. This chapter only focused on one form of conversational humour, that is, jocular flattery. Given the heterogeneous nature of conversational humour, future studies could be conducted on the roles emojis play in interactionally accomplishing other types of conversational humour. We also caution that new findings may emerge from studies of the role of emojis in jocular flattery sequences in larger, more diverse datasets and across different languages.

It is also pertinent to mention here that there appear to be both cross-cultural similarities and differences in the employment of specific emojis in the interactional accomplishment of conversational humour. In terms of similarities, the emoji of face with tears of joy seems to have become conventionalized for indicating laughter in response to humour on WeChat (Messerli & Locher, 2021; Sampietro, 2021a, 2021b). This emoji is overwhelmingly employed in this dataset by the target to endorse jocularity and is frequently used by the audience to echo jocularity through expressing (ostensible) amusement. Laughing emojis, as well as exaggerated emojis, generally mimic the facial expressions and gestures commonly used in accomplishing humour in face-to-face communication. These emojis can be used by the teaser to indicate or intensify jocularity, and by the target or the audience to endorse or support jocularity as well. Their connection with humour also seems to be conventionalized, though the tendency to use specific emoji within this board category may vary according to the situated context.

As to potential differences, these include emojis commonly used to indicate approval or compliments. Typical examples include 'thumbs-up', 'red rose', 'cupping one's fist in the other hand', and 'clapping-hands', which can be used in instances of jocular flattery to intensify jocularity through emphasizing (ostensible) approval. This different usage is closely related to the specific form of conversational humour we have focused on in this chapter, as jocular flattery involves (ostensible) other-elevation. Moreover, there are also emojis that seem to be culturally specific more generally, such as 'cupping one's fist in the other hand', a traditional Chinese gesture for showing politeness and approval.

In sum, in examining how emojis contribute to the multimodal co-construction of jocular flattery, we have deepened our understanding of the pragmatic functions of emojis. We have also contributed to the growing body of work on multimodal dimensions of conversational humour in technology-mediated communication across different linguistic and cultural contexts by shedding light on how emojis are used in jocular flattery sequences in the context of multiparty instant messaging interactions among speakers of (Mandarin) Chinese. While there are clearly cross-cultural similarities in the ways in which emojis contribute to the multimodal co-construction of conversational humour, we maintain that their supposed universality has been overstated, and we need further research on their usage across linguistic and cultural contexts.

References

Al Rashdi, Fathiya. 2018. Functions of emojis in WhatsApp interaction among Omanis. *Discourse, Context & Media* 26. 117–126.

Attardo, Salvatore, Lucy Pickering, Fofo Lomotey & Shigehito Menjo. 2013. Multimodality in conversational humour. *Review of Cognitive Linguistics* 11(2). 402–416.

Aull, Bethany. 2019. A study of phatic emoji use in WhatsApp communication. *Internet Pragmatics* 2(2). 206–232.

Bertrand, Roxanne & Béatrice Priego-Valverde. 2011. Does prosody play a specific role in conversational humour? *Pragmatics and Cognition* 19. 333–356.

Brône, Geert. 2021. The multimodal negotiation of irony and humor in interaction. On the role of eye gaze in joint pretense. In A. Soares da Silva (ed.), *Figurative language – subjectivity and usage*, 109–136. Amsterdam: John Benjamins.

Buján, Marta. 2019. The function of face gestures and head movements in spontaneous humorous communication. *European Journal of Humour Research* 7(2). 1–29.

Chang, Wei-Lin Melody. 2016. *Face and face practices in Chinese talk-in-interaction*. London: Equinox.

Chovanec, Jan. 2011. Humour in quasi-conversations. Constructing fun in online sports journalism. In Marta Dynel (ed.), *Humour across discourse domains*, 243–264. Amsterdam: John Benjamins.

Cruz-Moya, Olga & Alfonso Sánchez-Moya. 2021. Humour in multimodal times. Insights from online interactions among senior users of a WhatsApp group. *Internet Pragmatics* 4(1). 52–86.

Drew, Paul. 1987. Po-faced receipts of teases. *Linguistics* 25. 219–253.

Dürscheid, Christa & Christina Margrit Siever. 2017. Beyond the alphabet – communication with emojis. *Zeitschrift für Germanistische Linguistik* 45(2). 256–285.

Dynel, Marta. 2009. Beyond a joke: types of conversational humour. *Language and Linguistics Compass* 3(5). 1284–1299.

Fei, Xiaotong. 2019. *Earthbound China* [乡土中国]. Beijing: CITIC Press Group. (Original work published in 1948).

Gibson, Will, Pingping Huang & Qianyun Yu. 2018. Emoji and communicative action: the semiotics, sequence and gestural actions of 'face covering hand'. *Discourse Context & Media* 26. 91–99.

Giles, David, Wyke Stommel, Trena Paulus, Jessica Lester & Darren Reed. 2015. Microanalysis of online data: the methodological development of 'digital CA'. *Discourse, Context and Media* 7. 45–51.

Giles, David, Wyke Stommel & Trena Paulus. 2017. The microanalysis of online data: the next stage. *Journal of Pragmatics* 115. 37–41.

Gironzetti, Elisa. 2022. *The multimodal performance of conversational humor*. Amsterdam: John Benjamins.

Graham, Sage L. 2019. A wink and a nod: the role of emojis in forming digital communities. *Multilingua* 38(4). 377–400.

Hancock, Jeffrey. 2004. Verbal irony use in face-to-face and computer-mediated conversations. *Journal of Language and Social Psychology* 23(4). 447–463.

Haugh, Michael. 2010. Jocular mockery, (dis)affiliation and face. *Journal of Pragmatics* 42(8). 2106–2119.

Haugh, Michael. 2014. Jocular mockery as interactional practice in everyday Anglo-Australian conversation. *Australian Journal of Linguistics* 34(1). 76–99.

Haugh, Michael. 2016. "Just kidding": teasing and claims to non-serious intent. *Journal of Pragmatics* 95. 120–136.

Haugh, Michael. 2017. Teasing. In Salvatore Attardo (ed.), *Handbook of language and humor*, 204–218. London: Routledge.

Haugh, Michael & Danielle Pillet-Shore. 2018. Getting to know you: Teasing as an invitation to intimacy in initial interactions. *Discourse Studies* 20(2). 246–269.

Haugh, Michael and Béatrice Priego-Valverde. Forthcoming. Conversational humour. In Thomas E. Ford, Władysław Chłopicki & Giselinde Kuipers (eds.), *Handbook of humor research*. Berlin: Mouton de Gruyter.

Herring, Susan. 2019. The coevolution of computer-mediated communication and computer-mediated discourse analysis. In Pilar Gárces-Conejos Blitvich & Patricia Bou-Franch (eds.), *Analysing digital discourse*, 25–67. Cham: Palgrave Macmillan

Herring, Susan C. & Ashley Dainas. 2017. "Nice picture comment!": graphicons in Facebook comment threads. In *Proceedings of the 50th Hawaii International Conference on System Sciences (HICSS-50)*, 2185–2194. Los Alamitos, CA: IEEE.

Hübler, Mike & Diana Calhoun Bell. 2003. Computer-mediated humor and ethos: exploring threads of constitutive laughter in online communities. *Computers and Composition* 20. 277–294.

Keltner, Dacher, Lisa Capps, Ann M. Kring, Randall C. Young & Erin A. Heerey. 2001. Just teasing: a conceptual analysis and empirical review. *Psychological Bulletin* 127(2). 229–248.

Keltner, Dacher, Randall C. Young, Erin A. Heerey, Carmen Oemig & Natalie D. Monarch. 1998. Teasing in hierarchical and intimate relations. *Journal of Personality and Social Psychology* 75(5). 1231–1247.

König, Katharina. 2019. Stance taking with 'laugh' particles and emojis – sequential and functional patterns of 'laughter' in a corpus of German WhatsApp chats. *Journal of Pragmatics* 142. 156–170.

Kotthoff, Helga. 2006. Pragmatics of performance and the analysis of conversational humor. *HUMOR: International Journal of Humor Research* 19(3). 271–304.

Kowalski, Robin M. 2000. "I was only kidding!": victims' and perpetrators' perceptions of teasing. *Personality and Social Psychology Bulletin* 26(2). 231–241.

Li, Li & Yue Yang. 2018. Pragmatic functions of emoji in internet-based communication – a corpus-based study. *Asian-Pacific Journal of Second and Foreign Language Education* 3(1). Article 16.

Li, Xiaoting. 2020. Interpersonal touch in conversational joking. *Research on Language and Social Interaction* 53(3). 357–379.

Mao, Luming R. 1994. Beyond politeness theory: "face" revisited and renewed. *Journal of Pragmatics* 21(5). 451–486.

Messerli, Thomas C. & Miriam A. Locher. 2021. Humour support and emotive stance in comments on Korean TV drama. *Journal of Pragmatics* 178. 408–425.

Mullan, Kerry. 2020. Pile of dead leaves free to a good home: humour and belonging in a Facebook community. In In Kerry Mullan, Bert Peeters & Lauren Sadow (eds.), *Studies in ethnopragmatics, cultural semantics and intercultural communication*, 135–159. New York: Springer.

Norrick, Neal. 1993. *Conversational joking*. Bloomington, IN: Indiana University Press.

North, Sarah. 2007. 'The voices, the voices': creativity in online conversation. *Applied Linguistics* 28(4). 538–555.

Parkwell, Corina. 2019. Emoji as social semiotic resources for meaning-making in discourse: mapping the functions of the toilet emoji in Cher's tweets about Donald Trump. *Discourse Context & Media* 30. 100307.

Qiu, Jia, Xinren Chen & Michael Haugh. 2021. Jocular flattery in Chinese multi-party instant messaging interactions. *Journal of Pragmatics* 178. 225–241.

Riordan, Monica A. 2017. Emojis as tools for emotion work: communicating affect in text messages. *Journal of Language and Social Psychology* 36 (5). 549–567.

Sampietro, Agnese. 2019. Emoji and rapport management in Spanish WhatsApp chats. *Journal of Pragmatics* 143. 109–120.

Sampietro, Agnese. 2020. Use and interpretation of emoji in electronic-mediated communication: a survey. *Visual Communication Quarterly* 27(1). 27–39.

Sampietro, Agnese. 2021a. Emojis and the performance of humour in everyday electronically-mediated conversation. A corpus study of WhatsApp chats. *Internet Pragmatics* 4(1). 87–110.

Sampietro, Agnese. 2021b. The use of 'face with tears of joy' emoji on WhatsApp: A conversation-analytical approach. Paper presented at *Emoji 2021.4th International Workshop on Emoji Understanding and Applications in Social Media* (co-located with the 15th ICWSM). (doi:10.36190/2021.03)

Sampietro, Agnese, Samuel Felder & Beat Siebenhaar. 2022. Do you kiss when you text? Cross-cultural differences in the use of the kissing emojis in three WhatsApp corpora. *Intercultural Pragmatics* 19(2). 183–208.

Schnurr, Stephanie & Charley Rowe. 2008. The 'dark side' of humour. An analysis of subversive humour in workplace emails. *Lodz Papers in Pragmatics* 4(1). 109–130.

Togans, LaCount J., Thomas Holtgraves, Gyeongnam Kwon & Tania E. Morales Zelaya. 2021. Digitally saving face: an experimental investigation of cross-cultural differences in the use of emoticons and emoji. *Journal of Pragmatics* 186. 277–288.

Vandergriff, Ilona & Carolin Fuchs. 2012. Humor support in synchronous computer-mediated discussions. *HUMOR: International Journal of Humor Research* 25(4). 437–458.

Vásquez, Maria Simmaro, Nabiha El Khatib, Phillip Hamrick & Salvatore Attardo. 2021. On the order of processing of humorous tweets with visual and verbal elements. *Internet Pragmatics* 4(1). 150–175.

Weitz, Eric. 2017. Online and internet humor. In Salvatore Attardo (ed.), *Handbook of language and humor*, 504–518. London: Routledge.

Wolf, Alecia. 2000. Emotional expression online: gender differences in emoticon use. *CyberPsychology & Behavior* 3(2). 827–833.

Xie, Chaoqun & Bingyun Li. 2021. Understanding Chinese social media. *Internet Pragmatics* 4(2). 177–189.

Yus, Francisco. 2021. Pragmatics, humour and the internet. *Internet Pragmatics* 4(1): 1–11.

Zhang, Leticia Tian & Daniel Cassany. 2021. "The murderer is him ✓": multimodal humor in *danmu* video comments. *Internet Pragmatics* 4(2). 272–294.

Zhang, Yiqiong, Min Wang & Ying Li. 2021. More than playfulness. Emojis in the comments of a WeChat official account. *Internet Pragmatics* 4(2). 247–271.

Agnese Sampietro

9 More than laughter: Multimodal humour and the negotiation of in-group identities in mobile instant messaging interactions

Abstract: One form of maintaining sociability and cohesion in mobile instant messaging (MIM) interactions is posting humorous content (Cruz-Moya and Sánchez-Moya 2021; Yus 2018, 2021). Online humour can be multimodal since smartphone users can easily publish verbal, auditory, and visual content. This chapter focuses on the production, negotiation, and response to humorous multimodal posts in a single WhatsApp group chat among sixteen men. Methods combine computer-mediated discourse analysis (Herring and Androutsopoulos 2015), digital conversation analysis (Giles et al. 2015), and the study of interactional humour (see Chovanec and Tsakona 2018).

The analysis showed that humour in this chat was typically initiated by static images (i.e., photos, screenshots, or memes) or videos. Like other online contexts, such as Twitter and Instagram (Messerli and Yu 2018) or dyadic MIM chats (Sampietro 2021b), laughing emojis helped signal humour and show appreciation for it. Other emojis were used in a more playful manner, such as when repeating visually humorous discourse. Emojis were also a non-threatening way of bringing failed humour to an end. In addition to humorous memes, personal anecdotes and pictures of participants were elaborated upon in sustained humorous exchanges. Ageing and sex were common scripts for humour in the chat, and were used to negotiate in-group identity and reaffirm participants' masculinity.

Keywords: Digital Discourse Analysis, Emojis, Humour support, Instant Messaging, Interactional Humour, Memes, Multimodal Humour, WhatsApp

Acknowledgements: This work was partially supported by EXP.2138/2022 grant (SIB program) from the Universidad Nacional del Noroeste de la Provincia de Buenos Aires (UNNOBA, Argentina). The author would like to thank the informants for generously allowing her to study their private WhatsApp interactions, and the anonymous reviewers and the editor for their insightful comments and suggestions.

https://doi.org/10.1515/9783110983128-010

1 Introduction

Everyday interactions among peers often include humour (Chovanec and Tsakona 2018). As digital devices and applications mediate many interpersonal interactions today, it is unsurprising to encounter humour online, such as in interactions on mobile instant messaging applications (MIM), like Facebook Messenger, WhatsApp, WeChat, Telegram, QQ, to name a few. One of the most popular MIM applications worldwide is WhatsApp (We are Social, DataReportal and Meltwater 2023). It is generally considered a private communication channel for communicating with one or more friends or family members (Waterloo et al. 2018). Besides calling or sending text and voice messages to other contacts, WhatsApp users can share images, videos, emojis, stickers, GIFs, and other attachments. Due to the inclusion of various semiotic resources, or "modes", communication on WhatsApp and other MIM is, therefore, multimodal (see Kress and van Leeuwen 2011).

Although WhatsApp chats are not humorous per se, humour does appear in many of these digital interactions, especially those among friends and acquaintances (Yus 2022). Users of MIM applications resort to humour to connect with others at a distance and increase in-group bonding (Yus 2021). Although physical distance and communication asynchrony may affect humour performance in this application, other affordances can facilitate it, for instance, the available variety of visual resources. This chapter focuses on the use of visual resources in humorous WhatsApp interactions. Specifically, it studies multimodal production, negotiation, and response to humour in a single WhatsApp group chat among 16 men aged 40–45 years. As we shall see, the group participants took advantage of the affordances of the application to produce and sustain humorous interactions on WhatsApp.

The remainder of this chapter is structured as follows. First (§ 2), it reviews relevant literature on multimodal discourse analysis and online humour. Section 3 details the methods by describing the corpus and the procedure for analysis, which is largely based on the study of humour in interaction and digital discourse analysis. Section 4 presents the analysis of the selected humorous excerpts from the chat; given the interactional focus of the analysis, it distinguishes between initiating a humorous interaction and responding to it. The sections Discussion (§ 5) and Conclusion (§ 6) provide an overview of the main results and comment on the implications of the results for the study of digital humour.

2 Literature review

2.1 The multimodal turn in discourse analysis

Discourse analysis has shifted from an exclusively text-based to a multimodal approach (Kress 2012). "Multimodality" refers to the interplay of different resources for meaning making (Kress and van Leeuwen 2011), such as speech and gesture, image and sound, or pictures and writing. These are different "modes" or "semiotic resources". Research on interactional humour, i.e., humour "co-constructed by more than one interlocutor" (Chovanec and Tsakona 2018: 9) followed the same path, and nowadays, there is a recognised research agenda for multimodal approaches to humour in interaction (Gironzetti 2022). Research on face-to-face conversational humour has adopted an embodied approach (Gironzetti 2022: 2), thus considering how speakers use smiling, behavioural and emotional alignment and gaze to co-construct and negotiate humorous conversations (see, for example, Gironzetti 2022; Priego-Valverde et al. 2018).

This "multimodal turn" has also affected digital discourse analysis. During what Androutsopoulos (2006) calls the "first wave" of linguistic research on online communication, the written text was the only concern of digital discourse analysts (see Herring 2015). However, in recent years, scholars have inevitably turned their attention to semiotic resources other than writing in digital communication (Herring 2015; Herring and Androutsopoulos 2015). Multimodality has become increasingly popular as a framework for studying online interactions because digital technologies have enabled people to easily combine semiotic resources (e.g., mixing text and images) in their everyday interactions. Although multimodal texts have always existed, today it is almost impossible to find digital texts that do not mix different semiotic resources (Jewitt, Bezemer and O'Halloran 2016: 3). For example, various graphical devices (or "graphicons", as named by Herring and Dainas 2017), such as emojis, stickers, GIFs, images, and videos, are incorporated into the most popular social media platforms these days. Indeed, over 700 million emojis are used daily on Facebook posts (World Emoji Day n.d.). At the same time, 2020 data suggest that more than three billion images and 720,000 hours of video content are shared daily on social media (Thomson et al. 2020: 3). Like other social media platforms and MIM applications, WhatsApp integrates various graphical devices and multimodal resources, which also helps construct and manage humorous online interactions.[1]

---

[1] The analysis of multimodality in digital discourse–and in particular of the interaction of written language and images in contemporary communication– is usually approached and defined

2.2 Multimodal humour in online interactions

Research on online humour has primarily focused on memes, "digital items that are [...] circulated, imitated, and transformed via the internet by multiple users" (Shifman 2013: 41). Although not all memes are funny (see, for example, Gal, Shifman, and Kampf 2016; Milner 2016), humorous memes have received significant academic attention in a range of fields (Shifman 2013, but cfr. Dynel and Chovanec 2021, for an account of other forms of online multimodal humour). Research on humorous memes has mostly considered how they create humour multimodally (Ambrus 2017; Dynel 2016; Yus 2018). Few studies have addressed interactional factors in online meme communication. For instance, Messerli and Yu (2018) analysed how humour in football-related accounts was not only constructed (both verbally and multimodally) but also responded to on Twitter and Instagram. Cruz-Moya and Sánchez-Moya (2021) examined a WhatsApp group chat among seniors and found that humorous content was an ordinary component of their interactions; in this context, users posted memes and used avatars with the sole purpose of amusement. Recent studies have also found that images (with or without text) are consistently used to set the topic of subsequent interactions on Tumblr (Fichman and Dainas 2019) or to open humorous conversations on WhatsApp (Yus 2022). Yus (2022) analysed a corpus of WhatsApp group chats written in Spanish and found different responses to funny images or memes: users can resort to written text, emojis, laughing interjections, or a combination of these as a response to humour.

In recent years, researchers have analysed the contribution of other multimodal resources, especially emojis, to the "performance" of humour in WhatsApp interactions (Sampietro 2021a; Yus 2022). For example, emojis can be used to signal and respond to humour. Studies using digital conversation analysis found that the winking and the tongue-out emojis (😉 😛 😜 🤪) can distinguish different humour stances (König 2019; Sampietro 2021b). Furthermore, the popular "face with tears of joy" 😂 is a common way to reproduce laughter in response to humour in WhatsApp interactions (König 2019; Sampietro 2021a, 2021b). Specifically, Sampietro (2021b) observed that the emoji "face with tears of joy" 😂, when typed multiple times, was a quick way to show understanding and appreciation of humour in dyadic WhatsApp interactions among Spaniards. Research also shows that emojis are a flexible resource in humorous interactions. Besides sig-

---

differently depending on the discipline. Social semiotic approaches to multimodality refer to different "modes" or "semiotic resources" (Jewitt, Bezemer and O'Halloran 2016), while digital discourse analysts have introduced notions such as "graphical devices" or "graphicons" (Herring and Dainas 2017). Despite the different epistemological premises, I will use freely the terminology proposed by both currents in this chapter.

nalling and responding to humour, users also play with emojis (Sampietro 2019, 2021a) and use these pictographs to sustain extended humorous exchanges (Sampietro 2021a). In short, in informal digital interactions on WhatsApp, emojis contribute to all stages of humorous interactions (Sampietro 2021a): from initiating humour to responding to and sustaining it.

Studies on other graphical devices, such as stickers, GIFs, and personal avatars, are still in their infancy. Therefore, their use in humorous exchanges has been largely unexplored. One of the first analyses of multimodal resources in conversational interactions was Herring and Dainas's (2017) study of Facebook group threads, which observed that only emojis fulfilled various functions. Conversely, other "graphicons" tended to "specialise for certain functions more than others" (Herring and Dainas 2017: 2192): the main function of images and videos was to riff (this is, as a playful elaboration of the previous comment), GIFs and stickers to react to the preceding messages. Likewise, GIFs on Tumblr typically expressed reactions to previous posts (Fichman and Dainas 2019; Petersen 2014).

This contribution fills this gap in the literature by analysing how different visual cues help create and sustain humour in WhatsApp interactions. It is based on a corpus of messages exchanged in a single WhatsApp group chat among 16 friends (all males aged 40–45 years). Humour is a relevant component of these interactions. The research questions guiding this study are as follows:
1) What multimodal resources are used in humorous interactions on WhatsApp?
2) How do WhatsApp users exploit the application's affordances to manage humorous interactions?

3 Method

The corpus analysed in this chapter comes from a single WhatsApp group chat composed of 16 Spanish men aged around 40 years (17,901 messages). All participants provided written informed consent to participate in the study. The chat was exported to plain text by one member of the group and forwarded via email to the author, who anonymised the transcript by replacing names with pseudonyms. Data included text, emojis and metadata for each message; for this study, I consider a "message" or "posting" each unit of content posted by a user (it may include written text, emojis, stickers, images, videos, or links). Photos, images, videos, stickers, and audio files were received as attachments. Because many users regularly delete media files on their phones to free up storage, only a limited number of attachments were initially available for analysis. To increase their number and variety, an informant agreed to save the files received in the chat for three weeks and then export the chat again. In total, the corpus included 128 images (photos, memes, screenshots, etc.), 40 videos, 15 audio files, and 33 stickers. Many messages included emojis, but they were not counted separately. Messages were pasted onto a spreadsheet, and the attached media files were numbered and located in the transcript.

Participants in the chat were long-time friends; when they were younger, they lived in the same town and met regularly, and many of them played together on a local basketball team. At the time of data collection (late 2021, early 2022), they lived in different cities; all but three were married and had children. Due to work and family commitments, now they rarely met. However, the WhatsApp group is active every day; members use it for casual conversations, sharing information (i.e., job vacancies, updates on local Covid restrictions), and commenting on news and sporting events. Members' participation was uneven: Juan, the most active member, sent 4,438 messages (mainly multimedia files), while Valentín only 74.

Methods for the analysis combine computer-mediated discourse analysis (Herring 2004, 2015; Herring and Androutsopoulos 2015), the study of interactional humour (Chovanec and Tsakona 2018), and, to a lesser extent, digital conversation analysis (Giles et al. 2015, Giles, Stommel, and Paulus 2017).[2] The analysis started by looking at the data to find possible humorous episodes, and within these, it considered how participants use multimodal resources in different ways to initiate and respond to humour. Given the interest in the multimodal management of humour, this study focuses on humorous episodes with at least one visual component (even a single emoji). First, humorous episodes were identified based on verbal (jokes, puns, irony, teasing, etc.; see Dynel 2009) or visual prompts (humorous memes, videos, photos, or stickers; see Yus 2022). Users' reactions (playing along, laughter interjections and emojis, and other indicators of appreciation) and cultural knowledge helped identify these humorous episodes (Attardo and Raskin 2017). Later, I analysed the contribution of multimodal resources at two stages of humorous interaction: initiating humour and responding to it. As this study is inherently qualitative and interpretive, I will not present any quantitative data other than numbers in this section.

---

[2] In this chapter, I do not follow a strict conversation-analytical (CA) approach, as CA scholars regard humour as "an abstract category that is insufficiently specific for describing social actions and sequences or the visible orientations of the participants" (Glenn and Holt 2017; see also Attardo 2020). The analytical approach is inspired by conversation analysis as it pursues the "microanalytic goals of interpreting specific episodes of interaction" (Giles, Stommel, and Paulus 2017: 40).

4 Analysis

4.1 Initiating humour

4.1.1 Teller-initiated humour

This section examines the introduction of multimodal humour in a conversation. In this case, humour is initiated by the "teller". In other words, a user's post is intended to be humorous. Participants in the chat began humorous exchanges in a variety of ways: 1) by posting memes or other humorous material produced by others, 2) by creating their own humorous multimodal content, 3) by humorously re-contextualising non-humorous material, or 4) by using emojis in conjunction with verbal humour.

Posting a meme or humorous video first thing in the morning was a common practice for members of this chat to stay in touch with one another. As some participants, such as David or Federico, were more likely to send funny content to the chat, it could be expected that a file sent by them without further commentary would be a meme. Certain topics, regardless of sender, tended to result in humour. For instance, the participants were aware that some public events could inspire memes. Although the most famous and long-lasting memes are those based on stock images (Ambrus 2017), popular topics, such as sports and politics, can encourage Internet users' creativity. For example, after losing the Euro 2020 football cup shoot-out, some chat members knew that there would be plenty of memes about Álvaro Morata's failed penalty the following day. After the match, Martín wrote: *Mañana memes a saco* ('Tomorrow tons of memes');[3] indeed, memes around this incident blossomed in the chat over the following days. In early 2022, a political scandal involving the Spanish People's Party was judged as a possible source of memes. Shortly after the president of the Madrid region criticised her party's top leader, Pedro wrote *Ya empiezan los memes . . .* ('Here we go with the memes'), and participants posted various memes related to the incident. Posting multiple memes related to a particular issue is a way of commenting on current affairs. This is true not only for members of this chat but also across platforms and geographical contexts. Political memes, for example, have been extensively researched in the fields

---

[3] All messages were written in Spanish, with occasional switches to other languages (French, English, Catalan). It should be noted that the examples in this chapter are transcribed as they were typed, and no highlighting or marking is used to identify grammatical or spelling mistakes. I provide an English translation of the examples for readers' convenience. Messages in longer excerpts are always numbered starting at 1.

of political communication and digital media discourse (see, for example, Mortensen and Neumayer 2021).

There are different types of memes: those with pictures and text (image macros, i.e., an image with text at the top and bottom or a captioned picture) are the most common (Ambrus 2017). For instance, a few memes posted at different times in the corpus featured the same image with different captions; this is a vivid example of the circulation and mutation of some memetic images (Shifman 2013). The receiver can perceive the humorous nature of a post, even prior to reading its caption, simply by identifying the image or template.

Starting an interaction with a meme is one of the most common forms of teller-initiated humour in this chat. Other studies with wider corpora or different demographics have also confirmed that posting memes or other images (i.e., a screenshot of a humorous twit, a funny photo) is a common way to initiate humour on WhatsApp (Cruz-Moya and Sánchez-Moya 2021; Yus 2022). Indeed, one reason for the popularity of memes is the ease with which they circulate (Shifman 2013). Less common is producing multimodal humour, such as posting or editing a picture to initiate a humour bid.

Another way of exploiting the affordances of WhatsApp is by recontextualising a non-humorous message by means of a humorous comment. For example, Juan posted a screenshot of a piece of news from a local news outlet about a campaign to promote local organic products, whose slogan was *caga bien* ('shit well'), accompanied by the following comment: *Te han contratado Andrés?* [. . .] ('Did they hire you, Andrés? [. . .]'). In this case, a non-humorous bid (the news) was recontextualised as humorous by the teasing comment directed at Andrés accompanying it.

The latter example shows that verbal humour is still widely deployed in WhatsApp. Yus (2022) even considered verbal humour as a prototypical way of initiating humorous interaction in this application. A common and minimal way to mark a verbal message as humorous is to use emojis (see Sampietro 2021a, 2021b; Yus 2022). Two emojis stand out for this purpose: the popular "face with tears of joy" 😂 emoji (Sampietro 2021b) and the more recent "rolling on the floor laughing" 🤣 (released in 2016). Remarkably, the latter was the most common emoji posted in the chat. It was usually included at the end of a message (usually to mark it as humorous) or repeated several times to reproduce a burst of laughter. See, for example, Excerpt 1, the extract of the chat immediately after obtaining consent for the analysis (Mateo was the informant who sent the chat to the researcher): Jacobo frames Message #1 as humorous by adding three emojis "rolling on the floor laughing" 🤣; Juan in Message #2 elaborates on this utterance by adding more humour and using once again to this emoji. Martín (#3) and David (#6) post this same emoji to reproduce laughter.

Excerpt 1	Message number	Participant	Original message and translation
	1	Jacobo	*Mateo, dile q la investigadora que cuando ponen estos memes nos reímos. Que lo analice. Igual tenemos un problema sexual* 🤣🤣🤣 'Mateo, tell the researcher we're laughing when posting these memes. She should analyse this. Maybe we have a sexual issue 🤣🤣🤣'
	2	Juan	*Eso ya te lo digo yo sin necesidad de estudio* 🤣🤣🤣🤣 'I can tell you that myself with no need for a study 🤣🤣🤣🤣'
	3	Martín	🤣🤣🤣
	4	Pedro	😭🤣
	5	Mateo	*¡Correcto!* 'That's right!'
	6	David	🤣🤣🤣

These observations are consistent with König's (2019) and Sampietro's (2021b) studies of interactional patterns in the use of laughing emojis. In König's (2019: 161) example from a dyadic WhatsApp chat among German women, the initiator of the interaction likewise used "face with tears of joy" 😂 emojis at the end of the message to frame it as humorous, similar to Message #2 in Excerpt 1. The respondent accepted the humour bid by typing a laughter interjection or repeating the same emoji. In short, instances of user-initiated verbal humour marked by emojis were also present in König's (2019) study, despite examining different demographics and cultures. Although emojis are losing some of their pragmatic force and are likely to be replaced by stickers in the future (see Konrad, Herring, and Choi 2021), they are still useful for explicitly marking and responding to verbal humour in instant messaging interactions.

4.1.2 Recipient-initiated humour

Sometimes, a message intended to be non-humorous may be reframed as humorous by another user (see also Yus 2022). Photos showing actual participants in the chat were a regular source of joking re-elaboration. Farina (2018: 60) calls images posted to elicit comments from other chat members "photo tellings". Similar to spoken conversations, responses to these first-pair tellings usually involve evaluations or requests for clarifications (Farina 2018: 56). In this chat, this form of re-elaboration is often humorous. For example, while Pedro and Daniel were spending the weekend with a friend at a cottage house, they sent photos of them having fun, drinking and eating. They also sent a picture of Pedro cooking paella over an open flame. Once the dish was ready, Pedro and his friends took a photo holding the paella pan before serving it (photo telling). The image triggered several humorous comments, as shown in Excerpt (2).

Excerpt 2	Message number	Participant	Original message and translation
	1	Pedro	<Photo of the three friends, one of them holding a paella pan>
	2	Andrés	*Que tal estaba eso cabrones?* 'How was that, assholes?'
	3	Andrés	*2 horas para hacer una paella, no está mal eh jaja* '2 hours to make a paella, not too bad huh haha'
	4	Hugo	*Pero si esa paellica es pa uno cabrones* 😂😂😂😂😂 'But that baby paella is for one assholes' 😂😂😂😂😂
	5	Martín	*Solucionado* 😏 'Problem solved' 😏
	6	Martín	<Edited photo: each man holds their own paella pan>
	7	Pedro	😭 🤣
	8	Pedro	*Fill de puta, se mean todos con la foto.* 'Son of a bitch, they pee themselves laughing at the photo.'
	9	Pedro	😭 😭
	10	Andrés	*Ajajajajajajjja* 'Hahahahahaa'

Pedro does not intend the photo (Message #1) to be funny; he only displays the dish and waits for appreciative comments. The first humorous comment from Andrés related to the time it took to cook the dish (#3). Hugo also makes fun of them, claiming that the paella is too small to serve more than one person (#4). Martín edits the photo by copying and pasting the image of the pan so that each man is holding his own paella (Message #6) and comments on the photo, saying that the tiny portions "problem" has been "solved" (5). Some participants laughed (with interjections or laughing emojis) at the edited image as a token of appreciation. Note that the insults in this context are not intended to be offensive; instead, they should be seen verbal expressions of closeness, which is common among male friends in Spain (Bernal 2007).

This exchange illustrates one of the basic principles of humour: unexpectedness. First, the edited image is unexpected since reactions to photo tellings are usually written comments (Farina 2018). Additionally, we do not typically expect to receive a photo from someone who is not present at an event (in this example, Martín). Finally, humour in this context comes from Martín taking Hugo's comment at face value and editing the photo accordingly. This example shows how users can create multimodal humour by manipulating a photo of the participants (which the application's affordances easily allow).

A distinctive feature of this chat is the omnipresence of humour. Except for a few tragic events, all the topics were dealt with in a joking manner by the participants: soccer games, public or private events, planning meetings, politics, birthdays, financial matters, and even the infection with the coronavirus could be the starting point for jokes. If the prompt was "serious", the recipients were those who re-contextualised the message to create humorous effects. See, for example, the news of Pedro's injury in Excerpt 3 (expressed through a photo telling followed by an additional written commentary), which prompted several playful remarks from various participants.

Excerpt 3	Message number	Participant	Original and translation
	1	Pedro	<Picture of the injured ankle >
	2	Pedro	*Anoche tobillo por el aire.* 'Yesterday ankle sprained.'
	3	Pedro	🙁
	4	David	*Vacunado tú también* 'You vaccinated too'
	5	David	*Si es que tenemos una edad y'a . . .* 🥴🥴 'Well, we're of an age now . . .' 🥴🥴
	6	Pedro	👴
	7	Pedro	🦽

8	Martín	*joder . . . . sólo ver esa imagen y ya me duele* 'fuck . . . . only looking at the picture hurts'
9	Martín	*animo!!!* 'cheer up!!!'
10	David	*Pero si son unas patatas* 'Wait, they're just potatoes'
11	David	*Y la patata que hay debajo?* 'And the potato underneath?'
12	Martín	😂😂 *tú ves la comida . . . Yo me imagino el huevo debajo y el no poder ni apoyar* '😂😂 you see the food . . . . I imagine the bollock under it and not even being able to lean on the foot'
13	Martín	*cuando veo a alguien en muletas, sufro* 'Whenever I see someone with crutches, I feel the pain'
14	Martín	*muchos años de esguinces* 'many years suffering from sprains'
15	Jacobo	🧖 *ya no estamos para deporte de contacto. . . . . El deporte que nos toca es andar por la ruta del Colesterol. . . . . Que recuerdos me traen los esguinces . . . . . . Que no sea mucho.* '🧖 we are no longer fit for contact sports. . . . . The sport for us is walking to burn cholesterol . . . . Sprains bring back such memories to me. . . . . . I hope it won't be too bad.'
16	Pedro	*Total. Me cuesta reconocer que no puedo correr y saltar con chavales de 25 años. ¿Que será lo siguiente? ¿Que no se me levante?* 'Absolutely. It's hard for me to admit that I can't run and jump with 25-year-olds. What's next, that it won't get hard anymore?'
17	Pedro	😨
18	Martín	*Ahora toca ser perro viejo . . . .El que se compre la primera pastillita azul que nos lo cuente para ir comprandola cuando toque* 'Now it's time to be an old fox . . . . The first one who buys the blue pill should tell us

about it so we can go and buy it when the time comes'

David (#4) attempted unsuccessfully to create a humorous link between the injury and his recent COVID-19 vaccine. Then, in Message #5, he makes a self-deprecating remark about their age. Pedro (Messages #6 and #7) added two unusual emojis—an older man and a person in a wheelchair—to sustain David's humorous comment about becoming older. According to previous research, the use of less common emojis, such as animals or objects, is typically playful (Sampietro 2021a). As Attardo (2020: 295) observes, repeating the previous turn is a strategy to support humour. This repetition can be multimodal on WhatsApp: one message includes text (Message #5), while the following one repeats the same content using pictographs (#6).

After another failed attempt by David to lighten the tone of the conversation by focusing on trivial details in Pedro's photo (some potatoes), Jacobo stepped in to balance humour and empathy (Message #15): he joked about ageing and at the same time showed compassion for Pedro. Through humour and empathy, the group managed to overcome the possible disruption caused by David's failed humour bids.

Finally, Pedro, the injured man, steered the conversation into a humorous tone by pointing out another possible consequence of the passage of time: impotence (#16). Martín now added humour to the dialogue. It should be noted that after mentioning sexuality, a common source of humour in chat (as discussed later in this chapter), the interaction took on a joking tone for at least 26 more messages, with participants making retorts about the effects of Viagra. As we will see in the following section, adding more humour is a typical response to a successful humour bid.

In summary, this example shows how respondents reframed a non-humorous topic (injury) as humorous or, as Yus (2022) described, offered a humorous response to non-humorous initial discourse. This excerpt also shows that WhatsApp affordances can help manage the interaction in the case of both failed and successful humour: Martín included two laughing emojis as a minimal face-saving response to David's unsuccessful remark on potatoes in the picture. Pedro used two uncommon emojis to acknowledge visually the remark on ageing. Two topics stand out in the chat as successful sources of humour: ageing and sex.

While the latter is "the default script for humour" (Attardo 2020: 172), getting older is a form of group self-deprecation, as all members of this chat are around the same age; they strengthen their in-group relationships and overcome problems by jokingly complaining about shared life experiences (Zajdman 1995).

4.2 Responding to a humour bid

4.2.1 Laughter

For a humorous intent to be successful, it should be recognised and appreciated by its recipients, since interactional humour is a shared endeavour (Chovanec and Tsakona 2018: 7; Hay 2001). One of the reactions to humour (but as Attardo 2020 convincingly explains, not the only one) is laughter, which marks its referent as potentially humorous.

Laughter and smiling can occur in face-to-face and mediated interactions (Trouvain and Truong 2017: 340). In the WhatsApp chat analysed in this chapter, in addition to the laughing interjection *haha* (written in Spanish as *ja ja* or *jaja* repeated various times), the two emojis that signal humour (😂 and 🤣) are also used to reproduce laughter, as shown in all the excerpts included in the previous section. For example, in Excerpt 2, participants mimicked laughter using the interjections *jaja* (Message #2) and *Ajajajajajajjja* (#10). In addition, users posted with the same purpose sequences of the emoji "face with tears of joy" 😂😂😂 or "rolling on the floor laughing" 🤣🤣🤣. Remarkably, Pedro (see Excerpts 2 and 3) is the only participant in the chat using "loudly crying" 😭 and "rolling on the floor laughing" 🤣 in a sequence to reproduce laughter; his idiosyncratic use of "loudly crying" 😭 suggests that he might mistakenly interpret this emoji as reproducing a face laughing at the point of tears.[4]

Although stickers will likely replace emojis in the future (Konrad, Herring, and Choi 2020; Sampietro 2023), emojis are still very common in this chat: at least one of these pictographs appears in one out of every four messages. Among the 33 stickers compiled, at least seven showed famous people smiling or laughing, which were used to reproduce laughter in this chat. Interestingly, two stickers exhibited the emoji "face with tears of joy" 😂: one of these stickers (Figure 1) showed a truck full of laughing emojis, while the other displayed a series of 😂 placed in the shape of a phallus. According to Konrad, Herring, and Choi (2020: 232), stickers are more pragmatically marked than emojis for expressivity and playfulness, among other aspects. In this case, the sticker of a truck full of laughing emojis may suggest greater amusement than a burst of laughter reproduced exclusively by emojis.

---

4 Outside this idiosyncratic use by Pedro, the "loudly crying" emoji 😭 was also common in specific contexts, such as when jokingly coping with unpleasant situations, e.g., not being able to meet due to COVID-19 restrictions, or balding.

Figure 1: a sticker posted in the chat.
Source: author's corpus

However, emojis can sometimes serve as a more appropriate reaction to humour: they offer a fast and convenient way of supporting and non-conflicting means of rejecting it. As I have already commented, conversations about sex in the chat always have a nuance of fun: besides memes implying sex, participants complained about the need for more sex, other people's sexual experiences and habits, and even shared porn, which "grants participants an aura of heterosexual masculinity" (Toder and Barak-Brandes 2022). Over the timespan analysed, a couple of group members consistently shared pornographic content for enjoyment or to convey bodily and grotesque humour (Alexander 1997: 84). Nonetheless, not all participants shared or seemed to appreciate this kind of content. In that case, pornographic content was often ignored or responded to with a couple of laughing emojis 😂, clapping hands 👏, or very brief comments.

In their analysis of responses to improprieties, Jefferson, Sacks, and Schegloff (1987:160) observed that hearers could resort to different formulations, from overt disaffiliation (the least affiliative response) to escalation with new impropriety (the most affiliative one). At the midpoint, we found other responses, such as laughter or silence. Indeed, according to Glenn (2003: 151), treating indecorum as play rules out a possible offence. Silence is a way of showing the failure of humour or expressing disapproval of it (Bell 2015). Although the studies cited thus far refer to face-to-face interaction, some forms of less-conflicting responses to failed humour are also found in this chat. For instance, in response to 11 unclothing clips from TikTok shared by Federico, only two people responded: Juan (with a simple interjection) and David, who commented on the use of the platform (*más de uno por aquí con tiktok*, 'more than one guy over here using tiktok'). He also added a humorous video in response (featuring a Spanish comedian watching sexy women dance while unconvincingly complaining about the TikTok algorithm). A laughing emoji (🤣) sent more than half an hour later by Hugo can be interpreted as a response to David's funny video, while Federico's earlier sequence of videos is not commented on any more. In this case, users treated indecorum as play (Glenn 2003).

On another occasion, in response to a grotesque porn video posted by Martín, only Hugo responded with a series of laughing emojis (😂😂😂😂😂) and no more comments or responses were posted: not supporting the speaker's playful posting is a clue that humour failed (Bell 2015: 113). In sum, participants in this chat can show resistance to obscenities or their irrelevance by generating minimal responses (such as Juan's interjection, Hugo's laughing emojis), reframing them as humorous (David's humorous clip) or with silence, i.e., ignoring them. It is worth noting that silence plays a different role in face-to-face humorous interactions than in computer-mediated ones (Vandergriff and Fuchs 2012). According to Hay (2001: 70), silence is a way of openly withholding to support humour in face-to-face interaction. Although silence in WhatsApp chats can also be a way to break away from a humour attempt, sometimes it works simply as a non-threatening way to end a conversation.

In summary, laughing faces, clapping hands emojis, or a simple interjection can be minimal ways to support humour (appreciated or not) without engaging in it further. Other ways of supporting humour are more elaborate, as discussed in the following section.

4.2.2 Adding more humour

Research on humour in interaction has shown that not every instance of humour is marked or responded to with laughter (see Jefferson's 1979 seminal paper on this topic). As in face-to-face conversation (Hay 2001), the most common reaction to a humorous utterance, image, or video posted in a chat was the addition of more humour. As shown in the previous section, sending a few emojis without further engagement with humorous content is insufficient to sustain a longer humorous exchange. A more successful humour bid usually opens humorous sequences co-constructed by participants in the chat. Participants add humour by providing minimal (verbal and multimodal) or more extended responses. As an example of minimal addition of humour, see, for instance, two concise responses that elaborated on the meme reproduced in Figure 2, whose caption reads: 'This is what Predator sees after chasing me for 5 minutes'.[5] David replied: *2*; Mateo: *o 0* ('or 0').

---

[5] Predators are extra-terrestrial humanoid creatures featured in the science-fiction franchise by the same name (Wikipedia 2022).

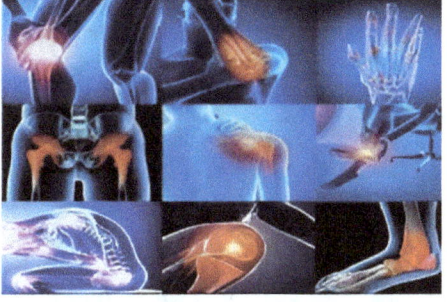

Figure 2: Predators' meme.
Source: Author's corpus (possibly translated from a meme published in Memedroid (https://www.memedroid.com/memes/detail/3757696)

These short replies continued to expand on the meme's humour: Predator, with its infra-red vision, will be able to see medical images of aching joints and bones, not after five minutes, but even after two (David) or even zero (as stated by Mateo). As shown in Excerpt 2, the effects of ageing were a recurring topic for teasing and self-deprecation in chat. As participants were all in their forties, complaints about the early physical signs and effects of ageing were common: canes, balding, weight gain, or not being able to exercise as accustomed (see Excerpt 3), were the age stereotypes around which many instances of humour revolved. Self-deprecating or deriding other participants for showing signs of physical deterioration serves an affiliative function here (Zajdman 1995): although negativity around ageing is deep-rooted in Western culture, laughing about it reinforces group identity and shows empathy.

The exchange in Figure 2 is an example of a short, humorous conversation co-constructed by different people, where the respondents' contributions are minimal. Humorous interactions can also be more extended and made multimodal. For instance, if a (non-grotesque) meme starts a conversation, other users are also very likely to post other memes, as Yus (2022) observed. I have already mentioned that some events are perceived as prompting the creation of memes, including Álvaro Morata's failed penalty in the 2020 Euro Cup. When Santiago posted a meme about this event, David replied with a different one and the comment *otro* ('another one'). This response showed engagement and supports humour in ways other than sending emojis, stickers, or typing simple laughter interjections.

An example of a longer humorous interaction is the news of Pedro's injury, already commented on in Excerpt 3; the passage reproduced was only the beginning of a longer humorous exchange, with the interaction keeping a humorous tone for around 26 more messages posted over 15 minutes. This heightened involvement is one way to support and react positively to humour (Hay 2001). It should be observed that only three of these 26 messages were multimodal. In contrast, the others included only text or text and emoji, suggesting that verbal humour is more effective in sustaining humour across multiple turns, even in the highly multimodal environment of a WhatsApp chat.

5 Discussion

This chapter examined humorous excerpts in a single WhatsApp group chat among 16 men aged around 40 to respond to two general research questions. First, the chapter analysed the multimodal resources used in humorous WhatsApp interactions in this chat. The findings showed that members of this chat used various affordances to produce and respond to humour. On the one hand, they posted pre-designed materials, such as memes (photos or videos). Memes were sometimes shared at the start of an interaction with a clear phatic purpose: staying in contact at a distance through shared humour (Yus 2022). Other pre-designed resources, such as emojis or stickers, were also involved in the performance of humour in the chat. As shown in previous studies (see Sampietro 2021a, 2021b), participants used emojis at every stage of the humorous interaction, from keying humour to acknowledging it. Two laughing emojis, in particular, were useful in humorous exchanges: 😄 and 🤣; these were used to mark and respond to humour. As observed in other contexts (see Sampietro 2021a; Yus 2022), laughing emojis (😄 or 🤣) worked as a contextualisation cue for humour. Sequences of the same laughing faces (such as 😄😄😄😄 or 🤣🤣🤣) were also a typical response to a humorous message or multimedia file, along with laughing interjections (*jaja*) and stickers (Sampietro 2023, 2021b). Other emojis, especially the least common ones (objects, people), were also involved in humorous discourse. Sequences of pictographs were sometimes used as a joking "visual language" (Sampietro 2019, 2021a) or to visually repeat part of the previous message as a token of acknowledgment, similar to repetitions that happen in face-to-face interaction (Attardo 2020). Although the use of stickers is growing (Konrad, Herring, and Choi 2020; Sampietro 2023), they were uncommon in this group chat. As observed by Herring and Dainas (2017) in studying Facebook groups, their primary use was to react to previous messages.

Participants not only shared humour created by other people (such as memes) or included pre-designed resources in their messages (as in the case of emojis) but also produced multimodal humorous materials themselves. Photo and video tellings (see Farina 2018) posted by participants were commonly reframed humorously by the other chat members. On some occasions, the participants themselves edited the images with humorous purposes.

As for the second research question, which concerned how humorous interactions unfolded, the analysis showed that participants used different multimodal resources to initiate and respond to humour. As commented, sharing memes was a common way to open up humorous interactions, the purpose of which was just to keep in touch through laughter. In this case, humour was framed by the teller. In posts that contained memes, humour could be identified by who is sending the meme (some participants send more memes than others), the situation or event they are laughing at (e.g., politics, celebrations, sporting events), or because they recognised the template of the meme. However, the variety of multimodal affordances available on WhatsApp does not overshadow the importance of verbal humour. Verbal humour was widely used and very effective in sustaining prolonged humorous exchanges.

As with face-to-face interactions, the most successful way to acknowledge and respond to humour is to add more humour (Attardo 2020; Glenn 2003; Hay 2001) verbally (with banter) or multimodally (as in the case of meme sequences related to the same topic). The analysis included an excerpt of an extended humorous interaction with more than 30 messages (Excerpt 3). Attardo (2020: 296) mentions that one of the longer humorous interactions described in the literature on face-to-face humour lasts up to 13 turns. Although it is difficult to compare face-to-face and digital interactions, it is noticeable that a single humorous WhatsApp episode from the chat analysed in this study is significantly longer. It is likely that the quickness of adding a simple emoji or a laughing interjection versus speaking up in a face-to-face interaction justifies these differences. While we cannot draw general conclusions about the differences between face-to-face humorous exchanges and WhatsApp, comparing face-to-face and mediated humorous interactions between the same people may be a fruitful topic for future research.

Several multimodal resources helped initiate and sustain humorous interactions, from posting funny images and videos to sending emojis and visually reproducing laughter. Topics such as ageing, sex, and personal anecdotes were common humour triggers. The analysis confirmed several findings already observed by other researchers in digital discourse analysis. First, in digital interactions, users exploit the affordances of the application (i.e., emojis) or texting conventions (e.g., laughing interjections) to signal their communicative intentions (see Herring and Dainas 2017; Sampietro 2019). Additionally, laughing emojis and interjections are used as contextualisation cues for humour (Sampietro 2021b), and memes are a typical means of initiating humorous interactions (Yus 2022). These and other affordances are also common reactions to humour: repeated laughing emojis, interjections, and stickers depicting laughing people are ways to acknowledge and respond to humour (Herring and Dainas 2017; Sampietro 2021b).

Finally, the analysis considered how participants disengaged from humour. Even if some participants consistently share sexist and grotesque material, this was largely ignored by the chat members. Usually only two or three chat members responded to such humour with a few emojis (such as clapping hands or a yellow face) or short comments or interjections. Including a simple emoji, a laughing interjection, or a quick remark can be a way to take the distance from a humour bid if it is not appreciated or even to disengage from it while saving the face of the sender. Although it is difficult to study silence in mediated conversations, particularly in multiparty interactions, we can assume the lack of response to be a non-conflicting way to deal with failed or unappreciated humour or even to end a conversation.

6 Conclusion

This chapter has analysed the unfolding of multimodal humorous interactions in a WhatsApp group chat among 16 middle-aged men. They post memes daily, make fun of current events or joke about their own lives, thus maintaining sociability and cohesion through shared laughter. In the chat, humour helps them to keep in touch from a distance, cope with difficult life circumstances, and align with shared topics, values, and experiences.

The novelty of this study is twofold. On the one hand, it analyses the role of emojis, stickers, and other less-explored visual cues in dealing with interactional humour online. In particular, the analysis has shown that pictures of participants, even if not humorous (e.g., an injured ankle), are consistently mocked, especially if participants associate the picture with sex or ageing. In addition, users can also manipulate photos of other participants for humorous purposes. Manipulation, one of the mechanisms underlying the success of mainstream memes (Shifman 2013: 41), can also be a source of humour on a more personal, intra-group level. On the other hand, the analysis also considered how multimodal resources helped manage interactions involving successful and failed humour, thus contributing to the emerging literature on multimodal interactional humour.

This chapter emphasises group-specific activities and interactional dynamics. Some of the practices described herein are specific to this group. Nevertheless, it is not to say that some of these would not be found in other data (Virtanen, Vepsäläinen and Koivisto 2021). For example, previous studies have found that emojis are key in framing different laughing stances (König 2019) or signalling and responding to humour (Sampietro 2021a) on WhatsApp. Other researchers have also observed the importance of memes in opening humorous instant messaging interactions with pure phatic purposes (Cruz-Moya and Sánchez-Moya 2021; Yus 2021) and the emerging use of stickers as reactions to humour (Sampietro 2023; Herring and Dainas 2017).

While the results of this study are based on the specific sample interactions examined, the findings provide valuable insights into the underlying mechanisms of multimodal humour in online group interactions and could be applied to other contexts. In future studies, the analysis presented in this chapter could benefit from in-depth interviews with participants, especially in defining the role of silence in coping with failed humour. Another natural extension of the study presented in this chapter is the examination of a group chat composed of women. In addition to gender differences in face-to-face humour (see, for example, Boxer and Cortés-Conde 1997), previous studies have found that in WhatsApp group chats women explicitly negotiate topics and tend to avoid conflict (Pérez-Sabater 2019). Humorous interactions are likely to differ from the characteristics presented in this chapter, from the obvious choice of topics to be made fun of, to the signalling of humour, to the presence of teasing and laughter. Another follow-up is analysing video or photo-based humorous interactions on other platforms. Although some of the results of this study can be applied to other applications (e.g., how humour is framed by the sender or receiver), the study of multimodal humour can benefit from the analysis of other platforms. For example, filters on Instagram, Snapchat, or TikTok can convey humour, such as placing cartoon cat ears or huge eyebrows in a photo or distorting one's face on a video (Snapchat n.d.). From an interactional perspective, while on Instagram and TikTok, users can write comments on a photo or video post (thus offering verbal responses to a multimodal humour bid), on Snapchat the entire exchange is visual, with users posting only pictures and videos back and forth with their contacts. Analysing how humorous interactions unfold in this app can shed light on emerging conventions in online visual humour.

Despite its limitations, this chapter contributes to the research on multimodal humour in digital interactions by examining how a group of men uses the visual affordances available on WhatsApp to initiate, respond to, and disengage from humour while negotiating in-group and personal identities.

References

Alexander, Richard. 1997. *Aspects of Verbal Humour in English*. Tübingen: Narr.
Ambrus, Laura. 2017. Categorisation of memes. *Opus et Educatio* 4(2). http://opuseteducatio.hu/index.php/opusHU/article/view/190/286 (2 May 2023).
Androutsopoulos, Jannis. 2006. Introduction: Sociolinguistics and computer-mediated communication. *Journal of Sociolinguistics* 10(4). 419–438. https://doi.org/10.1111/j.1467-9841.2006.00286.x.
Attardo, Salvatore. 2020. *The linguistics of humor. An introduction*. Oxford University Press.
Attardo, Salvatore &Victor Raskin. 2017. Linguistics and humor theory. In Salvatore Attardo (ed.), *The Routledge Handbook of Language and Humor*, 49–63. Abingdon/New York: Routledge.
Bell, Nancy. 2015. *We Are Not Amused. Failed Humor in Interaction*. Berlin/Boston: De Gruyter Mouton.
Bernal, María. 2007. *Categorización sociopragmática de la cortesía y de la descortesía*. Stockholm: Stockholm University dissertation.
Boxer, Diana & Florencia Cortés-Conde. 1997. From bonding to biting: Conversational joking and identity play. *Journal of Pragmatics* 27. 275–294.
Chovanec, Jan & Villy Tsakona. 2018. Investigating the dynamics of humor. Towards a theory of interactional humor. In Villy Tsakona & Jan Chovanec (eds.), *The Dynamics of Interactional Humor: Creating and Negotiating Humor in Everyday Encounters*, 1–26. Amsterdam: John Benjamins.
Cruz-Moya, Olga & Alfonso Sánchez-Moya. 2021. Humour in multimodal times. Insights from online interactions among senior users of a WhatsApp group. *Internet Pragmatics* 4(1). 52–86. https://doi.org/10.1075/ip.00061.cru
Dynel, Marta. 2016. "I has seen image macros!" Advice animals memes as visual-verbal jokes. *International Journal Of Communication* 10. 660–688. https://ijoc.org/index.php/ijoc/article/view/4101 (2 May, 2023)
Dynel, Marta. 2009. Beyond a joke: Types of conversational humour. *Language and Linguistics Compass* 3(5), 1284–1299. https://doi.org/10.1111/j.1749-818X.2009.00152.x
Dynel, Marta & Jan Chovanec. 2021. Creating and sharing public humour across traditional and new media. *Journal of Pragmatics* 177, 151–156. https://doi.org/10.1016/j.pragma.2021.02.020
Farina, Matteo. 2018. *Facebook and Conversation Analysis*. London: Bloomsbury.
Fichman, Pnina & Ashley R. Dainas. 2019. Graphicons and tactics in satirical trolling on Tumblr.com. *International Journal of Communication* 13. 4261–4286.
Gal, Noam, Limor Shifman & Zohar Kampf. 2016. "It Gets Better": Internet memes and the construction of collective identity. *New Media & Society* 18(8). 1698–1714. https://doi.org/10.1177/1461444814568784
Giles, David, Wyke Stommel, Trena Paulus, Jessica Lester & Darren Reed. 2015. Microanalysis of online data: The methodological development of "digital CA". *Discourse, Context & Media* 7. 45–51. https://doi.org/10.1016/j.dcm.2014.12.002
Giles, David, Wyke Stommel & Trena Paulus. 2017. The microanalysis of online data: The next stage. *Journal of Pragmatics* 115. 37–41. https://doi.org/10.1016/J.PRAGMA.2017.02.007

Gironzetti, Elisa. 2022. *The Multimodal Performance of Conversational Humor*. Amsterdam: John Benjamins.
Glenn, Phillip. 2003. *Laughter in Interaction*. Cambridge: Cambridge University Press.
Hay, Jennifer. 2001. The Pragmatics of humor support. *Humor – International Journal of Humor Research* 14(1). 55–82. https://doi.org/10.1515/humr.14.1.55
Herring, Susan C. 2015. New frontiers in interactive multimodal communication. In Alexandra Georgakopoulou & Tereza Spilloti (eds.), *The Routledge Handbook of Language and Digital Communication*, 398–402. Abingdon/New York: Routledge.
Herring, Susan C. 2004. Computer-mediated discourse analysis: An approach to researching online behavior. In Sasha Barab, Rob Kling & James H. Gray (eds.), *Designing for Virtual Communities in the Service of Learning*, 338–376. Cambridge: Cambridge University Press.
Herring, Susan C. & Jannis Androutsopoulos. 2015. Computer-mediated discourse 2.0. In Deborah Tannen, Heidi E. Hamilton & Deborah Schiffrin (eds.), *The Handbook of Discourse Analysis*, Vol. I, 127–151. Chilchester, UK: John Wiley & Sons.
Herring, Susan C. & Ashley R. Dainas. 2017. 'Nice picture comment!' Graphicons in Facebook comment threads. In *Proceedings of the Fiftieth Hawaii International Conference on System Sciences*, 2185–2194. https://doi.org/10.24251/HICSS.2017.264
Jefferson, Gail. 1979. A technique for inviting laughter and its subsequent acceptance/declination. In George Psathas (ed.), *Everyday Language: Studies in Ethnomethodology*, 79–96. New York: Irvington.
Jefferson, Gail, Harvey Sacks & Emmanuel A. Schegloff. 1987. Notes on laughter in the pursuit of intimacy. In Graham Button & John R.E. Lee (eds.), *Talk and Social Organisation*, 152–205. Clevedon: Multilingual Matters.
Jewitt, Carey, Jeff Bezemer & Kay O'Halloran. 2016. *Introducing Multimodality*. Abingdon/New York: Routledge.
Konrad, Artie, Susan C. Herring & David Choi. 2020. Sticker and emoji use in Facebook Messenger: Implications for graphicon change. *Journal of Computer-Mediated Communication* 25(3). 217–235. https://doi.org/10.1093/jcmc/zmaa003
König, Katharina. 2019. Stance taking with 'laugh' particles and emojis – Sequential and functional patterns of 'laughter' in a corpus of German WhatsApp chats. *Journal of Pragmatics* 142. 156–170. https://doi.org/10.1016/J.PRAGMA.2019.01.008
Kress, Gunther. 2012. Multimodal discourse analysis. In James Paul Gee & Michael Handford (eds.), *The Routledge Handbook of Discourse Analysis*, 35–50. Abingdon/New York: Routledge.
Kress, Gunther & Theo van Leeuwen. 2011. *Multimodal Discourse. The Modes and Media of Contemporary Communication*. London: Arnold.
Messerli, Thomas & Di Yu. 2018. Multimodal construction of soccer-related humor on Twitter and Instagram. In Ridvan Askin, Catherine Diederich & Aline Bieri (eds.), *The Aesthetics, Poetics, and Rhetoric of Soccer*, 227–255. Abingdon/New York: Routledge.
Milner, Ryan M. 2016. *The World Made Meme: Public Conversations and Participatory Media*. Cambridge, Massachusetts: MIT Press.
Mortensen, Mette & Christina Neumayer. 2021. The playful politics of memes. *Information, Communication & Society* 24(16). 2367–2377. https://doi.org/10.1080/1369118X.2021.1979622
Petersen, Line N. 2014. Sherlock fans talk: Mediatised talk on tumblr. *Northern Lights: Film & Media Studies Yearbook* 12(1). 87–104. https://doi.org/10.1386/nl.12.1.87_1

Pérez-Sabater, Carmen (2019). Emoticons in relational writing practices on whatsapp: Some reflections on gender. In Patricia Bou-Franch & Pilar Garcés-Conejos Blitvich (eds.), *Analysing Digital Discourse: New Insights and Future Directions*, 163–189. Cham: Springer International Publishing. https://doi.org/10.1007/978-3-319-92663-6_6

Priego-Valverde, Béatrice, Brigitte Bigi, Salvatore Attardo, Lucy Pickering & Elisa Gironzetti. 2018. Is smiling during humor so obvious? A cross-cultural comparison of smiling behavior in humorous sequences in American English and French interactions. *Intercultural Pragmatics* 15(4). 563–591. https://doi.org/10.1515/ip-2018-0020

Sampietro, Agnese. 2019. Emoji and rapport management in Spanish WhatsApp chats. *Journal of Pragmatics* 143. 109–120. https://doi.org/10.1016/j.pragma.2019.02.009

Sampietro, Agnese. 2021a. Emojis and the performance of humour in everyday electronically-mediated conversation: A corpus study of WhatsApp chats. *Internet Pragmatics* 4(1). 87–110. https://doi.org/10.1075/ip.00062.samp

Sampietro, Agnese. 2021b. The use of the 'face with tears of joy' emoji on WhatsApp: A conversation-analytical approach. Paper presented at *Emoji 2021. 4th International Workshop on Emoji Understanding and Applications in Social Media (co-located with the 15th ICWSM)*. https://doi.org/10.36190/2021.03

Sampietro, Agnese. 2023. El auge de los stickers en WhatsApp y la evolución de la comunicación digital. *Círculo de Lingüística Aplicada a la Comunicación* 94. 271–285. https://doi.org/10.5209/clac.83860

Shifman, Limor 2013. *Memes in Digital Culture*. Cambridge, Massachusetts: MIT Press.

Snapchat, n.d. Top Lenses and Filters on Snapchat. https://lens.snapchat.com/ (12 May 2023).

Thomson, T.J., Daniel Angus, Paula Dootson, Edward Hurcombe & Adam Smith. 2020. Visual mis/disinformation in journalism and public communications: Current verification practices, challenges, and future opportunities. *Journalism Practice* 16(5). 938–962. https://doi.org/10.1080/17512786.2020.1832139

Toder, Noa & Sigal Barak-Brandes. 2022. A booty of booties: Men accumulating capital by homosocial porn exchange on WhatsApp. *Porn Studies* 9(2). 145–158. https://doi.org/10.1080/23268743.2021.1947880

Trouvain, Jürgen & Khiet P. Truong. (2017). Laughter. In Salvatore Attardo (ed.), *The Routledge Handbook of Language and Humour*, 340–355. Abingdon/New York: Routledge.

Vandergriff, Ilona & Carolin Fuchs (2012). Humor support in synchronous computer-mediated classroom discussions. *Humor* 25(4). 437–458. https://doi.org/10.1515/humor-2012-0022

Virtanen, Mikko T., Heidi Vepsäläinen & Aino Koivisto. 2021. Managing several simultaneous lines of talk in Finnish multiparty mobile messaging. *Discourse, Context & Media*, 39. 100460. https://doi.org/10.1016/j.dcm.2020.100460.

Waterloo, Sophie F., Susanne E. Baumgartner, Jochen Peterand & Patti M. Valkenburg. 2018. Norms of online expressions of emotion: Comparing Facebook, Twitter, Instagram, and WhatsApp. *New Media & Society* 20(15). 1813–1831. https://doi.org/10.1177/1461444817707349

We Are Social, DataReportal & Meltwater. 2023. "Most popular global mobile messenger apps as of January 2023, based on number of monthly active users (in millions)". January 26, 2023. Statista. https://www.statista.com/statistics/258749/most-popular-global-mobile-messenger-apps/ (12 May 2023).

Wikipedia. 2022. "Predators (film)". https://en.wikipedia.org/wiki/Predators_(film) (23 March 2022).

World Emoji Day. n.d. "Statistics". https://worldemojiday.com/statistics (24 March 2022)

Yus, Francisco. 2018. Identity-related issues in meme communication. *Internet Pragmatics* 1(1). 113–133. https://doi.org/10.1075/ip.00006.yus

Yus, Francisco. 2021. *Smartphone Communication. Interactions in the App Ecosystem*. Abingdon/New York: Routledge.

Yus, Francisco. 2022. WhatsApp. Interacciones y humor en la mensajería instantánea. In Leonor Ruiz Gurillo (ed.), *Interactividad en modo humorístico: Géneros orales, escritos y tecnológicos*, 161–192. Madrid: Iberoamericana Vervuert.

Zajdman, Anat. 1995. Humorous face-threatening acts: Humor as strategy. *Journal of Pragmatics* 23(3). 325–339.

Kerry Mullan
10 Humour and creativity in a family of strangers on Facebook

Abstract: This chapter will examine the creative and multimodal aspects of collaborative humour in a local community Facebook group, whose aim is to provide members of an inner suburb of an Australian city with the opportunity to request and offer help with recommendations for local services, house-, pet-, or babysitting, and/or to exchange free goods.

The analysis focuses on the way in which multimodal "everyday creativity" (Carter 2015) and humour mechanisms (Norrick 2003) are employed in online interactions to foster a sense of belonging in this group of strangers. Particular aspects of linguistic play and discursive strategies will be examined in a selection of posts. These include puns, word play, joint fictionalisation, lexically creative terms of address for the group, and frequent references to certain recurring themes in the group, such as a popular local plumber and a particular group member who often requests a lift to/from the airport. The examples chosen – many of which are accompanied by emojis, images or memes – all illustrate how the jointly constructed humour is used to contribute to a sense of affiliation and belonging in this group of strangers.

Keywords: humour, creativity, multimodal, belonging, Facebook, online community

1 Introduction

As pointed out by Haugh (2017), it is well-known that language is not used purely for transactional purposes. In addition to performing important relational and interactional work, language is often used creatively for pleasure or entertainment, where "people manipulate the forms and functions of language as a source of fun for themselves and/or for the people they are with" (Crystal 1996: 328). However, it has been shown that such linguistic creativity can also play a key role in constructing and reaffirming (group and individual) identities (Bell 2012). As Thurlow points out (2012: 179), "creative practice is motivated by . . . the pragmatic, relational needs of participants as much as it is by their deliberate attempts to play with the norms of spelling, punctuation and grammar". For example, North (2007) showed how creative language use and punning contributed to constructing a sense of community and building and maintaining interpersonal connections rather than exchanging information. This is in no small part thanks to the interactive and collaborative nature of language play and the fact that it is co-constructed by participants. According to Vásquez (2019), linguistic creativity is a social phenomenon, something that is shared and co-constructed, and intended to construct a sense of mutuality. It can be performed by anyone and can consist of "everyday (linguistic[1]) creativity" (Carter 2015) such as puns, metaphors, repetition, idioms, slang, hyperbole, rhyme, alliteration, wordplay (Vásquez 2019).

Digital media have provided new opportunities and platforms for such creativity to be performed, co-constructed and shared. In addition to the creative language play that takes place in spoken interaction, such as puns, word play, metaphors, idioms, exaggeration, alliteration etc., the Internet offers a platform for additional and multimodal creative practices, including gifs, memes, images, reactions ('likes' and emojis), laughter tokens (e.g., *lol, ha ha*), sharing posts, unconventional spelling and punctuation, and the like. Extensive research into linguistic creativity online has been carried out for over two decades (for an overview see Vasquez 2019 chapter 2), and it is generally agreed that it entails some kind of performance or presentation to an audience (Lewin-Jones 2015). Goddard (2016) found that creative language use online was a way for individuals to invite others to judge their performance and to connect with them, announcing themselves as a sociable conversational partner or group member. North (2007) found that the participants in her study not only manipulated language to create humorous effects, but did so with self-awareness, making the humour[2] part of an online performance.

Digital communication has also radically changed the way we interact with each other, redefining our notions of friendship, relationships and identity (Lambert Gordon 2016). Maranto and Barton describe Facebook as a space that "disregard[s] traditional cultural boundaries between private and public spheres" (2010: 43). Not only can we connect with one another constantly, we can form relationships and communities with complete strangers. The definition and constitution of a community has long been debated by scholars. As Angouri (2016) points out, the term typically refers to a group of people brought together by a set of shared characteristics, therefore implying cohesion and belonging. A more nuanced description (and particularly

---

1 My addition.
2 I borrow Holmes and Marra's oft–quoted definition of humour as "utterances which are identified by the analyst, on the basis of paralinguistic, prosodic and discursive clues, as intended by the speaker(s) to be amusing and perceived to be amusing by at least some of the participants" (2002: 67).

suited to the complexity of online communities) involves the notion of a community emerging and being negotiated between members who claim/reject membership. In her discussion on on-/off–line communities, Angouri (2016: 324–6) explains that early research referred to communities such as the one in this study as virtual communities, but that more recent work has extended the original meaning of Communities of Practice (Lave and Wenger 1991) to "groups of people who share a concern, a set of problems, or a passion about a topic, and who deepen their knowledge and expertise in this area by interacting on an ongoing basis" (Wenger, McDermott and Snyder 2002: 4) – a suitable description of the online community under examination here.

The links between creative language play, performance, the online environment, community, and humour are therefore evident, albeit complex. As Thurlow (2012: 170) states, "creative practice is more often than not shot through with humour", and Carr, Schrock and Dauterman (2012) found humour in approximately 20% of Facebook updates. While Yus (2018) is no doubt correct when he proposes that humour encourages interaction and participation in many online spaces, I would argue that the reverse is also true, resulting in a type of virtuous circle. Yus also states that humour brings people together, creating a sense of "closeness and an in-group feeling" (2018: 297). This feeling comes when members share the cultural and background knowledge required in order to interpret humour and to create it in context. These shared values and views in turn create solidarity and intimacy, reinforce group boundaries, and create a pleasant atmosphere and a sense of belonging.

The remainder of this chapter will demonstrate the way in which this online community of practice uses multimodal creativity to create humour, which in turn fosters a sense of affiliation and belonging in the group. The next section describes the dataset and the methodology employed for the analysis of the data. The third section presents an analysis and discussion of the examples, divided into four categories of creative humour mechanisms: "ping-pong punning" (Chiaro 2018) and word play, online joint fictionalisations, playful affectionate terms of address, and recurring humour themes. Section 4 is the conclusion.

2 Data and methodology

The data are taken from a private Facebook group established in April 2016 for residents of an inner suburb of Melbourne, Australia. The group describes itself as "a safe and positive online group where people are empowered to ask for help and respond to requests for help from others in their community", and whose values are "collaborative problem solving, compassion and empathy, positivity, unity and inclusion, openness, empowerment and action". At the time of writing, the group comprised 10,916 members. According to the 2021 census, there were 10,745 residents in this area.³ The group offers a platform for members to ask for recommendations for local tradespeople or businesses, to advertise local events, to enquire about house/pet sitting and/or gardening services, to post messages about lost and found items (including pets), and/or to offer superfluous household goods or food to other members at no cost. There are typically around 30 posts a day with threads of varying lengths, depending on the topic. These are primarily textual, with accompanying photographs when free goods are being offered. Although the group can be considered a common-identity online community according to Schwämmlein and Wodzicki (2012) due to the shared interests and values of its members, the vast majority of members do not know each other personally. As a member of the group myself, I became interested in the way in which humour was being used collaboratively to create a strong sense of belonging in this group of strangers.⁴

A number of humorous multimodal posts were collected between 2016 and 2018 and have been chosen for qualitative analysis here on the basis that they illustrated the use of "everyday creativity" – described by Carter (2015) as language play which is spontaneous and co-constructed in interaction – and were identified as successfully performing humour by means of the group's appreciative responses, metalinguistic comments, laughter tokens, and positive reactions such as 'likes' and laughing emojis. The creative humour mechanisms (Norrick 2003) selected from the data included puns, word play, lexically creative terms of endearment for the group, "incorrect" spelling (Thurlow 2012), joint online fictionalisation, and frequent humorous references to certain recurring themes in the group, such as a popular local plumber and a particular group member who regularly requested a lift to/from the airport. This set of humour mechanisms was chosen for their prevalence and for their clear connection to fostering a sense of group belonging. The posts do not represent all instances of humour in the group over the period of collection, but they exemplify the most popular types of creative humour mechanisms performed by the group for this purpose.

The posts were analysed qualitatively according to the linguistic theoretical and methodological approaches (e.g., interactional pragmatics and discourse analysis) outlined in computer-mediated discourse analysis (CMDA) (Herring 2004), looking particularly at the core linguistic features identified by Herring when an-

---

3 These figures are slightly ambiguous because some residents of a neighbouring suburb are also members of this Facebook group, and some residents remain members even when they move out of the local area.
4 I was granted permission from the founder and moderator of the group to research the humour in the group. University ethics approval was also obtained (reference CHEAN B 21054-08/17).

alysing computer-mediated communication (CMC): structure, meaning, interaction and social function. This micro-level qualitative analysis provides a detailed description of how participants creatively contribute to humorous interactional practices in this specific online context.

In line with Androutsopoulos (2011), I also used a discourse-ethnographic approach, paying particular attention to the situated practices of language in the data. As a longstanding participatory member of the group, this participant-observer ethnographic approach allowed for identification of recurrent humour themes as well as the various contextualisation cues (Gumperz 1982) that signalled in-group humour, and enabled me to decode several insider jokes and otherwise seemingly obscure references. This combination of a micro-analysis of the creative linguistic features with a macro-analysis of the social and interactional practices being engaged in also aligns with what Jones (2016) refers to as a "discourse approach" to linguistic creativity, and follows the three broad organising principles in digital discourse research proposed in Thurlow (2018): discourse, multimodality, ideology.

3 Analysis and discussion

The examples presented below are taken directly from the Facebook page in the original formats (which differ slightly over time), with the exception of examples (1) and (5), which have been reformatted and appear without time markers and reactions for reasons of space. All names have either been removed or are pseudonyms which retain the gender and ethnicity of the participant's identity as far as can be determined (although my own contribution to example (1) retains my real name). Underlined names signify that the participant "tagged" another person, i.e., alerted them to the thread. OP refers to the original poster of the thread. The examples are presented in four sections, namely "ping-pong punning" (Chiaro 2018) and word play, online joint fictionalisations, affectionate terms of address, and recurring humour themes.

3.1 Ping-Pong Punning and word play

Punning is a well-known type of creative wordplay where a word or expression that has two (or more) interpretations is exploited purely for the purposes of amusement. The ambiguity can be phonological, lexical (semantic), syntactical, syllabic and/or morphological and combines with incongruity to create humour.

First coined by Chiaro (1992), the term "ping-pong punning" refers to sequences of semantically related puns produced by different participants in a conversation, and where the participants try to outplay each other by initiating clever verbal ambiguity (Chiaro 2018).

While punning was previously restricted to oral communication, the online environment lends itself to this type of creativity by allowing more time for contributors to think up puns and witty replies, as well as offering the opportunity to include emojis, memes and other images (although these were used sparingly in this instance). The following example illustrates such ping-pong punning, unfolding over an 18-and-a-half-hour period from 8 Jan 2017 17:17h to 9 Jan 11:49h, although all but the final two posts occurred within the first six hours. The 31 contributions shown here were made by 15 contributors. The original post was intended to be serious and was asking for advice regarding how to replace a cracked toilet bowl, accompanied by a photograph.

(1) **I'm sorry if this topples over into oversharing**
Rob
Good afternoon all, I'm sorry if this topples over into oversharing but if so, I plead the 'heat' ... I was cleaning my toilet with a regular loo brush and a crack appeared in the bowl. I've had a good few days to over think all possible scenarios and have ultimately decided that I'm not keen on my lav[5] cracking below me one day. The said W.C.[6] was purchased at Masters about 4 years ago, so I'm fresh out of luck. Has this happened to anyone out there? Thank you.

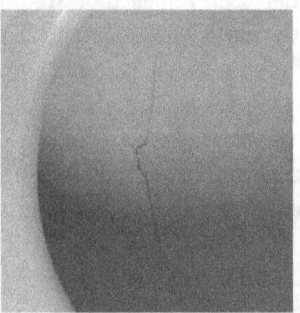

Yin Trying very hard not to **crack any jokes** ...
Rob Oh, that's good!

---

5 Lavatory.
6 Water closet (toilet).

Sian Melbourne city west water has specials for toilet replacements go to the web site

Rob Hi **Sian**, ah, yes, wonderful idea. Thank you.

Christina I am afraid I am of little help, but your post made our household (4 boys and 1 girl) giggle all afternoon as we are contemplating various scenarios.

Rob Excellent! I very much tried to use restraint . . . I could only imagine some of the scenarios!

Kerry And the wonderful Ronald Stoke will fit it for you . . .

Rob Yes! I've heard so much about Ronald.

Carla What exactly are you eating 😁

Yin It's not nice to laugh at **someone's expanse**.

Rob Ha! I know, it's a most unusual post isn't it?! Or perhaps I clean too vigorously?!

Yin Oh well, **them's the breaks** . . .

Craig Too much fibre?

Lynne You need to get it replaced asap as it's no longer stable and is also a health hazard (bacteria entering the crack (loo that is)).

Rob Thanks Lynne, I hadn't thought about the crack **(No pun intended)** and bacteria.

Ronald Stoke Please feel free to call me cheers Ronald

Rob Thank you Ronald, I've heard some great things about you. Will give you a buzz tomorrow.

Ronald Stoke No worries sit lightly on that pan please

Tess How I love this site . . . my evening entertainment done! (sorry Rob but this really is **a bum crack**!)

Rob I agree, it has been **a real pain in the behind**!

Tess well it will be if it breaks!

[Some comments omitted]

Tess and I'll be honest here **Rob**, I feel your pain! We have a similar problem with our Villeroy and Bosch . . . can't afford to eat off it but can afford to crap in it . . . until it explodes beneath us!

Cassandra Dear Kensington residents. I have a big grin on my face after reading all these posts. Rob, I hope all is back to normal tomorrow. It's great that Sir Ronald is ready to save the day.

Mary Cracking post

Tess 😁

Christina <u>Rob</u> we will all need an update, to calm our collective imagination and know the end of your saga. **It is a cracker** after all.
Dan I once dropped a scotch tumbler into a toilet and cracked the bowl . . . Also had a tenant once crack a bowl. I suspect weight was the issue in that case. He also went thru a floorboard . . .
Mary P.S. do you live on **McCracken** St by any chance? 😊
Tania Was someone in the household nervous about something and **shat bricks**? 😂
Ryan Toilet Bowls are **Crap** Today, if you can get an old type put it in.

Perhaps encouraged by Rob's light tone and the acknowledgement that this was a somewhat unusual scenario and request which might constitute "oversharing" (e.g., of information of an intimate nature) in the original post, as well as the irresistible temptation of the topic of 'toilet humour', the good-natured puns and humour started immediately and continued throughout the thread. Of the ten examples of puns and word play which appear, six of them are directly connected to the word *crack* (or *break* in one case) – including one which contains the name of a local street – where *crack* is understood as a common reference to the space between the buttocks. In addition, there are five further examples of word play based on scatological references.

The first response from Yin came five minutes after the original post in the form of a light-hearted tease, pretending that she did not really want to mock Rob's situation by seizing the opportunity to use the word *crack* in the expression "to crack (tell) a joke". Her third contribution is another show of mock sympathy, using the expression "them's the breaks" (meaning 'unfortunately, that's just the way it is'), with a clear lexical connection between the words *break* and *crack*. Tess's contribution "a bum crack" plays on the double meaning of *crack* (joke/ space between the buttocks) and *bum* (poor quality/buttocks). Mary's and Christina's puns rely on the meaning of 'excellent quality' in the terms "cracking" and "cracker". Mary then asks if Rob lives on McCracken Street, which is a real street in the neighbourhood. She follows this with the crying with laughter emoji, indicating appreciation for the quality of her own pun. As well as Tess's use of the word *bum*, the other scatological references are Rob's own "a real pain in the behind" (buttocks); Tania's question about "shitting bricks" (where the expression *to shit bricks* means 'to be scared of or nervous about something', but doubling here as referring to excreting something so heavy that it cracked the toilet bowl); Ryan's use of "crap" (synonym for *shit*, of poor quality); and the sole phonological pun by Yin, who says that it is not nice to laugh "at someone's expanse". The usual expression is *to laugh at someone's expense*, but "expanse" is being used here to refer to buttocks.

While the puns could have been seen as disruptive and derailing a serious request, Rob displays a sense of humour about the whole episode and responds appreciatively to all comments and suggestions as they move back and forth between humorous and serious, himself building on the scenario and inviting further comments in many instances. In one response he includes "no pun intended" after the word *crack*, acknowledging the punning and word play that was unfolding. Three posts simply stated how entertaining and amusing they found the thread, and yet another simply posted an image of a roll of toilet paper. My own contribution to the thread was a suggestion to call a popular local plumber, who, despite not being tagged, then also contributed to the thread and offered his services. This plumber – later referred to by Cassandra as "Sir Ronald" – is very well-known in the group and is frequently referred to across multiple threads (cf. section 4.3 Recurrent Humour Themes and Mullan Forthcoming).

It is important to note that the puns and word play interwoven throughout this thread are intended purely to amuse and to create an atmosphere of general silliness and enjoyment, with a friendly competitive element of 'one-upmanship' and banter involved in the creativity and cleverness of the puns and wordplay. This wordplay contributes to a textual cohesion which keeps the topic "in play" (North 2007: 553). This cohesion, like the humour, is jointly constructed, both reflecting and constituting the social cohesion of the group. What is also evident in this example is the solidarity and sense of light-hearted humour co-constructed by the contributors to this thread, whether by posting messages themselves, or by simply liking the posts or signalling laughter (likes and laughter reactions not reproduced here). In this way, through their punning, the contributors, who show no sign of knowing each other personally, have built on each other's contributions to create a "form of collective online laughter" (Chiaro 2018: 10), and strengthened the group rapport by demonstrating shared background knowledge and laughing together (Norrick, 2017).

3.2 Online joint fictionalisations

Joint fictionalisations are a well-known device for creating humour and have previously been examined in several languages and cultures (e.g., Mullan and Béal 2018, Chovanec 2012, Hay 2001, Stallone and Haugh 2017, Tsakona 2018, Winchatz and Kozin 2008). Also referred to as fantasy humour (among many other terms, cf. Stallone and Haugh 2017), these jointly constructed imaginary and scenarios escalate and take on a life of their own following their own internal logic. Australians have been found to favour this type of humour (Béal and Mullan 2013), particularly when the opener is delivered in a deadpan manner, without any overt indication that the speaker is not serious, as in the following examples. The participants recognise the situation as improbable and understand that the absurd scenario they are co-constructing is clearly a pretence.

The catalyst for the frequent examples of joint fictionalisations in the group was a post offering a pile of dead leaves free to a good home (cf. Mullan 2020). That thread was contributed to over four days, consisting of 91 contributions from 35 participants and prompting hundreds of reactions from other members. The thread has since attained an iconic status in the group, often referred to in other posts (and in another group, cf. Mullan 2022), and prompting a number of similar fictionalisations, such as those presented below. As a result this form of humour has become a particular feature of this online community, embodying a somewhat mocking tone towards both the perceived strict rules of the group, which only allow for posts asking for help or offering free goods, and the poor quality of some goods that are offered up for collection. This shared insider knowledge contributes to the sense of belonging and connection in the group.

Space does not permit a full analysis of all of the examples, especially those with extensive comments. Instead, the opening post of each thread is presented along with a brief description to illustrate the nature of these online joint fictionalisations, with a more in-depth analysis of example (5).

Example (2) below was the first online joint fictionalisation after the original "pile of dead leaves" thread. The enthusiasm for this new absurd fantasy scenario is evidenced by the number of comments (105) and reactions (126). The original poster (OP) claims to have made an extra cup of tea which they will make available to anyone who wants it by leaving it in their letterbox for collection.

(2) **Extra cup of tea**

The thread was co-constructed by twenty participants over three days and included four memes, two gifs and two images. A total of 101 reactions were posted throughout the thread. As well as the general absurd collaborative comments, the contributors made several references to Star Wars and Star Trek (cf. image of mug in original post), and two insider jokes, one pretending to report a comment to the (perceived as strict) group administrator, and the other to the local horseracing community. An interesting explicit comment was made about the nature of the humour in the thread and the community: "this could be the start of mildly amusing satire on suburbia and the connectedness of free tea and community . . . . . .".

On the other hand, the following two examples of joint fictionalisation did not have as much success, both in numbers of contributions and reactions, and in terms of escalation. The OP posted a picture of some glasses, claiming that they had found them in their pocket.

(3) Lost glasses

Perhaps because it was not immediately clear if this was a serious post or not, the first response was to suggest that they might belong to the owner. The OP then posted a large version of the glasses-wearing emoji. Several turns then ensued between the OP and another member who clearly knew each other, where the humour failed. This seemed to prevent the fictionalisation from being developed and it fizzled out after one further (successful) absurd exchange.

The following example was only slightly more successful, although the image in the original post clearly signalled absurd humour.

(4) Spotty Dog

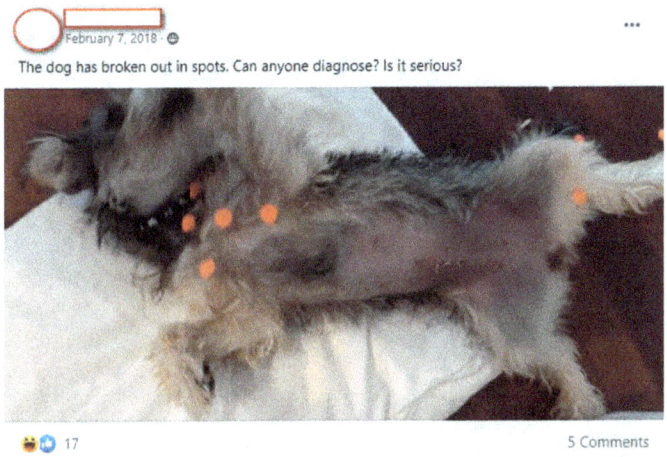

Despite the obviously photo-shopped image, the first two comments by the same poster were seemingly serious suggestions to change pet food and to contact a (real) pet supply shop and enquire about skin cream. Two other comments included puns and wordplay, but the final comment was a cryptic reference to a film, which put an end to the thread. What we see in both of these examples of failed humour is that when the values and/or creativity are not shared or understood by all the participants, the collaboration in the fantasy scenario comes to an end fairly rapidly, and the contributors respond primarily to the original post rather than interacting with each other and building a humorous scenario. Without the joint escalation, the sense of group solidarity is not present.

The next example is of a successful joint fictionalisation, opened by an apparently serious request for an ink cartridge for a Bic pen. The request is clearly absurd, given the availability and cheap price of Bic pens – nobody would seriously ask for a spare ink cartridge for a Bic. The target of this opening message is primarily the OP himself. He is publicly declaring that he has found a useless broken pen among his belongings – one that should have been thrown away earlier. The humour is also directed at those members who offer up free goods of questionable quality and utility. At the same time, there is an inference that some others in the group may also be disorganised and have broken pens lying around the house. The shared recognition of this scenario prompted 41 initial reactions and 22 comments from 18 contributors, and a further 55 reactions throughout the thread.

(5) Empty Bic

June 8, 2017

Hey Guys,

Just doing some winter cleaning today and found this Bic Kilometrico pen, only problem is that it seems to be missing the ink cartridge.

Please PM me if anyone has one that they think could go with.

👍😆 41   22 Comments

Chrissy Love it
David Here's the finished product fyi

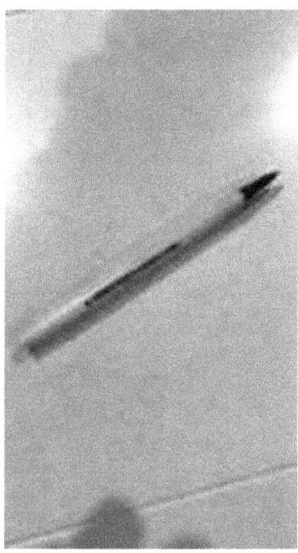

Gary I have one but the nib part is missing. Still has most of the ink in it, for now. If anyone has just the nib, please let me know.
George <u>Elaine H</u>
Gary Actually, I just checked the tube and all the ink has now run out of it. If you have the specific ink that Papermate loads that tube with, can I please have a couple of ml of it?
Still need a nib, by the way.
Bridie Hilarious, I'll go to Woolies[7] and buy you some.
Mary Oh! I think that might be mine. I have the ink cartridge here.
Arnie <u>Alf T</u>
Alf Ha, saw that and thought of you!!
Fred I think someone stuck the tube in my flower pot . . .
Margaret I have a lid if you need it
Carl I have this which I think will fit. I'm in Albury at the moment, but I knock off at six and we drive it down to you. Just pm your address. Have to be back for a wedding tomorrow unfortunately so can't stay for a Earl grey.

---

7 Woolworths supermarket.

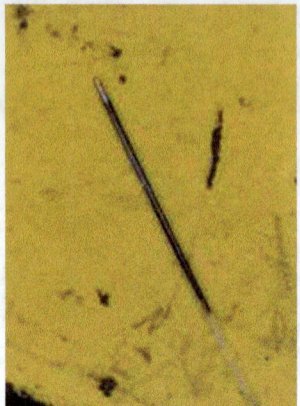

Alf <u>Arnie F</u>
Danielle How many k's does it have on the clock?
Ron <u>Melanie K</u> <u>Julie K</u>
Denise tell him he's dreaming!
Adam I have one but it's Empirical so probably not compatible with the Kilometrico system
Alan Keep it handy in case someone needs an emergency tracheotomy
Danielle In that case, I have some alcohol wipes to put with it
Gary NIL for the wipes.
Mia This thread is so awesome

The first comment indicates that the humour has been understood and appreciated, and the following several turns all enter into the spirit of the fantasy scenario, offering to supply (or in turn further request) spare parts for the Bic pen. Two contributors post images to enhance their responses, including Carl who offers to drive an approximately seven-hour round trip before attending a wedding just to drop off his ink cartridge. Danielle asks how many kilometres the pen has done, referencing the name of the type of Bic (*Kilometrico*), to which Denise responds with a pertinent famous quote from a well-known Australian film (*The Castle*). Adam offers the OP Dean his own pen, but points out that his is an *Empirical Bic* (which does not actually exist), so the ink cartridges may not be compatible. Towards the end of the thread Alan suggests absurdly that Dean should keep the empty Bic in case of an emergency tracheotomy, at which point Danielle helpfully offers some alcohol wipes for this medical procedure. Gary quickly responds, asking to be considered "next in line" for the wipes, a reference to the usual responses to free goods in the group. The thread concludes with another expression of appreciation for the humour and the entertainment.

The final two examples open with posts that can be understood as not entirely nonserious.[8] The situations themselves are not imagined but deemed amusing enough to be shared with the group, and, as with the previous examples, there is a desire to entertain, and invite participation from, other members. As well as the twenty or so comments for each example, the number of likes and reactions show the success and popularity of these threads. In the first example, the OP had mislaid their remote control and jokingly calls for help from any psychics in the group who might be able to help them find it. Similar to the previous example, there is an inclusiveness in the scenario; while the humour is self-directed in the first instance, the OP knows that everyone can relate to losing objects around the house.

(6) Psychics

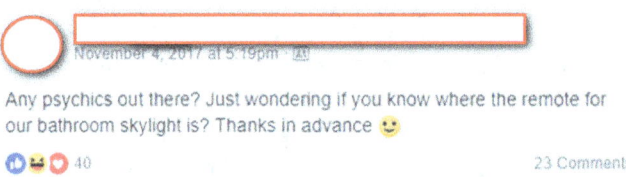

The responses were a mixture of serious suggestions intended to be helpful, and humorous comments such as "If you find one (a psychic, not the remote) can you ask about Tuesday's winner?" (referring to the weekly lottery), and "It's in that place outside where you have already looked", which was fittingly the final post. The thread demonstrates empathy for the owner of a lost object, and a desire to enter into the spirit of the game and the absurd scenario – absurd because the participants do not know each other and cannot possibly have any idea of where the remote control might be located, nor of the layout or contents of the owner's house.

The next example is another invitation to group members to enjoy the image conveyed by the post, and to participate in the scenario, which here again, is not totally imaginary.

---

[8] It is interesting to note – although no firm conclusions can be drawn – that no images accompany the initial posts in these half-serious examples. This may indicate the OP's desire to replicate a serious post, but further research would be required to validate this.

(7) Spice Girls

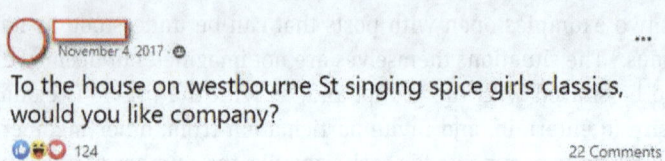

November 4, 2017

To the house on westbourne St singing spice girls classics, would you like company?

124   22 Comments

The responses express appreciation for the post ("Haha. This status is gold!"), and a desire to join in the fun and singing ("These are clearly my people", "I'm right behind you", "Totally wanting an invite"). The final comment "What a great thread! Such lovely peeps live in [the neighbourhood]!" indicates the success of these types of posts in generating a sense of solidarity and connection across the group.

This sense of solidarity or "complicity" (Priego-Valverde, 2006) is created through the sharing of experiences and values in these joint fictionalisations, and through displays of creativity (Tsakona 2018). As Norrick (2003: 1342) points out, "joking works to establish and enhance group cohesion, and serves as a control on what sorts of talk and behaviour are acceptable to participants in the interaction." By virtue of their collaboration, participants demonstrate their shared understanding and appreciation of an increasingly absurd scenario, collectively assuming responsibility for the entertainment and for keeping the interaction alive. This in turn helps to build trust amongst members of the group who begin to see each other as like-minded. As Tsakona (2018) also points out, the collective aspect and the solidarity functions of online humour are particularly important for group members who do not know each other personally, as in this case. Indeed, the online joint fictionalisation actually brings participants together (Tsakona 2018): in spoken joint fictionalisation the participants are brought together by the activity from which the scenario emerges; in these online joint fictionalisations the participants are brought together by the scenarios themselves.

3.3 Affectionate terms of address

While most research on address practices to date has focussed on spoken interaction, the basic principles can be transferred to the online environment. The way individuals address each other is fundamental to expressing and establishing social relationships (Norrby and Warren 2012). As such, address terms are a form of phatic rather than informative communication, serving to establish and maintain relationships, strengthen solidarity, express affiliation and belonging, and sustain in-group cohesion (Mensah 2021). Senft (1995: 3) describes phatic communion as:

> utterances that are said to have exclusively social, bonding functions like establishing and maintaining a friendly and harmonious atmosphere in interpersonal relations, especially during the opening and closing stages of social – verbal – encounters. These utterances are understood as a means for keeping the communication channels open.

In his study on language play in conversation, Norrick (2017), points out that, as well as terms of address performing dual pragmatic functions of summoning attention and identifying the addressee(s) while maintaining and reinforcing social relationships, they also offer opportunities for language play. The terms of address used in this online community display creativity through innovative word play, inventive spelling, and acronyms, all of which appear frequently in the group. Over the period of the data collection, 112 different ways of addressing the group were identified (apart from generalised greetings such as "Hi everyone"). These have been classified into five broad categories (although there are several instances of cross-over between them), one of which (Community) contains four sub-categories.

The terms of address all display a certain warmth and affection towards the group, prompting amusement among members, if not always 'laugh out loud' humour. There is a general sense of inclusiveness and informality in the way fellow group members are addressed. The first three categories of address terms comprise more general ones which frequently include the name of the group (*Good Karma Crew, Karma People, brains trust*), those which include flattery and compliments (*Morning amazing network!!, Hello lovelies!, Kenso heroes!*), and posts addressed to particular sets of people within the group (*beer drinkers, bird watchers, KenX women*), although we already see references to community and examples of creativity and wordplay – the two final categories. In the Community category (the largest), we see overt references to the idea of collectivity (*Fellow Kensos, gang, team, K-Crew, Karma Kollective*), and the idea of the group as family (*KGKN family, Kenso Karma-Fam*), friends (*community friends, Good Karma Network Friends, Kensfrens*), and neighbours (*neighborinos, Kenso-neighbours*). The final category is made up exclusively of examples of wordplay based on the name of the group and/or the neighbourhood(s). Many examples in this category combine wordplay and unconventional spelling with references to friendship (*Frensingtons, Kensichums)* or creative terms for the local community *KenXnation, karmakameleons, Karmites, KenXians, KenXnation Kensotopians*).

Using a particular address term indicates shared values in a community of practice (Wenger et al. 2002) such as this. Frequent interactions between members enhance a sense of group identity through shared assumptions, beliefs and knowl-

Table 1: Terms of address.

General (25)	Complimentary (20)	Special interest (15)	Community (30) Collectivity (11)	Play on name of group/neighbourhood (2)
Hello KenX	Hello lovely people of KenX	Hi Scrapbookers!	Fellow Kensos	Frensingtons
Ok hive mind	hi beautiful kensos!!	To all the bokashi and potential bokashi users	Hi, hello, hey fellow KGKN!	good karmaterians
Hey KGKN	Hi lovely KGKN!	Calling all green thumbs!	Hello fellow Kensingites	Hey kenstolians
Morning Kenso folk	Hello wonderful people of KGKN	Hi Kenso Goddess!		Hi Karma Llamas
Brains Trust	Hello lovelies!	Hi mums	Hi gang	Kensokarmarites
People of KenX	Hello lovely community	Australiana fans	Hi team	Kensichums
Hi Ken 😊	Kind Folks	To all the bird watchers out there	K-Crew	Good Karmeleons
Kensos	Hello lovely Good Karma Network	Hello beer drinkers	Hey Duderinos!	Karma-ites
Yo Karma People	Good people of KenX	Hello swim fans	Calling on the collective wisdom of the hive mind.....	Dear KenXians!
Hello Good Karma Crew!	Hi loving networkers!	Hi KenX patch workers	Hello Karma Kollective	Evening Karmites;)
Good morning Good Karma'ers!	Hello Lovely KenX Folk	To all chook loving Kensos	Hi Good Karma community!	Hello again good good karmingtons!

10 Humour and creativity in a family of strangers on Facebook — **309**

Hello People of KenX	hi amazing people of KenX	KenX women	Hey lovely community! ♥	Hi Friendsington!
Hello Good Karma Network	Hello my lovely KenX Community!	Fellow catsingtonians		Hi friendsington peeps
Hello Good Karma	Hello lovely karmic people	Hi cat-lovers		Hey Kenso Pickers
karma network	Blessed day good pple (reference to Handmaid's Tale by Margaret Attwood)	Hi handypeople of the network	**Family (3)**	Hey KenXites
			Hiya KGKN family!!	
Hi KenX	Hi legends		A bit of an odd one Kensofam-	Heyo KenXnation
Good morning KenX!	Morning amazing network!!		Hey Kenso Karma-Fam!	Good evening Karmanites
KGKNers	Hello possums! (Post about a possum and reference to Australian comedic figure *Dame Edna Everage*)			KensiSUN (posted on a sunny day)
Hi GK	Hi Kenso heroes!		**Friends (12)**	Hello KenX Residence
Hi Kenso	Hey Kensolegends		Hi community friends	Hi Ken Karmers
Hi Good Karma folk of KenX			Hi friends	karmakameleons!
Morning kens			Kensing-friends	Hello my lovely Kensotopians
Hello karma networkers			Hi Good Karma Network Friends	

(continued)

Table 1 (continued)

General (25)	Complimentary (20)	Special interest (15)	Community (30)	Play on name of group/neighbourhood (2)
Hi KGKN-tons			Hi, the most friendly bunch of ppl on earth!	
Dear kenso knights and ladies			Hi there friendlies	
			Dear KenX friends	
			Hello dear friends of KenX!	
			Hi kensfrens!	
			Hello dear friends of KenX!	
			Kenso friendos	
			Morning fellow friends!	
			Neighbours (4)	
			Happy sunny Sunday neighborinos	
			Hello neighbours	
			Kenso-neighbours (and Kenso-cats)	
			Hello friendly neighbours!	

edge, and in turn reinforce their "common ground" (Svennevig 1999: 55–56). This common ground is negotiated in interaction, where interlocutors position themselves in relation to the other(s), notably through the use of address terms. Norrick and Bubel (2009: 44) point out that the humorous deployment of address terms (or "vocatives" as they refer to them) demonstrates how participants invest creative energy into their interactions in order to entertain and enhance interpersonal relationships.

In this particular community of practice approximately fifty per cent of all posts include terms of address. Interestingly, most of these are posts requesting help or information, showing how they are being used as interactional tools to manage interactional outcomes, such as the following examples:

> *Hello Good Karma Crew! Does anyone have an i-phone 4 (yes old school!) charger I could borrow today & tomorrow morning? Cheers, Rachel*
>
> *Hey Kenso Karma-Fam! Just wondering if anyone had a 27 x40" inch frame that they had taking up space in their house that they'd like to sell. . . . . Halp! X*
>
> *Hello my lovely Kensotopians. I've decided that I need a couple of things, and thought I'd see if anyone is looking to offload or sell cheap before I go down the road of buying new: – Clothes Dryer – Pod Coffee Machine – Office Chair – Dining Chair x 2 Many thanks in advance* 😊

Vásquez (2019) suggests that creative language draws attention to itself, allowing it to stand out from more standard text in an overcrowded online environment where multiple items compete for our attention. All of the above examples include additional creative and or playful phatic devices such as exclamation marks, humour, creative spelling (*halp!*), a kiss (X), smiling emoji etc. There is a clear connection between aiming for a favourable outcome (i.e., an answer to one's question or request for help) and the choice of an attention-grabbing complimentary and/or affectionate address term.

3.4 Recurrent humour themes

According to Fine and de Soucey (2015: 1):

> every interacting social group develops, over time, a joking culture: a set of humorous references that are known to members of the group to which members can refer and that serve as the basis of further interaction. Joking, thus, has a historical, retrospective, and reflexive character. . . . . group joking is embedded, interactive, and referential, and these features give it power within the group context. Elements of the joking culture serve to smooth group interaction, share affiliation, separate the group from outsiders, and secure the compliance of group members through social control.

As groups form, they develop a set of humorous themes that are recognised and returned to repeatedly in interaction (Fine and de Soucey 2015), consolidating their joking culture and strengthening the group's bonds by constructing commonalities and a shared history. Maybin (2006: 29) refers to this as a 'long conversation', where particular themes are repeatedly returned to across different conversations. As North (2007) also points out, successful humour builds on previous contributions, playing an important role in developing a sense of social cohesion.

There have been several recurring humour themes in this group over the course of its existence. As well as references to the post with the offer of a pile of dead leaves (Section 3.2, Mullan 2020) and regularly asking if anyone is going to IKEA and can buy something for them (Mullan, 2022), the most frequent recurring themes are a highly respected and popular local plumber (Mullan, forthcoming), and a member who travels regularly for work for her job as a stand-up comedian and frequently asks for a lift to or from the airport. Listed below are three such posts (note the use of complimentary and affectionate address terms in these requests in line with the discussion in Section 3.3). Space does not allow for a list or an analysis of all airport references in the group, but in addition to the following original posts, there appeared numerous (at least twenty) other playful references to lifts to/from the airport in a range of posts concerning other (unrelated) topics.

The first post indicates that this member has made several previous requests for lifts to/from the airport, thus making an explicit reference to this recurring theme herself.

(8) Airport post 1

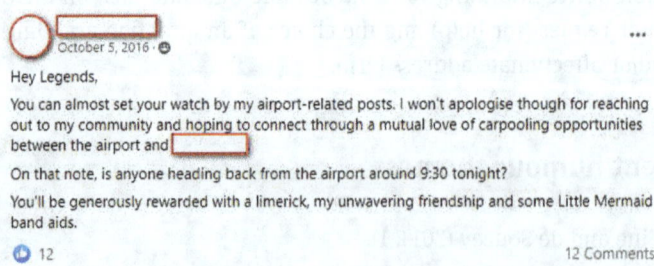

Hey Legends,

You can almost set your watch by my airport-related posts. I won't apologise though for reaching out to my community and hoping to connect through a mutual love of carpooling opportunities between the airport and ▭

On that note, is anyone heading back from the airport around 9:30 tonight?

You'll be generously rewarded with a limerick, my unwavering friendship and some Little Mermaid band aids.

👍 12   12 Comments

The humour here is self-oriented; the OP uses self-deprecation to construct a personal narrative, identifying herself as someone who is always posting requests for lifts to/from the airport. In case this implies that she is someone who does not like to spend money on taxis or time on public transport, she frames her request as an inclusive invitation to other like-minded group members who value carpooling to help her out. She then ironically offers a "generous" reward of a limerick, her loyal friendship (which one might imagine would involve frequent trips to/from the airport) and some (rather incongruous and childish) Little Mermaid band aids. The post attracted twelve 'likes' and twelve humorous comments: two references to the quality of the rewards, and a side sequence of ten messages between the OP and one other member who offered to take her back to the airport later that night.

In the next post, the member jokingly announces that her chauffeur is unwell and she therefore needs a lift to the airport. She includes an image of an aeroplane for good measure.

(9) **Airport post 2**

The member again uses irony (and fictionalisation) here; the group is well aware that she does not have a chauffeur (particularly given the frequency with which she requests lifts). The post attracted only two 'likes', but eighteen comments (nine of which were serious, including two genuine offers of a lift) involving six people. The remaining comments primarily consisted of another side sequence of banter between the OP and the same group member as in the post above concerning misaligned airport schedules.

On announcing that she (the OP) "[was] going to buy a car soon and put the KGKN [online group] out of its misery", another member suggested that the local popular plumber would be able to build her a car (given his supposed general superpowers). Here we see an example of the two most frequent recurring themes overlapping, which happened on other occasions involving this OP. Although she had not met the plumber at this point, she frequently referenced and venerated him, including a post she initiated with: "Look, I've never met him or required his services, but let's quit messing around and just call it now: Ronald Stoke is the King Of Kensington." This post generated 44 'likes' and fifteen comments, including one by the OP asking the plumber for a lift to the airport. These constant cross-references keep these topics "in play" (North 2007: 553) over time, generating further cohesive ties.

In the final example post, the member reports back to the group on finally receiving a lift to the airport from another member.

(10)   Airport post 3

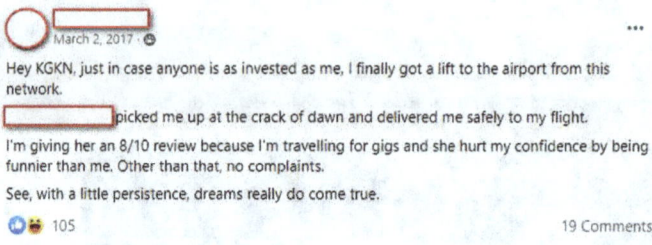

This post attracted 105 'likes' and laughing emojis, as well as nineteen comments, ten of which were another side-sequence of banter with the same group member as in the above posts. These comments in turn also received multiple 'likes' and laughing emojis, many from members who did not post comments themselves, indicating that these recurrent side-sequences were also appreciated by the group, and often prompting further humorous turns. This illustrates that recipients are just as important as speakers for maintaining a play frame (Kochman 1983). Other comments included a short side-sequence with the member who provided the lift to the airport, and another member posting the hashtag #shepersisted, to which the OP replied "Haha! Yes! Despite resistance from the KGKN #stillshepersisted!".

Since the OP left the neighbourhood (and the online group) in late 2017, references to her requests for lifts to/from the airport have continued, albeit less frequently. The most recent one was a post in October 2020, advising that "[former local] comedian [X] (the one that used to be permanently looking for lifts to the airport)" had started doing corporate workshops to make Zoom presentations more interesting. This prompted a flurry of compliments and fond memories in the group, including another member's comment that "aside from requesting lifts to the airport, she was also the self-appointed president of the I love Ronald Stoke [popular local plumber] fan club!".

Although Fine and De Soucey (2005: 3) claim that for a joking culture to be established, an ongoing relationship is required where individuals are aware of and are considerate of each other's identity, where the joker must know the target and the audience and vice versa (to give the joker the right to joke), this is not the case here.[9] On the contrary, the frequent joking between strangers, including the recurrent themes, actually created the joking culture, thereby forming and strengthening the group's identity, in turn fostering a sense of affiliation and belonging to the group. Indeed, as already mentioned, online humour is particularly important for creating a sense of solidarity when group members do not know each other personally (Tsakona 2018).

4 Conclusion

This chapter examined several examples of creative and multimodal humour in a local community Facebook group, with a particular focus on the way in which the humour was co-constructed and employed affiliatively to foster a sense of belonging in this group of strangers. The humour mechanisms (Norrick 2003) chosen for analysis were: punning and word play; joint fictionalisations; lexically creative and affectionate terms of address for the group; and recurrent themes, in particular a member of the community who often requests a lift to/from the airport.

The analysis illustrated the creative and collaborative nature of punning in the group, employed for no other purpose than to entertain others and to create a friendly atmosphere of light-hearted silliness, where participants compete with each other with examples of clever puns and wordplay. Participants and observers express their appreciation for the puns through comments and reactions in the thread, demonstrating their shared background knowledge and enjoying laughing together. Similarly, the shared recognition of the absurdity in the joint fictionalisations leads to a sense of solidarity and responsibility for co-constructing and maintaining the humorous scenario, in turn building trust amongst members of the group who consider themselves like-minded. The creative and affectionate address terms for the group also display and reinforce shared values. When address terms were used, there was a clear pragmatic link between the choice of a complimentary

---

[9] I would argue that, while this may be the case for American English speakers, it is not necessarily so for other English-speaking nations, particularly Australia, where joking with friends and strangers alike is highly valued (cf. Goddard 2006, 2009). (See also Béal & Mullan 2017, p. 33, for an anecdote describing a misunderstanding caused by this author using humour with an American colleague when meeting for the first time.)

and/or affectionate address term and a request for help or information, thereby displaying positive face management strategies. The majority of the terms created symbolise community, collectivity, and the idea of the group as family or friends. Finally, the recurrent humour themes were seen to both create and strengthen the joking culture (Fine and De Soucey 2005) of this online community, helping to create its identity and foster a sense of belonging; the members recognise that they share the background knowledge required to appropriately interpret and create humour in this in-group.

Online humour has been shown to be especially important for creating a sense of solidarity in groups where the members do not know each other personally (Tsakona 2018), and this is certainly the case in this community (see also Mullan 2020, 2022, and Forthcoming for further examples of this). What we have seen in these examples is a desire by the participants to engage in language play and to display creativity for the sole purpose of connecting with others in the group through humour. The participants could not be sure who (if anyone) would read their posts, and in almost all cases would not personally know the other members who might read or react to them. However, when posts are liked, built on, or otherwise responded to favourably, this creates a feeling of being connected to the group. These shared experiences and values all contribute to the sense of belonging to this family of strangers.

References

Androutsopoulos, Jannis. 2011. From variation to heteroglossia in the study of computer-mediated discourse. In Crispin Thurlow & Kristine Mroczek (eds.), *Digital Discourse: Language in the New Media*, 277–298. New York/London: Oxford University Press.
Angouri, Jo. 2016. Online communities and communities of practice. In Alexandra Georgakopoulou & Tereza Spilioti (eds.), *The Routledge Handbook of Language and Digital Communication*, 323–338. London/New York: Routledge.
Béal, Christine &Kerry Mullan. 2013. Issues in conversational humour from a cross-cultural perspective: comparing French and Australian corpora. In Bert Peeters, Kerry Mullan & Christine Béal (eds.), *Cross-culturally Speaking, Speaking Cross-culturally*, 107–139. Newcastle upon Tyne: Cambridge Scholars Publishing.
Béal, Christine & Kerry Mullan. 2017. The pragmatics of conversational humour in social visits: French and Australian English. *Language and Communication* 55. 24–40.
Bell, Nancy. 2012. Formulaic language, creativity, and language play in a second language. *Annual Review of Applied Linguistics* 32. 189–205.
Carr, Caleb T., David B. Schrock & Patricia Dauterman. 2012. Speech acts within Facebook status messages. *Journal of Language and Social Psychology* 31(2). 176–196.
Carter, Ronald. 2015. *Language and Creativity: The Art of Common Talk* (2nd edition). London: Routledge.

Chiaro, Delia. 1992. *The Language of Jokes: Analyzing Verbal Play*. London: Routledge.
Chiaro, Delia. 2018. *The Language of Jokes in the Digital Age*. London: Routledge.
Chovanec, Jan. 2012. Conversational humour and joint fantasising in online journalism. In Jan Chovanec & Isabel Ermida (eds.), *Language and Humour in the Media*, 139–161. Newcastle upon Tyne: Cambridge Scholars Publishing.
Crystal, David. 1996. Language play and linguistic intervention. *Child Language Teaching and Therapy* 12(3). 329–344.
Fine, Gary Alan & Michaela de Soucey. 2005. Joking cultures: Humor themes as social regulation in group life. *HUMOR: International Journal of Humor Research* 18(1). 1–22.
Goddard, Angela. 2016. Creativity and Internet communication. In Rodney Jones, (ed.), *Routledge Handbook of Language and Creativity*, 61–77. London: Routledge.
Goddard, Cliff. 2006. 'Lift your game, Martina!': Deadpan jocular irony and the ethnopragmatics of Australian English. In Cliff Goddard (ed.), *Ethnopragmatics: Understanding Discourse in Cultural Context*, 367–381. Berlin/Boston: Mouton de Gruyter.
Goddard, Cliff. 2009. Not taking yourself too seriously in Australian English: Semantic explications, cultural scripts, corpus evidence. *Intercultural Pragmatics* 6(1). 29–53.
Gumperz, John J. 1982. *Discourse Strategies*. Cambridge: Cambridge University Press.
Haugh, Michael. 2017. Jocular language play, social action and (dis)affiliation in conversational interaction. In Nancy Bell (ed.), *Multiple Perspectives on Language Play*, 143–168. Berlin/Boston: Mouton De Gruyter.
Hay, Jennifer. 2001. The pragmatics of humor support. *HUMOR: International Journal of Humor Research* 14(1). 55–82.
Herring, Susan C. 2004. Computer-mediated discourse analysis: An approach to researching online behaviour. In Sasha Barab, Rob Kling & James H. Gray (eds.), *Designing for Virtual Communities in the Service of Learning*, 338–376. New York: Cambridge University Press.
Holmes, Janet & Meredith Marra. 2002. Over the edge? Subversive humor between colleagues and friends. *HUMOR: International Journal of Humor Research* 15(1). 65–87.
Jones, Rodney. 2016. Creativity and discourse analysis. In Rodney Jones (ed.), *Routledge Handbook of Language and Creativity*, 61–77. London: Routledge.
Kochman, Thomas. 1983. The boundary between play and nonplay in black verbal duelling. *Language in Society* 12. 329–337.
Lambert Gordon, Sage. 2016. Relationality, friendship, and identity in digital communication. In Alexandra Georgakopoulou & Tereza Spilioti (eds.), *The Routledge Handbook of Language and Digital Communication*, 305–320. London/New York: Routledge.
Lave, Jean & Etienne Wenger. 1991. *Situated learning: Legitimate peripheral participation*. Cambridge: Cambridge University Press.
Lewin-Jones, Jenny. 2015. Humour with a purpose: Creativity with language in Facebook status updates. *Linguistik Online* 72(3). https://doi.org/10.13092/lo.72.1973
Maranto, Gina. & Matt Barton. 2010. Paradox and promise: MySpace, Facebook, and the sociopolitics of social networking in the writing classroom. *Computers and Composition* 27(1). 36–47.
Maybin, Janet. 2006. *Children's Voices: Talk, Knowledge and Identity*. Basingstoke: Palgrave Macmillan.
Mensah, Eyo O. 2021. A sociolinguistic study of address terms in a Nigerian university's staff club. *Poznan Studies in Contemporary Linguistics* 57(4). 677–707.
Mullan, Kerry. 2020. Pile of dead leaves free to a good home: Humour and belonging in a Facebook community. In Kerry Mullan, Bert Peeters & Lauren Sadow (eds.), *Studies in Ethnopragmatics, Cultural Semantics, and Intercultural Communication. Volume 1: Ethnopragmatics and Semantic Analysis*, 135–159. Singapore: Springer.

Mullan, Kerry. 2022. On the dark side: Facebook humour used for inclusion and exclusion. *European Journal of Humour Research: Humour and Belonging* 10(2). 96–115. http://dx.doi.org/10.7592/EJHR2022.10.2.644

Mullan, Kerry. Forthcoming. "Resident Superhero": community veneration on Facebook. *Internet Pragmatics*.

Mullan, Kerry & Christine Béal. 2018. Conversational humor in French and Australian English: What makes an utterance (un)funny? *Intercultural Pragmatics: Conversational humor: Forms, functions and practices across cultures* 15(4). 457–485.

Norrby, Catrin. & Jane Warren. 2012. Address practices and social relationships in European languages. *Language and Linguistics Compass* 6(4). 225–235.

Norrick, Neal R. 2003. Issues in conversational joking. *Journal of Pragmatics* 35(9). 1333–1359.

Norrick, Neal R. 2017. Language play in conversation. In Nancy Bell (ed.), *Multiple Perspectives on Language Play*, 11–45. Berlin: Mouton De Gruyter.

Norrick, Neal R. & Claudia Bubel. 2009. Direct address as a resource of humour. In Neal R. Norrick & Delia Chiaro (eds.), *Humor in Interaction*, 29–47. Amsterdam: John Benjamins.

North, Sarah. 2007. 'The Voices, the Voices': Creativity in online conversation. *Applied Linguistics* 28(4). 538–555.

Priego-Valverde, Béatrice. 2006. How funny it is when everyone gets going! A case of co-construction of humour in conversation. *CÍRCULO de Lingüística Aplicada a la Comunicación* 27. https://dialnet.unirioja.es/servlet/articulo?codigo=2122995

Schwämmlein, Eva & Katrin Wodzicki. 2012. 'What to tell about me?' Self-presentation in online communities. *Journal of Computer-Mediated Communication* 17(4). 387–407.

Senft, Gunter. 1995. Phatic communion. In Jef Verschueren, Jan-Ola Östman & Jan Blommaert (eds.), *Handbook of Pragmatics*, 1–10. Amsterdam: John Benjamins.

Stallone, Letícia. & Michael Haugh. 2017. Joint fantasising as relational practice in Brazilian Portuguese interactions. *Language and Communication* 55. 10–23.

Svennevig, Jan. 1999. *Getting acquainted in conversation. A study of initial interactions*. Amsterdam: John Benjamins.

Thurlow, Crispin. 2012. Determined creativity: Language play in new media discourse. In Rodney Jones (ed.), *Discourse and Creativity*, 169–190. London: Pearson.

Thurlow, Crispin. 2018. Digital discourse: Locating language in new/social media. In Jean Burgess, Alice Marwick & Thomas Poell (eds.), *The Sage Handbook of Social Media*, 135–145. New York: SAGE Publications.

Tsakona, Villy. 2018. Online joint fictionalization. In Villy Tsakona & Jan Chovanec (eds.), *The Dynamics of Interactional Humour: Creating and Negotiating Humor in Everyday Encounters*, 229–255. Amsterdam: John Benjamins.

Vásquez, Camilla. 2019. *Language, Creativity and Humour Online*. London: Routledge.

Wenger, Etienne, Richard A. McDermott & William Snyder. 2002. *Cultivating Communities of Practice: A Guide to Managing Knowledge*. Cambridge: MA Harvard Business Press.

Winchatz, Michaela R. & Alexander Kozin. 2008. Comical hypothetical: arguing for a conversational phenomenon. *Discourse Studies* 10 (3). 383–405.

Yus, Francisco. 2018. Positive non-humorous effects of humor on the Internet. In Villy Tsakona & Jan Chovanec (eds.), *The Dynamics of Interactional Humour: Creating and Negotiating Humor in Everyday Encounters*, 283–304. Amsterdam: John Benjamins.

Villy Tsakona

11 "Loanword translation and corrective acts are incongruous": Debating metapragmatic stereotypes through humorous memes

Abstract: Internet memes constitute multimodal ideological texts (Wiggins 2019) conveying speakers' views and values concerning language use, among other things. Such memes may either support "correct" language use or criticize and parody those who support "correct" language use (White-Farnham 2019). Thus, they are employed by speakers participating in metapragmatic debates to convey their (often opposing) metapragmatic stereotypes, namely their culture-dependent and context-specific internalized models on how language should (not) be used (Agha 2007). The present study investigates a corpus of Greek memes produced as part of an online debate concerning the translation of specific English loanwords into Greek. The analysis concentrates on the humor attested in these memes, which expresses participants' conflicting views about, and resistance to, loanword translation. More specifically, it is shown that humor is employed to frame the proposed translation practices and equivalents as incongruous. Its analysis also brings to the surface participants' metapragmatic stereotypes concerning when a translation equivalent is deemed (un)successful, (un)usuable, stylistically (in)appropriate, etc.

Keywords: online humor, metapragmatics, citizen sociolinguistics, metapragmatic stereotypes, memes, corrective acts, translation, loanwords

1 Introduction

It is a truism by now to say that the past few decades a significant part of our daily interactions has been taking place online. In online environments, speakers employ a wide variety of semiotic resources to convey meanings, build identities, and con-

---

Acknowledgments: The author would like to thank Argiris Archakis, the anonymous reviewers, as well as the audiences of the 13th Humor Research Conference (Commerce, Texas, USA, 31 March-1 April 2023), the 5th International Communication Styles Conference: Communication in Times of Permacrisis (Krakow, Poland, 24–25 April 2023), and the 18th International Pragmatics Association (IPrA) Conference (Brussels, Belgium, 9-14 July 2023) for invaluable feedback on earlier versions of the present study.

https://doi.org/10.1515/9783110983128-012

struct representations of social reality while interacting with other speakers whom they may or may not meet offline. They express their views and stances about all kinds of topics, creating online communities and extending discussions which may have started offline or may simultaneously take place offline (see among others Zappavigna 2012; Tsakona 2017a, 2018; Vásquez 2019).

In this context, the present study will discuss how participants in social media platforms debate language–related topics; in other words, how they participate in metapragmatic debates about language. More specifically, I will explore how speakers use humorous memes as multimodal contributions to debates concerning how language should (not) be used. My aim is to demonstrate that memes and the humor included therein could provide us with interesting and precious information about how speakers conceptualize aspects of language use. In particular, the data under scrutiny show speakers' opposition and resistance to promoting translation as the "appropriate" way to handle loanwords, and to publicly performed corrective acts concerning loanword translation.

The theoretical framework of the study draws on *metapragmatics* (Verschueren 2000; Bublitz and Hübler 2007) and *citizen sociolinguistics* (Rymes and Leone 2014). Both fields investigate talk about talk, but the latter places emphasis on how such talk emerges and is negotiated in online environments (see Section 2). The metapragmatic discourse scrutinized here consists of Greek humorous memes referring to loanword translation and respective corrective acts. Hence, Section (3) explores memes as metapragmatic and ideological texts using humor to argue and criticize. The sociocultural context where the data examined were produced and interpreted is presented in Section (4). Then, in Section (5), the goals and methodology of the analysis are discussed, while Section (6) includes the analysis of indicative examples of the data. Finally, Section (7) summarizes the findings of the study, points out some limitations, and maps further areas of inquiry.

2 In between metapragmatics and citizen sociolinguistics

Metapragmatic research[1] aims to investigate speakers' implicit or explicit views and norms concerning language use and underlines the inseparability between speakers' understanding of sociopragmatic phenomena and their own practices

---

1 The brief theoretical discussion of metapragmatics draws on Tsakona (2020a: 19–27).

in various contexts. Jaworski, Coupland, and Galasiński (2004: 3) provide a comprehensive account of what the study of metapragmatics can bring to the surface:

> How people represent language and communication processes is, at one level, important data for understanding how social groups value and orient to language and communication (varieties, processes, effects). This approach includes the study of folk beliefs about language, language attitudes and language awareness, and these overlapping perspectives have established histories within sociolinguistics. Metalinguistic representations may enter public consciousness and come to constitute structured understandings, perhaps even "common sense" understandings – of how language works, what it is usually like, what certain ways of speaking connote and imply, what they ought to be like. That is, metalanguage can work at an ideological level, and influence people's actions and priorities in a wide range of ways, some clearly visible and others much less so (emphasis in the original).

In other words, metapragmatic research not only brings to the surface more or less latent norms of language use, but also reveals how such norms are circulated, debated, and eventually become entrenched and often naturalized among speakers. It may help us trace the interplay between pragmatic norms and actual use: pragmatic norms and conventions shape actual use which in turn reinforces or weakens the dissemination and validity of the norms, depending on whether speakers decide to comply with them or challenge them. In Verschueren's (1999: 196) words, "in social life, *conceptualizations and practices* are inseparable. Consequently, there is no way of understanding forms of social behavior without gaining insight into the way in which the social actors themselves habitually conceptualize what it is they are doing" (emphasis in the original; see also Verschueren 2000: 451; Kádár and Haugh 2013: 183).

Agha (1998, 2004, 2007) calls speakers' conceptualizations and understandings of sociopragmatic phenomena *metapragmatic stereotypes*: speakers internalize models of language use which guide their own linguistic behavior and enable them to make judgments about their own language use or that of others. Such models aim at fixing and stabilizing the variation attested in language use. Metapragmatic stereotypes influence speakers' linguistic performance and interpretation of discourse in real settings, and are culturally–specific and context–dependent. They are shaped by the sociocultural context speakers interact in and, more specifically, by the ways discourse is used and evaluated therein.[2]

---

[2] It should be noted here that the concept of *language ideologies* is similar to that of *metapragmatic stereotypes*. The former consists of "habitual ways of thinking and speaking about language and language use" (Verschueren 1999: 198), or of "persistent frames of interpretation related to the nature and social functioning of language" (Verschueren 2000: 450; see also Kádár and Haugh 2013: 200–204). The discussion of the similarities and subtle differences (if any) between these concepts lies beyond the scope of the present study.

Speakers often have different views on how language is or should be used: the metapragmatic stereotype of one speaker may, to a greater or lesser degree, deviate from, or even compete with, that of the other, thus leading to conflicts and negotiations on the "(un)common", "(un)desirable", "(in)appropriate", and "(in)correct" language use as well as to defending specific interpretations as "the only valid/correct ones". A single speaker's metapragmatic stereotype may even exhibit differences from one communicative setting to another. As a result, metapragmatic stereotypes may mark group boundaries (e.g. between those who agree and those who disagree on the definition and/or functions of a sociopragmatic phenomenon) and may acquire an exclusive/inclusive potential and function in context.

When it comes to investigating metapragmatics, Kádár and Haugh (2013: 192–204) discuss a wide variety of methodological approaches including corpus analysis, lexical/conceptual mapping, metapragmatic interviews and questionnaires, naturally occurring discourse (e.g. face–to–face interactions, media commentary, historical documents/texts) or elicited discourse (e.g. interviews, diaries, reports; see also Verschueren 1999: 196; Bublitz and Hübler 2007; Xydopoulos, Tzortzatou, and Archakis 2019). Through such methods, scholars concentrate on metapragmatic resources such as language descriptions (whether scholarly or not), speech representation, deixis, hedges, contextualization cues, labeling of speech acts, cohesive devices, and explicit comments on language use.

The investigation of metapragmatic discourse is not, however, without limitations and challenges. In case metapragmatic discourse is elicited, it may be influenced by what Labov (1972) calls *observer's paradox*, namely the effect the presence of a researcher has on the collected data. Speakers are more or less likely to conform to (what they think are) the expectations of the researcher, whether consciously or subconsciously. On the other hand, authentic, spontaneous data which would be preferable is not particularly easy to obtain. It is often difficult to know in advance when and where participants will spontaneously discuss sociopragmatic phenomena, and to manage to record such discussions.

In an effort to search for and collect metapragmatic discourse, researchers tend to resort to online discussions concerning sociopragmatic phenomena (see among others Tsakona 2013, 2017b, 2020a; Aslan and Vásquez 2018). Such development comes as no surprise if we consider the fact that a significant part of our communication nowadays takes place in online environments and its traces may remain available for collection and analysis for quite some time. Given the above, Rymes and Leone (2014) advocate for what they call *citizen sociolinguistics*, namely the study of speakers' understandings of sociopragmatic phenomena, focusing on the views (i.e. metapragmatic stereotypes) expressed online by non–experts (i.e. *citizen sociolinguists*). Online environments become the places where speakers' metapragmatic stereotypes are not only expressed and disseminated, but also shaped and negotiated, as in such contexts a wide range of linguistic varieties and uses are attested and social meanings and values are ascribed to them. In Rymes and Leone's (2014: 38–39) terms, citizen sociolinguistics involves

> the study of the world of language and communication by the people who use it and who, as such, have devised ways to understand it that may be more relevant than the ways supercomputers or professional sociolinguistics have developed. What we can learn from citizen sociolinguistics, which we can learn neither from a disciplinary sociolinguist nor a supercomputer, is the nuanced social value that people put on certain ways of speaking: value that is itself developed through networks of participatory culture.

What the study of metapragmatics and citizen sociolinguistics have in common is a focus on talk about talk as an invaluable source of sociopragmatic meanings and information. Citizen sociolinguistics, however, seeks for such meanings and information specifically in online environments, where speakers discuss and negotiate those sociopragmatic phenomena which attract their attention. Citizen sociolinguists pose the questions they attempt to explore, and choose the sociopragmatic phenomena they concentrate on.

For the purposes of the present study, I draw on the concept of metapragmatic stereotypes to account for Greek speakers' views about corrective acts and loanword translation. The fact that such stereotypes will be explored in memes produced by citizen sociolinguists, disseminated through, and collected from online sources renders my endeavor a study not only in metapragmatics but also in citizen sociolinguistics. In this sense, memes and the humor included therein will be perceived as valuable material allowing me to bring to the surface speakers' metapragmatic stereotypes.

3 Memes as metapragmatic discourse

In recent years, research on memes has proliferated. Given that memes constitute a significant part of speakers' online experiences, especially if they participate in social media platforms, it is not accidental that this genre has attracted the attention of scholars coming from different fields (linguistics, semiotics, sociology, media studies, political communication, folklore, etc.). In most cases, memes are perceived as digital artefacts conveying cultural information and sociopolitical stances, while drawing on diverse intertextual sources and multiplying rather quickly, as speakers redesign them to suit their own communicative and social purposes. Memes are considered prototypical instances of contemporary internet culture reflecting and enhancing speaker involvement and everyday creativity.

Given that memes are based on the combination of semiotic resources coming from different sources and carrying various connotations, they can be used for the representation and dissemination of complex ideas and values, often in an unconventional manner (see among others Shifman 2014; Wiggins and Bowers 2015; Tsakona 2018; Denisova 2019; Wiggins 2019; Piata 2020).

Humor appears to be an important ingredient of memes, even though it is pointed out that not all memes are humorous (Wiggins and Bowers 2015: 1899). Several studies concentrate on the humorous dimension of memes, which turns out to be a key factor in increasing their popularity and speeding up their dissemination. Shifman observes that memetic humor "augments sharing, as people wish to amuse their friends and to be associated with wittiness" (Shifman 2014: 96), while at the same time "meme genres play an important role in the construction of group identity and social boundaries" (Shifman 2014: 100; see also Tsakona 2017a, 2018).

The presence of humor in memes as well as their (sometimes) trivial, mundane topics have led some scholars to perceive them as *phatic communion* (in Malinowski's [1923] 1989 sense) enhancing connectivity, dissolving silence among online participants, and projecting identities related to the communities created in social media platforms (see among others Zappavigna 2012; Varis and Blommaert 2015). Such perspectives on memes tend to undermine or overlook the fact that memes more often than not address large audiences to convey more or less latent ideological messages (see among others Yoon 2016; Tsakona 2017a, 2018; Denisova 2019; Archakis and Tsakona 2021). Like all texts, memes are *ideological* texts conveying social meanings and stereotypes concerning a wide variety of sociopolitical topics and events. More specifically, Wiggins (2019: 11) suggests that a meme is defined

> as a remixed, iterated message that can be rapidly diffused by members of participatory digital culture for the purpose of satire, parody, critique, or other discursive activity. (. . .) Its function is to posit an argument, visually, in order to commence, extend, counter, or influence a discourse. Naturally this can occur within humorous contexts; however, humor is merely the surface–level entry point for social salience. Digging deeper, one can view the argument within the meme which is usually if not always representative of an ideological practice.

Wiggins (2019) also refers to the significance of intertextuality for the creation and dissemination of memes. In particular, drawing on Giddens (1984), he insists on the importance of *memory traces* resulting in memes exhibiting structural (e.g. thematic, semiotic) similarities and eventually in memetic systems or cycles (see also Attardo 2020; Tsakona 2020b):

> Memetic systems are defined by the presence of an emergent meme (an altered form of spreadable media) that is recursively reproduced in a process in which agents adhere to an

unstated but known structure. (. . .) In memetic terms, *memory traces* (or structures) are the procedures of designing specific memetic content in such a way to be recognized as memes in order to promote a recursive reconstitution of related memes (Wiggins 2019: 50, emphasis in the original).

Research on memes has also pointed out that they often constitute a "discursive response" (Wiggins 2019: 52) to events that become well-known through the media. In such cases, meme creators and disseminators comment on various aspects of the related events, offer their criticism, and build online communities on the basis of common values and/or interests, even though the members of such communities may never meet offline. Understanding the meanings put forward by memes presupposes not only familiarity with the event commented on, but also alignment with the stances or ideologies expressed therein (Zappavigna 2012; Shifman 2014: 4; Tsakona 2017a, 2017b, 2018, 2020a, 2020b; Aslan & Vásquez 2018; Wiggins 2019; Attardo 2020; Vásquez and Aslan 2021).

In sum, the present study considers memes as ideological texts aimed at criticizing specific events. For the creation of memes, intertextuality and constant redesigning play a significant role resulting in the formation of meme cycles on a specific topic. The ideologies expressed in memes are, in the present study, related to language: speakers use humorous memes to participate in metapragmatic debates and to convey their metapragmatic stereotypes concerning loanword translation and relevant corrective acts, thus becoming citizen sociolinguists (see Section 2).

Research on memes including metapragmatic stereotypes, namely conveying speakers' views about how language should (not) be used, is, to the best of my knowledge, scarce but not non–existent. Švelch and Sherman (2018) investigate the use of humor for stigmatizing and "correcting" linguistic "errors", thus contributing to *language policing* (in Blommaert's 2013 sense) and to enacting standard language ideologies. More specifically, Švelch and Sherman (2018) argue that memes, among other forms of humor, are often employed by participants in social media platforms to note and negatively evaluate "deviant" language use and to design and put forward "correct" uses instead. Thus, humor serves as a conservative disciplinary force (in Billig's 2005 sense) imposing standard language use and deterring speakers from using non–standard expressions (see also Sherman and Švelch 2015; Vásquez and Aslan 2021).

In addition, White–Farnham (2019: 210) concentrates on what she calls *grammar memes* which "resist the growing and progressive position that a wide range of Englishes exist and their usage is acceptable" and "perpetuate beliefs about the use of correct English by making claims of superiority". Such memes, she claims (White–Farnham 2019: 213–215), constitute arguments in ongoing conversations

and debates about grammar usage. White–Farnham (2019: 216–218) distinguishes three categories of grammar memes:
1) *traditionalist grammar memes* which are the most numerous in her dataset: they mock "grammar misuse", involve extreme expressions of strictness, and support claims of superiority for those who follow "grammar rules";
2) *backlash memes* which overturn traditionalist grammar ones, highlight the negative social consequences of constantly correcting people's language use, and criticize and parody those who do it;
3) *narrative/instructional memes* which expressly teach "correct grammar" in friendlier terms than traditionalist ones do.

In a similar vein, Tsakona and Tsami (2021) analyze memes stigmatizing dialectal varieties and promoting the use of standard and prestigious varieties in the media. Their findings suggest that humorous memes function as commentary promoting metapragmatic stereotypes according to which a strict distinction should exist between those standard and/or prestigious varieties that are "allowed" in public and those non–standard varieties which are "forbidden" in public. Speakers not abiding by this distinction end up being stigmatized and ridiculed. Consequently, the conceptualization of language varieties as strictly defined entities meant for use in certain, well–defined sociocultural contexts is confirmed and further reinforced through memetic humor.

It therefore seems that memes and humor are often exploited by citizen sociolinguists to comment on language use. In most cases, such contributions appear to favor standard language use and to stigmatize non–standard use. However, there may be cases when standard language use and respective corrective acts are humorously denigrated and resisted – and this is achieved through what White–Farnham (2019) calls *backlash memes*. The data examined here seem to belong to this category.

4 Loanword translation in Greece: Contextualizing the data under scrutiny

On November 3rd, 2020, only a few days before the second lockdown began in Greece due to the COVID–19 pandemic, Georgios Babiniotis, Emeritus and Honorary Professor of Linguistics at the National and Kapodistrian University of Athens, posted on his personal Facebook account his proposal concerning the translation of three English loanwords, which are part of everyday use in colloquial Greek. In particular, he suggested that Greek speakers replace the words *lockdown*, *deliv-*

ery, and *takeaway* with the Greek equivalents *απαγορευτικό* (lit. 'prohibition'), *τροφοδιανομή* (lit. 'food-delivery') and *για το σπίτι* (lit. '[to be taken/consumed] at home') respectively. His proposals quickly became viral as online news articles reproduced and commented on them (either positively or negatively).

Simultaneously, a significant number of memes[3] were produced and posted online, also becoming viral. So, the data of the present study originate mostly in social media but also in news articles reporting specifically on the creation and dissemination of such material, and were collected from November 4th, 2020 until June 17th, 2021. The collection started immediately after Babiniotis' online proposal was posted on November 3rd, 2020, and lasted until the production and dissemination of such memes seemed to fade out. The dataset includes 174 memes: 106 of them (60.93%) refer specifically to loanword translation and related phenomena, while the rest of them (68 memes, 39.08%) refer to political and social issues (e.g. the COVID-19 pandemic and the measures the Greek government took to contain it, Greek celebrities, football slogans, Christmas holidays). For the purposes of the present study I will concentrate on the first category.

Why such a commotion over the translation of English loanwords into Greek and how does this relate to Prof. Babiniotis? Some contextual information is deemed necessary here. Like many languages around the globe, since the end of World War II, Greek has received a significant number of loanwords from English, both as part of everyday use and as part of specialized registers. Such loanwords have often been adjusted phonologically, morphologically, and semantically to the particularities of the Greek language, so they remain more or less easily recognizable by Greek speakers; or they have been translated, thus becoming calques and are more or less invisible to Greek speakers.[4] Given the above, it is not uncommon to hear or read in the Greek public sphere complaints or even protests against loanwords from English (especially against the visible ones), which are perceived as a threat to the Greek language and its "purity", potentially contributing to its "distortion" and even "death". According to such metapragmatic stereotypes, the Greek language should not contain English (or other) loanwords at all. These stereotypes

---

[3] The dataset examined here includes exclusively a specific kind of meme, namely *image macros*: "an image macro consists of text script superimposed over an image. In this genre, the particular background image tends to remain fairly constant within the meme; it is the text script that users continually modify" (Brideau and Berret 2014: 309). The term *meme* is preferred here for ease of reference.

[4] For example, the English word *lady* has been assimilated into Greek as *λαίδη* [léði] 'a woman of high social position' (cf. loanword adjustment), while the word *mouse* referring to the handheld device of a computer has been translated into Greek as *ποντίκι* (thus becoming a calque).

are also reproduced within Greek education (see among others Apostolou–Panara 1997; Anastasiadi–Symeonidi 2001; Tatsioka 2010; Papadopoulou 2020).

On the other hand, such metapragmatic stereotypes have triggered extensive research on the loanwords used by Greek speakers, focusing mostly but not exclusively on English ones (see among others Triandafyllidis 1905; Swanson 1958; Anastasiadi–Symeonidi 1994; Apostolou–Panara 1997; Tatsioka 2010; Papadopoulou 2020). Such research usually places emphasis on the phonological, morphological, semantic, etc. adjustment of loanwords to Greek linguistic particularities, but also on sociolinguistic factors considering borrowing to be a result of bilingualism, the high international prestige of English, globalization, etc. Even among researchers, however, one can trace negative metapragmatic stereotypes concerning loanwords, according to which borrowing is metaphorically framed as a disease which needs to be prevented early on (i.e. before they spread) rather than cured later on (see among others Anastasiadi–Symeonidi 2001: 69–70).

Research on loanword translation extends to putting forward and trying to establish specific criteria for what is deemed as a "successful" translation equivalent or calque (see Goutsos 1999b; Tsakona 2007: 126–129, and references therein). According to such criteria, translation equivalents would rather:
1) follow the grammatical rules and conventions and be compatible with the style/register of the (con)texts where they are expected to be used;
2) be brief and simple;
3) be semantically transparent and precise;
4) avoid synonymy, polysemy, and unwarranted or inappropriate connotations;
5) be reversible (i.e. those who speak the language of the original term are expected to be able to infer the term when exposed to the translation equivalent).

Needless to say, all such criteria are in fact metapragmatic stereotypes accepted, disseminated, and perhaps eventually imposed by linguists and translators reflecting their own evaluations on the "(un)successful" translation of loanwords in Greek. As such, they constitute their contributions to the ongoing metapragmatic debate on this topic.

To the best of my knowledge, the only study investigating Greek speakers' views and attitudes (i.e. their metapragmatic stereotypes) on the use of English loanwords in Greek is Tatsioka's (2010). Among other things, Tatsioka argues that there are intergenerational differences concerning such use: older speakers of Greek use fewer such loanwords than younger ones do, most probably because the latter are more familiar with English and their contact with this language is more intense through education, contemporary media, marketing, products, etc. Interestingly, both generations consider English loanwords to be a threat for the Greek language (the younger one even more so), without however suggesting that they should be avoided and, most importantly, without trying to refrain from using them themselves. Tatsioka's study thus maps an interesting contradiction between speakers' views/metapragmatic stereotypes and practices.

It is exactly in this context that Babiniotis makes his suggestions. His reputation as a linguistics professor is remarkable as he has been a prolific author, has taught generations of Greek language teachers and linguists (including the present author), has edited a significant number of dictionaries of Modern Greek, and co-authored grammars of Modern Greek. He has also served as Rector of the National and Kapodistrian University of Athens and Minister of Education and Religious Affairs, among many other administrative posts. He is also particularly well-known for his articles in the press and his frequent participation in TV shows since the 1980s, where he often discusses the "correct" use of Greek, "correct" spelling and grammar, and the "correct" translation of loanwords, among other things.[5] He could therefore be perceived as a *language missionary*, namely

> a person who has a much greater role in influencing the course of linguistic change in a community than one would normally expect to be the case for a particular individual. Such individuals will usually be people who for some reason are respected and accepted as insiders by members of the community, but who differ from the other members of the community in their linguistic characteristics (Trudgill 2003: 76).

Given the above, it is hardly surprising that Babiniotis uses social media to propose the translation of three English loanwords into Greek (i.e. *lockdown, delivery*, and *takeaway*). Two of these words (i.e. *delivery* and *takeaway*) were not recently introduced; on the contrary, they have been used by Greek speakers for quite some time. But due to the measures imposed by the Greek government to prevent the spread of COVID-19 disease, all three words have become prominent. Since restaurants were closed for months and people were forced to eat at their homes, those restaurants which provided takeaway and delivery services were the only ones which could stay open and offer their services during the lockdown. Needless to say, during the pandemic, the number of restaurants, bars, coffee shops, etc. which offered delivery and/or takeaway services increased significantly, together with the number of people who worked in such places. So, the words were repeatedly heard not only in casual conversations but also in public discussions concerning the state measures against the disease.

---

[5] The use of the term *correct* instead of *standard* is not accidental here. Babiniotis' proposals do not always coincide with standard use or may not turn out to be included in it, after all. On the contrary, he often attempts to modify what is perceived as standard (e.g. in spelling; see among others Goutsos 1999a: 167–168).

As we will discuss extensively in the analysis (Section 6), Babiniotis' translation proposals appear to have been evaluated by citizen sociolinguists as inappropriate and untimely, given that Greek people were faced with far more complex problems and conditions due to the pandemic than to how to speak "correct" Greek. This is clearly reflected in the data collected for the purposes of the present study, where meme creators and reproducers seem to make fun of such endeavors and eventually impositions, and to question their effectiveness. Interestingly, the "untimeliness" of his proposals is commented on by Babiniotis himself in the introduction of his post, yet he does not refrain from posting it. It could therefore be suggested that Babiniotis and meme creators operate under two different and opposing metapragmatic stereotypes concerning loanword translation: the former rejects the use of "visible" English loanwords in Greek and proposes their replacement with calques (*τροφοδιανομή/delivery*) or Greek equivalents already in use (*απαγορευτικό/lockdown, για το σπίτι/takeaway*), thus reproducing a negative evaluation of loanwords; the latter seem to prefer the English loanwords which are already in wide circulation and to reject not only their translation but also Babiniotis' corrective intervention. In other words, the metapragmatic stereotypes expressed by meme creators as citizen sociolinguists are positive for English loanwords but negative for loanword translation as well as for Babiniotis' corrective intervention.[6]

Babiniotis' proposal could be perceived in terms of what Moschonas (2022) calls a *corrective act* or *corrective*.[7] *Correctives* constitute directive speech acts (in Austin's 1962 sense) with a metalanguage–to–language direction of fit (Searle 1983); in other words, they constitute metalinguistic directives meant to influence language use (Moschonas 2022). They consist of three parts:
1) a *prohibitive/proscriptive* part – e.g. *one should neither say nor write X*;
2) a *normative* part – e.g. *one should say or write Y*; and
3) an *explicative* part – e.g. *because Z*, which offers a justification or invokes a general "rule", but is optional (Moschonas 2022: 319).

Babiniotis' intervention takes the exact form of a corrective aimed at stigmatizing the loanwords (i.e. the *prohibitive/proscriptive* part) and at replacing the loanwords with Greek equivalents (i.e. the *normative* part). Babiniotis' introductory comment in his post concerning the "need" to avoid English loanwords could be perceived as an *explicative* part. Babiniotis' decision to post his proposals (among

---

6 On opposing metapragmatic stereotypes concerning "correct" Greek language use, see also Xydopoulos, Tzortzatou, and Archakis (2019).
7 Moschonas (2022) distinguishes between two kinds of *correctives*: *correctives proper* and *prescriptives*. Babiniotis' proposal constitutes a corrective proper. The term *corrective (act)* will be used here for ease of reference.

numerous others) online indicates his awareness of the potential of the medium: in order for correctives to reach wider audiences they need to be reproduced in different media and platforms (Moschonas 2022: 327). The reproduction of his post in online articles and its extensive re-posting confirm this. As a matter of fact, the word *απαγορευτικό* instead of *lockdown* was adopted by some newspapers, TV channels, and other media for some time, but it seems that it was eventually abandoned by most of them.

Explicit resistance to the correctives came in the form of memes posted online and parodying Babiniotis' proposals (cf. White-Farnham's 2019 *backlash* memes in Section 3). Hence, here I consider memes as part of the online metapragmatic debate between a language missionary and citizen sociolinguists. Memes are more often than not investigated as cycles of artefacts sharing a common theme or drawing from the same intertextual resources. The present dataset further allows us to explore memes as multimodal contributions to an ongoing metapragmatic discussion in the Greek public sphere concerning loanword translation and, by extension, publicly performed corrective acts.

5 Goals and methodology

The aim of the present analysis is to investigate the role of memes and humor as metapragmatic commentary on the ongoing public debate concerning English loanword translation into Greek and respective corrective acts. In particular, it will be shown that meme creators and reproducers as citizen sociolinguists resist the translation of English loanwords commonly used in Greek and, by extension, object to corrective acts by considering both the translation and the correctives to be incongruous and hence funny. Interestingly, in the dataset examined here no one defended Babiniotis' proposals. Furthermore, I intend to bring to the surface exactly which metapragmatic stereotypes citizen sociolinguists put forward via humorous memes, namely what and why they consider to be (in)appropriate concerning loanword translation and publicly performed corrective acts.

To this end, I will use the *Discourse Theory of Humor* (henceforth DTH; see Tsakona 2020a; Tsakona and Tsami 2021; Archakis and Tsakona 2021). The DTH draws on previous linguistic theories of humor such as the *Semantic Script Theory of Humor* (Raskin 1985) and the *General Theory of Verbal Humor* (Attardo 2001) when it comes to defining humor: humor is based on an incongruity/script opposition,[8] namely on the incompatibility between two different scripts evoked

---

[8] The terms are used interchangeably.

within a single text. The first one is usually "expected", "normal", or "conventional" in the specific context, while the second one is perceived as "unexpected", "abnormal", or "unconventional", subverting or even canceling the meanings evoked within the first script and context in general. The DTH places particular emphasis on the contextual parameters affecting the production and interpretation of humorous discourse. Analyses in DTH terms are meant to highlight the interplay among the sociocultural context of humor production and reception, the generic particularities of humorous texts, and their semiotic ones. This analytical model includes three Analytical Foci (AF) for analyzing humorous texts:

Analytical Focus 1: Sociocultural Assumptions

Sociocultural Assumptions include the background knowledge that is deemed necessary for processing humor and is co-constructed as shared. Such knowledge may differ more or less from one community to another and shapes individual preferences and differences in humor use. Participants' background knowledge determines what is considered expected, conventional, or normal in a specific community, and simultaneously what is considered unexpected, unconventional, and abnormal therein (i.e. the script opposition), and eventually defines who is held responsible for potential deviations (i.e. the target of humor). In other words, sociocultural assumptions form the basis for evaluating or perceiving specific actions or people as incongruous.

Here, the sociocultural assumptions necessary for creating, comprehending, and analyzing the memes in question involve the background knowledge concerning the translation of English loanwords into Greek and the respective metapragmatic debates (see Section 4). It is within such sociocultural assumptions that diverse and opposing metapragmatic stereotypes emerge and are negotiated (see Section 6).

Analytical Focus 2: Genre

Genre pertains to the types of texts where humor appears. Humor may be indispensable to certain genres (e.g. canned jokes, stand-up comedy), more or less common in others (e.g. informal conversation among peers, advertisements), and usually absent from some (e.g. legal or religious texts). Genre also determines (or may be determined by) the sociopragmatic goals and functions of humor: humor may highlight ingroup/outgroup boundaries, create solidarity and reinforce intimacy, express criticism, mitigate aggressive or face–threatening moves/acts, disparage the Other, build gender, ethnic, political, or other identities, etc.

In the present case, genre pertains to memes including metapragmatic comments on loanword translation and relevant corrective acts. Such memes constitute a multimodal response to Babiniotis' Facebook post showing speakers' disagreement with, and resistance to, his proposals. Such a function is compatible with the conceptualization of memes as ideological texts conveying criticism concerning various sociopragmatic phenomena (see Section 3).

Analytical Focus 3: Text

Text involves the semantic content, the stylistic choices of a stretch of discourse (e.g. wordplay, style), the placement of humorous utterances (e.g. punch or jab lines), and the visual, slapstick, acoustic/musical elements, etc. therein. It also involves the contextualization cues accompanying this stretch of discourse as well as the various, perhaps also multimodal, reactions offered by the recipients.

As we are about to see (in Section 6), in most cases, meme creators employ fictional corrective acts (see Section 4) mimicking Babiniotis' style and, in general, parodying his frequent public interventions in the media. From a semiotic point of view, they are designed so as to be clear as to their purposes and attitudes: they employ photos of Babiniotis, expressions constituting corrective acts (e.g. *It's not X, it's Y; Why say X since we have the word Y; Let's not say X, let's say Y*), the specific words/translation equivalents Babiniotis referred to or similar ones, etc., in an effort, on the one hand, to establish intertextual links to Babiniotis' post and other of his interventions; and, on the other, to undermine the significance of his proposal and to imply that it is not going to be accepted, after all. All these semiotic resources could be perceived as memory traces (see Section 3) connecting not only the memes to each other but also connecting the memes to Babiniotis' proposal and to the wider metapragmatic debate on loanword translation through corrective acts.

6 Data analysis

The analysis of the data in DTH terms brings to the surface six metapragmatic stereotypes offering justifications for avoiding loanword translation and respective corrective acts (see Sections 6.1–6.6). Even though the categories identified may overlap in some cases (e.g. Figure 8), I have attempted a quantitative analysis of my sample (see Table 1):

Table 1: Quantitative account of the data.

	Metapragmatic stereotypes attested in the memes examined	Number of memes (%)
1	Translation equivalents should not carry inappropriate connotations.	11 (10.37%)
2	Translation equivalents should not sound uncommon and unusable.	17 (16.03%)
3	Loanword translation should take into consideration stylistic effects and differences.	41 (38.67%)
4	Loanword translation should be proposed by speakers who are proficient in English.	9 (8.49%)
5	Common informal expressions should be used in colloquial speech.	14 (13.20%)
6	Corrective acts should not be performed.	14 (13.20%)
	Total	106 (100%)

It is also interesting to note here that most of the memes examined here constitute instances of *stylistic/register humor* (see Attardo 2001; Piata 2020; Tsakona and Tsami 2021), as they juxtapose expressions perceived as belonging to different, incompatible styles and highlight stylistic incongruities between actual (colloquial) language use and the proposed "corrections". The only ones which may not constitute register humor in this sense are those which frame corrective acts *per se* as incongruous (see Section 6.6).

6.1 Translation equivalents should not carry inappropriate connotations

The first metapragmatic stereotype emerging from the data under scrutiny relates to the connotations surrounding the Greek equivalents proposed for the translation of English loanwords. In particular, citizen sociolinguists seem to suggest that loanwords should not be translated because the proposed equivalents may carry inappropriate connotations; or that translation equivalents should be carefully chosen/created so as not to carry inappropriate connotations. The following examples (Figures 1–2) refer to fictional translation proposals involving equivalents with inappropriate connotations:[9]

Figure 1: Babiniotis (on the left): Let's not say Big Brother!
Interviewer (on the right): What shall we say?
Babiniotis: Big brother/faggot!

In Figure 1, a photo of Babiniotis is chosen from a TV show. He is represented to propose a translation equivalent for *Big Brother* referring either to Orwell's *1984* novel or to the popular reality show. The proposed Greek equivalent *αδερφάρα* is indeed a literal translation of the English term: the suffix –*άρα* meaning 'big, great' is added to the noun *αδερφός* 'brother'. However, the word *αδερφάρα* is already commonly used in informal Greek as a derogatory term meaning 'faggot'. Humor is built on the pun and the semantic distance between the common/derogatory and the uncommon/literal meanings of the word *αδερφάρα*.

Figure 2 involves a similar case. The photo employed to create this meme features Babiniotis talking about one of the dictionaries he has edited, and has been commonly exploited for the creation of such memes, thus serving as a template (see also Figures 6, 8–10). Babiniotis is here represented to supposedly propose a translation equivalent for the name of the American rock band Red Hot Chili Peppers. The

---

[9] All the data presented here were translated by the author for the purposes of the present study. Some humor may have been lost along the way.

Figure 2: "It's not Red Hot Chili Peppers, it's red pepper flakes".

translation equivalent proposed is μπούκοβο 'red pepper flakes', which is a commonly used word in the Greek culinary register.[10] The proposed translation equivalent carries inappropriate connotations *vis–á–vis* the original English proper name, so humor is built on a pun involving different uses of the word *red hot chili pepper*, either as a spice or as the proper name of a rock band. In addition, such proper names are hardly ever translated into Greek (unless for humorous effect), hence humor is also based on exaggeration: corrective acts may sometimes be taken to extremes.

Via such memes, citizen sociolinguists suggest that loanword translation may result in recontextualizing widely used words whose meaning is irrelevant to the intended one. So, humor is based on the script opposition "Greek translation equivalents should not carry/carry inappropriate connotations". This script opposition resonates and reproduces the metapragmatic stereotype put forward by linguists and translators, according to which translation equivalents would rather avoid synonymy, polysemy, and unwarranted or inappropriate connotations (see Section 4). What is more, it indirectly criticizes Babiniotis' suggestion concerning the translation of *lockdown*: the proposed term *απαγορευτικό* is already commonly employed in Greek, mostly referring to the prohibition of departure imposed on ships due to bad weather conditions, hence it carries inappropriate

---

10 Ironically, the Greek word *μπούκοβο* is an assimilated loanword of Slavic origin, hence a Slavic word is here used to replace an English one.

connotations when recontextualized to refer to movement restrictions imposed on citizens due to the pandemic. Inappropriate connotations could be the problem with the translation of *takeaway* as για το σπίτι '[to be taken/consumed] at home' as well. Products offered for takeaway can be taken and consumed not only at home (as the translation suggests) but also at the office, in the car, outside the shop, while walking, commuting, etc.

6.2 Translation equivalents should not sound uncommon and unusable

According to the memes belonging to this category, loanword translation may result in the creation of calques/neologisms, which, at least at first sight, sound strange, uncommon, and unusable. Figures 3–4 are illustrative of this category:

Figure 3: Robin: Batm . . . .
Batman: Batman

In Figures 3–4, the humor is untranslatable. In Figure 3, a panel from the Batman comics series is employed featuring Batman slapping his partner Robin on the face, because he tried to call him by his English name. Batman performs a corrective act (verbally and through physical violence) similar to that of Babiniotis' when it comes to English loanwords: Robin should have called him Νυχτεριδάντρα, which is a compound word literally translating 'Batman' into Greek (νυχτερίδα 'bat' + άντρας 'man'). Humor is produced through Batman's exaggerated reaction (i.e. slapping) and, most importantly, through the creation of a calque/neologism which sounds quite uncommon, if not weird, and hence funny in Greek. Similarly, Figure 4 represents Babiniotis in his gown for official ceremonies as a Rector of the National

Figure 4: "It's not 'hot dog', it's 'hot dog'".

and Kapodistrian University of Athens supposedly proposing a translation equivalent for the English loanword *hot dog* which is most commonly used in Greek and whose literal translation (*ζεστό σκυλί* 'hot dog') would also result in a calque/neologism sounding incongruous and hence funny in Greek.

Even though in such cases the proposed translation equivalents capture the literal meanings of the English loanwords with remarkable accuracy, it seems that citizen sociolinguists resist the replacement of such common words with new, so far non–existent ones. The script opposition producing humor in such examples could be formulated as follows: "Translation equivalents should not sound/sound uncommon and unusable". In other words, humor reproduces a metapragmatic stereotype according to which a translation equivalent may not be successful if it sounds uncommon and is eventually judged as unusable by speakers. In such cases, loanwords should not be translated. The memes in this category echo experts' metapragmatic stereotypes concerning the grammatical, semantic, etc. conventions to be followed in loanword translation (see Section 4). Such a stereotype seems to be related to Babiniotis' proposal concerning the English word *delivery* (specifically referring to restaurants' delivery services): this word is tentatively replaced with the calque/neologism *τροφοδιανομή* 'food–delivery'. Although the translation equivalent is the most accurate, it may also sound uncommon and unusable.

6.3 Loanword translation should take into consideration stylistic effects and differences

This category comprises memes suggesting that loanword translation may result in words or expressions which seem to belong to a higher or lower style than the one attested in the expected context of use for this word or expression. Figures 5–6 belong to this category:

Figure 5: "It's not click away, it's take what you want and hit the road".

Figure 6: "Don't say click away, say *molon labe*/come and take them".

In both examples, the translated word is the same: the term *click away* appears to be a Greek neologism (or a pseudo–loanword) created by the Greek government out of English words, equivalent to the English expression *click and collect*. *Click away* refers to a shopping method which was not very common in the past, but became so during the Greek lockdown: customers would place their order online (or via the telephone), the shop would prepare their package, and customers would visit the shop only to pick up their order (and perhaps pay, if they had not already paid online). This would limit personal contact to a minimum, thus preventing the coronavirus from spreading through such service encounters. In Figure 5, Babiniotis is represented as speaking in public and proposing a rather low style equivalent for *click away*: the idiomatic expression *και πούλο* 'and hit the road' in particular could be perceived as too informal and perhaps also rude. On the contrary, in Figure 6, his fictional proposal involves replacing *click away* with what the ancient king of Sparta Leonidas is reported to have said when Persians asked Spartans to surrender before the Battle of Thermopylae (480 BC): *μολών λαβέ/molon labe* 'come and take them'. The Ancient Greek phrase reproduces the meaning of *click away* but simultaneously sounds too formal (and out of context) for everyday shopping.

Humor is employed here to criticize translation equivalents which do not take into consideration stylistic effects and differences and end up being stylistically "inappropriate". The relevant script opposition could be formulated as follows: "Loanword translation should/does not take into consideration stylistic effects and differences". The emerging metapragmatic stereotype proposes that loanword translation should provide us with expressions not only semantically but also stylistically appropriate. In other words, translation equivalents are perceived as appropriate and hence successful only when the proposed equivalent seems to be stylistically compatible with its context of use. Otherwise, loanwords should not be translated. This stereotype may not be directly related to the specific proposals Babiniotis made, but it seems to coincide with widespread metapragmatic stereotypes followed by experts when translating loanwords (see Section 4).

6.4 Loanword translation should be proposed by speakers who are proficient in English

Another category of memes identified in the data examined here employs humor to put forward a metapragmatic stereotype which suggests that loanword translations presuppose proficiency in English: they should only be attempted by speakers who are proficient in English. The following examples are indicative.

In Figure 7, Babiniotis' face is superimposed on the *Portrait of Szczęsny Jerzy Potocki* by Johann Baptist von Lampi the Elder (circa 1792–1793). The choice does

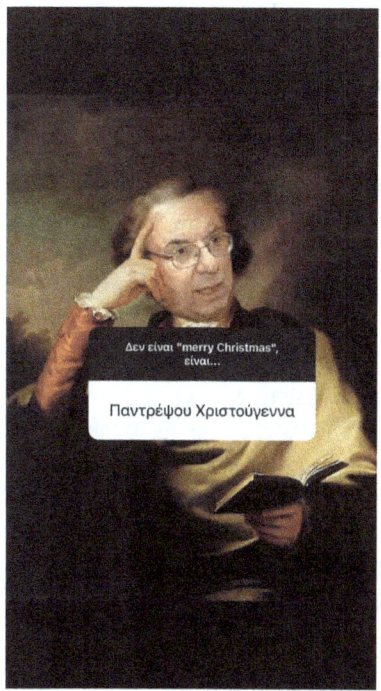

Figure 7: "It's not Merry Christmas, it's marry to Christmas/on Christmas day".

Figure 8: "It's not 'WebEx crashed', it's 'web-former collapsed'".

not appear to be accidental as Potocki is portrayed as pensive and holding a book, perhaps resembling an intellectual and an author, like Babiniotis. The humor is produced by a pun based on the similarity between the English adjective *merry* 'happy' and the English verb *marry* 'to wed'. Instead of translating *Merry Christmas* into *Ευτυχισμένα Χριστούγεννα* (as is usually the case), the well-known wish is translated as *παντρέψου Χριστούγεννα* meaning either 'marry to Christmas' (which is absurd) and 'marry on Christmas day' (which makes sense but is not semantically equivalent).

Similarly, Figure 8 represents Babiniotis proposing a translation equivalent for the Greek phrase *κράσαρε το WebEx* 'WebEx crashed'.[11] First, he appears to propose an equivalent for the verb *κράσαρε* 'crashed' (3rd person singular of the past tense of the verb *κρασάρω*). The Greek verb *κρασάρω* is a compound word consisting of the English verb *to crash* and the verb ending *–άρω*, which is very productive in Greek, yet of Italian origin (cf. *–are*). So, he replaces the loanword/neologism *κράσαρε* with the Greek equivalent *κατέρρευσε* 'collapsed', which may sound slightly more formal than *κράσαρε* and would not necessarily belong to the technological register (cf. Sections 6.1 and 6.3). Most importantly in the context of this category of memes, he supposedly offers a translation equivalent for the proper name *WebEx* as a compound word consisting of the words *web* 'ιστός' and *ex* in the sense of *former* 'πρώην'. Such a fictional etymological/semantic analysis results in the non-existent, nonsensical, and hence humorous Greek calque *ιστός–πρώην*.

Such absurd humor based on "failed" or incongruous translations is particularly popular among Greek speakers of English wishing to show off their skills in detecting when English is "correctly" translated into Greek and when it is not. In other words, in such cases, meme creators come up with deliberately incongruous translations that would not normally be made by Greek speakers who are proficient in English.[12] The respective script opposition is as follows: "Loanword translation should be/is not proposed by speakers who are proficient in English". The emerging metapragmatic stereotype suggests that loanword translations should be attempted by speakers who are proficient in English. Otherwise, they may not make sense, and hence sound funny, in Greek. This stereotype is not directly related to Babiniotis' proposal, but rather exploits the corrective speech act and Ba-

---

[11] This meme alludes to the following event. The teaching platform WebEx was officially used by students and teachers in Greek primary and secondary education during the COVID–19 pandemic. On the first day of its use (November 9th, 2020), the platform crashed due to overload and its function was restored gradually within the next few days (Anonymous 2020).

[12] In the memes of this category, humor is employed to stigmatize those who attempt to translate English (loan)words even though their skills in English may be "limited", and, in general, those who do not speak Standard English (script opposition: "Greek speakers should/do not speak Standard English"). In this sense, a second metapragmatic stereotype is relevant here, which does not relate to loanword translation, but to Standard English: Greek speakers of English are expected to use exclusively Standard English (cf. Tsakona and Tsami 2021).

biniotis' photos (as memory traces) to ridicule what speakers judge as failed attempts to translate, even if such attempts are fictional ones.

6.5 Common informal expressions should be used in colloquial speech

This category of memes does not involve loanword translation, but rather attempts to "correct" informal Greek expressions by replacing them with more formal ones. Figures 9–10 belong to this category:

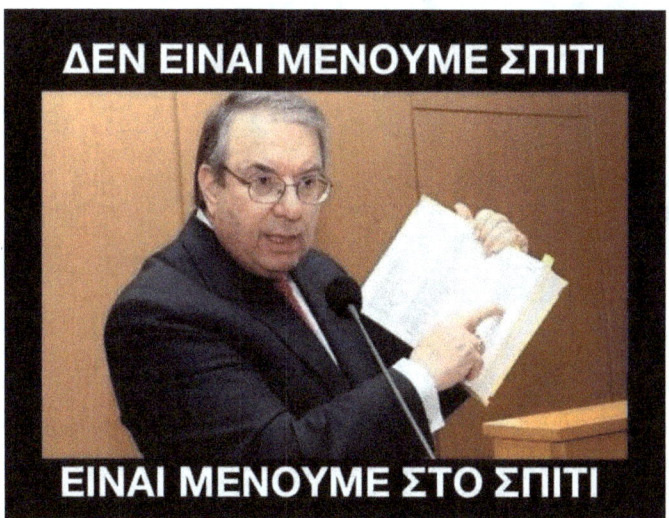

Figure 9: "It's not 'we stay home', it's 'we stay at home'".

In Figure 9, meme creators use the same template as Figures 2 and 8 to suggest that Greek speakers should not say *μένουμε σπίτι* 'we stay home' but instead say *μένουμε στο σπίτι* 'we stay at home', the first expression being perceived as more informal than the second one. This correction is not entirely fictional: on the one hand, *μένουμε σπίτι* 'we stay home' was the main slogan put forward by the Greek government to convince Greeks of the necessity of the first lockdown due to the pandemic (March–May 2020), so Greek people are most familiar with it. On the other, the omission of the preposition in such phrases has been stigmatized as a "common mistake" of Greek speakers since at least the 1990s, so many people may be familiar with the relevant discussions in the media, in education, and elsewhere, concerning the "correct" use.

On November 9th, 2020, namely only a few days after Babiniotis posted his translation proposals online, the popular Greek singer Notis Sfakianakis was arrested for drug possession and illegal weapon possession. Figure 10 alludes to this event to "correct" the informal Greek calque *κοκαΐνη* 'cocaine' with its Greek formal equivalent *βενζοϋλομεθυλεκγονίνη* 'benzoylmethylecgonine', which (ironically) is a calque used in chemistry and medicine. Thus, humor is created by the juxtaposition between a commonly used word and a specialized term known only to experts:

Figure 10: "It's not cocaine, it's benzoylmethylecgonine". BabiNotis.

It should also be noted that the humor of Figure 10 is enhanced by the replacement of Babiniotis' face with Sfakianakis' one in the template of the meme (see Figures 2, 6, 8–9), so as to contextualize the corrective act as relevant to the latter's arrest. It is also enhanced by a pun involving the proper names of Babiniotis and Sfakianakis: a signature appears below the corrective act consisting of *Μπαμπι* 'Babi' (from *Babi–niotis*) and *Νότης* 'Notis' (i.e. Sfakianakis' first name – instead of *Babi–niotis*) also framing the meme as relevant not only to Babiniotis' intervention but also to Sfakianakis' arrest.

In such memes, humor frames the use of formal expressions as incongruous, so the emerging script opposition is "Common informal expressions should be used in colloquial speech/should be replaced with formal ones".[13] The emerging metapragmatic stereotype therefore favors the use of informal expressions in colloquial speech at the expense of formal ones and does not necessarily consider

---

13 The face replacement and the signature pun create an additional incongruity: "Babiniotis as an expert/Sfakianakis as a popular singer performs corrective acts concerning language use".

the former to be incorrect. Such fictional correctives and the respective metapragmatic stereotypes may not be directly related to Babiniotis' specific proposals which triggered the memes of this dataset, but they are related to Babiniotis' practices and interventions (in the media, his courses, etc.), where he advocates for a more formal style of Greek as the "only correct" one. So, meme creators recontextualize the corrective act and some of the semiotic resources commonly employed in this meme cycle to produce humor parodying such corrective acts.

6.6 Corrective acts should not be performed

The final category identified in the data includes memes which evaluate the corrective acts *per se* as incongruous. Figures 11–12 are illustrative:

Figure 11: Babiniotis versus lockdown, click away, self-test, delivery, internet.[14]

Figure 11 exploits a photo from the ship *Ever Given* which blocked the Suez Canal in March 2021. It seems that, in an effort to solve the problem, a comparatively small bulldozer was sent to dislodge the ship.[15] The photo is employed here to underline the futility and ineffectiveness of Babiniotis' proposals through anal-

---

14 The English loanwords are transliterated into Greek in the meme as an indication of their adoption and adjustment to Greek by its speakers.
15 The photo triggered a significant number of memes all over the world (see among others Shukla 2021).

ogy: Babiniotis and his corrective acts are metaphorically represented as the small bulldozer trying to dislodge the huge ship; Greek speakers and their use of English loanwords are metaphorically represented as the lodged ship which cannot be dislodged by the small bulldozer. Babiniotis' efforts to convince Greek speakers not to use English loanwords and to prefer Greek equivalents instead, is represented as impossible and hence as incongruous.

Citizen sociolinguists' resistance to Babiniotis' corrective acts is also shown in Figure 12, where they go a step further by suggesting that the English discourse marker *by the way* (often used in oral colloquial Greek and here written in the Greek alphabet as *μπαϊδεγουέι*) should officially be documented as a Greek word and included in the Greek dictionaries Babiniotis has been editing:

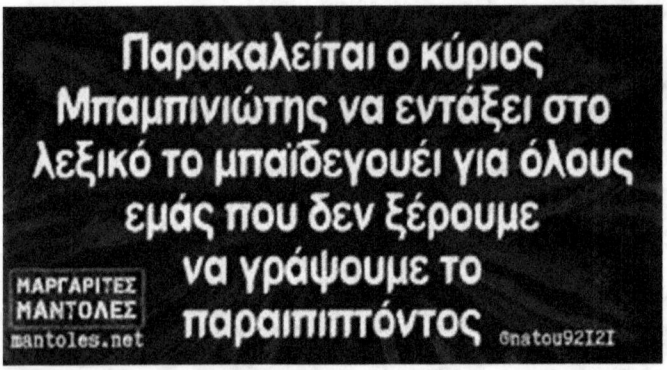

Figure 12: "Mr. Babiniotis is [kindly] requested to include in the dictionary [the English word] *by the way* for all of us who do not know how to write *παραιπιπτόντος* 'by the way'".

Thus, citizen sociolinguists adopt a more "aggressive" approach by reversing Babiniotis' argumentation and proposing the inclusion of one more English loanword in the Greek language (and dictionaries). In order to support their proposal, they argue that *μπαϊδεγουέι* 'by the way' is easier to write than the Greek formal equivalent *παρεμπιπτόντως* 'by the way', here deliberately spelt "incorrectly" as *παραιπιπτόντος* to prove their point. Humor is here created through the role reversal between Babiniotis and citizen sociolinguists and through the unconventional spelling of *παρεμπιπτόντως* as an argument in favor of adopting more English loanwords in Greek.

In such examples, the overarching script opposition is "Linguists as experts propose Greek translation equivalents for English loanwords/Citizen sociolinguists as non–experts resist the Greek translation equivalents proposed by experts for English loanwords". Several metapragmatic stereotypes are related to this script opposition. A prominent and most interesting one concerns metapragmatic discourse, in particular corrective acts publicly performed by experts: such corrective acts are pointless and ineffective and hence should not be performed. Citizen sociolinguists thus clearly question the role of experts in monitoring language use and defend the choices made by non-expert speakers like themselves.

Other related metapragmatic stereotypes pertain to loanword translation (similarly to the ones identified in Sections 6.1–6.5): English loanwords should be perceived and treated as part of the Greek language and not to be removed or replaced with Greek translation equivalents. Interestingly, citizen sociolinguists refrain from "protecting" the "purity" of the Greek language from the "disease" of loanwords (see Section 4) and seem to put forward a more inclusive and multilingual perspective on what constitutes their language. This brings them closer to what García and Wei (2014: 2) call *translanguaging*, namely "an approach to the use of language (. . .) that considers the language practices of bilinguals not as two autonomous language systems as has been traditionally the case, but as one linguistic repertoire with features that have been societally constructed as belonging to two separate languages".

7 Conclusions

The present study has a metapragmatic orientation as it investigates speakers' views on sociopragmatic phenomena. In particular, it focuses on Greek speakers' metapragmatic stereotypes concerning the translation and use of English loanwords into Greek and the performance of relevant corrective acts in the Greek public sphere. The data under scrutiny include a corpus of humorous memes which were produced and circulated as a negative and resistant response to an attempt for loanword translation made by a well-known Greek linguistics professor. Given that the data come from online sources, the study also draws on citizen sociolinguistics (Rymes and Leone 2014) placing emphasis on how citizen sociolinguists (i.e. non-expert speakers) create, negotiate, and disseminate sociopragmatic meanings and values online.

Memes are not texts devoid of social meaning: like all texts, they convey ideologies which often go unnoticed not only by their creators and consumers but also by researchers themselves. As such, they have been used to convey speakers' ideologies related to language, namely their metapragmatic stereotypes, mostly promoting standard varieties and stigmatizing non-standard ones. Less often, humorous memes are created to resist standard use and respective metapragmatic stereotypes (see Section 3). The data examined here are a case in point. Through the identification of incongruities forming the core of humorous meaning, the present analysis has attempted to bring to the surface citizen sociolinguists' metapragmatic stereotypes concerning loanword translation and the respective corrective acts. Citizen sociolinguists use humor to participate in metapragmatic debates and, in particular, to convey their metapragmatic stereotypes concerning English loanword translation into Greek. Their humor also parodies corrective acts aiming to replace informal Greek expressions with formal ones (see Section 6.5). Table 2 summarizes the findings of the present study.

Table 2: The findings of the qualitative analysis.

Section (Figures)	Script oppositions	Citizen sociolinguists' metapragmatic stereotypes	Experts' metapragmatic stereotypes
6.1 Inappropriate connotations (1–2)	Translation equivalents should not carry/carry inappropriate connotations.	Loanwords should not be translated because the proposed equivalents may carry inappropriate connotations. Translation equivalents should be carefully chosen/created so as not to carry inappropriate connotations.	Translation equivalents would rather avoid synonymy, polysemy, and unwarranted or inappropriate connotations.
6.2 Uncommon and unusable translation equivalents (3–4)	Translation equivalents should not sound/sound uncommon and unusable.	Loanwords should not be translated because the proposed equivalents may sound uncommon and unusable. Translation equivalents should be carefully chosen/created so as not to sound uncommon and unusable.	Translation equivalents would rather follow the grammatical, semantic, etc. rules and conventions of the target language.
6.3 Lower or higher inappropriate style (5–6)	Loanword translation should/does not take into consideration stylistic effects and differences.	Loanwords should not be translated because the proposed equivalents may be stylistically inappropriate.	Translation equivalents would rather be compatible with the style/register of the (con)texts where they are expected to be used.

Table 2 (continued)

Section (Figures)	Script oppositions	Citizen sociolinguists' metapragmatic stereotypes	Experts' metapragmatic stereotypes
		Loanword translations are perceived as appropriate and hence successful only when the proposed equivalent seems to be stylistically compatible with its context of use.	
6.4 "Bad" English (7–8)	Loanword translation should be/is not proposed by speakers who are proficient in English.	Loanword translations should be attempted by speakers who are proficient in English. Otherwise, they may not make sense, and hence sound funny, in Greek.	–
6.5 Informal versus formal Greek (9–10)	Common informal expressions should be used in colloquial speech/ should be replaced with formal ones.	Informal expressions should be used in colloquial speech and not formal ones; informal expressions are not necessarily incorrect.	–
6.6 Corrective acts should not be performed (11–12)	Linguists as experts propose Greek translation equivalents for English loanwords/Citizen sociolinguists as non-experts resist the Greek translation equivalents proposed by experts for English loanwords	Experts' corrective acts are pointless and ineffective and hence should not be performed. English loanwords should be perceived and treated as part of the Greek language and not to be removed or replaced with Greek translation equivalents.	–

Table 2 also shows that some of the citizen sociolinguists' metapragmatic stereotypes are compatible with (if not identical to) those put forward by linguists and translators in the relevant research (see Goutsos 1999b; Tsakona 2007 in Section 4). This comes as no surprise if we consider that citizen sociolinguists use, and are thus capable of evaluating, the choices made by translators and linguists when translating loanwords. And vice versa, it should not be forgotten that such experts are first and foremost users of translation equivalents themselves, so their expertise cannot but rely (at least partly) on their own experiences as speakers: what they propose as criteria for "successful" loanword translation are nothing but their own –theorized– metapragmatic stereotypes as speakers (see also a similar discussion in Tsakona 2017b: 196–199, 2020a: 58–62).

The analysis proposed here highlights the significance of humor in framing specific translation practices and corrective acts as incongruous. It seems that humor, even in the mundane form of memes circulating in social media platforms, exhibits remarkable ideological/metapragmatic functions and helps us identify what citizen sociolinguists consider (in)appropriate language use. Interestingly, a comparison between earlier studies (see Section 3) and this one reveals that humor may either support or undermine "correct" language use. More specifically, the majority of language–related memes tend to reinforce standard varieties and to stigmatize non–standard ones (see Švelch and Sherman 2018; White–Farnham 2019; Tsakona and Tsami 2021 in Section 3), but there also exist some memes which counterattack standard language ideologies and corrective practices, such as White–Farnham's (2019) *backlash memes* and the ones examined here. Consequently, memes may turn out to be an invaluable resource for metapragmatic knowledge and inquiry within metapragmatic research and citizen sociolinguistics. As Wiggins (2019: 143) suggests, "with internet memes, (. . .) it is crucial to be able to step back, and consider what the big picture is, to see beyond the humor of the initial moment, to view a particular meme, its iteration, or even a series of memes as a discourse and not simple bon mot". Needless to say, more research is needed to investigate metapragmatic stereotypes conveyed through humorous discourse (whether digital or not) referring to other sociopragmatic phenomena and coming from different linguacultural contexts.

A most interesting question which, however, goes beyond the scope and potential of the present study, involves the reasons why some publicly performed corrective acts attract citizen sociolinguists' attention and others do not. In the present case, it seems that Babiniotis posts such proposals quite frequently on his personal Facebook account, yet only these translations became the object of memetic reframing and commentary. The online news websites may play their role in this process: they may be the first which transmit the "news" and bring it to the attention of the wider audience. The lockdown/pandemic conditions may also play a significant role: stuck in front of their computer screens for several hours per day, citizen sociolinguists may feel like dedicating more time and effort to offer their metapragmatic comments on "timely" topics. A comparative perspective on different studies on memes with metapragmatic content and function may shed more light on the reasons why some topics become viral while others do not.

Last but not least, diachronic studies could be most revealing when it comes to ongoing metapragmatic debates. As already discussed (in Section 4), the metapragmatic debate on the use and translation of English loanwords into Greek is definitely not a recent one and many scholars have contributed to it. The present study has offered us a digital snapshot of what form this debate takes nowadays on social media and between experts in linguistics and citizen sociolinguists. It is interesting to note here that the present findings which reveal a negative metapragmatic stereotype concerning loanword translation and a positive stance towards using English loanwords, is partly in contrast with Tatsioka's (2010) earlier findings. Her informants perceived English loanwords as threats to the Greek language and evaluated them negatively, but this did not seem to affect their (reported) use. Future studies could further explore such a trend towards gradually more positive metapragmatic stereotypes concerning the use of English loanwords in Greek.

References

Agha, Asif. 1998. Stereotypes and registers of honorific language. *Language in Society* 27(2). 151–193.
Agha, Asif. 2004. Registers of language. In Alessandro Duranti (ed.), *A Companion to Linguistic Anthropology* (Blackwell Companions to Anthropology 1), 23–45. Malden: Blackwell.
Agha, Asif. 2007. *Language and Social Relations* (Studies in the Social and Cultural Foundations of Language). Cambridge: Cambridge University Press.
Anastasiadi–Symeonidi, Anna. 1994. *Νεολογικός δανεισμός της νεοελληνικής: Άμεσα δάνεια από τη γαλλική και αγγλοαμερικανική. Μορφοφωνολογική ανάλυση* [Neological borrowing in Modern Greek: direct loanwords from French and American English. A morphophonological analysis]. Thessaloniki: Aristotle University of Thessaloniki. [in Greek]
Anastasiadi–Simeonidi, Anna. 2001. Ιδεολογία και δανεισμός [Ideology and borrowing]. In Yannis I. Haris (ed.), *Δέκα μύθοι για την ελληνική γλώσσα* [Ten myths about the Greek language], 63–71, Athens: Patakis. [in Greek]
Anonymous. 2020. November 9. Greece's Online Education Crashes on Day One under Lockdown. *Keep Talking Greece: Greek News in English, Blog, Wit & Drama*. https://www.keeptalkinggreece.com/2020/11/09/greece-online-education-crash-webex-cisco-lockdown

Apostolou-Panara, Athena-Maria. 1997. *Language Change in Modern Greek: The Morphological Integration of English Loanwords* (Parousia Journal Monograph Series 40). Athens: Parousia.

Archakis, Argiris & Villy Tsakona. 2021. Greek migrant jokes online: A diachronic-comparative study on racist humorous representations. *Internet Pragmatics* 4(1). 28–51.

Aslan, Erhan & Camilla Vásquez. 2018. "Cash me ousside": A citizen sociolinguistic analysis of online metalinguistic commentary. *Journal of Sociolinguistics* 22(4). 406–431.

Attardo, Salvatore. 2001. *Humorous Texts: A Semantic and Pragmatic Analysis* (Humor Research 6). Berlin: Mouton de Gruyter.

Attardo, Salvatore. 2020. Memes, memeiosis, and memetic drift: Cheryl's Chichier She Shed. *Media Linguistics/Медиалингвистика* 7(2). 146–168.

Austin, John L. 1962. *How to Do Things with Words*. Oxford: Clarendon Press.

Billig, Michael. 2005. *Laughter and Ridicule: Towards a Social Critique of Humor* (Theory, Culture and Society). London: Sage.

Blommaert, Jan. 2013. Policy, policing and the ecology of social norms: Ethnographic monitoring revisited. *International Journal of the Sociology of Language* 219. 123–140.

Brideau, Kate & Charles Berret. 2014. A brief introduction to impact: "The meme font". *Journal of Visual Culture* 13(3). 307–313.

Bublitz, Wolfram & Axel Hübler (eds.). 2007. *Metapragmatics in Use* (Pragmatics and Beyond New Series 165). Amsterdam: John Benjamins.

Denisova, Anastasia. 2019. *Internet Memes and Society: Social, Context, and Political Contexts* (Routledge Advances in Internationalizing Media Studies 25). New York: Routledge.

García, Ophelia & Li Wei. 2014. *Translanguaging: Language, Bilingualism and Education* (Palgrave Pivot). Basingstoke: Palgrave Macmillan.

Giddens, Anthony. 1984. *The Constitution of Society: Outline of the Theory of Structure*. Berkeley: University of California Press.

Goutsos, Dionysis. 1999a. Essay review: George D. Babiniotis. *Λεξικό της νέας ελληνικής γλώσσας* [Dictionary of Modern Greek]. Athens: Center for Lexicography. 1998. *Journal of Modern Greek Studies* 17(1). 163–170.

Goutsos, Dionysis. 1999b. Translation in bilingual lexicography: Editing a new English-Greek dictionary. *Babel* 45(2). 107–126.

Jaworski, Adam, Nikolas Coupland & Dariusz Galasiński. 2004. Metalanguage: Why now? In Adam Jaworski, Nikolas Coupland & Dariusz Galasiński (eds.), *Metalanguage: Social and Ideological Perspectives* (Language, Power and Social Process 11), 3–8. Berlin: Mouton de Gruyter.

Kádár, Dániel Z. & Michael Haugh. 2013. *Understanding Politeness*. Cambridge: Cambridge University Press.

Labov, William. 1972. *Language in the Inner City: Studies in Black English Vernacular*. Philadelphia: University of Pennsylvania Press.

Malinowski, Bronislaw. 1989 [1923]. The problem of meaning in primitive languages. In Charles Kay Ogden & Ivor Armstrong Richards, *The Meaning of Meaning: A Study of the Influence of Language upon Thought and the Science of Symbolism*, 296–336. San Diego: Harvest/Harcourt Brace Jovanovich.

Moschonas, Spiros A. 2022. Detecting prescriptivism's effects on language change: The corpus-linguistic approach. In Nikolaos Lavidas & Kiki Nikiforidou (eds.), *Studying Language Change in the 21st Century: Theory and Methodologies* (Brill's Studies in Historical Linguistics 16), 315–357. Leiden: Brill.

Papadopoulou, Rania. 2020. *Evaluating anglicization in Modern Greek: A qualitative and quantitative survey*. Patras & Lyon: University of Lyon & University of Patras dissertation.

Piata, Anna. 2020. Stylistic humor across modalities: The case of classical art memes. *Internet Pragmatics* 3(2). 174–201.

Raskin, Victor. 1985. *Semantic Mechanisms of Humor* (Studies in Linguistics and Philosophy 24). Dordrecht: D. Reidel.

Rymes, Betsy & Andrea R. Leone. 2014. Citizen sociolinguistics: A new media methodology for understanding language and social life. *Working Papers in Educational Linguistics* 29(2). 25–43.

Searle, J. R. 1983. *Intentionality: An Essay in the Philosophy of Mind*. New York: Cambridge University Press.

Sherman, Tamah & Jaroslav Švelch. 2015. "Grammar Nazis never sleep": Facebook humor and the management of standard written language. *Language Policy* 14(4). 315–334.

Shifman, Limor. 2014. *Memes in Digital Culture* (The MIT Essential Knowledge Series). Cambridge: MIT Press.

Shukla, Ridhima. 2021. March 26. Tiny Bulldozer and a Giant Ship in Suez Canal Inspire Wave of Memes. *NDTV*. https://www.ndtv.com/offbeat/tiny-bulldozer-and-a-giant-ship-in-suez-canal-inspire-wave-of-memes-2399213

Švelch, Jaroslav & Tamah Sherman. 2018. "I see your garbage": Participatory practices and literacy privilege on "Grammar Nazi" Facebook pages in different sociolinguistic contexts. *New Media and Society* 20(7). 2391–2410.

Swanson, Donald C. 1958. English loanwords in Modern Greek. *Word* 14(1). 26–46.

Tatsioka, Zoi. 2010. *English loanwords and code-switching on the Greek television: The effects and the attitude of the public*. Edinburgh: Heriot-Watt University dissertation.

Triantafyllidis, Manolis. 1905. Ξενηλασία ή ισοτέλεια; Μελέτη περί των ξένων λέξεων της νέας ελληνικής ["Deportation of aliens" or equality? A study on loanwords in Modern Greek]. http://www.ins.web.auth.gr/images/Apanta_pliri/%CE%86%CF%80%CE%B1%CE%BD%CF%84%CE%B1%201_1_297.pdf (accessed 25 July 2021). [in Greek]

Trudgill, Peter. 2003. *A Glossary of Sociolinguistics* (Glossaries in Linguistics). Edinburgh: Edinburgh University Press.

Tsakona, Villy. 2007. Bilingualization in practice: Terminological issues in bilingualizing a specialized glossary. *International Journal of Lexicography* 20(2). 119–145.

Tsakona, Villy. 2013. Okras and the metapragmatic stereotypes of humor: Towards an expansion of the GTVH. In Marta Dynel (ed.), *Developments in Linguistic Humor Theory* (Topics in Humor Research 1), 25–48. Amsterdam: John Benjamins.

Tsakona, Villy. 2017a. Constructing local identities via/for humor: A Cretan-Greek case study. *Styles of Communication* 9(2). 118–147.

Tsakona, Villy. 2017b. Humor research and humor reception: Far away, so close. In Władysław Chłopicki & Dorota Brzozowska (eds.), *Humorous Discourse* (Humor Research 11), 179–201. Berlin: Mouton De Gruyter.

Tsakona, Villy. 2018. Online joint fictionalization. In Villy Tsakona & Jan Chovanec (eds.), *The Dynamics of Interactional Humor: Creating and Negotiating Humor in Everyday Encounters* (Topics in Humor Research 7), 229–255. Amsterdam: John Benjamins.

Tsakona, Villy. 2020a. *Recontextualizing Humor: Rethinking the Analysis and Teaching of Humor* (Language and Creativity 4). Boston: De Gruyter Mouton.

Tsakona, Villy. 2020b. Tracing the trajectories of contemporary online joking. *Media Linguistics/Медиалингвистика* 7(2). 169–183.

Tsakona, Villy & Vasia Tsami. 2021. "Did you hear the crunch sound?": Humor and metapragmatic stereotypes in the Greek *Master Chef* contest. *Journal of Pragmatics* 172. 197–214.

Varis, Piia & Jan Blommaert. 2015. Conviviality and collectives on social media: Virality, memes, and new social structures. *Multilingual Margins* 2(1). 31–45.

Vásquez, Camilla. 2019. *Language, Creativity and Humor Online* (Language and Digital Media). London: Routledge.

Vásquez, Camilla & Erhan Aslan. 2021. "Cats be outside, how about meow": Multimodal humor and creativity in an internet meme. *Journal of Pragmatics* 171. 101–117.

Verschueren, Jef. 1999. *Understanding Pragmatics*. London: Edward Arnold.

Verschueren, Jef. 2000. Notes on the role of metapragmatic awareness in language use. *Pragmatics* 10(4). 439–456.

White-Farnham, Jamie. 2019. Resisting "Let's eat grandma": The rhetorical potential of grammar memes. *Computers and Composition* 52. 210–221.

Wiggins, Bradley E. 2019. *The Discursive Power of Memes in Digital Culture: Ideology, Semiotics, and Intertextuality* (Routledge Studies in New Media and Cyberculture). New York: Routledge.

Wiggins, Bradley E. & Bret G. Bowers. 2015. Memes as a genre: A structurational analysis of the memescape. *New Media and Society* 17(1). 1886–1906.

Xydopoulos, George J., Kyriakoula Tzortzatou & Argiris Archakis. 2019. The perception of Greek national orthography and Greeklish at the threshold of the post-modern era: Investigating attitudes towards orthography in Greek education. *Journal of Modern Greek Studies* 37(2). 397–424.

Yoon, InJeong. 2016. Why is it not just a joke? Analysis of internet memes associated with racism and hidden ideology of colorblindness. *Journal of Cultural Research in Art Education* 33. 92–123.

Zappavigna, Michele. 2012. *Discourse on Twitter and Social Media: How We Use Language to Create Affiliation on the Web* (Bloomsbury Discourse Series). London: Bloomsbury.

Index

Amusement 15–19, 21–24, 27, 29–38, 40–43, 45, 48, 54, 253, 254, 257, 258, 266, 276, 293, 307
– shared amusement. See amusement

Emoji 2, 4, 5, 6, 8, 182, 232–259, 263–271, 273, 275–278, 280–283, 289, 290, 292, 294, 296, 300, 311, 314
Enjoyment 27, 28, 89, 248, 256–258, 277, 297
Eyebrow 4, 5, 8, 67–70, 72, 73, 80, 182, 209, 212–228, 247, 248, 252, 283

Facial expression 5–8, 15, 16, 20, 23, 28, 30, 42, 46–48, 77–90, 109, 110, 113, 115, 118, 131, 136, 140, 141, 150, 156–158, 169–171, 174, 181–185, 189, 193, 194, 197, 198, 209, 211–213, 215, 217, 219–221, 223–228, 232–234, 247, 248, 252, 258
Facial gesture 2, 4, 7, 131, 133, 136, 140, 141
Fictionalization 140, 289, 291, 292, 293, 298, 299, 300, 301, 306, 313, 315
– joint fictionalization. See fictionalization
Frame 4, 22, 54, 55, 61, 63, 68, 70, 73, 87, 92, 99, 132–135, 149, 150, 152, 153, 190, 209, 210, 215, 218–221, 224, 225, 227, 231, 234, 235, 238, 247, 249, 252–254, 256–258, 270, 271, 311, 312, 314, 319, 334
– nonserious frame. See frame
– playful frame. See frame
– humorous frame. See frame

Gaze 1, 2, 5, 7, 15, 19, 20, 23, 28–33, 35–38, 40–43, 46–48, 53–67, 69–82, 169, 170, 180–185, 189, 192, 194, 197, 198, 211, 232, 265
– eye-gaze. See gaze
GIFs 2, 4, 5, 9, 232, 264, 265, 267, 290, 299

Hand gesture 1, 5, 56, 72, 225, 228
Humor
– canned humor 1, 138, 139, 146, 169, 171, 172, 174–181, 183, 189–191, 196, 198, 199, 332
– canned joke. See canned humor

– conversational humor 8, 87, 90–93, 96, 97, 99, 101 104, 105, 139, 149, 171–175, 177–181, 195, 198, 231–237, 252, 257–259, 265
– device 1, 3–5, 132, 139, 140, 149, 155–158, 174, 175, 181–183, 189, 190, 196–198, 298, 311
– failed humor 2, 101, 102, 105, 133, 135, 159, 263, 275, 277, 283, 301
– generation 4, 8, 171, 183, 186–190, 192, 193, 196–199
– implementation 8, 169, 171, 180, 184, 188, 189, 197–199
– interactional humor 2–6, 8, 9, 49, 58, 131, 132, 136, 139, 156, 263, 265, 268, 276, 282, 283
– sequence 6, 8, 16, 19, 22, 31, 133, 135–138, 140, 150, 152, 153, 156–158, 179, 278

Incongruity 17, 18, 23, 24, 31–33, 35, 40, 42, 43, 46, 48, 136, 209, 210, 212, 252, 224, 242, 248, 250, 251, 293, 331, 334, 344, 348
– incongruous 17, 18, 24, 32–35, 38, 40, 41, 43, 156, 228, 239, 240, 242, 313, 319, 331, 332, 334, 338, 342, 344–346, 350
Interaction
– computer-mediated 6, 9, 87, 91, 93, 132, 232, 234, 263, 268, 278, 29A2, 293
– dyadic 3, 4, 8, 57, 60, 77, 80, 87,91, 92, 94, 96, 97, 99, 101, 102, 105, 120, 122, 131, 136, 137, 234, 235, 236, 263, 266, 271
– dyad. See dyadic
– face-to-face 2, 3, 4, 6, 7, 53, 54, 56, 62, 66, 81, 87, 91, 92, 105, 131, 132, 156, 212, 227, 231–233, 258, 265, 276–278, 280, 281, 283, 322
– human-robot 8, 169, 185, 192
– online 3–5, 231, 237, 256, 265, 266, 289
– spontaneous 15, 16, 19, 21, 48, 53, 58, 60, 61, 81, 87, 138, 213, 224, 228, 292, 322
– triadic 3, 7, 53, 54, 57, 59, 60, 61, 81, 77, 81
– triad. See triadic
Irony 30, 54, 55, 56, 58, 59, 63, 72, 76, 80, 92, 169, 173, 174, 180–184, 186, 188, 189, 192–194, 196, 198, 199, 250, 268, 313
– ironic. See irony

Jocularity 55, 63, 231–259
– jocular. See jocularity

Laughter 5, 8, 16, 17, 24, 25, 28–32, 34, 35, 37–39, 41, 42, 55, 56, 59, 63, 69, 70, 73, 74, 77, 80, 89, 92, 93, 96, 98, 104, 109, 131, 134–139, 141–153, 155–158, 174, 176, 179–186, 190–193, 197, 198, 212, 214, 216, 219, 221, 223, 224, 234, 258, 263, 266, 268, 270, 271, 276, 277, 278, 280–283, 290, 292, 296, 297
– shared laughter 155, 282

Marker 3, 8, 16, 21, 46, 53, 54, 104, 109, 123, 132, 133, 169, 179, 176, 178, 181, 182, 192–194, 209, 212, 213, 225, 227, 228, 235, 246, 293
Meme 2, 4, 5, 9, 232, 263, 266, 268–271, 277–283, 289, 290, 294, 299, 319, 320, 323–327, 330–340, 342–345, 347, 348, 350, 351
Mockery 54, 59, 63, 78, 214, 239, 246, 256
– jocular mockery. See mockery

Negotiation 56, 57, 92, 131–133, 135, 153, 157, 158, 175, 263, 264, 322

Prosody 1, 2, 5, 15, 16, 22–24, 28, 31, 34, 37, 38, 42, 47–49, 92, 132, 139, 169, 170, 174, 177, 178, 180–183, 189–194, 197, 198, 212, 228, 232, 234, 290
– prosodic. See prosody

Resource 1–7, 9, 15, 16, 19–22, 30, 31, 33, 37, 38, 42, 48, 56, 57, 59, 72, 80, 81, 105, 131, 134, 136, 137, 139, 140, 150, 157, 158, 170, 175, 188, 232, 253, 256, 264–268, 280–282, 319, 322, 324, 331, 333, 345, 350
– nonverbal. See resource
– semiotic. See resource

Sarcasm 8, 58, 80, 173, 182, 196, 209, 214, 216, 220, 222, 226, 228
– Sarcastic. See sarcasm
Smile 1, 2, 6–8, 26–31, 33–37, 39–43, 44, 46, 75–77, 88–91, 94, 98, 109–115, 117, 118, 123, 124, 131, 135, 136, 138, 140–147, 150, 152, 153, 155, 157, 158, 179, 180, 183, 186, 192, 194, 197, 198, 218, 221, 225, 232, 240, 243, 247, 248
Smiling. 5, 7, 15, 17, 23–27, 31, 36, 49, 56, 80, 87–97, 99–105, 109–115, 118–123, 134, 135, 137, 139, 140–142, 144–147, 150, 152, 157, 159, 179–182, 184, 190, 192, 197, 212, 218, 228, 240, 241, 246, 247–249, 252, 254, 256, 257, 265, 276, 311
Smiling Intensity Scale 5, 6, 7, 87, 90, 91, 93, 94, 96–105, 109, 112–24, 127, 140–145
– SIS. See smiling intensity scale
Synchrony 28, 92, 93, 94, 96, 99, 104, 109, 123, 173
– synchronicity. See synchrony
– synchronic. See synchrony
– synchronous. See synchrony

Tease 7, 53–56, 58–60, 62–67, 69–81, 149, 150, 155, 156, 173, 231, 232, 235–238, 245–250, 252–254, 256–258, 268, 270, 279, 283, 295
– teaser. See tease
– teasing. See tease